"*Pigmentocracies* is a signal achievement in the comparative sociology of race and racism, punctuating Edward Telles's already distinctive and pioneering research on racial and ethno-national classification and categorization. The innovations of Telles and PERLA in both demographic and conceptual methodologies will enable students of racial and ethnic politics to apprehend the crucial but often ignored distinction between identity and identification, as well as to explore the tensions and disjunctions between the concerns of governments and elites, on the one hand, and those of poor and marginalized populations, on the other. In providing and unpacking multicountry data, *Pigmentocracies*' conclusions highlight the relationship between identification and inequality often obscured in both nationalist and scholarly explanations of racial exceptionalism, with implications for both North and South America."

—MICHAEL HANCHARD, The Johns Hopkins University

"This book breaks new ground with its rigorous comparative approach, which reveals the variety of Latin American attitudes toward and perceptions of racial difference, and with its systematic use of questionnaire data, which allow many standard ideas about race in Latin American countries to be tested in detail—and confirmed in some cases, but challenged in others. Indispensable reading for all scholars and students of race and ethnicity in Latin America."

—PETER WADE, University of Manchester

"Based on imaginative, meticulous, and ambitious comparative research, this pathbreaking book shatters the traditional indigenous-black divide and takes the study of race, color, ethnicity, and mestizaje in Latin America to a whole new level. A must read."

—ALEJANDRO DE LA FUENTE, Harvard University

"For some time now, national ideologies of racial democracy and mestizaje in Latin America have been under critical pressure, from academics and Black and indigenous rights activists alike. *Pigmentocracies* shatters these ideologies' veneer of academic legitimacy, marshaling data that definitively links racial difference with enduring socioeconomic inequality. The study's color palette method is sure to generate intense controversy, and by extension, healthy debate on how racialization affects people's wellbeing. Rarely has academic research—through a combination of compelling evidence and actionable arguments—had so much potential to make tangible contributions to racial justice in the Americas."

—CHARLES R. HALE, University of Texas at Austin

"*Pigmentocracies* presents fascinating new findings about racial stratification and attitudes in contemporary Latin America. No other book exists with data like these; no other book can speak directly to the empirical questions addressed in these chapters. A valuable and distinctive contribution to scholarship on race and ethnicity in a major region of the world."

—MARA LOVEMAN, University of California at Berkeley

"*Pigmentocracies* is a significant resource and a welcome addition to the literature on race and ethnicity in Latin America, providing up-to-date findings and analyses rarely found elsewhere. Includes fascinating data that are important for a deeper understanding of race and ethnicity in Latin America."

—JAN HOFFMAN FRENCH, University of Richmond

"We have needed this book for a long time. Based on a rigorously comparative survey of racial attitudes and identities in four Latin American countries, it identifies important differences among those countries and one fundamental similarity: the effects of skin color on socioeconomic outcomes and individual life chances. The book is a major research achievement and a model of how to carry out international scholarly collaboration."

—GEORGE REID ANDREWS, University of Pittsburgh

# PIGMENTOCRACIES

# PIGMENTOCRACIES

Ethnicity, Race, and Color in Latin America

## EDWARD TELLES

and the Project on Ethnicity and Race in Latin America (PERLA)

The University of North Carolina Press
*Chapel Hill*

Cover illustration: The PERLA skin color palette © 2014 by Edward
Telles and PERLA. This key PERLA instrument represents respondents'
self-reported facial skin color according to a palette of eleven skin
tones, with 1 indicating the lightest skin color and 11 the darkest.

Library of Congress Cataloging-in-Publication Data
Telles, Edward Eric, 1956–
Pigmentocracies : ethnicity, race, and color in Latin America /
Edward Telles and the Project on Ethnicity and Race in Latin America
(PERLA).—1 Edition.
pages cm
Includes bibliographical references and index.
ISBN 978-1-4696-1783-1 (pbk : alk. paper)
ISBN 978-1-4696-1784-8 (ebook)
1. Ethnic groups—Latin America—Cross-cultural studies. 2. Latin
America—Race relations—Cross-cultural studies. I. Project on
Ethnicity and Race in Latin America. II. Title.
GN562.T45 2014
305.80098—dc23
2014024703

18  17  16  15  14    5  4  3  2  1

# CONTENTS

# FIGURES, TABLES, AND MAPS

# ACKNOWLEDGMENTS

This book would not have been possible without the enthusiasm and collegiality of the twelve collaborators of the Project on Ethnicity and Race in Latin America (PERLA). As director of the PERLA project, I am particularly indebted to the PERListas whose intellectual fervor, solidarity, and loyalty to the project were outstanding. Through our multinational, multilingual and multidisciplinary cooperation, we hope to have taken the study of race and ethnicity in the region to another level, thanks to their work and the work of many individuals beyond the PERLA team.

First of all, Ana Maria Goldani participated in the PERLA discussions, providing valuable substantive input, and her generosity and spirit made Princeton a welcoming place for the PERLA meetings. From the beginning, Mitchell Seligson of the Latin American Public Opinion Project (LAPOP) gave generously of his time in helping us to think carefully about the full range of issues in carrying out such surveys in the region.

We also thank Abby Cordova, Rubi Araña, Fernanda Boldi, Dominique Zephyr, and Liz Zechmeister of LAPOP as well as Pablo Parás, who led the Mexico survey, for their valuable assistance regarding the design of the PERLA surveys. Appreciation also goes out to the survey staff at each of the four institutes that carried out the surveys, in which we discovered that their reputations as top-rate survey firms are well deserved. In addition, George Reid Andrews and Guillermo de la Peña directly participated in PERLA meetings and gave valuable commentary based on their extensive substantive knowledge.

Without the enthusiasm of Felipe Aguero, Mario Bronfman, Martín Abregú, Carmen Feijóo, Todd Cox, and Sara Rios, all of the Ford Foundation, this book would never have been possible. We thank the Ford Foundation and Princeton University for their generous financial support.

We thank Elaine Maisner of the University of North Carolina Press for her enthusiasm and support for the project from nearly the beginning of the multi-year process, which involved several stages of writing and revising; thanks go as well to Paul Betz for his careful handling of the production of this book. We are also grateful to our formerly anonymous reviewers, Mara Loveman and Jan Hoffman French. They provided us with valuable comments that raised the quality of the individual chapters and the manuscript as a whole. Before that, Miguel Centeno, Douglas Massey, and Alejandro Portes of the Princeton Sociology Department and George Reid Andrews brilliantly commented on individual country chapters. Between those early drafts and the almost finished manuscripts, we also benefited from the comments of Jerome Branch and Cesar Rodriguez Garavito at an annual meeting of the Latin American Studies Association.

We are grateful to Sylvia Zamora, Rachel Ferguson, and Jane Katz for their assistance in copyediting and Steven Server for his assistance in compiling and checking data. We especially thank Nancy Doolan of Princeton's Center for Migration and Development for the many hours and attention to detail that she spent preparing the text and corresponding with the authors.

Because of the scale of the project, which extended across the twelve collaborators in five countries, we may not be able to recognize everyone by name, but we express our appreciation for everyone involved. In the following paragraphs we acknowledge many of those whose support and assistance made possible the completion of the book's individual country chapters.

## Mexico

This chapter is the result of the interdisciplinary, cross-national collaborative effort of the authors, whose knowledge of Mexico derives from distinct personal and professional perspectives. We received valuable comments and criticisms from Guillermo de la Peña, Casey Walsh, and Douglas Massey. We extend our gratitude to Georganne Welles for her help in the translation and to the anonymous reviewers whose input encouraged us to clarify our contribution to the vast literature of race and ethnicity. Data Opinión Pública, headed by Pablo Parás and Carlos López, worked closely with us in carrying out the survey. We were also aided by several students from CIESAS and the Universidad Iberoamericana, to whom we are grateful.

We are indebted to our respective institutions for facilitating and supporting our participation in PERLA. CIESAS provided technical and logistic support and the Program in Latin American Studies of Princeton University provided institutional space for the first author during the final stages of analysis and writing. We are equally grateful for the help of Mario Bronfman, the Ford Foundation representative in Mexico, for making this research possible.

Several colleagues were instrumental to the dissemination of our findings throughout Mexico and other countries. In particular, Francois Lartigue (†) organized meetings and seminars with academics, public officials, and NGO leaders to discuss the impact of our research on Mexican ethnoracial dynamics. Mónica Figueroa, Alicia Castellanos, and Mariana Mora also contributed to the discussion and diffusion of the results from PERLA.

Last, but not least, we express gratitude to our respective families for their patience during the time-consuming research process, which took us on journeys far from home, to carry out fieldwork and ensure communication with our whole team.


## Colombia

In Bogotá, we thank Franklin Gil, Pietro Pisano, Klará Hellebrandová, and Sergio Lesmes of the research team "Escape from genealogical misfortune. The emergence and participation of the middle 'black' middle classes in Colombian national life," led by Maria Viveros and supported by COLCIENCIAS (Colombian Department for Science, Technology and Innovation).

In Cali, we are grateful to Diego Ocasiones Canaval, Mónica Holguín D. Caicedo, and Diego Alejandro Rodriguez Sanchez for their support in translation to English of various versions of the chapter, and Diego Alejandro and Sol Kizzy Ruíz of the Universidad del Valle for the statistical processing and analysis of the survey.

We also thank the Interdisciplinary Group of Gender Studies (GIEG) at the Universidad Nacional de Colombia, which provided support for Viveros, and the research group "Ethnic-racial and labor studies and their various components" of CIDSE (Center for Socioeconomic Research and Documentation) of the Universidad del Valle, which provided support for Urrea. The enthusiasm of Luis Carlos Castillo Gómez and Jeanny Posso Quiceno as researchers of CIDSE (Universidad del Valle) and members of this group have been particularly important for disseminating PERLA findings throughout Colombian academia.

Comments and criticisms from Alejandro Portes were important for clarifying our arguments. We acknowledge the Centro Nacional de Consultoría (CNC), which designed the sample and fielded the Colombia survey, for their flexibility and technical expertise, which assured an excellent survey. Peter Wade has long been an academic partner to the Colombia PERLA team and has helped to understand the logic of social inequality in Colombia.

Felipe Agüero of the Ford Foundation in Santiago has been an ardent supporter of research at the Universidad del Valle on ethnoracial statistics for Afrodescendant and Indigenous people in Colombia. We also thank César Rodríguez Garavito, who has closely followed and consulted on the PERLA study findings.

## Peru

Many of the ideas in this chapter are the result of valuable discussions among colleagues of the PERLA project. Their insights were fundamental in order to explore the complex realities of ethnicity and race in Peruvian society using different questions and approaches from other Latin American societies.

Comments and criticisms from Miguel Angel Centeno (Princeton University) and Martín Benavides (PUCP and GRADE) were extremely useful to clarify some of the main arguments in our text. We are indebted to Néstor Valdivia (GRADE) for sharing with us his work on the use of ethnic categories in national censuses and official surveys in Peru. We also thank Narda Henriquez, director of the Master's Program in Sociology of the PUCP, for inviting us to present and discuss some of the findings of this chapter at the International Seminar on Inequality and Politics, which took place in Lima in March 2012.

The support of Gavina Córdova and Alejandra Villanueva was fundamental in order to carry out and analyze the results of the pilot test of PERLA's questionnaire in Peru, and to adapt the core questions to the Peruvian context. Several students from the PUCP also participated in this process. The fieldwork for the Peruvian survey was conducted by Ipsos Apoyo in close coordination with us.

We are particularly grateful to the Social Sciences Department of the Pontificia Universidad Católica del Perú and its head, Aldo Panfichi, for encouraging and facilitating our participation in this project.

## Brazil

Most of the ideas discussed in this chapter were constructed in the debates and discussions with the other participants of the PERLA project. Meeting them has been an invaluable intellectual and personal asset. Our multidisciplinary and open approach was key to exploring the Brazilian reality through a different comparative and Latin American frame.

During the PERLA meetings in Princeton, comments and criticisms from George Reid Andrews (University of Pittsburgh) were also extremely useful for clarifying some of the main arguments in our text. The chapter was also enriched by the constant intellectual dialogue with Elisa Reis (UFRJ) and Michèle Lamont (Harvard University).

We also thank Narda Henriquez, director of the Master's Program in Sociology of the PUCP, for inviting us to present and discuss some of the findings of this chapter at the International Seminar on Inequality and Politics, which took place in Lima in March 2012.

In Brazil, we have also benefited from the support and partnership of the researchers at NIED (Network for the Study of Inequality) and LAESER (Laboratório de Análise Econômicas, Históricas, Sociais e Estatísticas das Relações), at UFRJ. We also thank Alberto Carlos Almeida and his staff at Institute Análise for carrying out the survey and Irene Rossetto for the tabulation of data. Both authors also received grants by the Ford Foundation, FAPERJ and CNPq, which made this project possible.

# PIGMENTOCRACIES

## CHAPTER ONE

# The Project on Ethnicity and Race in Latin America (PERLA)

## Hard Data and What Is at Stake

EDWARD TELLES

Social distinctions and ethnic hierarchies based on phenotype, ancestry, and language have been prominent features of social life throughout the Western Hemisphere for more than five hundred years. Since 1492, Europeans' incursions into the Americas brought them into contact with the native peoples of the continent, whom they would soon decimate through war and disease or would enslave or subject to various forms of servitude and harsh labor systems. Facing the growing labor demand in these rapidly expanding economies, the decimation of indigenous labor from disease and war, and prohibitions against enslaving indigenous peoples, the Spanish and Portuguese would enslave and forcibly transport millions of Africans to the Americas for nearly four hundred years, up to the nineteenth century. Fully fifteen times as many Africans— eleven times in Brazil only—were brought to Latin America compared to those shipped to the United States.

The region's ethnoracial complexity increased further through the extensive mixture of Indians, Africans, and Europeans and a racial hierarchy, with Europeans at the top and blacks and indigenous peoples at the bottom. Race mixture and large nonwhite populations would become a central concern in the nineteenth century with the new independence of these republics when elites became concerned that these factors would doom national development and thus they sought ways to whiten their population. By the mid-twentieth century, as race science was becoming discredited and openly racist societies were becoming global pariahs, many Latin American elites turned their race mixture into virtues, with a new ideology of *mestizaje*, Though the elites moved from centuries of explicit racial domination toward proclaiming harmonious race relations, social hierarchies based on race, color, and language have nonetheless persisted (Patrinos and Psacharoupolos 1994; Flórez et al. 2001; Ñopo et al. 2007; Telles 2007).

Today, most Latin American countries have constitutionally declared themselves multiculturalist, and with this multiculturalist turn many Latin American countries have, at least officially, begun to recognize ethnoracial distinctions and to acknowledge the disadvantages and discrimination suffered by indigenous and Afrodescendants. Brazil, as well as other countries to a lesser extent, has even instituted social policies to redress minority disadvantages. Multiculturalism has also been accompanied by a growing consciousness of ethnic diversity and the adoption of ethnoracial identification in the censuses of nearly all Latin American countries, many for the first time in decades. Census recognition of indigenous and Afrodescendant people is an important first step that permits understanding how many they are, what their sociodemographic profiles are, and how much ethnoracial inequality there is.

In 2008, the Project on Ethnicity and Race in Latin America (PERLA) was formed in an effort to collect and analyze new data to explore a wide range of ethnoracial issues in the region, providing much-needed data on ethnoracial conditions in the region. By designing nationally representative surveys on a broad range of ethnoracial issues, PERLA has gone well beyond the one or two ethnoracial classification questions found in national censuses and other official surveys. PERLA surveys include several ethnoracial classification and inequality items, questions on perceived discrimination, and public opinion questions about ethnoracial minorities, social policies, and social movements. Our analyses of these surveys provides new truths based on solid data for a region that has long been in denial about deep-seated ethnoracial inequalities, injustices, and prejudiced attitudes, not to mention the need for policies that seek to redress them.

This book summarizes the findings from PERLA's five-year effort—two years designing the surveys and three years dedicated to the analysis of PERLA data and the production of this book. With this book, PERLA seeks to inform academic analysis, official and other data collection efforts, policy making, and public opinion in the region. In the four countries we analyze (Brazil, Colombia, Mexico, and Peru), like many others in the region, social movements of black and indigenous people now demand that they be recognized, including in national censuses. As these nation-states begin to democratize, political decisions can no longer be fully inattentive to their demands for recognition and social justice. Thus the time is ripe for rich empirical analyses that can inform academic discussions and policy making about race and ethnicity in many Latin American countries, although the extent of receptiveness varies among them. In particular, policy discussions, including those about the census and how to collect such data, have become increasingly common in Colombia and Peru. In Mexico, academic discussions have only just begun, and policies to redress ethnoracial inequality still seem out of reach. In the absence of ethnoracial data, such studies have been relatively scant in those three countries. But Brazil seems to have moved fairly quickly from socially denying racial discrimination to widely recognizing racism and working to reverse it, partly as a result of studies that directly challenged its racial democracy ideology.

With the PERLA surveys, we are able to empirically examine critical issues in race and ethnicity that cannot be assessed using available data sources. We pay particular attention to the factors involved in the formation of ethnic identities, the extent and nature of inequality and discrimination, the degree of ethnic inequality, and the nature of social relations across ethnic boundaries, all set within the particular national context. We examine a wide range of methods for classifying race and ethnicity, from asking respondents various self-identification questions and using interviewer-classification, employing different category schemes; an innovative feature of our study for all countries is the use of a color rating by the interviewer. We are also interested in public opinion about ethnicity and race, including individuals' experiences of discrimination against themselves or others, and their attitudes about black and indigenous social movements and policies that may alleviate ethnic and racial inequality and discrimination.

We emphasize a comparative sociology of the contemporary situation, though one that is embedded within a particular historical and political context. We draw on PERLA's in-depth surveys of the four countries and the scholarly literature to better understand the current situation. Rather than a series of chapters in an edited volume, this book is the product of a five-year multinational and multidisciplinary collaboration involving leading specialists in each country, the design of common surveys, and collective research framing and analysis. The book's chapters are thus in dialogue with each other and address common issues and themes that draw from the perspectives of various disciplines and both national and international debates.

*Pigmentocracies* highlights our finding that skin color is a central axis of social stratification in at least several Latin American countries, though it is often ignored. The term *pigmentocracy* was coined by Chilean anthropologist

Alejandro Lipschutz in 1944 to refer to inequalities or hierarchies based on both ethnoracial categories, such as indigenous and black, and a skin color continuum. While Lipschutz referred to ethnoracial categories and skin color, he described them interchangeably. We separate and closely examine these two dimensions of race and their effect on inequality. Fully seventy years after the coining of the term, we have found that *pigmentocracy* is quite appropriate for describing Latin America's ethnoracial inequality.

Throughout this book, we present numerous findings, but we highlight five sets of findings based on the analysis of the PERLA surveys, which stand out in all four countries. We further discuss these in chapter 6. The major findings can be summed up as follows:

1. Race/Ethnicity is multidimensional and can be measured in multiple ways, including how ethnoracial questions are worded, which categories are used, and who answers the question. These have implications for population counts of ethnoracial groups and estimates of ethnoracial inequality (Measurement).

2. Estimates of inequality based on ethnoracial classification do not consistently support expectations of pigmentocracy (Categorical Pigmentocracy).

3. Skin color is a more consistent but overlooked dimension of ethnoracial inequality in Latin America (Continuous Pigmentocracy).

4. Ethnoracial discrimination is commonly experienced and witnessed in Latin America (Perceived Discrimination).

5. Most Latin Americans support ethnic and race-based social movements and public policies to promote black and indigenous people (Minority Support).

Despite many similarities in PERLA survey outcomes, the ethnoracial histories and contexts of the four countries are often distinct, as we show in the separate chapters. We thus invite readers to explore these differences and similarities across chapters, which are set in a collaboratively defined set of common intellectual concerns, forged in PERLA's deliberations. In the rest of this chapter, we examine the history of PERLA and the research questions we developed. We then present a short history of race and ethnicity in the region and a background on the new ethnoracial census data. Finally, we examine major conceptual issues, such as distinctions between race and ethnicity, as well as color and language, and our decision to examine both black and indigenous populations.

## The Project on Ethnicity and Race in Latin America

The PERLA research team is made up of leading analysts of ethnicity and race in each of the four countries, along with the principal investigator who has worked extensively on Brazil. Moreover, PERLA collaborators represent the fields of sociology, anthropology, linguistics, history, and (socio)economics; in combination, they also cover the literature in English, Spanish, and Portuguese in each of the countries. Thus a main goal of this project, has been to explore and engage each other on conceptual and empirical issues in the study of race and ethnicity, across national and linguistic boundaries. In so doing, we have sought to make a rich tradition of academic analysis available in English that was often only in Spanish and Portuguese.

The four countries we have chosen to analyze together represent about 65 percent of Latin America's population. Mexico and Peru are home to more than half of the indigenous people in Latin America. Brazil alone is the home of a large majority of Afro–Latin Americans—a full 90 million—while Colombia has the region's second largest population of Afrodescendants. Moreover, these four countries represent a variety of historical nation-building processes and several configurations of ethnoracial dominance, thus providing an excellent place to begin developing a quantitative empirical base for understanding ethnicity and race in the region.

Altogether we conducted six separate surveys: four national surveys, one for each country, an indigenous oversample survey in Mexico, and an Afrodescendant oversample survey in Colombia. We conducted the oversample surveys because the latter two groups officially represent less than 15 percent of the population of Mexico and Colombia, and including additional cases (the oversample) assured that we would have enough cases for analysis. For the national representative surveys, we conducted approximately fifteen hundred randomly sampled interviews in Peru and one thousand each in Mexico, Colombia,[1] and Brazil; for the oversamples, we interviewed five hundred indigenous Mexicans and five hundred Afro-Colombians. The national surveys are self-weighted in Brazil, Mexico, and Peru and are adjusted with sampling weights in Colombia.

The surveys were conducted by leading survey institutes in each of the four countries: Instituto Análise in Brazil, Centro Nacional de Consultoría in Colombia, Data Opinión Publica y Mercados in Mexico, and IPSOS Apoyo in Peru. These institutions collaborated directly with the PERLA authors in each country in the survey design, pretesting of the questionnaire, and interviewer training. We were fortunate to be able to work interactively with the staff of these firms, each of which was quite cognizant about the rigors of academic survey research. They were attentive to our methodological concerns, such as question wording, pretesting surveys, and training interviewers. Although the sample sizes are moderate by survey standards, resulting in margins of error of about 3 percent (plus or minus), these limitations are overcome by the innovative nature of these data. Getting exact percentage estimates was not our goal; rather, we sought to provide an extensive profile of ethnoracial issues in a region where little is known about such matters, using representative data.

We decided to focus on Afrodescendants in Brazil and Colombia and indigenous people in Mexico and Peru, although we also attend to the indigenous in Colombia and Brazil and Afrodescendants in Mexico and Peru. The reason for this choice was largely practical: facing limits on the number of questions we could ask in the surveys, we decided to focus on one particular group in pairs of countries, rather than have less depth on both groups in all countries.

The PERLA surveys are the first cross-national representative surveys of race and ethnicity in Latin America, as far we know. Representative surveys like these are very important because of their fairly large samples and their ability to measure a variety of phenomena that can be generalized to the entire population. Surveys like PERLA's, with their agility, are able to examine a much wider range of issues than censuses, including alternative forms of ethnoracial classification; this approach facilitates scholarly analysis, and yields both suggestions for policy making and ideas on improving census taking itself. Admittedly, censuses are valuable for providing information for entire populations and for small areas. But censuses are very expensive and logistically complicated, and they have only one or two questions measuring race and ethnicity—generally using ethnoracial identification.

At about the same time as the in-depth surveys analyzed in this book were undertaken, PERLA also added a short ethnicity module to the 2010 AmericasBarometer (LAPOP), which included the color palette in all the countries they surveyed in 2010—a feature that has remained in their subsequent surveys. In eight countries, the 2010 AmericasBarometer also included several questions on racial attitudes, parental occupation, and perceived discrimination, which are analyzed in separate articles (Telles and Bailey 2013; Telles and Garcia 2013; Telles and Steele 2012; Canache et al. 2014; Telles and Paschel forthcoming).

## Research Concerns and Ethnoracial Classifications

Over the course of nearly two years, the PERLA team designed a common survey instrument for the four countries across the six surveys, with additional questions that were specific to each survey. Our discussions (in three languages) involved three international meetings, seven major revisions of the questionnaire, numerous Skype calls, hundreds of emails, survey pretesting, and trips by the primary author to each of the Latin American sites. We had intensive discussions and, as can be expected with such a diverse set of collaborators, we often did not agree. But these disagreements were productive: they often pushed us to better resolution and sometimes, when they involved an empirical issue, to testing our competing hypotheses in the field.

Most of us started out with a concern for understanding various kinds of ethnoracial inequalities in Latin America, but we also brought various questions that emerged with our deliberations. The issue of ethnoracial classification became central, especially considering the various methods that censuses have used to classify populations and the fact that the census has been the most important multicultural initiative taken by some Latin America states. Substantively, we suspected that the choice of method for classification would have implications for determining a country's ethnoracial composition and thus for how the nation is to be understood. Indeed, the ethnoracial categories that censuses create often guide how nations and individuals understand their own identities and assign identities to others (Kertzer and Ariel 2002). Moreover, we believed that alternative methods of classification were also likely to affect the extent of ethnoracial inequality. We also recognized that particular classification methods might be equipped to explain some social phenomena better than others. As we came to see that there was no one-size-fits-all approach, we set out to explore alternatives using the PERLA surveys.

Although we wanted to test several possible alternative questions and response categories, we also recognized that we could not ask all of them because of limited space in the questionnaire and because asking several similar questions in the same questionnaire could prime respondents, or set them up to answer subsequent questions in certain ways. At that point we prioritized particular questions. More difficult, though, was getting the right question for each of our concerns. What kind of questions would capture the essence of our concerns and what was the best way to phrase them so that they could be understood by as wide a range of people as possible, in all four countries? This often involved field pretesting of various alternatives, which also presented a challenge regarding the Spanish-Portuguese translations and, in some cases, translations of questions that had been employed in the United States. Finally, we had to decide on the order of questions in order to make the interviews as smooth and understandable as possible for respondents and to minimize priming. After all that, we could begin to carry out the surveys and do the analysis.

PERLA team members would often describe the particular way ethnoracial classifications were made in their own country; by comparing experiences across the four countries, we came to realize that we should test these alternatives against each other in the same questionnaire. We discussed the "polysemy" of categories such as indigenous and mestizo, in whom the core of the concept is the same but with wide variations in meanings, often depending on the situation, but in our case often depending on the way the question was asked. We were motivated by the idea that race or ethnic classification is fluid in the region; we also knew about researchers' experiences with changing the ethnoracial questions in national censuses and surveys, as occurred in Colombia, Mexico, and Peru. We challenged the idea that race or ethnicity is static or one-dimensional and came to agree that it could not be fully understood with a single census question. Therefore we included several questions on ethnoracial classification.

Even among the four countries we examine, there was wide variation in how questions were asked. For example, the 1993 Colombian census asked individuals if they identified as belonging to a black community; this question captured only 1.5 percent of the Colombian population as black. However, the 2005 census found 10.6 percent of the Colombian population was black or mulatto; it asked respondents if they were black or mulatto on the basis of their "culture or physical features." Thus the earlier census seems to have missed a large majority of Afro-Colombians. A similar change occurred in Costa Rica: because of a comparable change in wording, the black and mulatto population grew from 2.0 to 7.8 percent between the 2000 and 2011 censuses. A notable change was the huge decrease in Bolivia's indigenous population from 62 percent to 42 percent between the 2001 and 2012 national censuses. Not surprisingly, the statistical disappearance of so many indigenous Bolivians led to much discussion in that country, including questioning the very nature of the Bolivian nation; even though the change may have been largely due to changes in the wording of the census question (Fontana 2013). Finally, Argentina and Uruguay asked respondents in their recent censuses if they are of indigenous or African *descent*, so we also included such a question.

The PERLA collaborators were also concerned about the response categories used. We noted that the Colombian, Brazilian, and Mexican censuses simply asked if respondents were "indigenous," though the question wording varied, and the 2007 Peruvian census did not have a question on indigenous identification (but did on language); meanwhile countries like Bolivia and Guatemala queried respondents on whether they belonged to one among several indigenous categories, including Aymara and Quechua in Bolivia and Kaqchikel and Kiche in Guatemala. We expected that persons who identify in the latter kinds of categories may be loath to identify in the highly stigmatized category of indigenous, as de la Cadena (2000) has documented for Peru in her aptly titled *Indigenous Mestizos*. Indeed, we found that only 4.7 percent of Peruvians in the PERLA sample self-identified as indigenous when the category "indigenous" was used but fully 23.3 percent identified as indigenous when the categories included Quechua, Aymara, and other indigenous groups.

Another issue was asking respondents whether they consider themselves to be white or mestizo. Brazil is exemplary in that the ethnoracial question in its census asks whether one's race or color is white, brown (*pardo*), black (*preto*), indigenous, or Asian. Ecuador also includes the categories of white and mestizo in addition to indigenous and black. However, the Population Division of the UN's Economic Commission on Latin America and the Caribbean (CELADE) exhorts countries to ask people only whether they are a minority group member, such as indigenous or black, since including the other categories may draw persons away from the more stigmatized black and indigenous categories (del Popolo and Schkolnik 2012). Indeed, most countries do not include a white or mestizo term (Telles and Flores 2013). Colombia offers only the minority group categories including black/mulatto and indigenous, and Mexico's only ethnoracial question asks if the population identifies as indigenous.

Self-identification has become the standard method for collecting racial and ethnic data around the world (Morning 2009). This follows from a rights perspective that considers that all people have the right to identify themselves as they want. CELADE follows the mandate set by the International Labor Organization's (ILO) Convention 169: self-identification is the primary criterion for counting indigenous people. CELADE seeks to extend this approach for counting Afrodescendants (del Popolo and Schkolnik 2012), although it seems to violate the right of all people to self-identify by recommending that ethnoracial identification be limited to only the disadvantaged groups such as indigenous and black.

The census interviewers' practice of ethnoracially classifying respondents in the past is considered today to disregard respondents' identities and as state-controlled efforts to categorize them (Nobles 2000). Ironically, however, one could argue that states often violate the right to self-identification by imposing particular census questions and ethnoracial categories and forcing people to identify with—or reject—them. Moreover, the rule of self-identification is rarely followed, even where it is mandated. Censuses tend to rely on responses by a single person in the household who responds for the other household members—so most ethnoracial classification in censuses is actually based on classification by others (Telles 2004). Finally, census takers are known to avoid asking the ethnoracial question because of time constraints, or out of politeness; instead, they classify the respondent themselves (Martínez 2008 ).

Analyzing these issues, we thought that self-identification is especially useful for understanding phenomena such as identity, willingness to join ethnic social movements, and other social phenomena that tend to involve ethnoracial self-understanding. We have found that self-identification is less adequate for understanding social phenomena like discrimination, where others do the classifying, in ways that may be independent of how the person facing discrimination self-identifies. Since Latin America's system of ethnoracial classification is quite fluid (de la Cadena 2000; Telles and Flores 2013), self-identification also allows individuals to escape from stigmatized cultural and phenotypic categories and identify with the dominant group. Thus it may hide or underestimate the actual disadvantages of indigenous and Afrodescendant peoples and those whose looks are especially typical of indigenous people and Afrodescendants (according to social stereotypes), as others have found (Telles and Lim 1998; Bailey, Loveman, and Muniz 2012; Telles et al. unpublished).

How then do we monitor racial inequality and discrimination, a goal of modern ethnoracial statistics gathering (Morning 2009; del Popolo and Schkolnik 2012)? After all, isn't the appropriate monitoring of racial inequality and discrimination also a right? That is why we also examined external classifications as made by interviewers: ethnicity may be self-identified but it is also regularly defined by others. Even in the case of the indigenous, as Rachel Sieder (2002, 2) notes, identity involves "a complex dynamic of self-identification and ascription." Ethnoracial self-identification is clearly endogenous as it may involve a calculus based not only on appearance but also on variables such as culture, personal trajectory, and social status. Thus, for the purpose of understanding ethnoracial inequality and disadvantage, we believe Latin American states should consider alternatives based on external classification. Race and ethnicity are not simply a matter of identity or consciousness. They also involve the gaze of the other.

## Skin Color and Its Measurement

We had particular concerns with skin color and its measurement. As our title *Pigmentocracy* suggests, we paid particular attention to the issue of skin color, which is a dimension of race that cannot be subsumed under the traditional category-based notions of ethnicity and race. While one's race is often named and recognized in categories such as mestizo, indigenous, or black, the continuous aspect of skin color is less often so-named and thus often lies hidden from analysts and others who do not probe for racial differences beyond the ethnoracial categories. As Jablonski (2012, 196) notes, "The ordering of races according to skin color has been one of the most stable intellectual constructs of all time, even though the number, inclusivity and acceptability of racial categories have varied greatly." We believe that its absence from data collection and analysis in Latin America has helped to keep it as an invisible and unacknowledged dimension of inequality, and thus we chose to draw attention to this important variable. In particular, we hypothesized that actual skin color is a primary stratifying variable in Latin America and that social disadvantages are correlated with successively darker skin tones. In particular, since we believed that Latin Americans often use skin color to assign greater worth to lighter-toned persons and lesser value to progressively darker persons, some of us thought that we needed a direct measure of color to capture this phenomenon. Thus, we went beyond ethnoracial evaluation by the interviewer and sought to directly capture this relatively exogenous variable. In sum, racial self-identification, classification by others or interviewers, and actual skin color are all different ways to measure various dimensions of ethnicity and race, but they are all socially meaningful because of notions of white superiority and a societal urge to classify in such ways. Needless to say, these meanings and the various constructs that convey them are socially created—i.e., they are social constructions.

Skin color is a continuous and clearly visible characteristic that may discriminate among people who identify in the same race category but who are actually of different colors. This is particularly true of the quasi-national category of mestizo, which may hide much physical or skin color variation and thus distinct racialized experiences. One could ask respondents to self-identify on the basis of color, as the Brazilian census does (Nobles 2000; Telles 2004; Petrucelli 2012), or one could have the interviewer evaluate color as was done in a survey of Mexico (Villarreal 2010). We felt that these were useful alternatives, but we could further reduce the subjectivity and endogeneity in classification by providing actual color samples to match to each respondent's color. We thus created a color palette, which interviewers used to rate the facial skin tone of respondents. Thus we created a variable denoting skin color as observed by the interviewer using an actual color palette; that allowed us to reasonably fix skin tone, arguably the primary physical characteristic associated with racial differences in Latin America (Gravlee 2005; Guimarães 2012). Members of the

PERLA team held differing views on using the color palette, but through an interactive process we agreed that it was valuable, though there was disagreement about the extent of its exogeneity or objectivity.

Interviewer-rated skin color based on a color scale has been used in several surveys about racial discrimination and racial attitudes in the United States (Gullickson 2005; Keith and Herring 1991; Massey and Sánchez 2010), but it has not, to our knowledge, been used in Latin America. Although skin color evaluations by interviewers are by no means perfect,[2] we believe that in most cases they closely capture the respondent's skin color, especially in the aggregate where large numbers tend to even out deviations.

To minimize distortions in the interviewers' ratings, we instructed them to rate each respondent's facial skin color according to a palette of eleven skin tones (1 = lightest, 11 = darkest), which we took from Internet photographs.[3] We told them not to take into account any other factor when assessing a respondent's skin color. Both surveys in all countries used the same palette, produced by a single printing company. We pretested the palette extensively in several countries to ensure it would be easy for interviewers to use and that it covered the range of skin tones found in the field. We also trained the interviewers in all four countries using a uniform training manual.

At first glance, some might consider the color palette to be an exercise in racial measurement like those conducted by the scientific racial classifiers of the nineteenth century who used instruments to measure cranial and other bodily features to determine racial and psychological traits. Of course, we used it for a completely different reason: to understand how social cognition of skin color variations affects social stratification and discrimination, and to assess whether social inequalities are based on skin color. Why not use a measure of skin color if that is what humans notice when they encounter others and decide how to treat them?

Another justification for our use of the color palette derives from classic sociological theories of social determinism, as developed by such theorists as Durkheim and Mauss (1963), as well as the more current theory of Pierre Bourdieu (1984).[4] For them, perceived differences in bodies or appearances often have the effect of "othering" individuals based on social criteria or rules that people use to establish order or hierarchy. Social psychologists interpret these as cognitive perceptions that rely on stereotypes or shortcuts for locating others in a social order. In racialized societies, humans use skin color as a criterion for how they value and treat others. (See also the idea of "chromophobia" as discussed in chapter 3.)

On the basis of our discussions with the team and outside colleagues, and through pretesting, we found both benefits and costs to using the color palette, but we concluded that the benefits clearly outweigh the costs. Thus, we aim to be entirely transparent about our use of it. We did encounter some resistance to the palette because it reifies socially constructed distinctions that are stigmatizing, distinctions we all wish did not exist. We encountered two types of negative reactions. Some came from dark-skinned persons themselves. During a couple of presentations to groups made up mostly of black movement activists, dark-skinned persons told us they felt objectified in a way they did not feel otherwise. However, they said they also recognized its potential net benefits: we could use it to verify the negative social consequences of dark skin color and bring them out into the open. Being objectified like this, they said, would be a small price to pay for the benefits of better understanding how color shapes inequality in the region.

Second, Latin American social scientists who attended some of our early presentations warned us about the potential for the media to misuse our research: they could say we were making color distinctions that would potentially create new social divisions in these countries, where color presumably did not matter. More troubling, it appeared that at least one analyst thought that the success of the mestizaje project had actually ended nineteenth-century racial distinctions and that our methodology would threaten to reinstate those distinctions. In response, we explained that it was important to test the hypothesis, for which there was more than reasonable evidence that Latin Americans are attentive to color differences and use them to discriminate against others. The racist motives of nineteenth-century scientists are hardly a reason for us to avoid evaluating skin color, especially given our motives: we seek to understand the social phenomenon of racism, not to reify biology. Thus we were willing to challenge perceptions that color does not matter in parts of Latin America or that it simply should not be discussed, ideas that evolve from the presumably progressive notion of mestizaje.

Ultimately, our analysis of skin color proved us right: skin color cut through the cover of mestizaje and revealed an unambiguous pigmentocracy in the four countries we examined. We found both that skin color tended to be a better predictor of ethnoracial inequality than the traditional ethnoracial categories and that it was closely related to reported discrimination (see Telles and Steele 2012 on the relation between skin color and educational attainment throughout the Americas). Let us be clear here: we are not advocating that governments use such a skin color measure in censuses, as doing so would create considerable political resistance and require vast technical resources. But that decision does not diminish its importance for understanding the continuous color-based dimension of societal inequalities. We strongly advocate, at least for now, that researchers use color measures in surveys in order to understand and monitor color-based inequalities.

We also spent much time in developing questions about experiences of racial discrimination. We were interested in whether respondents experienced discrimination, whether they understood it as discrimination on the basis of color or language, and also whether they witnessed others experiencing discrimination. Were the ideas that Latin Americans did not perceive ethnoracial discrimination accurate? Moreover, where did those experiences most occur? Were they at government institutions such as health posts or schools, or were they in public in general?

Finally, we were interested in the large area of inquiry known as racial attitudes, which are well known in surveys in the United States but less known in Latin America. What did normal Colombians, Brazilians, Mexicans, and Peruvians think about indigenous people and Afrodescendants? Why did they think they tended to be poor? What did they think about intermarriage occurring in their own family, about having black or indigenous neighbors or schoolmates, or about creating multicultural policies? In particular what did the population think about bilingual programs or having quotas for ethnoracial minorities in higher education? What about people joining black or indigenous social movements that demand greater social inclusion? There has hardly been any data to answer these questions for Colombia, Mexico, or Peru. Although Brazil has had several social surveys with some of these questions, many of the PERLA questions have never been used in that country.

## A Short Ethnoracial History

No one can completely understand the current ethnic situation of Latin America without understanding its historical foundations. Here and in the country chapters, we draw from the rich body of historical research. Historians have generally focused on the unique histories of each nation-state, but in this introduction and throughout the chapters we emphasize comparative elements. In this historical section, I largely rely on the histories presented in chapters 2–5 to cite the appropriate references.

Today, the basic elements of colonization, slavery, whitening, mestizaje, and multiculturalism are often thought of as similar in all Latin American countries, although in reality they vary substantially among countries. The authors of each of the four chapters discuss the development of racialist thinking in their countries and how this process was shaped by distinct social structures, including labor systems, nationalist and international discourse, development plans, and social movements. The importance of ideologies and regimes of whitening, mestizaje, and multiculturalism are often mentioned in the historiographic literature on race in the post-independence periods of all four countries that we examine, and they provide the context for the current ethnoracial configurations with important national variations, as we describe here. They are also important in several other countries in the region, though clearly not in all. These stand in contrast to the U.S. case, which includes race-based legal segregation and a civil rights revolution ironically set within a system that long defended democracy, factors that were largely absent in Latin America.

## Colonization, Independence, and Whitening

Throughout the colonial period, the biological reproduction of whites was generally constrained by the high sex ratio among Spanish and Portuguese colonists because their immigration to the Americas was largely male. Spanish and Portuguese males, seeking to escape poverty in Europe, came to the New World in search of wealth; in contrast, the English settlement of the United States tended to be more family oriented, beginning with many families that were escaping religious persecution. In Latin America the result was a relatively small, and mostly male, European population; they, and their *criollo* (American-born) descendants were oriented toward resource extraction economies, fueled by a large black, indigenous, and mixed-race population. The paucity of white women led to high rates of mixture between nonwhite women and white men, especially lower-class white men whose status reduced their marital prospects but whose whiteness gave them access to nonwhite women. The result was extensive race mixture (mestizaje), which was apparently greater than in the United States where a more balanced sex ratio among whites emerged from a more family-based immigration in the colonial period (Telles 2004; Martínez-Alier 1974; McCaa et al. 1979).

Though the idea of race came into being in the eighteenth and nineteenth centuries, systems of domination and power, based partly on ancestry, were clearly present before that. The extensive mixture that was occurring in the Spanish colonies became a concern for colonial authorities who sought to regulate relations among persons of varying ancestry. During much of the seventeenth and eighteenth centuries and until independence in the early nineteenth century, Spanish colonial authorities established a system of *castas* (literally, castes), which defined the proportion of Spanish blood that people carried. Spanish royal edicts mandated that subjects be taxed and assigned trades and offices according to their *casta*. The casta system was not a unified, coherent system throughout Spanish America because each *audiencia* could introduce local casta regulations. However, the authorities often used phenotype or skin color or other phenotypic markers because genealogies were rarely available except in the most elite families. Spaniards and their "pure-blooded" descendants were clearly aware of their privileged status as they were given full legal and social rights, which granted them access to elite jobs, schools, occupations, and various economic opportunities. Whiteness also bestowed pureblood Spaniards with honor and pride; even lower-class whites treasured their racial purity as their "most precious and inalienable asset, an inheritance which entitled them to unquestioned legal superiority over non-whites" (Andrews 1980, 18). Whiteness also became a valued property in the marriage market for both whites and nonwhites, allowing the former to maintain high status for their children and permitting the latter higher status for themselves and especially their children (Acuña Leon and Chavarria Lopez 1991; Martínez-Alier 1974).

Eventually, Spaniards began to deploy the term *raza* (literally, race) instead of *casta*, especially in reference to persons of full or partial African ancestry (Martinez 2009). But local elites began to suspend casta laws with Spain's liberal constitution of 1812, making Spain and its colonies a single nation, and these laws everywhere would fall with the independence movements of the 1820s, when most people (except slaves) became formally equal before the law. Moreover, as generations of race mixing made castes unsustainable and as mercantile capitalism expanded, feudal-like ideas about lineage were gradually replaced by informal discourses about physical appearance (Martinez 2008; Graham 1990). The movement out of one casta and into another, often associated with changing professions, seems to be early evidence of Latin America's substantial racial fluidity, which we document for the current period.

Until the later nineteenth century, Latin American societies were predominately rural and mostly nonwhite. Andrews (2004) estimates that in 1800 only 18 percent of Mexicans, 26 percent of both Colombians and Peruvians, and 30 percent of Brazilians were white, although it was usually impossible to distinguish between whites and mestizos. By contrast, 67 percent of Brazilians and 39 percent of Colombians were Afrodescendants, while 60 percent of Mexicans and 63 percent of Peruvians were indigenous. In addition, fully 20 percent of Colombians were indigenous, and 10 percent of Mexicans and 6 percent of Peruvians were Afrodescendants. At that point, even Argentina's population was fully 37 percent Africans or of African origin (Andrews 1980; 2004).

Beginning in the nineteenth century, Latin American elites set out to create independent nations out of the remnants of the old Iberian colonies in the New World; they often debated extensively about how to incorporate indigenous and black people. Their concepts of nation were built largely around ideas of race and mixture, motivated by concerns over their large nonwhite populations. Considering the large size of their mixed-race, black, and indigenous populations, and often fearing dissension from them, Latin American elites often sought to include them in vital areas such as the military but limited them from becoming part of the elite and middle classes. In their fights for independence and during civil wars, as in Gran Colombia and Cuba, many criollo leaders sought alliances with nonwhites, largely because they perceived them as essential in the fight for independence from European powers. Thus they sometimes promised nonwhites citizenship and freedom in the new nations, though often as racial subordinates. Later wars in the nineteenth century also involved slaves and indigenous persons who enlisted in the hope of being freed or acquiring land.

Brazil was the last country in the Americas to abolish slavery, in 1888, and had by far the largest slave population. Moreover, its independence period was much different from that in Spanish Latin America. In 1821 Brazil became independent from Portugal, but it remained a monarchy headed by the son of the Portuguese monarch, who had previously fled Portugal in advance of Napoleon's army. Because of this relatively smooth transition, it had no significant war of independence with the great losses of life seen in the former Spanish republics. Brazil became the exception to a relatively warless nineteenth century when the Brazilian monarchy entered the bloody Paraguayan War of 1864 to 1870 and promised manumission to its largely slave army recruits. By that time, though, most of the descendants of Africans had been freed, although a significant African-born population was still largely enslaved, as the slave trade ended in that country only in 1850 (Andrews 2004).

From the late nineteenth to the early twentieth century, Latin American elites became increasingly concerned that their often large, nonwhite populations might imperil national development, mainly in response to contemporary scientifically endorsed ideas of a biological white supremacy. Elite thinkers ranging from Domingo Sarmiento of Argentina in the 1880s to Brazil's Francisco Oliveira Vianna in the 1920s believed that only Europeans were capable of achieving full progress and that their large nonwhite populations would doom them to perpetual second-class status (Skidmore 1976; Helg 1990). To be modern like Europe and the United States, they thought that a white population was essential.

During that time, national elites shared a common concern: to make their countries modern. Early pseudoscientific theories that linked race to intelligence had turned their large nonwhite populations into liabilities. Nevertheless, the neo-Lamarckian ideas about the mutability of race and constructive miscegenation in which white genes would predominate in successive generations gave these elites hope that their populations could be whitened and could thus become a modern nation (Skidmore 1976; Stepan 1991).

Although Argentina, Cuba, Venezuela, and (southern) Brazil succeeded in attracting European immigrants, most other Latin American countries did not, despite their efforts. Soon after its 1880s war with Chile, the loss of which they blamed partly on indigenous blood, Peruvian elites made similar attempts to attract European immigrants (Larson 2004b; Sulmont and Callirgos, chap. 4 in this volume) but mostly failed. Mexico was able to attract only a few European immigrants in the twentieth century. Colombian elites, who seemed more eager for Argentine-like whitening than those in the other three countries, probably fared the worst as they attracted almost no European immigrants and thus fell miserably short of their goal.

## Mestizaje

By the 1930s, leading thinkers in many Latin American countries (clearly not all)[5] would turn the previous racialist thinking of whitening on its head, with their innovative nation-building ideas of mestizaje. Scientific racism, the basis for whitening strategies in Latin America, began to come under fire in the early twentieth century in the United States, Europe, and Latin America. Its scientific undoing was largely at the hands of anthropologist Franz Boas, who argued that so-called racial differences were rooted not in biology but rather in culture. Moreover, Boas had a tremendous influence in Latin America as he trained arguably the most important thinkers of the new mestizaje discourse in Brazil and Mexico: Gilberto Freyre and Manuel Gamio (see chapters 2 and 5). Through such thinkers, the scientifically backed but increasingly discredited ideas of whitening began to lose support in favor of progressive ideologies that viewed race mixture as positive. Throughout much of the twentieth century, Brazil touted itself as a racial democracy, which could be contrasted with the horrors of explicitly racist regimes in the United States under Jim Crow, South Africa with Apartheid, and Nazi Germany. Mestizaje, referring to both biological and cultural mixture, had become a central trope for understanding ethnicity, race, and nation in much of Latin America; it continues to be used as a point of contrast with the United States. All four countries examined in this book developed some version of mestizaje ideas for nation building, with their own national particularities.

In contrast to whitening, mestizaje would put a positive spin on the region's biological and cultural mixing by glorifying it as central to the nation (though not necessarily discarding the scientifically endorsed ideas of white biological supremacy). Latin American elites would often claim that mestizaje signaled racial harmony; at the same time, they promoted the idea that Latin America was morally superior to a racially segregated United States. Moreover, Latin American societies did not face the "American" dilemma of ethnoracial injustice in a country that considered itself democratic and egalitarian, since they were clearly authoritarian and racial hierarchies were widely accepted.

More than just ideologies of race and ethnicity, mestizaje ideologies would present racial mixture as an essential feature of these new nations and of a national peoplehood, as they sought to proclaim that race and nation were coterminous. Elites sought to create visions of the nation as homogeneous; in these visions, national or mestizo identities would seek to replace the previous ethnoracial identities (Wade 1993; Telles 2004; Knight 1990). Their narratives presented Brazilians, Mexicans, and other national subjects as metaraces that fused white, indigenous, and (sometimes) black blood or culture; now, mestizos or mixed-race persons would be considered the ideal or prototypical citizens (Whitten 2004; Knight 1990; Mallon 1992; Skidmore 1976). Mestizo identities would be taken up by many in the population, even those who would often be seen as, and otherwise identify themselves as indigenous, black and mulatto (de la Cadena 2004; Roca 2008; also see chapters in this book).

Nevertheless, mestizaje ideologies varied within the region (Wade 2009; Telles and Garcia 2013). For example, nation-building elites in Mexico and Brazil and at times in Peru ("the living synthesis") provided particularly strong mestizaje ideologies that largely transcended whitening. By contrast, mestizaje had particularly low resonance in the so-called white nations of the Southern Cone (Argentina, Uruguay, and, to some extent, Chile) and Costa Rica (Andrews 1980, 2010; Telles and Flores 2013), which continued to value whitening. Among the four cases examined in this book, elites in Colombia most closely embraced whitening, explicitly embracing mestizaje as a way to move the population toward whiteness. On the other hand, Colombian social movements would stress the indigenous and black essence of that mostly mestizo country, with its significant black and indigenous populations and relatively small white population. Elites in Peru would come to embrace a mestizaje that glorified an indigenous past but saw Hispanismo as the dominant element into which indigenous people could and would assimilate, achieving a "living synthesis" of the Peruvian people.

Elites in Mexico and Brazil were politically willing and able to promote particularly strong versions of these ideas, partly because their states had strong capacities to disseminate these ideas through educational and cultural campaigns (Mallon 1992; Wade 2009; Telles and Garcia 2013). Moreover, mestizaje thinkers like Manuel Gamio were well positioned in the Mexican state apparatus, and Freyre's ideas gained wide popularity in Brazilian literary circles as his project fit well with nation-making and modernizing efforts. In Mexico, mestizaje arose as a response to the social unrest of the Mexican Revolution. The new ideology was part of a nation-building project that sought to glorify its indigenous heritage and distance itself from Spain and Europe. For example, the state sponsored a mural campaign featuring Diego Rivera's depictions of a brown mestizo Mexico. In Brazil, national identity would form largely around Freyre's (1933) depictions of race mixing in his *Casa Grande e Senzala*, which would be consecrated in the racial democracy spectacles of *samba*, *futebol*, and *carnival* and would showcase Brazil's African origins. Although the narratives in Mexico and Brazil had mostly abandoned the earlier ideas of whitening or white supremacy, one can nevertheless find them grafted onto the elite-led mestizaje narratives of those countries (Wade 1997).

Andean countries tended to stress the binary racialized distinctions between the Spanish and the indigenous; to the extent that mestizaje ideologies existed, they were clearly weaker and shorter lasting than in Mexico, the country to which they are sometimes compared (Mallon 1992; de la Cadena 2000; Larson 2004b). Mallon (1992) found that, because Bolivia and Peru were unable to use state power to unite indigenous groups, the indigenous-Spanish bipolar distinctions remained, though one of the Peruvian versions (living synthesis) is more similar to the Mexican ideology of mestizaje (see chapter 4). Bolivia sought, not wholly successfully, a national mestizo project in its 1952 revolution of unity and integration, but Peru repudiated the indigenous in both its radical and its neoliberal projects (Mallon 1992). Even elite defenders of Indians in the Andes criticized race mixing (culturally and biologically), often suggesting that the pure Indian was better than the mestizo (de la Cadena 2000).

In Mexico, Colombia, and Peru, the mestizaje narratives tended to stress indigenous and Spanish contributions while downplaying or ignoring African contributions, even though all of these countries had imported hundreds of thousands of slaves from Africa. For example, Colombian narratives tended to ignore its African elements or relegated them to the marginalized provinces along the Pacific Coast (Wade 1993), even though blacks have lived in many other parts of the country and constitute at least 10 percent of the national population. Similarly, Mexico's national narratives of mestizaje rarely mention its African roots and, even today, rarely recognize their existence, even though at least 200,000 and perhaps as many as 380,000 Africans were brought to that country. This exclusion is arguably more severe in the Dominican Republic, where African features are apparent among much of the population and Santo Domingo was a major slave port, yet Africans are conspicuously absent from the national mestizaje narratives (Candelario 2007; Howard 2001; Roth 2012). On the other hand, mestizaje ideologies in Brazil and Cuba tended to stress the inclusion of African elements, as well as those of Europeans and Amerindians (Telles 2004; de la Fuente 2001).

Even though ideas on mestizaje were widely considered progressive, they also had critics who argued that they erased race and ethnicity from the consciousness of the general population. For some, mestizaje implied a cultural or statistical genocide of black and indigenous peoples (Nascimento 1979; Bonfil Batalla 1990). Whereas race and ethnicity had been so important in the eighteenth and nineteenth centuries, as the chapters show, the new national narrative would suddenly extinguish ethnoracial distinctions from official and popular discourses.

Although racial hierarchies characterize the socioeconomic structure of both Latin America and the United States, throughout the twentieth century national ideas of mestizaje have stood in contrast to the more long-standing ideas of white racial purity in the United States and the association of modernity with whiteness (Sollors 2000; Bost 2003; Holt 2000).[6] Mestizaje would serve as a useful narrative in these multiracial and racially mixed societies and could be contrasted with the harshness of formal racial segregation in the United States. Although the mestizaje narratives clearly served the interests of elites, they probably gained their wide popular appeal because they revealed more fluid and presumably superior social relations compared to those of their powerful neighbor, the United States. Latin Americans would point to their more widespread racial mixture in both the past and present and thus provide evidence that racial boundaries were blurred and ethnoracial relations more tolerant (and in the Peru case, that Indianness could be overcome). With a huge leap in logic, defenders of mestizaje would often argue that race and racism had consequently been transcended.

Mestizaje has become a widely shared Latin American experience. At the level of racial classification, racial categories are certainly numerous, and classification is more ambiguous and fluid across these categories than in the United States (Wade 1997; Telles 2004), although there is growing fluidity in that country (Rodriguez 2000; Harris and Sim 2002 ; Saperstein and Penner 2012), despite its historic racial classification laws. There was arguably greater actual racial mixture in Latin America simply because of its lopsided sex ratio among its colonizers and the region's near absence of legal prohibitions against intermarriage, which were common in the United States (Cottrol 2013). Today, black-white intermarriage is clearly higher than in the United States, at least in Brazil (Telles 2004), though in Guatemala it is very limited (Ishida 2003). Perhaps more importantly, the presence of mixed-race categories and large numbers of people identifying themselves as such demonstrates the widespread popularity of mixed-raced identification and the fact that mestizaje has become established in Latin America (Telles 2004; Telles and Flores 2013). As a lived experience, Wade (2005) also shows how mestizaje is reflected in family relationships and friendship networks. Mestizaje is also apparent in its cultural form, as in religion (Telles 2004; Andrews 2010; Hill 2010), music (Sansone 2003a; Wade 2005), and literary expression (Martínez-Echazábal 1998; Bost 2003; Miller 2004).

An ideology of mestizaje has also been consistent with a social scientific tradition in Latin America that has emphasized class and treats race as an epiphenomenon of class or as a distraction from class cleavages and class struggle (Altria 2004; Filguera 2001; González Casanova 1965; Portes and Hoffman 2003). According to various scholarly traditions in Latin America that derive from the Marxist, Weberian, Mertonian, and Bourdieuan traditions, stratification and mobility are based mostly on class origins and the class structure (Atria 2004; Filguera 2001). Indeed, current studies of mobility in Latin America tend to ignore the influence of race (Behrman et al. 2001; Torche and Spilerman 2009), whether for reasons of theory or data availability.

### The Multicultural Turn

The contexts for understanding race and ethnicity in much of Latin America are rapidly changing in what is often called the multicultural turn. This has occurred in the context of an economic transition and growing democratization. The domestically focused economic model of industrial growth of the 1980s, based on import substitution, seems to have run its course; now Latin Americans are involved in neoliberal and globalized models of economic development, which have exposed these countries to greater external pressure and scrutiny, including the monitoring of human rights norms by private international organizations and UN human rights committees, legislation, and forums (Van Cott 2000; Telles 2004).

In a rapid transition taking less than three decades, nearly all Latin American countries are now considered representative democracies, in contrast to only four of the nineteen in the mid-1970s (Mainwaring and Pérez Liñán 2014). As part of their democratization process, more nations are officially recognizing the identities, dignity, and rights of Afrodescendants and indigenous people; many have declared themselves multicultural in their constitutions, providing communal and other rights for the indigenous and sometimes for Afrodescendants (Hooker 2005).[7] Democratization and greater transparency are being promoted by domestic civil society, including black and indigenous movements. These forces have started to weaken the mestizaje ideas that tended to homogenize the nation.

Since the 1980s, black and indigenous movements have emerged as important new global and domestic actors, pointing out and challenging the region's inequalities. The 2001 United Nations Conference on Racism in Durban, South Africa, was promoted by black movements, including groups of Afro-Brazilians and Afro-Colombians; it increased awareness of racial inequalities throughout Latin America. At the same time, truth commissions in Peru and Guatemala discovered that most victims of internal armed conflict were indigenous peoples (Comisión de Esclarecimiento Histórico 1999), and the Zapatista rebellion, beginning in 1994 (and still unresolved), reminded Mexicans and the Mexican government that indigenous communities are severely marginalized and have the capacity to hinder national development plans. Often backed by an international network of human rights supporters and institutions, including UN forums to promote human rights, indigenous and black movement activists are now strong enough to pressure their governments to address their persistent social exclusion.

In some cases, new constitutions, laws, and social policies have sought to respond to claims for more racial, ethnic, and gender justice. New leftist and center-left governments, most notably in Brazil and Bolivia, have assumed power in various countries and addressed issues of ethnicity and race in their transformative platforms. In Brazil, the former world champion in income inequality, such inequalities are beginning to decline for the first time in decades, largely through policies designed to alleviate poverty. Moreover, both class- and race-based affirmative action now exists in most public institutes of higher education, upheld by the Brazilian Supreme Court and legislatively mandated for all federal universities and other federal institutes of higher education (Telles and Paixão 2013). On the other hand, race-based policies have also emerged in Colombia, where governments have been relatively conservative.

In sum, multiculturalism refers to a new stage of race thinking in Latin

America, one that recognizes, respects, and endorses the region's ethnic diversity and its benefits for national society. Under multiculturalism, ethnic and racial identities are finally being allowed to flourish, and discrimination can no longer be hidden easily. In reality, though, many people in contemporary Latin America seem to be sitting somewhere between mestizaje and multiculturalism, though that in-between point probably varies widely among these countries. Charles Hale (2002) considers multiculturalism a new form of mestizaje since the state continues to administer and provide a narrative for ethnoracial difference, despite the actions and sentiments of ethnoracial minorities. Thus, our surveys, conducted in 2010, are situated in this particular juncture in Latin American development, between mestizaje and multiculturalism, accompanied by greater state management of ethnicity and race, including in its data collection systems.

## Official Ethnic Statistics in Latin America

Official efforts at data collection largely run parallel to this history. As many countries sought to assess their progress in whitening their populations in the late nineteenth and early twentieth centuries, they took ethnoracial censuses (Loveman 2009; Stepan 1991; Applebaum et al. 2003). The inclusion of race queries peaked in the 1920s and was then dropped in many countries for ideological and political reasons but also because the scientific consensus began to invalidate race as a concept or category for understanding human behavior (Loveman 2014). Liberals and conservatives alike also believed that using the census to count their people by race would reify any belief that their country was racialized or even racist and would thus fuel the specter of a racially divided society.

By the 1990s, though, race and ethnic data began to appear with the shift to multiculturalism and the demand for ethnoracial recognition and the growing acceptance that race and ethnicity were social constructs that were associated with societal inequalities. Largely as a result of pressure by international human rights groups and international conventions, particularly the International Labor Organization's Convention 169 (Indigenous and Tribal Peoples Convention), adopted in 1989 and ratified by most Latin American countries by 2000, many Latin American countries began collecting ethnoracial data for the first time in decades. In addition, Latin American activists at the 2001 UN Conference against Racism, Racial Discrimination and Xenophobia in Durban, South Africa, demanded that their governments collect data on ethnicity and race. Having data to document ethnoracial inequities, governments would find it increasingly difficult to sustain a national mestizaje narrative of nondiscrimination, racial harmony, and equality. Collecting data on race and ethnicity was also considered an important first step in the transition to multiculturalism.

As of this writing, although almost all countries now have census data for ethnic minorities since 2000 although many, such as Mexico and Peru, do not collect data on Afrodescendants. Cuba has census information for its Afrodescendants but not for its indigenous people. Incidentally, Cuba is the only country in the region that still uses interviewer-classification. The Dominican Republic has not collected official data on race since 1960 but is considering it for its next census (Republica Dominicana 2012). Besides Brazil, only Cuba[8] has collected data on its black population in most of its censuses since the late nineteenth century, as have Bolivia and Mexico for their indigenous populations (del Popolo 2008; Loveman 2014).

Turning to the four countries that are our focus, Brazil has collected data for Afrodescendants since its first census in 1872, but Colombia began doing so only in 1993. Peru has plans to collect data on Afrodescendants in its next census in 2017 and has done so in several national surveys since 2001. Meanwhile Mexico has never collected Afrodescendant data. Among these four countries, Mexico has consistently collected data on persons who speak an indigenous language since 1895. Brazil has usually collected data on pretos and pardos since its first census in 1872 and began collecting data on the indigenous in its 1991 census. The Colombian and Peruvian censuses have collected indigenous data inconsistently (Angosto-Ferrández and Kradolfer 2012; Loveman 2014).

Table 1.1 shows the proportion of the population that identifies as indigenous or Afrodescendant for each Latin American country, according to, in order of priority: the latest census; where census information is not available, recent national survey data; and where neither is available, estimates from the 2010 AmericasBarometer (of the Latin American Public Opinion Project or LAPOP). The second, third, and fourth columns refer to the Afrodescendant population, whereas the fifth, sixth, and seventh columns refer to the indigenous population. The final column refers to the total national population according to the most recent census.

Using these figures, we calculated a range of 113 to 133 million Afrodescendants, or 20.4 to 24.0 percent of the entire Latin American population of 554 million. This range is due to the ambiguity inherent in particular categories in two countries: *moreno* in Venezuela and *Indio* in the Dominican Republic, both of which do not specifically name persons of African or black ancestry but may contain them and others as well. For that matter, estimates of who is black or

TABLE 1.1 Afrodescendant and Indigenous Population (in 1,000s) and Percentages in Latin America by Country Using Most Recent Census Data When Available (PERLA countries in bold)

| Countries | Year | Afro-descendant Population | Per-centage | Year | Indigenous Population | Per-centage | Total National Population |
|---|---|---|---|---|---|---|---|
| Argentina[1] | 2010 | 150 | 0.4 | 2010 | 955 | 2.4 | 40,117 |
| Bolivia[2] | 2012 | 24 | 0.2 | 2012 | 4,068 | 40.6 | 10,027 |
| **Brazil[3]** | **2010** | **97,083** | **50.9** | **2010** | **897** | **0.5** | **190,733** |
| Chile[4] | 2012 | 97 | 0.6[5] | 2012 | 1,700 | 10.2 | 16,636 |
| **Colombia[6]** | **2005** | **4,274** | **10.3** | **2005** | **1,393** | **3.4** | **41,468** |
| Costa Rica[7] | 2011 | 334 | 7.8 | 2011 | 104 | 2.4 | 4,302 |
| Cuba[8] | 2012 | 3,885 | 34.8[9] | 2012 | — | — | 11,163 |
| Dominican Republic[10] | 2010 | A) 2,267 B) 8,046 | A) 24.0 B) 89.0[11] | 2010 | — | — | 9,445 |
| Ecuador[12] | 2010 | 1,043 | 7.2 | 2010 | 1,014 | 7.0 | 14,484 |
| El Salvador[13] | 2007 | 7 | 0.1 | 2007 | 13 | 0.2 | 5,744 |
| Guatemala[14] | 2011 | 5 | 0.0 | 2011 | 4,428[15] | 30.1 | 14,713 |
| Honduras[16] | 2011 | 59 | 0.7 | 2001 | 428 | 5.1 | 8,448 |
| **Mexico[17]** | **2010** | **2,366** | **2.1[18]** | **2010** | **15,700** | **14.0** | **112,337** |
| Nicaragua[19] | 2005 | 23 | 0.4 | 2005 | 444 | 8.6 | 5,142 |
| Panama[20] | 2010 | 313 | 9.1 | 2010 | 418 | 12.1 | 3,454 |
| Paraguay[21] | 2012 | 234 | 3.5[22] | 2012 | 116 | 1.7 | 6,673 |
| **Peru[23]** | **2007** | **411** | **1.5[24]** | **2007** | **7,600** | **27.0[25]** | **28,221** |
| Uruguay[26] | 2011 | 255 | 7.8 | 2011 | 159 | 4.8 | 3,286 |
| Venezuela[27] | 2011 | A) 953 B) 14,534 | A) 3.5 B) 53.4[28] | 2011 | 953[29] | 3.5 | 27,228 |
| Total | | A) 113,783 B) 136,723 | A) 20.6 B) 24.7 | | 40,390 | 7.3 | 553,661 |

1. Argentine Census 2010, INDEC, http://www.censo2010.indec.gov.ar/archivos/censo2010_tomo1.pdf.

2. Bolivian census 2012, INE, http://www.ine.gob.bo:8081/censo2012/default.aspx. The Bolivian census counts only those 15 and older for indigenous and Afrodescendant affiliation. As such, the projected total number of indigenous and Afro-Colombians was calculated by multiplying the percentage of 15+ year olds by the total number of Bolivians.

3. Brazilian Census 2010, IBGE.

4. "Chile's "Official" Indigenous Population More than Doubles with New Census Results," Indigenous News, http://indigenousnews.org/2013/04/08/chiles-official-indigenous-population-more-than-doubles-with-new-census-results/. Upon time of research, the census data was undergoing an internal audit, and as such, was unavailable to corroborate the report of this news source.

5. 2010 AmericasBarometer (LAPOP).

6. La visibilización estadística de los grupos étnicos colombianos (2005), DANE, http://www.dane.gov.co/files/censo2005/etnia/sys/visibilidad_estadistica_etnicos.pdf.

7. Costa Rican Census 2011, INEC, http://www.inec.go.cr/Web/Home/GeneradorPagina.aspx, 2010 AmericasBarometer (LAPOP). Figure includes those who reported as "Indio."

8. Cuban Census 2012, ONE, http://www.one.cu/cifraspreliminares2012.htm.

9. Ibid., http://www.one.cu/publicaciones/08informacion/panorama2012/10%20Demograficos.pdf; the 2012 census showed that 10.4% of Cubans reported as "negro" and 24.8% reported as "mulatto."

10. Dominican Census 2010, ONE, http://censo2010.one.gob.do/index.php.

11. 2010 AmericasBarometer (LAPOP). Estimate A includes only persons identifying as negro, mulatto or Afro-Dominican. Estimate B also includes persons identifying as Indio.

12. Ecuadorian Census 2010, INEC, http://www.elcomercio.com/sociedad/resultados-censo-Censo_de_Poblacion_y_Vivienda-INEC_ECMFIL20110905_0005.pdf.

13. Salvadoran Census 2007, DIGESTYC, http://www.digestyc.gob.sv/servers/redatam/htdocs/CPV2007S/index.html.

14. Guatemalan Census 2011, INE, http://www.ine.gob.gt/np/poblacion/index.htm.

15. Includes Maya and Xinka.

16. Honduran census bureau site (http://www.ine.gob.hn/drupal/).

17. Bases de datos por municipio 2010, CDI (Comisión nacional para el desarrollo de los pueblos indígenas), http://www.cdi.gob.mx/index.php?option=com_content&view=article&id=1327:cedulas-de-informacionbasica-de-los-pueblos-indigenas-de-mexico-&catid=38:indicadores-y-estadisticas&Itemid=54.

18. 2010 AmericasBarometer (LAPOP).

19. Census 2005, INIDE, http://www.inide.gob.ni/censos2005/ResumenCensal/Resumen2.pdf.

20. Panamanian Census 2010, http://estadisticas.contraloria.gob.pa/Resultados2010/.

21. Paraguayan Census 2012, DGEEC, http://www.dgeec.gov.py/index.php.

22. Inter-American Development Bank projection, http://www.iadb.org/en/topics/gender-indigenous-peoples-and-african-descendants/percentage-of-afro-descendants-in-latin-america,6446.html.

23. Peruvian Census 2007, INEI, http://www.inei.gob.pe/.

24. ENCO 2006, INEI.

25. Ibid.

26. Uruguayan Census 2011, INE, http://www.ine.gub.uy/censos2011/index.html.

27. Venezuelan Census 2011, INE, http://www.redatam.ine.gob.ve/redatam/index.html. Estimate A includes only persons identifying as negro, mulatto, or Afro-Venezuelan. Estimate B also includes persons identifying as moreno.

28. The figure counts those who self-identified as "negro," "afrodescendiente," as well as those who identify as "moreno."

29. Primeros Resultados Censo Nacional 2011: Población Indígena De Venezuela, Ine, http://www.ine.gov.ve/documentos/Demografia/CensodePoblacionyVivienda/pdf/PrimerosResultadosIndigena.pdf.

Afrodescendant may also vary widely, as we show for Brazil in chapter 5 (see also Telles and Paschel forthcoming). Pardos and pretos are officially considered Afrodescendants in Brazil (Telles 2004). On the other hand, others might argue that even the 133 million figure is an underestimate because many Afrodescendants might not declare themselves as such because of their stigmatization and their ability to move out of these categories in the Latin American system.

By far, the largest Afrodescendant population resides in Brazil. Afro-Brazilians, comprising the preto and pardo categories, constitute roughly half (50.9 percent) of the population in the region's largest country and, as a result, a large majority (73.0 to 86.7 percent) of all Afrodescendants in Latin America. Relatively large numbers also reside in Colombia, Cuba, and the Dominican Republic. According to the 2010 AmericasBarometer, Mexico also registers a surprisingly large number of persons that self-identify as black or mulatto, although it is a small percentage of that large country's total population. By contrast, six countries in the region (Argentina, Bolivia, Chile, El Salvador, Guatemala, and Nicaragua) have Afrodescendant populations that constitute less than 1 percent. Indigenous people, according to these figures, number about 40 million people, which is 7.3 percent of the Latin American population. The largest numbers of indigenous people live in Mexico and Peru, although higher percentages of national populations are found in Guatemala and Bolivia. Like Afrodescendants, estimates of the indigenous population are often an artifact of question wording and the response categories available, as we show in chapters 2 and 4.

Despite these important beginnings in ethnoracial data collection in the region, we see at least two major barriers to further efforts at data collection. The first is making race or ethnicity a regular part of census taking. That will largely depend on politics, as it has in the past (Ferrández and Kandolfer 2012; Loveman 2014). While much progress has been made in collecting data on race, especially in the past decade or two, these efforts are far from institutionalized. Long-term commitments are questionable at this point (del Popolo 2008). The Brazilian case has shown that if countries are to consolidate a system for gathering data on race, they need more than resources and technical support: they must also find the political will and must engage in constant discussions with civil society.

A second issue, more central to this book, is how race and ethnicity are to be measured. National censuses are important because they become a template for understanding the composition of the nation and for how ethnoracial classification is made in other data collection efforts. Because such data collection in the region's censuses is apparently in formation, we hope that our ideas and evidence can contribute to their development.

## Conceptual Issues

Human relations in Latin America often involve relationships among persons of various phenotypes and cultures. Unfortunately, these relationships often involve power differentials (racism), in which humans are classified according to characteristics such as color, culture, or language, which are ranked on a hierarchy of worth (racialization). In the Americas, these characteristics are often denoted by categories that are popularly known as "races" (or, more politely, ethnic groups). While the idea of race is not considered a valid biological category today as it once was, it is important as a social construct, with very real consequences for one's life chances. Social science evidence shows that humans continue to treat others according to these arbitrary societal classifications in a wide variety of situations in contemporary United States, despite claims to colorblindness (Brown et al. 2003). As we reveal in this book, similar evidence is emerging for several Latin American countries, and discrimination is widely recognized.

Today, as in the past, one's ethnoracial position often becomes naturalized: whites or lighter-skinned mestizos tend to be privileged, while indigenous peoples, Afrodescendants, and dark-skinned persons are often seen and treated as less deserving. In this way, Latin Americans often use distinctions based on "race" and culture—whether real, self-identified, or putative—and skin color as markers of social worth. As people continue this everyday behavior, they reproduce ethnoracial hierarchies and inequalities. As a clear example of how white (or near white in the Latin American case) privilege is naturalized, consider television and magazine propaganda: light-skinned models predominate while dark-skinned persons, though they arguably represent most Latin Americans, are nearly absent. As a result, someone unfamiliar with Latin America who watches Latin American television, whether produced in Mexico, Brazil, or any other Latin American country, could mistakenly conclude that Latin Americans look like Europeans. This example is just at the level of representation. Or consider the multibillion-dollar industry of skin whitening products in Latin America. More compelling still is the emerging sociological evidence for several Latin American countries that shows that educators, employers, and voters use race to make important decisions (Telles 2004; Aguilar forthcoming; Rodriguez Garavito et al. 2013).

## Race versus Ethnicity

In this book, we have decided to use the term ethnoracial as an adjective and then use ethnicity and race to refer to the meaningful social boundaries that people create in their social interactions, whether they be based on phenotype or cultural distinctions, most notably language (Barth 1969; Wimmer 2013). In some cases, though, we continue to highlight race, given its importance as a social cleavage throughout the history of the Americas since at least the past two hundred years.

The terms *race* and *ethnicity* are often used as separate concepts and can be quite confusing because they have acquired popular meanings that may distort or hinder analysis. In popular discussions, race commonly refers to differences in particular physical features; ethnicity commonly refers to cultural differences. In Latin America, the experiences of blacks are often considered racial, while those of the indigenous are ethnic (Wade 1997). A similar line of thinking by U.S. analysts views ethnicity (understood as cultural) as involving particular soft social boundaries, like those among European-origin ethnic groups, whereas racial ones (understood as skin color and phenotypical differences) are relatively hard, such as those between blacks and whites (e.g., Omi and Winant 1994; Desmond and Emirbayer 2009), although Asians, indigenous people, and Latinos are more difficult to catalog using this scheme (Cornell and Hartmann 2007; Wimmer 2013). In both the United States and Latin America, ethnicity may also be seen as more politically correct even when referring to blacks than the more emotively charged and supposedly false idea of race, as when Senator Demosthenes Torres attempted to replace all references to race with ethnicity in Brazil's Racial Equality Statute of 2010. When examined beyond the United States and Latin America, such distinctions—arguably based primarily on a U.S. model—become murkier still. As Wimmer (2013) notes, social boundaries between Bosnians and Serbians, which are considered to be merely ethnic within this U.S. vision, may be more rigid than those between groups perceived to be racially different. Unfortunately, such popular and essentialist understandings of ethnicity often creep into scholarly attempts to provide analytic moorings for these concepts.

Beginning with the work of Frederik Barth (1969), scholars have emphasized that social interactions are key to the way ethnicity is created, rather than defining particular cultural traits that determine how individuals are to be ethnically categorized. More recent scholarship defines ethnicity, which may include the concept of race, as a social construct or classification system that is created by people with unequal levels of power (Bourdieu 1986; Brubaker 2009;

Wimmer 2013). For example, race in the Americas was socially constructed by Europeans on the basis of particular physical features that stood out culturally (Hannaford 1996; Wade 1997). Over time, these categories become embedded in social cognition as natural divisions of society, and as individuals identify with them to different extents. We do not wish to engage in a long debate about this process, since these and other scholars make the point so well. More importantly, it would distract us from our objectives: to illuminate how ethnicity and race play out in Latin America. The ethnoracial categories used by national censuses and in popular discourse such as negro, mulato, mestizo, indio, and blanco are well known, but there are other dimensions of race and ethnicity such as color (or phenotype) and language. As we earlier argued, the visible manifestation of color is particularly important in Latin America, which involves a continuum of visible difference rather than the usual ethnoracial categories. Scholars on Brazil observed that they, like Latin Americans seem to do generally, often make color distinctions on a continuum rather than the racial distinctions of the United States (Nogueira and Calvacanti 1998; Telles 2004).

Language is arguably the main marker distinguishing indigenous people from mestizos, a distinction that has been referred to as racial. However, language as a racial distinction has been absent from the literature, probably because the literature has been based mostly on the experience of Afrodescendants and especially the U.S. case. Today, however, many indigenous languages are being lost throughout Latin America as children become Spanish monolinguals, which leads to the increasing importance of indigenous self-identification.

## Indigenous and Afrodescendant Experiences

Most countries in the region have important black and indigenous roots if not significant black and indigenous populations today, though the predominance of one or the other generally varies by country. Brazil, for example, is largely weighted on the side of the black or mulatto categories, whereas Peru and especially Mexico have more people in the indigenous and mestizo categories; in Colombia, the two populations are more balanced. On the other hand, Argentina is largely white, though not entirely of course, and thus ethnicity and race are less central to its social stratification. Our study compares the experiences of black and indigenous populations across the two pairs of countries with the largest indigenous (Mexico and Peru) and Afrodescendant (Brazil and Columbia) populations.

Although they are generally treated as differently as apples and oranges and generally with two distinct literatures, both indigenous and Afrodescendant peoples have been clearly understood as racial groups and racialized through-out the region and throughout its history. At least in theory, whites or light-skinned persons occupy the apex of what we refer to as a pigmentocratic social pyramid; mixed-race persons in the middle; and blacks and indigenous peoples or dark-skinned persons tend to be at the bottom, as both Lipschutz (1944) and others since then (Wade 1993; Sidanius et al. 2001) have described, a half century apart.

As Wade (1997) notes, both groups are called races on the basis of their phe-notype, and that racialization has both physical and cultural roots. Afrodescen-dants are seen as culturally assimilated and part of an undifferentiated Latin American population, but they are socially excluded. Meanwhile the indige-nous are viewed as culturally distinct and often exoticized but also are socially excluded; however, they can become mestizos if they acculturate, perhaps by speaking Spanish or moving up the socioeconomic ladder, as in Peru, where the large majority of Quechua identify as mestizo. Mobility out of the indigenous category is often achieved through demographic, cultural, or status change as indigenous is often understood on the basis of community, language, and low socioeconomic status (Patrinos and Psachoroupoulos 1994; Friedlander 1975; Sieder 2002). One can become a mestizo by moving to an urban area, speaking Spanish, or moving out of poverty. Blacks and mulattos can sometimes move out of these categories through changes in status, as in the popular phrase "money whitens" (Schwartzman 2007), though such mobility has probably been overstated and may even be reversed (Mareletto 2012; Telles and Paschel forthcoming). Thus, social mobility seems less likely to change the racial status of individual Afrodescendants compared to that of indigenous people.

The cultural distinctions of the indigenous that are widely accepted have generally not been extended to Afrodescendants. For example, in the Gue-laguetza celebrations of ethnic diversity in the Mexican state of Oaxaca, the Afro-Mexican communities of the Costa Chica region are not recognized as part of the state's ethnic mosaic since they are not considered to be culturally different, although they do have particular dance and music forms, and other cultural distinctions. Afro-Colombians, on the other hand, have also used the example of indigenous Colombians to attain recognition and cultural rights by demonstrating their own cultural symbols and forms under that country's Law 70, which requires cultural distinction. In other cases, the mixture of black and indigenous people is too complex to be easily separated into the three points of Latin America's ethnic triangle. For example, French (2009) shows how a phenotypically similar population understands itself as indigenous in one town but as Afrodescendant in a neighboring town. An important point here is how race and ethnicity, regardless of whether they are categorical or based on skin color, are not natural or essential but rather social constructions, in which particular contexts make them more or less salient.

Moreover, distinct ideas about indigenous and Afrodescendant people emerged early in colonial Spanish America as well as in anthropological thought; however, ideas about one group or the other were often clearly related to each other. Von Vacano (2012) notes how American ideas of whiteness began in European encounters with natives, but the bulk of thinking about race was built on the population descended from enslaved Africans. Bartolomé de las Casas advocated strongly for an end to the indigenous slavery of the sixteenth century, although at first he suggested alternative sources of slaves, particularly Africans, an idea he would later renounce (Gutiérrez 1991). Indeed, Baker (2010) argues that the concept of culture developed by ethnologists to understand American Indian languages and customs in the nineteenth century formed the basis of the anthropological concept of race that was eventually used to confront "the Negro problem" in the twentieth century.

Although black and indigenous people tend to be studied separately by race/ethnicity scholars, some early scholars of Latin America studied both black and indigenous populations together. The studies by Marvin Harris (1964) and Pierre Van den Berghe (1967) were notable in that they compared ethnicity and race across the indigenous and black divide and across Latin American countries. Harris compared distinct ethnic systems that emerged from distinct labor needs in highland and lowland Latin America, while Van den Berghe compared Brazil and Mexico. Van den Berghe hardly mentions that the relationships he studied in Mexico largely included indigenous people, and that those in Brazil were largely about Afrodescendants. To their credit, both authors examined Latin America across the indigenous-black divide, but their work was driven by theory and probably did not reflect empirical realities.

With the turn to multiculturalism, such comparisons have become more important today, especially as governments seek to recognize ethnoracial minorities. In his comparisons of blacks and indigenous people, Wade (1997) argues that the indigenous have occupied a more privileged position than blacks in Latin America, and that early on the Catholic Church considered them more worthy of redemption and made more attempts to assimilate them, compared to Afrodescendants. Hooker (2005) also notes that national policies have often favored indigenous claims over those of Afrodescendants as a result of distinct ideas about the two groups. Moreover, the indigenous inhabited the Americas long before Columbus arrived, and therefore Latin Americans perceive that they are entitled to certain rights, such as their own land and way of life, that are often not extended to blacks (Hooker 2005). Symbolically and perhaps politically, then, the indigenous seem to occupy a higher status than Afrodescendants, especially in relation to nation-making narratives in the region. Still, as our results show, the indigenous have the lowest socioeconomic status of all ethnoracial groups in Latin America. In sum, we generally agree with Wade (1997) that scholars' tendencies to focus separately on blacks and indigenous people has hindered the development of a broad or systematic understanding of nation formation and social relations in Latin America. As we show in this book, such a comparison enriches our understanding of ethnicity in the region.

## Organization of the Book

Chapters 2–5 are organized by country: Mexico (chapter 2), Colombia (chapter 3), Peru (chapter 4), and Brazil (chapter 5). But because of the common questions we collectively asked and the data we collected, the structure of these chapters is similar. Each of the chapters highlights the country's particular historical, social, and political contexts and then reports important findings for our surveys, based on the in-depth PERLA surveys that we have described. To reach a wide audience, we mostly utilize descriptive or bivariate analyses. In contrast, to overcome the confounding effects inherent in descriptive analysis and to focus on particular issues, a series of directly comparative papers further examines many of the findings highlighted in this book, including classification/identification (Telles and Flores 2013; Telles and Paschel forthcoming), ethnoracial inequality (Flores and Telles 2012; Telles and Steele 2012, Telles et al. forthcoming), and racial attitudes (Telles and Bailey 2013; Telles and Garcia 2013) on a wider range of Latin American countries.

At the same time, each of the four chapters provides a unique story of a particular country, so that PERLA outcomes can be understood on their own terms. The historical circumstances in each country varied widely, as each country developed its own imagined community, formed its own internal alliances, created its own press, shaped particular kinds of ethnic social movements, faced particular forms of resistance by them, and responded in particular ways. Moreover, each country designed its own ideologies and censuses, responded to its particular ethnic and racial composition and has been influenced by local cultures, all shaped by its own previous development paths.

Nevertheless, these processes shared many broad similarities, as did the formation of nations whose stances on race went from whitening to mestizaje to multiculturalism. The authors introduce common elements that we discussed in our joint meetings, so they are in dialogue with each other, examining common themes and exploring particularities in each country. These elements include the histories of whitening and mestizaje ideas, which varied substantially across the four countries in the way they evolved, their importance, and the extent to which the former were grafted into the latter. The chapters also include material on black and indigenous social movements and a history of official statistics and academic production in each country.

At the same time, each chapter can be read as a stand-alone review of ethnic or racial matters in each country. Although we stress common themes, these chapters also emphasize particular historical and contemporary issues. While every chapter examines the cutting-edge issues in a specific country, they are organized around common themes and hypotheses, and about half of the figures are similar, so those themes can be compared across the chapters. In sum, they tell a particular country's ethnoracial story and report PERLA findings.

The findings and conclusions in each chapter are those of the respective authors. Also, findings based on the PERLA surveys are often presented without noting sampling margins of error, which are ±2.5 to 3 percent for 95 percent confidence intervals, given the sample sizes of 1,000–1,500 cases in the surveys. Thus, small differences, though suggestive, may not be statistically significant.

Chapter 6 concludes by directly comparing PERLA results across the four countries and elaborates on the five major findings that we highlighted earlier. We emphasize our cross-national findings on the many questions we raised about ethnicity, race, and color in the region regarding classification, inequality, perceptions of discrimination, and attitudes about ethnoracial issues and social policies. We have sought to advance our understanding of these critical questions, as governments and civil society increasingly engage ethnoracial issues throughout Latin America.

CHAPTER TWO

# The Different Faces of Mestizaje

*Ethnicity and Race in Mexico*

REGINA MARTÍNEZ CASAS

EMIKO SALDÍVAR

RENÉ D. FLORES

CHRISTINA A. SUE

> Fusion of races, convergence and fusion of cultural manifesta-
> tions, linguistic unification and economic equilibrium of social
> factors[1] . . . should characterize the Mexican population in order
> for Mexicans to constitute and embody a powerful homeland and
> a coherent and well-defined nationhood. (Gamio 2010 [1916], 183)

The ideology of *mestizaje* (race mixture) has strongly marked Mexican identity since the end of the Mexican revolution (Villoro 1996 [1950]). A year before the 1917 Mexican Constitution, the legal synthesis of the Mexican Revolution, was established, Manuel Gamio, one of the most influential anthropologists in post-revolutionary Mexico, published *Forging a Fatherland*. In his book, which embodies the ideology of mestizaje, Gamio refers to the creation of a new nationality that is neither European nor indigenous, but Mexican: "It is up to Mexico's revolutionaries to seize the mallet and tighten their apron strings to ensure that a new miraculous anvil will plow the ground and shape a new nation made of melted iron [Spaniards] and bronze [the indigenous]. Here's the iron, here's the bronze, go forth my brothers!" (Gamio 2010 [1916], 6).

Gamio's book was the forerunner of three other texts on mestizaje, all which became highly influential: *La raza cósmica* (The Cosmic Race), authored by José

Vasconcelos and published in 1925; *México integro* (Integral Mexico), by Moisés Sáenz, published in 1939; and *El proceso de aculturación* (The Acculturation Process), written by Gonzalo Aguirre Beltrán in 1982. A common thread running through all of these writings is that mestizaje would allow Mexico to become a modern and just nation. However, across these texts, each author took a slightly different approach in conceptualizing mestizaje.

Although the concepts of "race" and "race mixture" are present in Gamio's work, as a disciple of anthropologist Franz Boas, a preeminent critic of scientific racism who argued that racial differences were cultural rather than biological, Gamio emphasized mestizaje as the fusion of cultures (Gruzinski 2000; Walsh 2004). Consequently, he believed that linguistic homogenization was necessary to achieve a socially just society. In contrast, Vasconcelos referred to both racial mixing and cultural blending. He used the term "race" in the sense of "people," as German romanticism postulated. It is from this meaning that the motto of the National Autonomous University of Mexico (UNAM) emerged: "Por mi raza hablará el espíritu" (The spirit shall speak for my race). Vasconcelos argued that the Latin American subcontinent had given birth to a "fifth race," which represented a mixture of Europeans, Africans, indigenous people, and Asians. Sáenz, on the other hand, focused on cultural mestizaje, proposing that it would be achieved through a strong and unified school system. Finally, Aguirre Beltrán envisioned mestizaje as being a cultural synthesis, more than just a sum of parts. The different meanings, or "faces," of mestizaje evoked by these authors indicate its polysemic nature.[2] Mestizaje sometimes signals cultural markers such as language and, at other times, refers to ethnic or racial characteristics such as skin color and ancestry.

In this chapter, we explore the different meanings that underlie mestizaje ideology in Mexico by drawing on our analysis of the PERLA findings. We use data from the PERLA study to identify and explain the variations in and different components of ethnic and racial identities in Mexico, given the broader ideological context of mestizaje. Although most Mexicans identify as *mestizo* (mixed), our findings show that a significant number of Mexicans embrace a white identity and that many of them are not in positions of privilege or status. We also find that few Mexicans identify as being of African descent, despite the significant demographic flows of Africans to Mexico during the colonial era. Finally, our research highlights the multiple meanings, or polysemy, of mestizo identity in Mexico. It shows how the context in which people who were surveyed define themselves and are defined by others is crucial for fully understanding the different components of the mestizo identity (see Basave 2007; Wade 1997).

In Mexico, as in other Latin American countries, nation-building projects related to mestizaje have entailed the disavowal of ethnic and racial hierarchies and identities. In this context, the persistence of indigenous identities has been explained mainly by insufficient policies for the integration of indigenous populations, an issue that has preoccupied politicians and academics for most of the twentieth century. With the increased focus on multicultural and indigenous rights, indigenous groups have been conceived as distinct and separate units that deserve tolerance or respect but that are still different from the rest of Mexican society. Outside of issues of the cultural and structural integration of the indigenous population, academics have paid little attention until recently to how other features, such as skin color or phenotype, shape interethnic relations in Mexico. This oversight is unfortunate given that recent work shows that discrimination is based not only on cultural differences, such as language, but also on physical traits, including skin color and phenotype (Castellanos and Sandoval 1998).

In this chapter we seek to illustrate the multiplicity of factors that play a role in processes of discrimination and interethnic relations. We first present a brief overview of the history of ethnic and racial relations in Mexico as an ongoing cultural process, focusing on aspects we believe shed light on the present situation. Then we examine the ethnoracial identities of contemporary Mexicans and the factors involved in shaping their identities. Finally, we assess how race and ethnicity influence Mexicans' experiences with discrimination and their life outcomes.

## From Mexico's Glorious Indigenous Past and the Modern Global Nation

### Indigenous People and the Castas

When the Spaniards colonized New Spain, what we know today as Mexico, they created a series of sociopolitical institutions to regulate and control the *souls* of the native indigenous populations. They established "Reducciones," "Encomiendas," "Repúblicas de Indios" (Indigenous Republics) (1521), and "Repartimientos" (1542) so that the Spanish crown could colonize and control the territory and population (Aguirre Beltrán 1992 [1957]). These institutions were superimposed over the vast linguistic and ethnic differences of the native populations, creating a new social subject: the indigenous. While seeking to control indigenous people's labor and protect their spiritual well-being, these institutions were not able to protect the indigenous from the resistance wars, diseases for which they had no immunological defense, and the labor conditions, all of which resulted in a precipitous demographic decline in the indigenous population (Sánchez Albornoz 1973).[3]

To solve the subsequent labor shortage, Spanish colonizers imported African slaves into New Spain to work in mines, for textile industries, and on plantations (Beltrán 1967). Some historians have estimated that at least 380,000 African slaves arrived in Mexico between the sixteenth and eighteenth centuries (Vinson 2012), although the numbers could be higher because the illegal slave trade may have imported slaves from other Spanish colonies (Aguirre Beltrán 1944). Unlike the indigenous population, African slaves were not confined to well-defined territories. Instead, they were dispersed geographically, residing in the homes, in the mines, or on the haciendas where they worked. Because they originated from different regions in Africa and were dispersed, the Africans did not establish separate language communities; instead, they learned Spanish and gradually assimilated into the dominant culture.

During this same time period, the Spanish crown attempted to segregate indigenous people from the rest of the colonial population, though such efforts were often unsuccessful. The crown drafted legal prohibitions to prevent indigenous people from living in areas reserved for Spaniards, creoles, slaves, and mestizo craftsmen (Zavala et al. 1954; Cope 1994 [1980]). Instead, they lived in communities within the Repúblicas de Indios, with some rights and protection from Spanish settlers' greed and abuses. Each community received a plot grant of land, which native authorities owned and ruled collectively, under the supervision of clergymen and Spanish bureaucrats. The Repúblicas de Indios allowed for the preservation of indigenous languages and culture, and it gave inhabitants the possibility of bringing grievances against local creoles to the Spanish crown.

Colonial legal codes demarcated social status by defining the rights, responsibilities, and restrictions of the four major ethnoracial groups: Spaniards, indigenous people, slaves (mostly from Africa), and *castas* (mixed-race). Diverse laws regulated interethnic interactions and the rights of each group, dictating who paid taxes or different kinds of tribute, who might be educated, who could preach and to whom, who could rule, who was free, and whom one could marry (Kellogg 1995). Therefore, in addition to the system of the two republics—the indigenous and Spanish—and slavery, colonial authorities tried to regulate the mixed-race population through these laws. However, these regulations had little relevance for nonelites, who created a counterculture to defy authorities (Cope 1994 [1980]; Boyer 2000; Kellogg 1995). Nevertheless, despite uneven implementation, by the eighteenth century the "castas system" was well established.

The castas system reflected the concerns of Spanish and creole elites for maintaining a socioracial hierarchy in the presence of increased racial mixing (Katzew 2004). In this hierarchy, Spaniards were on top and indigenous people and Africans at the bottom, with mixed-race individuals falling somewhere in between, depending on the composition of their mixture. The castas system was captured through a series of images or paintings; these visual representations became one of the first exercises in social taxonomy based on descent, phenotype (i.e., skin color and facial features), class (i.e., occupation), culture (i.e., language, food habits, dress, etc.), and, most importantly, legal rights and obligations. Even though social and legal inequality was one consequence of the ethnic and racial categorizations that existed in New Spain, the castas system also represented the beginning of mestizaje practices that involved not only miscegenation but also cultural synthesis, of which indigenous peoples' contributions were especially important (Aguirre Beltrán 1992 [1957]; Gruzinski 2000).

## Independent Mexico: The Rise of a New Nation

When Mexico gained independence from Spain in 1821, one of the first actions of the leaders of the newly independent nation was to abolish the colonial hierarchy. All Mexicans were to be equal before the law. Under this philosophy, creole elites, both liberal and conservative, seized the opportunity to end the semiautonomy and protection of indigenous communities, which opened up access to their labor and resources.[4] These actions were supported by the ideas of individuals such as José María Mora, one of the founders of liberal thinking in Mexico, who attributed indigenous poverty to conditions under colonial paternalism (Mora 1950). He maintained that, under Spanish rule, indigenous people did not have the individual freedoms that came with being private land-owners. He thus saw colonial missions as hindering indigenous progress by perpetuating the notion of communal property: "Indigenous people, in their present state and until undergoing considerable changes cannot reach the degree of civilization and culture of Europeans nor have equal status in a society formed by the two [repúblicas]" (Mora 1950, 77).

After independence, the legal privileges of indigenous communities were abolished as the institutions charged with their protection disappeared. These policies culminated in the Lerdo Law (1856), which removed the legal standing (and therefore the possibility of landownership) from civil corporations (mayordomías, guilds, and indigenous communities), the church, and religious orders (Brading 1993 [1973], 106). Under the new liberal regime, indigenous people were denied collective rights over their territories, which resulted in increased social discontent and political instability. Between 1840 and 1860, some forty-four indigenous rebellions broke out, compared to the eight rebellions that had occurred over the previous twenty years (Florescano 1996, 376). Describing the climate under which these rebellions occurred, Friedrich Katz writes: "When Mexico won independence at the beginning of the 19th century, some 40 percent of agricultural land in the central and southern regions of the country was communal land that belonged to the Indigenous people. When Porfirio Díaz was beaten in 1911, only 5 percent remained in their hands. Since Independence, 90 percent of Mexican peasants (Indigenous people) had lost their lands" (quoted in Florescano 1996, 490). In almost all of these rebellions, participants demanded respect for communal lands and the abolition of the extremely high taxes placed on indigenous people and the church.

Many indigenous communities became allies of different factions of the elite and formed alliances with local chieftains and the military in an effort to protect their rights and political autonomy. In turn, creole (*criollo*) elites, both conservative and liberal, characterized these uprisings as an ethnic and racial war (*guerra de castas*) between civilization and barbarism, modernization and backwardness. The discourse of ethnic and racial fear further cemented the idea that Mexico's deep-seated social problems were associated with the presence of an indigenous population. It was during this period that the mestizaje ideology began to take shape. In this process, indigenous people became defined as "others" and were seen as being opposed to modernity and thus representing an obstacle to a prosperous Mexico.

The revitalized concern over the indigenous population motivated elites to find a solution in the ideology of mestizaje to guarantee "the total extinction of the castes" (Hale 1968). They believed that "infusion of European blood" was needed to "improve" Mexicans' blood and felt that the indigenous "problem" could be overcome through the expansion and education of the mestizo population. Such ideas, which echoed the liberal call for equity, small-scale property, and local power, were received with enthusiasm, particularly among the growing population of ranchers, small entrepreneurs, miners, and industrial workers. As Brading noted, "Neither the 'Glory of the Aztecs' nor the principle of communal land were appealing to ranchers, miners or craftsmen from the states of Jalisco, Guanajuato and Zacatecas. They wanted more equity, the redistribution of land and envied the higher social status of Spaniards and Creoles" (Brading 1993 [1973], 138). This middle sector, largely comprising mestizos, would grow in prominence and become an important social and political force that both liberals and conservatives had to take into account.

During this time there was also a growing sense of patriotism and the development of nationalistic discourse among Mexicans, which was fueled by the war with the United States (1846–48), the Liberal Reforms (1857), and the French Intervention (1863–67). Patriotic symbols—many of which were, paradoxically, pre-Hispanic in origin—were used to establish a sense of belonging and unity in a society profoundly divided after many years of conflict (Brading 1993 [1973], 141). A vision of the country as a homogeneous society in cultural, racial, and ethnic terms began to gain acceptance. In 1884 Vicente Riva Palacio was among the first to articulate a connection between mestizaje and Mexicanness in racial terms. For Riva Palacio, the blending of Spanish and indigenous blood was necessary to create a "New Mexican People." On the basis of evolutionary thought, Riva Palacio formulated an interesting synthesis between Darwinism and nationalism. He asserted that, although contemporary indigenous people did not have much to offer culturally or physically, the "mestizo race" was superior to the white race. As a nationalist, he agreed that homogeneity was essential but not necessarily limited to linguistic and cultural unification. Rather, he believed that Mexico needed not only linguistic and culturally unification but also *racial* homogeneity for successful national development.

The most innovative component of his argument was the idea that mestizos are the superior outcome of the evolutionary process, which led him to question the belief that racial purity was essentially superior and racial mixture inferior. Accordingly, the process of mestizaje did not represent a path to "whiteness" but was an end in itself. The mestizo, he argued, "had accumulated virtues and vices from various races and, by multiplying them over time, acquired the undisputable right to autonomy by formulating a new nationality in this land . . . destined to be the seat of an important nation in the American Continent" (Riva Palacio 1884, 471).

The increasing integration of mestizos through the state's actions, such as educational policy and colonization, marked the development of a racial ideology that operated to naturalize economic and political problems caused by capitalist expansion (Takaki 1990 [1979]). During the Porfiriato (1876–1911), intellectual and political elites used pseudoscientific racial theories in attempts to explain social inequality. Justo Sierra, a leading intellectual, synthesized this approach when he declared, "The nation has impoverished blood in its veins and this leads to skepticism, a lack of energy, resistance to being useful and premature old age. This situation can only be corrected by 'huge amounts of iron in the form of railroads and large intakes of strong blood from immigration'" (Sierra 1949, 125–69).[5] Prejudice against and distrust of the indigenous population impeded the Porfirian elite's ability to foresee the social antagonism that was to come about in Mexico, and which would eventually bring the country to a violent civil war, the Mexican Revolution (1910–20).

### The Consolidation of the Mestizo Nation (1930–1990)

In the aftermath of the revolution, the racial theories of the nineteenth century were redefined. New ideological frameworks were needed to explain the new social dynamics in the country. Although the mestizo project was originally conceived as a whitening project, in the post-revolutionary period it evolved into an ideology that celebrated mixture in itself. This new version of mestizaje drew on popular ideas of miscegenation, social justice, and economic development. José Vasconcelos (1985–1959), founder of the federal Ministry of Education (1921), was one of the main actors driving this formulation of the mestizaje ideology. Under the banner of "the cosmic race," Vasconcelos promoted a program of cultural missions, funded public mural paintings, and disseminated a vast program of publications, all of which touted this ideology. Under the aegis of a mestizaje policy, he aimed to consolidate a national identity based on the assimilation and integration of indigenous individuals and rural mestizos. The social imaginary of the mestizo nation, however, did not include the presence of Afrodescendants (Knight 1990).

In the same period, anthropologist Manuel Gamio founded the intellectual, ideological, and political movement known as indigenism (*indigenismo*).[6] This movement included both the positivist ideology of the Porfirian era and demands that surfaced during and after the revolution, by combining concerns for national unity, social justice, modernization, and the incorporation of new social actors (i.e., cultural brokers). Under the influence of his mentor Franz Boas,[7] Gamio proposed that the determining factor in human behavior and differentiation was *culture* and not race. In his view, understanding and modifying indigenous cultural practices were the best ways to lead indigenous groups toward cultural integration into the mestizo category. Yet Gamio also believed it was important to encourage the "racial fusion" of indigenous people through their assimilation into a more evolved mestizo society, combing Boas's cultural relativism with contemporary ideas on eugenics (Walsh 2004).[8] However, Gamio's perspective was more strongly rooted in the former indigenous cultures.

Boas's ideas influenced Gamio's definition of a mestizo Mexico. Boas himself had worked for a year and a half at the International School of American Archeology and Ethnology in Mexico City around 1910. In that position, he promoted a model of identity that was not based on race (Villoro 1996 [1950]). Despite some differences between his and Gamio's scholarship, Boas, just like his disciple, saw Mexico as an ideal platform for demonstrating that it was possible to build a modern society free of racism (Aguirre Beltrán 1982).[9] One consequence of positioning cultural homogeneity at the axis of mestizaje ideology was that "otherness" focused on cultural and linguistic differences as the way to differentiate what was indigenous from what was not, and to differentiate ethnic differences among indigenous people themselves.[10] Although Gamio considered language as one of the many cultural traits of indigeneity, over time language displaced other criteria (e.g., food, footwear, clothes), and in the latter half of the twentieth century it was the sole criterion used in the census to identify indigenous people. However, it was far from an "objective" measure of indigeneity as speaking an indigenous language was a sign of illiteracy, isolation, backwardness, and poverty.

Indigenist policy not only shaped relations between the state and indigenous peoples but also played a central role in constructing and defining mestizos as being *non*indigenous individuals. Thus, indigenismo in the twentieth century was an important factor in the development of the national ideology of mestizaje (Saldívar 2008); or, stated differently, the indigenous and mestizos were two sides of the same coin of Mexico's modernizing project (de la Peña 2002, 45–47). Indigenismo and mestizaje were both constructions created as part of national projects, and therefore both the indigenous and the mestizos represented state-fostered modernization. Thus, Mexico´s post-revolutionary ideology entailed the acculturation of these two populations into a solely mestizo identity.

An example of the institutionalization of indigenismo can be seen between 1917 and 1918 in the Department of Anthropology in the Ministry of Federal Education, which was founded by Gamio and encouraged regional studies that provided the scientific foundations for development projects. Mestizaje ideology was also institutionalized and disseminated in the school system. After the Ministry of Federal Education was established, the Mexican state invested large sums of money in building schools, training and hiring teachers, and designing curricula. A key player in designing the Mexican public school system was Moisés Sáenz. He had studied at Columbia University with John Dewey (and also with Boas), and with this background he designed the curriculum for a new form of secondary education. Unlike elementary school, which emphasized reading, writing, and arithmetic, Sáenz's model for middle school education went into detail about the type of knowledge adolescents needed to know about Mexican history and civics to become upstanding national citizens.

Regarding the indigenous population, Sáenz designed a plan to teach them

Spanish through literacy instruction in the various indigenous languages, as a transition between monolingualism in an indigenous language and monolingualism in Spanish (Sáenz 1939). To this end he contacted William C. Townsend, the founder of the Summer Institute of Linguistics and an expert in Mayan languages who had previously worked in Guatemala. Sáenz also invited an enthusiastic group of young linguists from the United States to study the different Mexican indigenous languages and to help in designing literacy primers (Martínez Casas 1998).[11] These efforts were illustrative of Sáenz's broader philosophy that national integration should be carried out with the active and democratic participation of indigenous people. He managed to gain President Cárdenas's support for establishing an indigenous institution in 1938, the Autonomous Department of Indian Affairs. Although this institution languished after Cárdenas left the presidency in 1940, in 1948 the Instituto Nacional Indigenista (INI) was created and charged with transforming indigenous peoples into Mexicans. By this time, the ideology of racial mestizaje was downplayed in official discourse in favor of a version of mestizaje based on the fusion of cultures. "Acculturation" became the key word to describe this process. As Aguirre Beltrán (1992 [1957]) pointed out, the policies of acculturation comprised crosscutting processes that involved not only the native population but also Mexicans of European and African origin.

The first period of the INI (1950–70) emphasized its modernizing role. For Mexico to become a modern nation, indigenous people had to embrace cultural mestizaje, which would allow them to transform economically their economies through access to technology and the marketplace, and their political organizations through participation in municipal life. Under this vision, the state often engaged in aggressive policies, such as the relocation of entire communities to make way for infrastructure projects such as the building of dams, highways, and agro-industrial complexes (Villa Rojas 1955). After 1970, indigenismo, as a component of the project to construct a unified national identity, received strong criticism (Stavenhagen 2001). Integration policies had not solved the country's vast social inequalities, and for this reason elites began to say there were no more indigenous, just peasants, and emphasized class over ethnicity. This in turn led to the questioning of the goal of cultural homogeneity for all Mexicans.

In the late 1980s, recurrent economic crises and growing political opposition from all sides of the political spectrum besieged the Mexican state. Seeking to regain legitimacy, the state endorsed pluralism and recognized Mexico as a pluricultural nation.[12] After the Zapatista rebellion, indigenous people's legal recognition became central in the multicultural model that would vindicate the permanence of the state recognition of cultural differences in Mexico.[13] And yet education continued to play a central role in advancing the process of mestizaje and constructing new identities. Through the public school system, the government was able to promote its own ideas about race and ethnicity. In primary school textbooks, which are distributed free of charge to public schoolchildren all over the country, indigenous people are portrayed as "folkloric," or as a vestige of Mexico's glorious past (Galván 2010). Folkloric tones are used to reference the language and culture of indigenous peoples, emphasizing differences, specificities, and local identities and their importance to Mexican identity (Stavenhagen 2001). These nostalgic and romantic representations of indigenous people further perpetuated the idea that they were somewhat distant and peripheral to contemporary Mexico. Moreover, the emphasis on their differences promoted the ideology of a mestizo identity as the national standard, from which ethnoracial difference is assessed.

Nevertheless, in the face of this nostalgic (and even essentialist) outlook by some anthropologists and politicians, even today there is a widely generalized disdain for indigenous persons in the country. Discourses that characterize indigenous identities as useful or valuable surface only occasionally and in particular social spaces. For example, while presenting oneself as indigenous may facilitate access to certain social programs (Martínez Casas 2010), this same identity could result in discrimination in other situations, such as when searching for jobs or trying to connect with nonindigenous social networks. For those who migrate to large cities or abroad, studies have found these individuals oftentimes over- or underemphasize their indigenous identity, depending on the situation (see Martínez Novo 2006; Martínez Casas 2007). In addition, complex relationships with an indigenous identity have been found to exist among members of so-called historical (primarily rural) indigenous communities, particularly among younger generations who have attended school.

## Mexico's Multiculturalism: Real or Just Legal?

Mexico's deep economic and political crisis in the 1990s eroded the political legitimacy of the revolutionary government and its institutions, serving as a catalyst for important changes in the legal treatment of ethnic groups. At the forefront was the decision to reform Article 4 of the constitution to recognize Mexico's "multicultural and pluriethnic" nature and to ensure equality of opportunity for all members of society (Olivé 1999). Some contemporary authors, such as Hale (2002), interpret multiculturalism, which manifested itself in constitutional changes aimed at recognizing diversity and which occurred throughout Latin America, as a new form of mestizaje.

In 2001 a more comprehensive reform was introduced in Mexico with a new version of Article 2, which proclaimed indigenous peoples' right to their own languages and cultures, as well as to political autonomy. In addition, Article 1 was expanded to penalize the perpetrators of discrimination based on ethnicity, language, or gender, among other things. These measures coincided with the introduction of neoliberal policies that cast aside old revolutionary promises of redistributive equity and replaced them with ideas of participation, free markets, and tolerance.

The Zapatista indigenous movement's uprising in 1994 questioned the notion of official pluralism and highlighted the consequences of neoliberal reforms (e.g., the scaling back of agrarian reform policies). Zapatistas' demands for effective indigenous autonomy and self-determination demonstrated that an abstract recognition of multiculturalism was insufficient. The Zapatista uprising challenged the relationship between the state and indigenous peoples as well as perceptions about ethnic diversity and equality in the country. The myth of the submissive indigenous was challenged by images presented in the news media, which showed indigenous people as political actors with agendas and making demands for equality and indigenous rights. Moreover, the idea that indigenous cultures were disappearing via assimilation was openly contested as large numbers of indigenous people came forward to articulate their demands on and make statements about contemporary and national issues.

Despite this massive and internationally visible uprising, the state has not been very responsive to indigenous demands. Federal and local legislation has been limited to issues of cultural recognition and educational policies (including bilingual education), the establishment of "intercultural universities" in isolated areas, and the incipient training of indigenous court interpreters (Hernández et al. 2002; Saldívar 2006). However, ethnic and racial identification trends appear to be shifting after the uprising. For example, there has been a dramatic, and still unexplained, growth over the past decade in the number of Mexicans who identify as indigenous on state forms: 6.2 percent in 2000 but 14.8 percent in 2010. Demographic factors alone cannot explain this rapid expansion of the indigenous category. Moreover, this population shift directly challenges INI predictions that indigenous ethnicity would disappear by the 1970s. Interestingly, indigenous peoples' significant out-migration from traditional indigenous communities has seemingly reenergized their ethnicity, contradicting the general belief that urbanization and modernization implied assimilation (Bonfil Batalla 1990). Increasing educational attainment for urban migrants has resulted in the emergence of better-trained spokespersons and better-formulated ethnic-based demands (de la Peña 2005). This increased visibility of ethnic identities has also stimulated a nascent Afro-Mexican movement.[14]

## The PERLA Survey

In this section, we use various data sources, including the PERLA survey conducted in 2010 and other demographic and qualitative data, to confront these long-held beliefs and to examine the different meanings associated with a mestizo identity. We also work to identify the factors that have helped to keep the mestizo ideology alive in twenty-first-century Mexico, despite the state's official turn to multiculturalism. Finally, we discuss Mexico's unique racial and ethnic characteristics relative to the other countries included in the PERLA survey.

### *The Components of Mestizo Identity and the "Mirror Game"*

Throughout Mexican history, various criteria have been used to define and classify people into ethnic and racial groups. These criteria have been influenced by changes in political processes, demographics (e.g., the arrival of slaves from Africa, immigrants from Europe and Asia), and ideologies (e.g., the rise of the mestizo project as a national identity). Even official systems of classification, like the national census, have shifted, reflecting domestic debates on race, diversity, and culture (Walsh 2004). For example, while the 1921 National Census included a race question with the categories of white, Indian (Indio), and mixed (*mezclado*), the 1930 census eliminated the race question, substituting it with a question on language. Consequently, in ethnic or racial terms, people were classified only as speakers or nonspeakers of an indigenous language (González Navarro 1968). The official justification for dropping the race question revolved around the idea that race was an unscientific concept (Gamio 1916) and that, because of high rates of miscegenation, most individuals were unaware of their ancestries (Dirección General de Estadística 1930; Loveman 1993). Since the national ideology of mestizaje fostered the idea that all nonindigenous individuals were, by definition, mestizos, the mestizo category was also dropped. This is just one illustration of how the defining of the mestizo category as Mexico's "national identity" has taken hold and powerfully shaped the collection and interpretation of social science data.

From 1930 to 1990, the indigenous category was defined by linguistic criteria and was the only ethnic category captured in Mexico's national censuses in

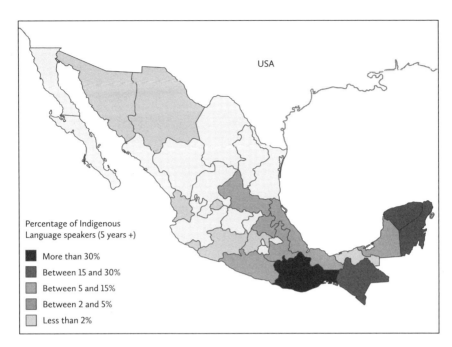

Percentage of Indigenous
Language speakers (5 years +)

- More than 30%
- Between 15 and 30%
- Between 5 and 15%
- Between 2 and 5%
- Less than 2%

MAP 2.1 Percent Indigenous Language Speakers in Mexico, by State Source: Census of Mexico, 2010

that period. Although other criteria have been used, language has been used as an ethnic marker since the 1895 census. Eventually, indigeneity was considered to be only a cultural identity, which could be diminished or eliminated through behaviors like learning Spanish, wearing Western clothes, and abandoning indigenous communities.

It was not until the 2000 and 2010 censuses that a question on indigenous self-identification was included.[15] As we mentioned previously, around 6.2 percent of Mexico's population self-identified as indigenous in 2000. This number rose to 14.8 percent in 2010, despite the fact that only 6.6 percent of the overall population self-identified as speaking an indigenous language. Perhaps this dramatic increase stems partially from changes in the wording of the questions. Whereas the 2000 census question was, "State if you are Náhuatl, Mayan, Zapotec, Mixtec or from another indigenous group," the 2010 census asked, "According to your culture, do you consider yourself indigenous?" In other words, the 2010 census changed the ethnolinguistic membership criteria to "culture" without mentioning specific groups and used the broad term "indigenous." The 2010 census also included a separate question on indigenous language, which listed sixty-four options.

Map 2.1 shows the percentage of residents who speak an indigenous lan-

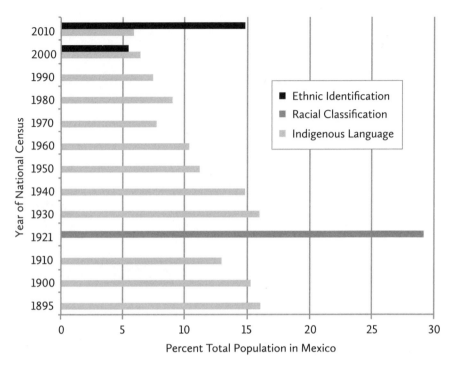

FIGURE 2.1  Size of Indigenous Population in Mexican National Censuses

guage by region according to 2010 census results. It shows that, as has historically been the case, indigenous language speakers continue to be concentrated in the southern states, particularly Oaxaca, Chiapas, and the Yucatan Peninsula.

As Figure 2.1 indicates, while the population identified by the state as indigenous, on the basis of their spoken language, has gradually decreased as a percentage of the total Mexican population, it has grown in absolute numbers. We hypothesize that, throughout the twentieth century, many indigenous people and their descendants collectively adopted both the Spanish language and a mainstream mestizo identity, leaving behind a population that has continued to speak indigenous languages and transmit its language to the next generation.

The PERLA data provide a unique opportunity to systematically and quantitatively explore the ethnic and racial identities of the Mexican people beyond indigenous identity and language. The PERLA survey includes several ways of measuring identity: a closed-ended question on ethnic self-identification (without specifying membership criteria), a closed-ended question based

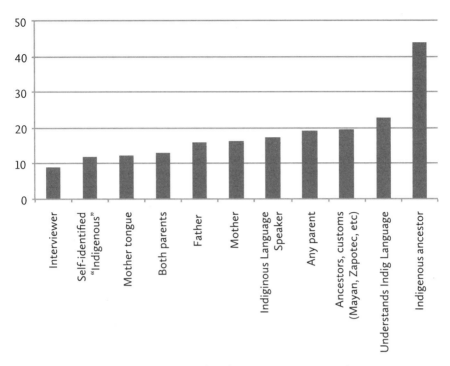

FIGURE 2.2 Percent Indigenous or with Indigenous Ancestry according to Various Criteria, Mexico

on "ancestors and customs," and an open-ended question on racial identity. Furthermore, survey takers classified respondents according to ethnic and racial categories, including white, mestizo, indigenous, black, and mulatto and categorized their skin color on the basis of a printed color palette, all prior to administering the survey.

These multiple measures of ethnic-racial identification and classification allow us to explore the multidimensionality of ethnicity and race. For example, we show in Figures 2.2 and 2.3 how the size of ethnic and racial groups change according to the criteria used to define them.

Figure 2.2 shows how the size of the indigenous population changes according to the criteria used to measure it. Most of the indicators used in the PERLA survey for linguistic criteria (i.e., language spoken, language understood, and parental language) are commonly used by the Mexican census, the Indigenous Development Commission (CDI), and the National population council (CONEVAL). Three of these measures are based on self-ascription. An important difference between the questions on "ancestors" and those on "self-identity as Náhuatl, Mayan, Zapotec, and Mixtec" is that, while the former was open to any ancestor, the latter included a list of the main ethnolinguistic groups in Mexico. Only one question, completed by the survey interviewer, represents external classification.

As we can see in Figure 2.2, asking respondents if they considered themselves "indigenous" produced one of the smallest population sizes (11.9 percent). Nevertheless, when we asked respondents about their identification based on their ancestors and customs, a surprisingly larger number identified as indigenous (19.4 percent). One key difference between these questions is that the latter did not use the term "indigenous" but instead included the names of the four largest indigenous groups in Mexico (Mayan, Zapotec, Mixtec, and Náhuatl). However, we believe that the key difference is that questions that are based on more flexible criteria such as cultural traits might result in larger number of self-identified indigenous individuals than questions that are based on more static conceptions of ethnic membership (i.e., asking respondents if they "are indigenous"). Indeed, as we mentioned above, when the Mexican Census asked Mexicans if they considered themselves indigenous "according to their culture," 14.9 percent of individuals responded affirmatively. This represents a 270 percent increase from the 2000 census, in which no references to culture were used. In addition, this "ethnic explosion" may also be related to recent social movements and the celebration of the 200th anniversary of the country's independence, which prompted multiple public discussions about different aspects of Mexican history and identity (Martinez and Barbary forthcoming).

In line with these findings, we also find that questions that reference other cultural traits such as language ability also return larger numbers of self-identified indigenous respondents.

It is telling that only 44 percent of respondents acknowledged an indigenous ancestor. This number seems low if we consider that more than 75 percent of respondents self-identified as either indigenous or mestizo. Therefore, we would expect a similar number of individuals recognizing indigenous ancestors since mestizos should technically be of partial indigenous ancestry. Perhaps the answer lies in the fact that cultural assimilation into mestizo culture took place several generations ago in many Mexican regions outside of the South. In such regions, many respondents may only recall having mestizo ancestors.

As Figure 2.3 indicates, there is a much higher degree of diversity in the ethnic and racial identities held by contemporary Mexicans than what is officially recognized. When respondents were asked to self-identify ("What do you consider yourself to be?"), more than 13 percent identified as white, 64.3 percent as mestizo, 11.9 percent as indigenous, and about 3 percent as either

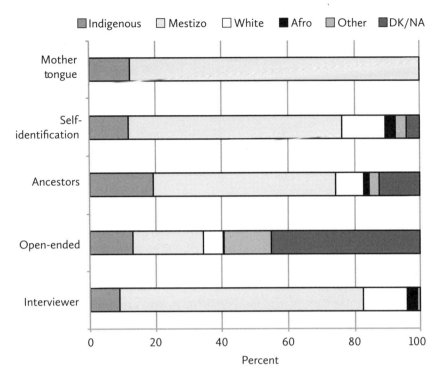

FIGURE 2.3 Ethnoracial Composition Using Various Criteria, Mexico

black or mulatto. The presence of these identities is a significant finding in and of itself since they challenge the long-held view, derived from mestizaje ideology, that Mexicans' only categories of self-identification are mestizo (for the large majority) and indigenous (for a small minority).

We also found that the relative size of the aforementioned ethnic or racial groups varied according to the wording of the question and the options provided. This fluidity points to the existence of different meanings and the multidimensionality of ethnic and racial identities. While almost 20 percent of the respondents identified with a specific indigenous group (e.g., Mayan, Mixtec, Zapotec), based on "ancestors or customs," only 12 percent defined themselves panethnically as indigenous[16] when no criteria (e.g., ancestors, customs)[17] were used. Similarly, the size of the white and mestizo populations varied according to the question format. This suggests that white and mestizo identities are not mutually exclusive. As scholars have found in Brazil, there seems to be "categorical ambiguity" or polysemy between ethnic and racial categories in Mexico (Harris 1970). Our findings also seem to confirm that these ethnic and racial identities are relative and contextual. However, they are not constructed

TABLE 2.1 Interviewer versus Self-Identification (%)

| | Interviewer Classification | | | | |
|---|---|---|---|---|---|
| | White | Mestizo | *Indigenous* | Other | Total |
| Self-Indentification | | | | | |
| White | 47.0 | 47.7 | 3.8 | 1.5 | 100.0 |
| Mestizo | 9.5 | 83.7 | 4.3 | 2.5 | 100.0 |
| *Indigenous* | 4.2 | 53.8 | 37.0 | 5.0 | 100.0 |

Source: PERLA 2010 (National Sample)

randomly; as we will show later, they are shaped by specific factors including region, education, community size, language, and ancestor characteristics.

As we mentioned in the introduction, the mestizaje ideology equated a mestizo identity with the national identity. The centrality, and even normative character of this identity, remains a powerful force, even today. For example, our own survey takers classified most of their respondents as mestizo (73 percent), and only 13 percent as white and 9 percent as indigenous.

As we know, external classification does not always coincide with how people perceive themselves. Table 2.1 presents our results regarding the relationship between the self-identification of PERLA respondents and how our survey takers classified them. It shows that most self-identified mestizos, 83 percent, were classified as such by the interviewers. Nevertheless, both self-identified whites and indigenous persons were more commonly classified by the survey takers in other categories, particularly as mestizo. This seems to suggest that the identities as white and indigenous do not necessarily depend solely on external characteristics that others can observe easily. Rather, there seems to be a tendency, perhaps owing to the strength of the mestizaje ideology, to classify most people as mestizo.

This polysemy raises an important question for researchers: How do ethnic and racial identities in Mexico correlate with social and demographic factors such as language, skin color, ancestors, region, and education? How does external classification or self-identification, in all its variants, shape ethnic and race relations in the country? Do individuals hold these identities in a flexible way? To address these questions, we turn to our findings based on regression analysis and contextualize them using ethnographic literature to explore the different meanings of ethnic and racial identity in Mexico. We concentrate on those who identified themselves as white, mestizo, or indigenous, since we have limited numbers of individuals who identified as black or mulatto.

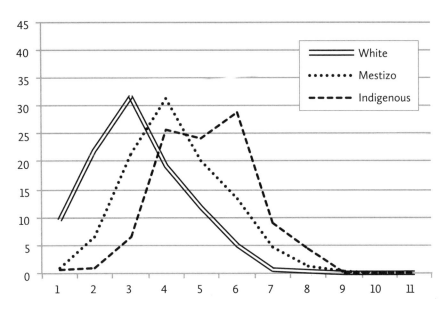

FIGURE 2.4 Ethnoracial Self-Identification by Skin Color, Mexico

One of the key variables in our study was skin color. As mentioned in the introduction, PERLA survey interviewers categorized the skin color of each respondent according to an eleven-point skin color palette. Such color measurements are not commonly used in Mexico, partly because of the mestizaje ideology, which promotes the idea that race and phenotype lack significance. However, a few recent studies have begun to consider the role of color in Mexican society (Flores and Telles 2012; Moreno Figueroa 2010; Sue 2013; Villarreal 2010). Even the government agency in charge of preventing discrimination (CONAPRED) has recently experimented with a color variable in a large-scale survey to assess the prevalence of discrimination (ENADIS 2010). The existence of this color variable shows that an important sector of Mexican society feels that skin color plays a relevant role in explaining discrimination in Mexico.

Figure 2.4 shows the distribution of skin color (as recorded by the interviewer) for each ethnic and racial category based on self-identification. While there was a tendency for self-identified whites to be categorized with lighter skin tones, 58 percent of them actually were categorized as having light brown or dark brown tones (colors 4–7 in the eleven-point color scale). The variation in skin color categorization within ethnic or racial groups was even clearer for people who self-identified as mestizos. These individuals are distributed across the entire color spectrum (1–9), and 24 percent of them were described as having light skin (1–3). Therefore, even though Figure 2.4 shows a clear bivariate association between identity and skin color, there is considerable overlap in the color distribution of the three categories.

Despite this ambiguity, being classified by the interviewer as having light skin was a powerful predictor of white self-identification. Indeed, multivariate regression analyses indicated that Mexicans whose perceived skin tone fell within the first three tones of the eleven-point scale were 35 percent more likely to identify as whites, holding all other variables constant. On the other hand, those who self-identified as indigenous or mestizo did not differ significantly in their skin tones.

The graph also shows that most of those surveyed were ranked in category 4 of the palette and that the distance between the skin tone of those who considered themselves white and those who identified as mestizo was small in terms of skin color, especially when compared to the results from other Latin American countries (see chapter 4). Therefore, while skin color seems important in constructing the boundaries of whiteness, it is not the fundamental component on which mestizo identity is determined in Mexico. Nevertheless, as we will see later, perceived skin tone rather than white or mestizo self-identification, seems to play a more important role in explaining inequality.

## What Is Mestizo Identity Built Upon?

Public schooling in Mexico underpins the processes involved in converting mestizo ideology into practice (Sáenz 1939). Figure 2.5 shows the relationship between formal education and identification as mestizo. Here we see that the predicted probabilities of identifying as mestizo increased almost linearly with educational attainment, when holding all other individual and contextual variables constant at their means.[18] These results will allow us to reflect on the efficiency of the national educational project in the construction of a Mexican mestizo identity: educated persons are exposed to a mestizaje discourse and are thus more likely to identify as mestizo.

In the PERLA study, the distribution of those individuals who considered themselves to be mestizos was fairly constant throughout the country; only the central-western zone showed a stronger trend. This is consistent with the national importance of ranch culture (known in Mexico as *cultura criolla* or *ranchera*) in the Bajío area (parts of the states of Guanajuato, Querétaro, and Michoacán) and in the highlands of the state of Jalisco (Barragán 1997) and with the argument that mestizo identity in Mexico is, above all, cultural. Most of the symbols of "being Mexican" (the so-called *mexicanidad*), such as rodeos, te-

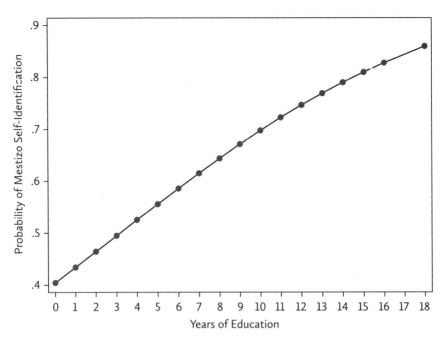

FIGURE 2.5 The Effect of Schooling on *Mestizo* Self-Identification (controlling for age, gender, skin color, size of community, geographic region, urban/rural), Mexico

quila, and mariachi music, are recognized both inside and outside the country as originating in this region (see Palomar 2004). Another possible explanation for increased mestizo self-identity in the central-western zone could relate to the tradition of migration from this Mexican region to the United States, and the role that the border plays in defining identity as well (see Lomnitz 2005).

Finally, the family is another important domain for constructing identity (Eriksen 1995). Using the PERLA data, we explored the different components of family origin that had an impact on interviewees' identity. As we can see from Figure 2.6, most of the respondents showed an overall consistency between their parents' ethnoracial origins and their own identity. It is particularly interesting that several respondents who self-identified as white reported having mestizo or indigenous ancestors, which challenges the notion of whiteness as a "pure" racial category that is prevalent in countries such as the United States (Telles and Flores 2013).

As we set forth at the beginning of this chapter, we do not intend to outline all the factors of mestizo identity. Rather, we hope to highlight its multidi-

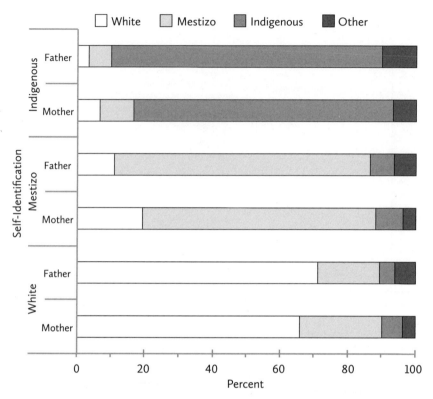

FIGURE 2.6 Ethnicity of Parents by Respondents' Self-Identification, Mexico

mensional nature and to show how this identity is relational (i.e., established vis-à-vis others). The relational and situational nature of identities has been amply examined in the literature. One of the aspects of identity that is particularly interesting in the PERLA results concerns those respondents who self-identified as white.

## Whiteness in Mexico

The study of whiteness as an identity category in Latin America has received little attention, especially in comparison to research on indigenous and Afrodescendant persons (Loveman 1993; Telles and Flores 2013). In what is probably the first systematic study on white identity in contemporary Latin America, Telles and Flores (2013) found that social class and country of residence, in addition to skin color, were important factors influencing the probability that contemporary Latin Americans would self-identify as white. In countries such as Argentina, Costa Rica, and Uruguay, where whiteness and racial purity were central to the construction of the national ideology, broad sectors of the population claim a white identity, regardless of skin color. In contrast, in countries such as Mexico, where the national ideology has extolled mestizo identity as the national one, people tend to avoid a white identity, especially as educational attainment increases. Rather, people tend to identify as mestizo, even when they have light skin or a European appearance;[19] in countries such as Mexico, this suggests there is a normative component to mestizo identity.

The data from the 2010 PERLA study also confirm these previous findings for the Mexican case. For example, in comparison to self-identified mestizos, respondents who identified as white tended to have fewer years of formal education (controlling for other sociodemographic factors and skin color). This finding seems to be in keeping with the idea of whiteness as a strategy for socioeconomic mobility: people of low socioeconomic status may have greater incentives to classify themselves as white than middle-class persons do, since whiteness continues to be a source of symbolic capital in Latin America (Telles and Flores 2013).

In Mexico, the geographic region that a person comes from is another important factor in constructing identity. In spite of the fact that the national ideology of mestizaje officially disregarded white identities and fostered identification with the mestizo category, there are regional identities that relate whiteness to ideas of progress and modernization.[20] According to the PERLA data white identity is more likely to be claimed in Mexico's northern regions. This could be due partly to a higher concentration of lighter-skinned people in that region (especially relative to the southern states)[21] but could also result from a strong regional ideology that identifies the Mexican North with both whiteness and industrial development. Many inhabitants in the North originally arrived as settlers, and they often treated local indigenous groups as enemy combatants within the context of the central government's general effort to forcefully "pacify the remaining nomadic indigenous groups, who were also called 'border Indians' (or *indios de frontera*)" (Sariego 1988). Also, the North had few state institutions before the twentieth century, because of its geographic distance and powerful regional chieftains (Aboites 1998). The whiteness of the North was widely referred to as an important component of capitalist development in the region.

Figure 2.7 shows the relationship between region, skin color, and identity and indicates that ethnic and racial identities in Mexico are associated not only

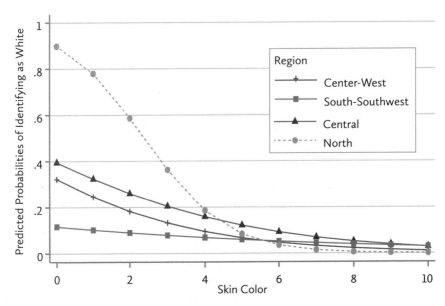

FIGURE 2.7 Predicted Probabilities of Identifying as *White* (controlling for age, gender, size of community, urban/rural), by Region and Skin Color, Mexico

with skin color but also with geographic context. This graph was constructed based on a logistic regression model that controls for several individual characteristics such as sex, age, community size, and educational attainment. Therefore, it allows us to examine how geography and skin color interact in shaping the probabilities that Mexicans will identify as white holding all those other control variables constant. We find that lighter-skinned people are significantly more like to identify as white, but that this correlation is substantially stronger in the north, where an average light-skinned person has a 90 percent probability of identifying as white. In contrast, a person of the same characteristics but living in the southern region has less than a 20 percent probability of self-classifying as white. The higher propensity among northern residents to identify as white is found even among light brown persons (those with skin color rated 4).

In contrast, in the more indigenous South, identification with whiteness bears almost no relation with skin tone, and it might depend more on social or cultural factors. For example, it is possible that the category white in these areas refers to being "nonindigenous" or not being poor, an idea we will explore when discussing inequality. These findings appear to confirm the role of regional ideologies, along with skin color, in shaping white identities.

## Indigenous Identities in Mexico

Results of the PERLA survey show that about 12 percent of those surveyed self-identified as being indigenous, a pan-ethnic category. Consistent with the literature, we found that most of those who self-identified as indigenous reside in the southern region of the country. Somewhat surprisingly, our survey also detected respondents in the northern region who self-identified as indigenous, even if they did not report speaking an indigenous tongue. In the past few years, the northern region of Mexico has received numerous immigrants from indigenous regions in the South. Recent work in the North has shown that the urban offspring of these indigenous immigrants often continue to identify as indigenous subsequent to the migration (Martínez Novo 2006). Therefore, internal migration may be playing an important role in reshaping the geography of interethnic relations in Mexico. Although internal migration would explain the geographic distribution of the indigenous population, it could not explain the national increase of indigenous population.

As we mentioned previously, there were no significant perceived skin color differences between respondents who identified as mestizo and those who claimed an indigenous identity in the PERLA survey. What, then, are the elements that shape a pan-ethnic indigenous identity? Multivariate regression models indicate that having a mother or father who speaks an indigenous language was the determining factor: having such a parent increased the likelihood of identifying as indigenous by more than sevenfold compared to having parents who are Spanish speakers. Community size was also an important factor: the probability of respondents identifying as indigenous increased by 19 percent when those respondents lived in a small community (less than twenty-five hundred residents). Furthermore, geographic context and parental language interacted dynamically. As Figure 2.8 shows, the probabilities that the children of speakers of an indigenous language would identify as indigenous diminished as the community size increased. While a person whose parents were indigenous-language speakers had a 38 percent chance of self-identifying as indigenous if he or she lived in a small locality, this probability decreased to 22 percent if that person lived in a metropolitan area such as Mexico City. In other words, those who move to larger cities and urban centers seem to have fewer incentives to maintain their indigenous identities. This is consistent with the classic model of cultural assimilation, as well as with findings regarding the stigma of indigenous identification in urban areas (Martínez Casas 2007; Martínez Novo 2006).

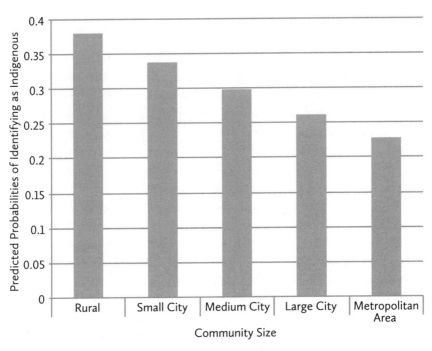

FIGURE 2.8 Predicted Probabilities of Identifying as *Indigenous* (controlling for age, gender, skin color, geographic region, urban/rural) by Community Size, Mexico

But does the term indigenous refer to a homogeneous category in Mexicans' minds? Guillermo de la Peña (2005) restated this question, initially posed by Aguirre Beltrán in 1957. De la Peña argued that, although a wealth of ethnographic studies highlights the existing heterogeneity within the indigenous population, state policies still perceive indigenous communities as a relatively undifferentiated block. Therefore, in some ways, the self-identification into a pan-ethnic indigenous category by speakers of indigenous languages may reflect assimilation to a national project, wherein indigenous people are considered to be a fundamentally homogeneous group, defined in opposition to the nonindigenous (i.e., mestizos).

Therefore, the question remains: How do the speakers of different indigenous languages choose to identify? Do Mixtec or Zapotec speakers identify as indigenous, as the Mexican census officials seem to assume, or as mestizo, or white? Are there significant differences in their identities based on the language they speak? Or do all speakers of indigenous languages, in fact, form a homogeneous identification-based group?

Our data show that the various ethnolinguistic groups in Mexico relate to the pan-ethnic indigenous category in profoundly different ways. Náhuatl

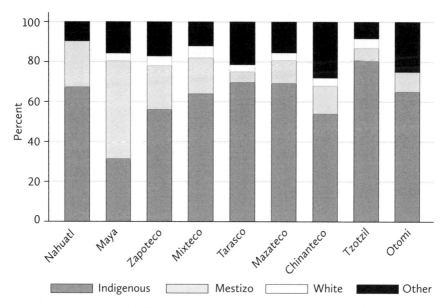

FIGURE 2.9 Ethnoracial Self-Identification by Indigenous Language Spoken (Based on "Ancestors and Customs"), Mexico

speakers were, on average, nine times more likely than Spanish speakers to identify as indigenous.[22] On the other hand, respondents who grew up in homes where Mayan-Yucatec or Mixtec languages were spoken were only three times more likely than the children of Spanish speakers to identify as indigenous. Figure 2.9 presents these relationships graphically, showing the percentage of each ethnolinguistic group that self-identified as white, mestizo, indigenous, or other. Figure 2.9 demonstrates, in effect, that each ethnolinguistic group relates to the pan-ethnic term "indigenous" in a different way.

Figure 2.9 indicates that close to 70 percent of Náhuatl speakers and more than 80 percent of Tzotzil speakers identified themselves as indigenous. On the other hand, only 30 percent of Maya-Yucatecan speakers, who live in the states of Quintana Roo and Yucatan, identified themselves pan-ethnically as indigenous. In fact, most Maya-Yucatecan speakers saw themselves as mestizo (and a small minority as white). The special relationship between Mayan speakers and the mestizo identity in the Yucatan Peninsula has historical roots. During the War of the Castes, which took place in the mid-nineteenth century, the Mexican government brutally repressed indigenous movements. This likely resulted in the retreat of local Mayans from the stigmatized indigenous category and in their adoption of the more neutral mestizo category.[23] In other words, in a process similar to what happened in Cuzco, Peru, with the Quechua identity, the Mayan identity was not constructed in opposition to the mestizo identity but became, to a certain degree, interchangeable with it (de la Cadena 2004). This reinforces the idea that the construction of ethnic and racial identities in Mexico is strongly anchored in the local context.

Besides language and community size, formal education also plays an important role in the construction of an indigenous identity. As our data indicate, respondents with more schooling tended to shy away from identifying pan-ethnically as indigenous and identified instead as members of particular ethnolinguistic groups (e.g., Mayan, Náhuatl, Zapotec). In fact, 11.9 percent of these respondents had at least one year of university education. This percentage dropped considerably (to 4.2 percent) for those who defined themselves as indigenous and was even lower for those who were classified as indigenous by survey interviewers. This significant drop in the educational attainment of members of the pan-ethnic indigenous group was caused, in part, by the exclusion of the Mayan-Yucatecan respondents, who generally had a higher socioeconomic status and tended to avoid the indigenous label and to identify as mestizo if the interviewer did not provide a Mayan category. This highlights the heterogeneity of the indigenous experience in Mexico and also shows how changes in the way indigeneity is assessed could directly impact the measurement of inequality (a topic we develop more in the inequality section).

A mestizo identity is not only the most frequent category mentioned in the PERLA results but also the identity that is linked to a Mexican identity; however, this identification also emerges in the form of whiteness (albeit rarely explicit) and especially in the form of indigenous identities. This face in the mirror is the one that leads to polysemous reflections: individuals can be Mayan and mestizo at the same time, even while the state-defined categories consider them indigenous (pan-ethnic). Mestizaje ideology has been particularly efficient in creating a national framework for a shared identity but has not achieved the homogeneity that intellectuals such as Gamio desired; nor has mestizaje ideology attained social equality. In the next two sections we analyze the consequences of the inconsistencies between ideology and reality.

## Mestizaje at Work: From Illusion of Equality to Discrimination

The political project of mestizaje has been the guiding ideology informing Mexican ethnic and racial relations since the end of the nineteenth century. Over time, racial mixture has been replaced by a policy that seeks a cultural mestizaje through education and economic development projects. Therefore, an important component of mestizaje is that it is an inclusive, homogenizing process, making ethnic and racial boundaries fairly irrelevant. It is on this basis that mestizaje has been presented as an antiracial and unifying project. The mestizaje ideology has become entwined with social policies and promises of social justice, which together have formed what is known as the "postrevolutionary national project" (see Vasconcelos 1982 [1925]). The result of development of this ideology is that there is a generalized belief that Mexico is an inclusive, not racist, country; at the very least, the topic of race is believed to have no relevance. However, racial and ethnic discrimination do exist, and has an impact on social interaction, educational attainment, and people's economic well-being.

## Discrimination: Perception versus Experience

In analyzing perceptions and reported experiences of discrimination, we have generally found that most perceived and experienced discrimination was economic-based and that people classified as having light- or medium-colored skin, self-identified mestizos, and highly educated people reported witnessing more discrimination against others but were less likely to see themselves as victims of discrimination. To explore differences among respondents, we classified these respondents on the basis of their skin color, ethnoracial identity, and educational attainment.

Table 2.2 shows that there was more perceived discrimination due to economic status (68.6 percent) than to due to skin color (58.5 percent) or use of an indigenous language (54.5 percent). The incidence of reported language discrimination is relatively high, given that only 6.5 percent of the national population speaks an indigenous language. Our data show that skin color, self-identification, and years of schooling were important factors shaping the likelihood that a respondent would report discrimination. Among lighter-skinned respondents, those who self-identified as mestizos and those who had more years of formal education reported having witnessed more discrimination than the other groups. This trend is markedly different from that in the United States, where African Americans consistently report more discrimination than whites (Appelbaum et al. 2003). A possible explanation is that the ideology of mestizaje acknowledges the existence of social inequality, especially economic inequality, for those who are seen as falling outside of the mestizo category. Given that indigenous people tend to be the most frequent victims of discrimination (see Stavenhagen 2001), it is telling that they reported having witnessed discrimination less frequently; for example, 57 percent of mestizos but only 47 percent of indigenous reported witnessing language discrimination. Never-

TABLE 2.2 Witnessed Discrimination due to Indigenous Language, Economic Situation, and Skin Color (%)

| | Witnessed | | |
| --- | --- | --- | --- |
| | *Indigenous* Language | Economic Situation | Skin Color |
| *Skin Color* | | | |
| Light | 62.9 | 73.8 | 65.7 |
| Medium | 51.4 | 67.7 | 56.4 |
| Dark | 48.5 | 64.5 | 55.0 |
| *Identity* | | | |
| *Indigenous* | 47.0 | 66.4 | 50.4 |
| Mestizo | 57.5 | 73.4 | 62.8 |
| White | 47.0 | 59.1 | 50.7 |
| *Education* | | | |
| Low | 42.8 | 57.7 | 45.6 |
| High | 66.4 | 80.5 | 70.4 |

Source: PERLA 2010 (National Sample).

theless, indigenous people reported experiencing discrimination more consistently than any other group.

"Indigenous language" and "accent" are not synonymous in these tables: the former refers to people who report speaking one of the Mexican indigenous languages, while the latter could include regional accents, which, even if they are not perceived as indigenous, are not considered "proper" Spanish. Both, however, refer to the importance of language as a significant marker of discrimination. In the PERLA results, people who identified as indigenous reported experiencing more discrimination because of how they speak. This is consistent with the state's linguistic policies, which are informed by the belief that continued linguistic diversity hinders the formation of a unified mestizo nation; these policies have framed indigenous languages as the greatest obstacle to the complete assimilation of indigenous people into Mexican society (Sierra 1947; Gamio 1916; Knight 2004).

Our survey also found that many Mexicans report having experienced discrimination. 33.8 percent reported having been mistreated due to their economic status, 20 percent due to accent, and 16 percent on the basis of skin color. The percentage of people who reported experiencing some form of dis-

TABLE 2.3 Experienced Some Type of Discrimination according to Skin Color, Self-identification, and Schooling (%)

| | Accent | Experienced Economic Situation | Skin Color |
|---|---|---|---|
| *Skin Color* | | | |
| Light | 16.5 | 33.0 | 12.5 |
| Medium | 19.2 | 31.1 | 13.4 |
| Dark | 24.7 | 39.8 | 26.0 |
| *Identity* | | | |
| *Indigenous* | 31.9 | 42.8 | 25.2 |
| Mestizo | 19.3 | 35.1 | 16.0 |
| White | 17.4 | 25.7 | 9.8 |
| *Education* | | | |
| Low | 19.3 | 30.9 | 15.2 |
| High | 19.4 | 33.5 | 21.5 |

Source: PERLA 2010 (National Sample).

crimination was considerably lower than the percentage that reported witnessing discrimination. Mestizos and respondents with lighter skin tones seemed to have experienced less discrimination than darker-skinned or indigenous respondents have. Moreover, it would appear that educational attainment was not a crucial factor in determining who will report experiencing discrimination. The only exception is discrimination based on skin color: respondents with more schooling reported experiencing more discrimination than did those with fewer years of schooling.

Reports of having experienced skin color discrimination also differed according to region (Figure 2.10). Survey participants from the Center and Center-West who reported having experienced less discrimination due to skin color were those categorized as having the lightest skin color. The North and South of Mexico showed the opposite: participants with medium skin color reported the lowest rates of skin color discrimination. Hence, the interaction of region and skin color shaped the probabilities of perceiving discrimination. Our findings indicate that people classified as dark skinned were more likely to perceive discrimination due to skin color, a situation that was particularly prevalent in Mexico's South, where the largest numbers of indigenous people and Afrodescendants live.

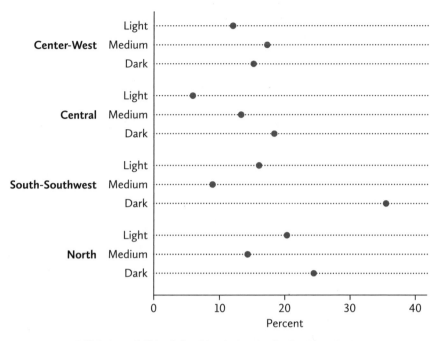

FIGURE 2.10  Self-Reported Skin Color Discrimination by Region, Mexico

## Social Distance

The perception of "others" is another topic that helps us understand the various faces of discrimination. In Mexico it is generally recognized that indigenous people are poor. In our analysis we examined respondents' explanations for indigenous poverty. Figure 2.11 shows that only a small part of the sample provided explicitly racist explanations, such as IQ level and personal habits for indigenous socioeconomic status, while external and cultural factors, such as injustice or the lack of education, were predominant explanations. This is consistent with official post-revolutionary discourse on social justice, in which indigenous people have historically been viewed as victims of abuse by the powerful (e.g., large landowners, *ladinos*, local chieftains). In response, the state has implemented social and educational policies to lift indigenous people out of poverty (e.g., cultural missions, bilingual education, indigenous boarding schools, Oportunidades).[24]

Nevertheless, when examining other possible explanations, we saw a tendency for respondents to give more weight to explanations of a personal and cultural nature such as, "They don't speak Spanish well," "They don't want to change their culture," and "They have little schooling." Respondents favor these

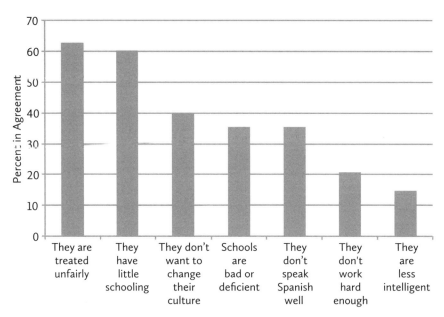

FIGURE 2.11  Reasons Given as to Why the Indigenous are Poor, Mexico

explanations over those of an institutional nature, such as "Schools are bad or deficient." The tendency to attribute poverty to personal and cultural factors (40 percent of respondents chose "customs" and 35.5 percent chose "They don't speak Spanish well") echoes the philosophies driving the acculturation and integration policies of the twentieth century. Similarly, educational explanations (60.3 percent) are consistent with state discourse, which highlighted education as a path to modernization and the attainment of a more equitable Mexican society. Moreover, educational explanations echo the dominance of human capital investment policies in the twenty-first century.

Our data indicate majority support for public policies that address ethnic and racial inequality such as affirmative action, antidiscrimination laws, and multicultural school curricula (Figure 2.12). Such strong public support could perhaps have roots in the post-revolutionary Mexican ideology that forwards social justice and equality ideals (at least at the level of public discourse). In fact, support for affirmative action is higher in Mexico than in any other country included in the PERLA study perhaps because Mexico has very few affirmative action programs directed at this population.[25] Support was slightly higher when affirmative action was aimed more at indigenous people than at blacks.[26] We note that support for these policies is 12.5 percent higher than it is in Brazil, a country in which the value of affirmative action has long been debated.

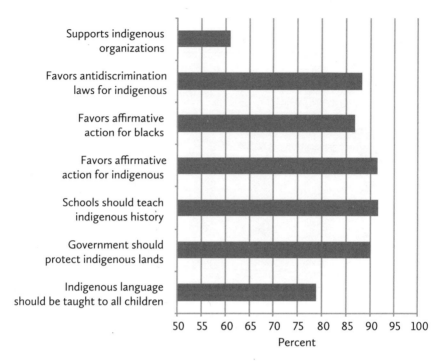

FIGURE 2.12 Support for Multiculturalism and Multicultural Policies, Mexico

Two social policies, however, enjoy less (yet still significant) support among Mexicans. First, 79 percent of respondents believe that indigenous languages should be taught to all children in school. This was significantly lower among self-identified whites (73 percent) and mestizos (78 percent) than among indigenous people (91 percent). There was also less support from highly educated Mexicans: respondents with a high school degree or more were 45 percent less likely than those without one to support indigenous language instruction.[27] Because indigenous languages are commonly associated with poverty and vulnerability in Mexico, they are highly stigmatized. Nevertheless, less-educated respondents and indigenous people (who are among the most disadvantaged groups) embraced indigenous languages more than members of the other groups.[28] These findings could challenge a simple self-interest story where we may expect vulnerable respondents to reject languages that could be perceived as obstacles to their children's social mobility. Rather, indigenous people might perceive the promotion of indigenous languages as an indirect defense of their collective worth. In addition, individuals with more formal education might have been more exposed to or be more invested in the normative aspects of mestizaje ideology in Mexico, which has long insisted that cultural differences are key reasons for "indigenous backwardness."[29] This could explain why highly educated respondents supported all multicultural policies except those directed at preserving indigenous cultural differences.

Second, respondents in Mexico expressed a lower level of support for indigenous organizations (61 percent) in comparison with those in Peru (72.6 percent) and Colombia (90.5 percent), but slightly higher than in Brazil (51.2 percent), where the political organization of a large section of the population might seem threatening to many non-black Brazilians. Despite the relatively small size of Mexico's indigenous population and its spatial concentration, the Zapatista uprising of the mid-1990s, which resulted in the widespread dissemination of images of highly organized and armed indigenous people, may have eroded support for indigenous organizations. Indeed, our analysis showed that such support is especially low in the heavily indigenous southern states, the general region where the conflict took place.[30] Nevertheless, important segments of the urban middle classes sympathized, at least symbolically, with the Zapatista movement. Our survey also found such support particularly among college-educated respondents and those living in the central states, where Mexico City is located.[31]

In sum, while we found general support for multicultural policies in Mexico, perhaps because of the national ideology's populist bent, there was considerably less support for indigenous political organizations. The support that did exist was found among the more educated, who were generally supportive overall of policies that seek to improve the living conditions of indigenous people. Ironically, such support might lead middle-class respondents to regard the teaching of indigenous languages to all children in schools with more skepticism, because they identify these languages as root causes of indigenous poverty.

Another core component of the mestizaje ideology is discourse on the advantages of racial and cultural mixture. The PERLA survey's array of questions aimed at measuring social distance and interethnic dynamics allows us to examine the issue of mixture and integration. For example, when asked, "Would it bother you if your son or daughter married an indigenous person?" more than 80 percent of our respondents said no, which signals a high degree of reported acceptance of mixed marriages, especially with people of indigenous origin.

On the basis of this information, we might suspect that interethnic marriages are common in Mexico. However, looking at couples' ethnic composition (Figure 2.13) reveals that between 67 and 75 percent of couples are endogamous.[32] This indicates that, despite the official endorsement of race mixing in

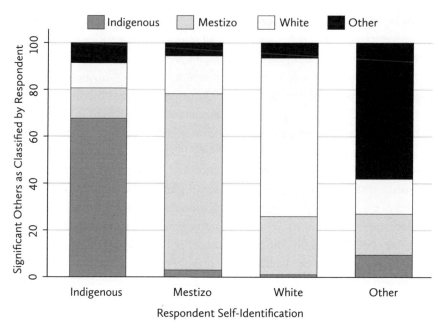

FIGURE 2.13 Ethnoracial Self-Identification and Ethnicity of *Significant Other*, Mexico

Mexico, in practice interethnic couples are not the norm. When interethnic marriages do occur, they almost never involve whites and indigenous persons, the two poles of the Mexican ethnoracial system.

Another measure of social distance is friendship ties. Figure 2.14 shows how many self-identified mestizos reported having indigenous friends or neighbors and supported indigenous rights organizations. As previous findings may lead us to expect, 72 percent of respondents in the South-Southeast, home to the largest numbers of indigenous people, reported having indigenous neighbors, and around 50 percent had indigenous friends and supported indigenous causes. This contrasts with other regions, where fewer reported having indigenous neighbors or friends, but where support for indigenous organizations was much higher (e.g., 75 percent in central Mexico). This reveals the complexity of interethnic relations. There is a recognition and celebration of cultural diversity through the promotion of indigenous rights to organize, even where interethnic relations are not a daily occurrence. On the other hand, mestizos who share common space with indigenous, are less likely to sympathize with their demands for legal recognition. The findings are also consistent with the Zapatista movement's support from those residing in large urban areas of Mexico (all located in the Center, Center-West, and North of the country),[33] in

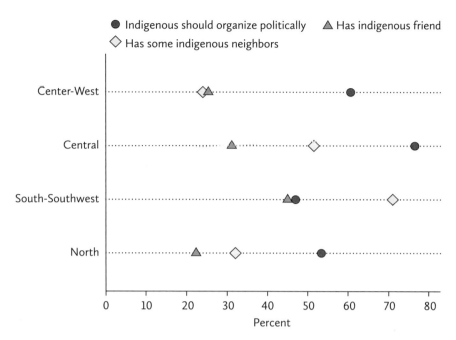

FIGURE 2.14 Support for Indigenous Organizations and Prevalence of Indigenous Friends and Neighbors (Only for *Mestizos*), Mexico

comparison to the fear awakened by more recent indigenous movements (such as APPO in Oaxaca),[34] which were deemed "a threat to national unity."

## Social Inequality

One of the central tenets of the mestizaje ideology in Mexico is that there are no significant racial differences among nonindigenous Mexicans. This assumption is reflected in the fact that most research on inequality in Mexico has focused on class and indigenous status. Mexican elites commonly assume that ethnoracial differences in socioeconomic status do not exist among the population at large. However, in this chapter we have shown that there is a significant and previously unrecognized level of ethnic and racial diversity even among the nonindigenous population. Recent research suggests that such differences may affect individuals' life chances (Villarreal 2010; Flores and Telles 2012). In this last section, we contribute to this incipient line of research by exploring whether the mestizaje ideology has led to social equality, as predicted by Gamio, or whether there are significant socioeconomic differences among Mexicans by ethnic identity and skin color.

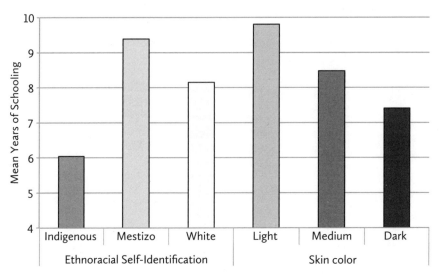

FIGURE 2.15 Mean Years of Schooling by Ethnoracial Self-Identification and Skin Color, Mexico

We first turn to the case of education. Figure 2.15 shows the average years of schooling for all respondents 25 and over by ethnic identity and skin color. Echoing findings from a vast literature, PERLA data show that indigenous people have very low levels of formal education. More surprisingly, Figure 2.15 also shows that Mexicans who self-identify as white are not the most educated respondents. Instead, mestizos have one more year of schooling on average than self-identified whites. This finding sets Mexico apart from other Latin American countries, like Brazil or Peru, where individuals who self-classify as white sit at the top of the social structure. Two factors may help explain this trend. First, highly educated Mexicans may be more likely to identify as mestizo since they are the most exposed to the national ideology of mestizaje through formal schooling. Second, low-status persons may be more likely to identify as "white" because whiteness may be of greater symbolic value to them.

Figure 2.16 also shows that there is a linear negative relationship between skin color and educational attainment. Individuals classified as having light skin had 2.5 more years of formal education than their dark-skinned counterparts. The educational gap between light and dark Mexicans shrank but remained statistically significant when we controlled, with regression analysis, for other factors related to educational attainment, including sex, age, parental occupation, region, indigenous status, and community size.

Critics could argue that the presence of indigenous people could explain these color gaps in education. Given indigenous peoples' low levels of educa-

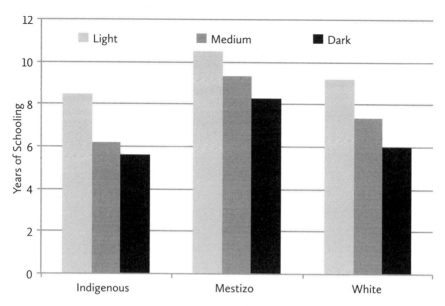

FIGURE 2.16 Mean Years of Schooling by Ethnoracial Self-Identification by Skin Color, Mexico

tion, if indigenous people are darker than the population at large, they could drive the negative association between color and education. In Figure 2.16 we test this proposition and show the level of schooling for individuals of different skin tones within each identity group. Figure 2.16 shows that the negative association between skin color and education is not only driven by indigenous people but that the same pattern is also found within each ethnoracial category. Such an educational advantage is particularly strong for light-skinned indigenous persons who have two years more of education, on average, than their dark-skinned counterparts. Our research design, based on survey data, cannot prove the existence of discrimination as driving these differences. Nevertheless, using regression analysis, we found that even after accounting for the other factors that could explain education (mentioned in the previous paragraph), these gaps remain. These findings highlight both the uniqueness of the Mexican case, where highly educated Mexicans prefer to identify as mestizo rather than white, perhaps because national identity is associated with being mestizo and Mexico's pigmentocratic commonality with the rest of the PERLA countries.

Finally, we look at occupational attainment. In Figure 2.17 we summarize the relationship between holding a nonmanual or high-status job[35] and respondents' ethnic identity and skin tone. While more than 8 percent of self-identified mestizos held high-status, nonmanual jobs, only about 5 percent

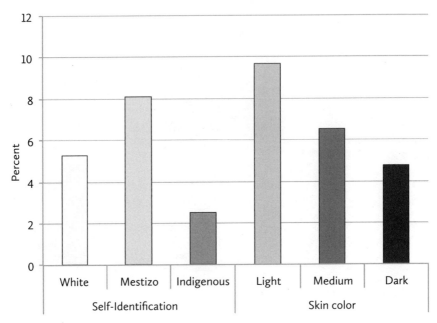

FIGURE 2.17  Percent in High-Status Nonmanual Jobs by Identity and Skin Color

of whites and less than 3 percent of indigenous people occupied similar positions.[36] Thus, we find the same pattern of mestizo advantage and indigenous
disadvantage that we found for educational attainment. However, the most
telling indicator of potential discrimination, as with education, is the fact that
skin color seems to be an important factor: those with lighter skin were more
likely to be employed in high status jobs.

## Conclusion

In this chapter we analyzed the 2010 PERLA survey data, contributing to the
discussion on ethnic and racial differences and the social construction of identity in Mexico. Here, we revisit important aspects of the sociohistorical and
ideological context of race and ethnicity in Mexico to interpret our findings.
We begin by looking at indigenous people. While indigenous people were segregated since the sixteenth century from the rest of society, Europeans and
Afrodescendants had greater geographic mobility, which facilitated interethnic
interactions and gave them more opportunities to improve their location in
the colonial social structure. On the other hand, the segregationist policies and
practices targeting the indigenous population contributed to the emergence of
indigenous community identities.

Toward the end of the seventeenth century, segregationist policies started to weaken and racial mixture increased (although significant mixing had taken place since the Spaniards' and Africans' arrival on the American continent). The social and legal system known as castes (*castas*) was established to regulate the various forms of mestizaje. Over time, there was a reconfiguration of the New Spain society, which involved many different ethnoracial groups, and most of them became involved in the Movement of Independence from 1810 to 1821, which in turn led to the first attempts to build a national identity. With the 1910 Revolution, the mestizo ideology was consolidated and became the foundation of Mexican identity. Policies were generated to assimilate or incorporate indigenous communities. By this time, Afrodescendants had become part of the mestizo population, largely disappearing from national discourse (Sue 2013).

Today, the policies that seek to integrate indigenous people into mainstream society have moved away from acculturation toward the much newer discourse of cultural recognition and respect for diversity. Despite this shift, the ethnic inequalities that were evident since the eighteenth century are still present today. As a result, indigenous people in contemporary Mexico continue to suffer from high levels of poverty and social exclusion. Our findings also highlight the multidimensionality and ambiguity surrounding a mestizo identity, the most common ethnic category used and claimed in Mexico. We found that the definition of mestizaje proposed by Manuel Gamio in 1916, which attributed all social differences to culture and obliterated all mention of race in Mexico, is still influential. We also found that two ideological and structural apparatuses contributed strongly, albeit in different ways, to the consolidation of this ideology: the educational system and indigenismo.[37] While the educational system played a significant role in fostering a mestizo identity (as part of being Mexican), indigenismo failed to integrate indigenous people into the nation. The discourse regarding indigenous integration had contradictory implications: although it protected the cultural heritage of the indigenous peoples, it also accentuated their differences vis-à-vis mestizos and thus contributed to the construction of mestizos as "others."

Our findings with respect to whiteness were especially novel and interesting. First off, whiteness was not solely determined by skin color; we found many cases of divergence between light skin and a white identity, especially in southern Mexico. Overall, our analysis also revealed that identifying oneself as white in Mexico was neither commonplace nor the highest status identity. A possible explanation for the relative lack of status associated with a white identity in Mexico (also found in other Latin American countries) may lie in

Mexico's immigration and population policies in the post-revolutionary period (see Gleizer 2012). After the revolution, Mexico's immigration policies shifted toward restriction in favor of natural population growth (Buchenau 2001). For those who were to be admitted to the country, government officials created immigration policies that aligned with the mestizaje ideology. These policies prioritized immigrants who were culturally similar to Mexicans, which was consistent with Gamio's belief that cultural (and more specifically linguistic) unity was a precondition for modernity and national development. In contrast, there were demanding citizenship requirements for foreigners thought to be culturally or linguistically different, and the children of foreigners were not considered "Mexican." The consequence of these policies was that large numbers of Spanish immigrants, fleeing the Spanish Civil War (1936–1939), and Latin Americans, were welcomed to Mexico. However, they entered Mexico under a refugee status (which is somewhat stigmatized) and not a privileged immigration status, a status that was further devalued by the general xenophobia of the post-revolutionary period (Buchenau 2001). These immigrants were generally lower class (Buchenau 2001), and many of them were considered white (e.g., many of those from Spain and Argentina), which may help explain our findings about the contemporary disassociation between whiteness and status. Furthermore, this may help explain why whiteness signifies something different in Mexico and other Latin American countries, a topic that is explored in Telles and Flores 2013.

Another likely consequence of the homogenizing power of mestizaje ideology relates to explanations of inequality focused on class differences. While poverty among mestizos was a "temporary" condition that was "solvable," indigenous people's poverty was a constituent part of their culture, condemning them to backwardness and exclusion. Thus, instead of forming part of the class system, indigenous people were considered a "problem" that needed to be solved; this could be achieved only through their cultural assimilation (as opposed to through social justice).

But our findings also demonstrated that, in spite of the presumed national homogeneity of the Mexican population, there is not only discrimination against indigenous people in society but also differential treatment based on skin color. Despite the fact that we found that many survey participants reported witnessing and experiencing discrimination due to skin color, this issue goes largely unmentioned in society, probably because of the eradication of racial categories in official discourse during the twentieth century.

Given recent challenges to the model of mestizaje by indigenous and Afro-descendant movements, and the nation's recent turn toward multiculturalism, we have to wonder whether mestizaje is still relevant in the twenty-first century. Indeed, our own findings regarding the role of racial characteristics in shaping people's lives seem to contradict many of the basic tenets of mestizaje. The strength of the nationalistic project from the second decade of the twentieth century until the dawn of the twenty-first century can provide us with clues about the power of a state that has tried to be a part of a community of modern nations, without losing its own identity of mestizaje. Many scholars of Mexican identity have examined ethnic and race relations but have ignored sociohistorical turning points that are important to contextualize these issues. For example, on the same day that NAFTA (the trade agreement that Mexico signed with the United States and Canada in the mid-1990s) went into effect, the indigenous revolt broke out in Chiapas and would go on to have international repercussions. The aftermath of these events brought about the end of seventy years of a one party dictatorship, and the recognition of Mexico as a plural society.

Nevertheless, these changes have not resulted in a new discourse of a Mexican identity like the one generated by Gamio, Vasconcelos, Sáenz, and Beltrán, among others, after the Revolution. Neoliberal multiculturalism, which has marked a series of constitutional changes since 1992, has not generated the same type of model for national identity as the mestizaje ideology, which was institutionalized and specified by law for nearly all of the twentieth century. It is against this backdrop that academics began writing about racism in Mexico (see Castellanos and Sandoval 1998; Moreno Figueroa 2010) and proposed an end to mestizaje ideology (Bartra and Otero 2007). Our results show not only that a mestizo identity continues to exist in Mexico but also that this is an identity with multiple faces.

While identity is linked to culture, the two are not synonymous. In spite of efforts to "culturalize" race by anthropologists who followed Boas, and who have worked for the Mexican state for decades (see Saldívar 2008), our findings clearly show the multiple faces that unfold from Mexican identity. To be mestizo in Mexico means different things to different people, and this varies according to region, schooling, socioeconomic position, and skin color. Gamio's and Aguirre Beltrán's visions saw mestizaje more as a means for establishing a Mexican identity rather than an end in itself. This is seen in the respondents who identified themselves as mestizos but also reported that they were of indigenous parentage. At the other end of the ethnoracial scale, we find those who self-identified as white but also reported having mestizo or even indigenous ancestors.

We found very interesting and important differences related to region. In the South and North of the country, mestizo identity is associated (among other things) with having medium skin color. This contrasts to the Center and Center-West, where many self-identified mestizos have light skin. Whiteness in the North is primarily shaped by skin color, whereas in the South (which has higher numbers of indigenous persons) it is more dependent on sociocultural factors. In terms of discrimination, those who reported having experienced less discrimination in the Center and Center-West were categorized as having the lightest skin, while in the North and South of Mexico those with medium skin color reported the lowest rates of skin color discrimination. These findings reveal that, although a unified mestizaje ideology was disseminated across the nation, it produced uneven meanings related to identity, interethnic relations, and understandings of discrimination. The different regional adoptions of mestizaje ideology are likely due to how this ideology has interacted with differing regional histories and constructions of race and ethnicity. Somewhat ironically then, what our regional analysis illustrates is that, although the mestizaje project was created to homogenize the nation, it has resulted in the creation of difference.

The results that have emerged from our analysis of the 2010 PERLA study in Mexico allow us to propose new agendas for social research. We know little about the consequences of the low returns on education according to identity. Furthermore, research on whiteness in Mexico is almost nonexistent. We also cannot easily explain the continuance of an ideology of mestizaje which was initially erected almost a century ago. Finally, we struggle to understand the mechanisms that trigger discrimination and inequality in a country that has its eyes set on using a national mestizo identity as the mainstay for modernization and which, according to Gamio (1916), "would achieve social equality."

## CHAPTER THREE

# From Whitened Miscegenation to Tri-Ethnic Multiculturalism

*Race and Ethnicity in Colombia*

FERNANDO URREA GIRALDO

CARLOS AUGUSTO VIÁFARA LÓPEZ

MARA VIVEROS VIGOYA

There are two main currents of thought among scholars regarding the role that race and ethnicity have played in Colombian history: the first posits that racism has been present only in specific time periods, most notably during the nineteenth century when the concept of "race" was popularized (Hering Torres 2007; Arias Vanegas 2007; Leal 2010); the second argues that racism has had a constant presence in Colombian history and that "racist practices in the colonial world preceded the birth of the concept [of race]" (Montoya and Jiménez 2010; Almario 2010a). For the latter group, the colonial practice of categorizing individuals into castes, on the basis of their perceived physical and cultural traits, preceded the emergence of the notion of race and left a legacy of racism and discrimination that is still felt in contemporary Colombian society.

During the colonial period, racism was evident in various forms, most obviously in slavery (Montoya y Jiménez 2010; Almario 2010a). Slaves were treated harshly in the mines, farms, and private homes where they labored; even pregnant slave women were signed burdensome jobs. Moreover, although free blacks could organize in *cabildos*,[1] they were constantly harassed because of their potential for inciting slave revolts. Racism was also apparent in the "Compiled Laws of the Indian Kingdoms" (1680), which dictated that indigenous and black people could not be elected to the *cabildos*.[2] In addition, the "Inquisition

Laws" attempted to purge the religious and cultural practices of African slaves and also prohibited interracial marriages between whites and blacks.[3]

After gaining independence from Spain, the newly appointed Colombian authorities passed a series of laws to undermine and finally outlaw slavery, including the Free Womb (1821) and Abolition laws (1851). Nevertheless, racist practices persisted. Though the colonial caste system was officially dismantled with Independence in 1810, it was replaced by racial categories rooted in social practices. This allowed for the continuation of social exclusion based on perceived physical and cultural differences. Thus, many social groups that were previously castes came to be considered new racial groups occupying similar positions in the new social hierarchy. This conversion from caste to race reflected the transition from a monarchical system during the colonial era to a republican model built on allegedly egalitarian and inclusive political ideals, which were in tension with the logic of colonial caste classifications.

During this time, race-mixing became increasingly perceived, along with education, as a possible path for black Colombians to achieve full citizenship. The black leader Diego Luis Córdoba, a prestigious lawyer and member of the left wing of the liberal party that sought progressive reforms for the black population, particularly emphasized education as the means to create a black intelligentsia and improve the social position of black people. At the same time, however, mulato and black leaders criticized him for having married an elite white woman (Pisano, 2012).

Whiteness then became a sought-after commodity. Hence, rather than undermining the concept of race, the liberal model adopted by the national elites in the nineteenth century strengthened it by associating whiteness with political membership, especially citizenship, in the development of the Colombian nation-state (Almario 2010a, 364). This pyramid of color, with light-skinned people at the top and dark-skinned people at the bottom, has profoundly influenced Colombian society and structured the social relations among people of different social classes. Though Colombia is commonly portrayed as having a homogeneous mestizo identity, whiteness is still widely perceived as a synonym of modernity, progress, and national unity even in the contemporary period.

The primacy of whiteness is unquestionable in Colombia, but there are important differences regarding indigenous and black peoples. Though both Afrodescendant and indigenous people have been historically marginalized in Colombia, they have faced sharply different circumstances. While black people were made invisible after the colonial period, as neither policy makers nor intellectuals recognized their existence, indigenous people were an integral part of the Colombian national consciousness, although often perceived as "exotic others" (Wade 1997). Afrodescendants were largely excluded from the national imagination, although they typically held formal citizenship even if they did not enjoy full citizenship rights (Agudelo 2005). Instead, blacks were devalued with very limited possibilities for social mobility. On the other hand, though mulattos were also stigmatized, they had greater mobility opportunities (Meisel and Aguilera 2003). Moreover, claims of racial discrimination were routinely rejected, even if a preference for whiteness and a concomitant rejection of blackness permeated Colombian society. These factors prevented Afrodescendants from building a cohesive ethnoracial identity that could have been used in the struggle for social and political inclusion.

With multiculturalism in the 1990s, blacks and indigenous people began to be differently conceived in the national imagination. The 1991 Colombian Constitution granted indigenous people collective rights over their communal lands on the basis of their perceived cultural differences vis-à-vis mainstream society. In contrast, black communities obtained similar rights only after a long and contentious process in which they attempted to prove that they too were culturally distinct.[4] In the end, the Colombian Congress granted collective rights only to blacks living in the Pacific region, an area with a significant Afro-Colombian population dating to the colonial era, and they failed to address issues regarding black urban populations, such as racial discrimination (Paschel 2010).

The pervasive race mixing that occurred in Colombia since colonial times partially blurred racial distinctions among social classes. Nevertheless, as casual observers have noted, physical traits such as skin color and hair texture continued to be markers of social stratification. Elites are seen and recognize themselves as white, while darker persons are at the bottom rungs of the social ladder. In this chapter, we use data from the PERLA project in Colombia to systematically assess whether and how skin color and hair texture are important elements that shape Colombians' ethnoracial identity, and we also explore whether these traits and identities are still associated with a specific position in the social hierarchy, something that many Colombian thinkers would deny, including the canonical Jaramillo Uribe (1994). Despite Colombia's large indigenous population, we emphasize its even larger black population in our empirical discussion.

In this chapter, we integrate the latest evidence from historiographic and anthropological research, along with our results from the Colombia PERLA survey to shed light on several crucial aspects related to race and ethnicity in contemporary Colombia. First, we provide a brief overview of how the notions of race and ethnicity have been incorporated in Colombian history. Then, we discuss how official statistics have attempted to capture ethnic and racial diversity in Colombia and, in the process, contributed to the creation and maintenance of race-based boundaries. Next, we rely on the results from the PERLA survey to systematically explore how race and ethnicity shape identity and inequality processes in contemporary Colombia. We take an intersectional approach to the analysis of Colombian historiography and the development of subordinate popular sectors, especially those comprising blacks and indigenous people, dark-skin mestizos, poor whites, and the black and mulatto urban middle class. We are attentive to relationships among dominated groups according to their ethnoracial, class, gender, and other characteristics.

## Historical Perspective

### The Colonial Period: Castes, Slavery, Segregation, and Rebellion

During the colonial period, New Granada, which was the name originally given by the Spanish crown to the area that today includes Colombia,[5] depended on mining and agriculture and, therefore, on lands and territories belonging to indigenous groups. As in other Latin American countries, indigenous people were decimated, and the survivors were forced to work. Moreover, indigenous lands were taken over by the Spanish crown, as well as by landlords, priests, and other individuals, who were often mestizos (Tovar 1988). In order to supply labor to the growing number of mines and plantations, indigenous people were *encomendados* (assigned) as legal servants to private persons or to the Spanish crown. Such arrangements lasted until the eighteenth century (Colmenares 1997, 29–108). As Colmenares (1983, 24–25) argues, "The most coveted resource was to own men. Each person who contributed to the conquest had the right to a certain number of indigenous people. The *repartimiento* (distribution) meant a privilege for the beneficiary: the privilege to receive tributes from the indigenous, though it did not include the possession of lands or other resources." Hence, resource extraction and the appropriation of indigenous labor allowed for the subsistence and development of colonial settlements, which explains why colonial settlements proliferated in areas with large indigenous populations (26).

The *encomienda* was a complex institution with religious, political, and financial dimensions. The *encomendero* was required by the Spanish crown to provide protection and spiritual development to the indigenous people under his jurisdiction in exchange for their labor. In practice, many *encomenderos* failed to comply with the rules on wages and working conditions set by the crown to protect indigenous people and treated the native population harshly (Tovar 1988, 65; Colmenares 1997). These slavelike working conditions along with the spread of various epidemics, resulted in a sharp decline in the local indigenous population, which prompted the Spanish crown to increasingly rely on African slave labor to meet labor demand in mining activities and domestic service.

The first recorded African slaves were imported to Colombia in 1510 (Palacios 1978). Estimates vary regarding the total number of slaves brought from Africa during the colonial period. Andrés Gallego (2005: 19) estimates about two hundred thousand, a figure that also includes slaves sent to Ecuador and Panama as well as Colombia. Most slaves were concentrated in the Pacific and southwestern regions in Colombia. During the last phase of the Republic of Nueva Granada (1830–53), slavery had largely ended. By the time the Abolition Law was issued in 1851, only sixteen thousand slaves remained in the territory (Klein 1987, 269). Unlike Cuba, Brazil, and the United States and other regions with large numbers of slaves, most slaves in New Granada worked outside of agriculture. Though slaves were clearly involved in sugar and coffee plantations,[6] most slaves were used in precious metal extraction (especially gold, silver, and copper), livestock production, and household service (Tovar 1988).[7]

Unlike Brazil and Cuba, the importation of slaves to Colombia decreased after 1750. However, this did not necessarily lead to a reduction in slave labor since there was a local supply of slaves coming from mines, haciendas, and urban centers (Tovar, 1988, 45–46; Colmenares 1983, 37–78). From the beginning of the slave trade, runaway slaves, commonly labeled as *cimarrones*, fled haciendas and mines and built *palenques*—social settlements where economic and military organizations operated far from colonial society. Though these runaway settlements took a toll on the institution of slavery, this institution was dismantled only when the use of free labor became feasible and profitable (Tovar 1988; Patiño 2011, 110–132).

In the eighteenth century, a population of free blacks and mulattos, who worked as urban artisans and peasants, developed in some Caribbean regions such as Cartagena (Meisel and Aguilera 2003, 234, 250–256, 270–279) and Antioquia (Patiño 2011). Many obtained their freedom through manumission and others were descendants of cimarrones. In contrast, in the Cauca Province and throughout the Pacific area, slavery remained strong until the mid-nineteenth century, even after the independence from Spain. Because the regional economy, which was based on old mining, cattle rising, and domestic servitude, was heavily dependent on enslaved men and women, local landowners and slaveholders fiercely resisted the 1851 Slavery Abolition Law.

Despite the Spanish crown's desire to maintain separate societies of indigenous and Spaniards, ruled by distinct laws, Colombia experienced a proliferation of castes that emerged because of the increasing intermixing of Europeans,[8] Africans, and natives. The resulting castes were granted specific symbolic and legal obligations by colonial authorities. The frontiers between castes were relatively porous, which allowed for some mobility by persons in lower castes, including free blacks (Almario 2010a). Notwithstanding, skin color, ancestry, and alleged racial purity endured as key elements in social ranking and assured the elite's monopolization of power and control over social mobility (Hering Torres 2010).

Many black slaves and indigenous people were initially ambivalent about joining the fight for independence from Spain because the two main parties involved in this conflict, New World criollos and mestizos, on one hand, and Spanish-born *peninsulares*, on the other, were not interested in a radical transformation of Colombian society. Under their initial plans, the economic structure of the colony, which depended heavily on labor by lower castes (free and slaved blacks, poor whites, mestizos, mixed black and indigenous [*zambos*], and indigenous people), would remained relatively untouched.

Pardos, free blacks, black slaves, and indigenous people had common interests, despite their differences, in challenging the designs of criollo elites (led by Bolivar) to support an aristocratic and republican project for a new republic, which sought to exclude them from their project (Almario 2010a, 2010b; Múnera 2010).

After gaining independence from Spain, the republican regime promoted the abstract notions of equality, freedom, and citizenship for all, including free blacks, indigenous people, mestizos, and pardos. However, it actually prevented these groups from fully enjoying such privileges. Criollos and light-skinned mestizos, who formulated the Independence project, delayed the manumission process until 1852,[9] prevented collective land titling, disintegrated indigenous lands known as *resguardos*,[10] and obstructed the collective organization of blacks (Mina 1975).

After the abolition of slavery in 1851, indigenous and blacks often came into conflict over ownership and possession of land. Blacks were supported by the liberal party and the radicals, while indigenous people looked for support in the conservative party and the Catholic Church (Sanders 2007). With the arrival of the centralist and highly Catholic Regeneración regime,[11] indigenous people kept their rights of the colonial period through Law 89, issued in 1890, by keeping their authority inherited from Spanish colonial laws, such as the system of *cabildos*[12] and the recognition of *resguardo* lands. Although this law was closely related to a specific indigenous colonial status, at the same time it tried to integrate the indigenous population into the nation in several ways: symbolically, through equality before the law and access to citizenship, even though this notion of equality considered indigenous people as children or savages; racially, in favoring biological miscegenation between indigenous and white people; socially, through education exclusively imparted by the church; and economically, through integration to the liberal market model (Safford 1991).

In contrast, legislation regarding Afro-Colombians—both constitutional and penal—was almost absent for the 140 years of the republican history of Colombia, which began about the time of Abolition and lasted until the promulgation of the new constitution in 1991 (de Roux, 2010). When the left-wing and populist Gaitanist project was defeated in 1948 with the murder of Gaitán himself, the liberal party's promise of universalism and equality and Gaitán's idea of miscegenation thus failed to transform the colonial-based racial hierarchy.

In short, the existence of laws for the indigenous and the lack of laws for the Afro-Colombians were closely related to the ideology of miscegenation, political liberalism, and conservative reaction during the Regeneración. At the same time, the political and legal differences between the indigenous population and the Afro-Colombian population, where the former was recognized and the latter was not, would play an important role in establishing the ethnic and cultural rights of the Constitution of 1991.

## Mestizaje in Colombia

The Colombian national ideology as represented by thinkers such as Jaramillo Uribe (1995) and Posada Carbó (2006) posits that Colombia is an egalitarian society, marked by substantial race-mixing and harmonious race relations while racism was a problem unique to the segregationist U.S. society (Pisano 2012). According to this ideology, ethnoracial minority groups enjoy the same privileges and rights as the majority, and racism was extirpated from Colombian society after the abolition of slavery and the dismantling of the caste system. For a critical analysis of the mestizaje ideology in Colombia, as a vehicle of harmonious race relations and social mobility, see Friedemann (1984, 1992) and Wade (1993).

However, mestizaje in Colombia is a complex ideology that has had two dimensions historically. On the one hand, since the Independence period, it has represented a means of consolidating national identity by making racial equality a constitutive part of the nation, transcending the social hierarchies of the Spanish caste system (Lasso 2007). In this sense, the inclusive dimension of mestizaje was supposed to do away with the caste divisions inherited from the colonial period: Spanish, criollo, mestizo, indigenous (*indio*), pardo, zambo, and black.[13] On the other hand, the mestizaje ideology has had a less egalitarian dimension. It has provided ideological support for the continuous domination of white people under the idea that—as stated by the conservative politician Sergio Arboleda (1822–1888)—this group would be the only one to have the "moral, physical, and intellectual resources to lead and control the society" (Arboleda [1869] 1972: 80–81). Nevertheless, while some elite intellectuals believed that mestizaje was a civilizing process for ethnoracial minorities (López de Mesa 1920; Gómez 1970), others regarded it as the main reason why Colombia could not achieve progress since it led to "racial degeneration" (Urrea Giraldo and Viáfara López 2007).

Intellectual elites in the late nineteenth and early twentieth centuries generally discussed mestizaje as an ideal, justifying the supposed inferiority of the indigenous and black population and the superiority of the white population, on the basis of physical features and cultural aspects (Solano 2011; Leal 2010; Albán 2010; Lasso 2006; Flórez 2010, Appelbaum 1999).[14] Besides these factors, geography was also used to justify ethnoracial differentiation. Under the influence of scientific racism, Colombian thinkers linked the alleged inferiority of Afrodescendant and indigenous people with their residence in specific topographies.[15]

Between 1930 and 1950, there were two competing models of mestizaje: a Mexican model, which regarded mestizaje as fundamental to national identity and democracy; and an Argentinean model, which sought to whiten the nation's racial composition by encouraging immigration from Europe and mixing the nonwhite population with the "superior white element," thus gradually eliminating its black and indigenous presence. Scholars such as Wade (1995), Appelbaum (1999), and Rojas (2000) have shown that that the Argentine version ultimately prevailed among most of the elite and in the national imagination. However, unlike Argentina, Brazil, and Venezuela, Colombia was unable to attract European immigration thus failing to achieve the whitened ideal.

The political project of charismatic left-wing leader Jorge Eliecer Gaitán[16] was the strongest challenge from "below" to the elitist model of whitening, in which he argued for a Mexican model of mestizaje and led a social movement

(Green 2000: 98–101, 113–124). During the 1940s, Gaitanismo sought to unite all "dark"-skinned people as well as poor whites, mestizos, and the urban middle class in Colombia. Gaitán first developed an explicit indigenista discourse to integrate indigenous people into national society, and he was able to secure the alliance of many black and mulatto intellectuals of the period in regions like Chocó, North of Cauca, Valle del Cauca, and several areas of the Caribbean region.[17] His eugenic views on race in which he elevated the biological contributions of black and especially indigenous people were mixed with his social views of their importance for the construction of the Colombian nation. Thus, Gaitán noted with pride how he was popularly nicknamed "Gaitán the indigenous" (el Indio Gaitán) and also "Gaitán the black" (el Negro Gaitán).

From the 1960s to the 1980s, with the development of social sciences in Colombia, ethnoracial issues came to be seen as epiphenomena of class. Colombia was seen as a mestizo nation, in which classes were the central social cleavages, and there were no ethnoracial minorities, except for isolated indigenous communities. Indigenous peoples represented savages and the only ethnoracial "other." In contrast, Afrodescendants were mostly rendered invisible or ignored, except to the extent they were part of the nation's mestizaje (Freidemann 1984). Thus, a new ideal of mestizaje emerged that portrayed Colombia as mostly homogeneous and glorified the mixture of white, indigenous, and black elements.

This perspective has been defended by a group of historians that emerged during the sixties, including Jaime Jaramillo Uribe.[18] By the 1990s, many Colombian historians (e.g., Alfonso Múnera) increasingly questioned these ideas,[19] pointing out that the vision of an integrating mestizaje and the suppression of racial tensions in the formation of the Colombian nation ignored a series of primary sources from the eighteenth and nineteenth centuries in which hierarchy, social exclusion, and societal conflict are clearly race based. The Gaitanist movement also served as a prime example of race-based Colombian politics well into the twentieth century.

The mulatto writer and anthropologist Manuel Zapata Olivella provided a bridge between mestizaje and multiculturalism in exalting the racial and cultural mixture among African, indigenous, and Spanish elements.[20] Zapata Olivella proposes a miscegenation that values the contribution of people with darker skins, blacks and indigenous, against the miscegenation project of the elite that values lighter skins and excludes the African and Amerindian. In 1977 he proposed "tri-ethnic miscegenation" in which he saw the three cultural and racial elements as constituent components of Colombian nationality.

The future of our country will not be the result of a historical determinism outside our conscience and will. Very little would we contribute to achieving a real racial and cultural balance if we were to persist in ignoring that we conform to a hybrid population with social inequalities under the colonial legacy. Our duty is to face this reality and take advantage of its excellent advantages. For this, of course, it is necessary to acknowledge the creative participation of Indigenous, Spanish and Africans in our culture. (Zapata Olivella, quoted by Mina 2011, 122).

The dominant idea of the mestizo nation began to be challenged by indigenous movements and some black intellectuals in the 1970s, and it was ultimately replaced by the constitutional recognition of the country as multiethnic and multicultural in 1991 (Castillo 2007). Multiculturalism opened a political space for black communities, but their participation in the nation depended on their participation as an ethnic group, thus producing the "indigenization" of rural blacks while excluding urban blacks and overlooking racial and social discrimination.

## Ethnoracial Movements

Nasa Indian Manuel Quintín Lame led a vigorous indigenous movement in the Colombian Andean region between 1914 and 1918. His struggles for land reform would be addressed by the Colombian government only in the 1960s. Under the influence of the Mexican Revolution, Gaitán's political movement provided a further impetus to indigenous and also black challenges, which suffered a serious blow with Gaitán's assassination and was repressed under subsequent conservative governments (1946–53). A new indigenismo emerged only in the 1960s, through the creation of the first anthropology departments at the Universidad de los Andes, Universidad Nacional de Colombia and through INCORA (Colombian Institute of Agrarian Reform), which encouraged the study of indigenous people. By the 1980s, these elements contributed to a new indigenous movement, which was influential in the Constitutional Assembly of 1991. Further constitutional reforms including Law 70 in 1993 recognized collective indigenous and black lands (Castillo 2007; Agudelo 2005). Indigenous movements would continue to be influential up to recent years, including during the Uribe Vélez administration (2002–10), when they became the primary social opposition to the Colombian government.

The first black organizations in Colombia emerged in the 1930s in response to their perceived marginalization and exclusion from national life, most notably the Democratic Action Movement founded in the Chocó (Pisano 2012). Ten years later, a group of students from the North of Cauca and the Atlantic Coast founded the Black Club of Colombia. Between the 1930s and 1950s, claims by the black population were made mainly through mainstream political channels, especially the liberal party (Pisano 2012; and de Roux 1994).

A modern black movement began with the Circle of Soweto Studies in 1976, which led to the first national political movement in 1982, known as the Cimarron National Movement. These and other 1970s organizations were influenced by the U.S. civil rights movement and the anticolonization and antiapartheid movements in several African countries (Agudelo 2005). A second wave of modern Afro-Colombian organizations was formed around the ethnic-territorial and environmental movements in the Colombian Pacific in 1985.[21] This included black peasant organizations' struggles for their collective territories under Law 70 of 1993, which protected ethnic-based (indigenous) claims to land. Between 1985 and 1990, the black movement became a national movement, expressed in the creation of the Coordinación Nacional de Comunidades Negras (National Coordination of Black Communities). By then, the black movement had largely adopted an ethnic-based discourse, raising tensions between those advancing ethnic and racial claims inside its ranks.

Relatedly, the Proceso de Comunidades Negras (PCN, Process of Black Communities) began in 1993 and gained strength by demanding government recognition of the multiethnic and multicultural character of the nation, according to the 1991 Constitution. The PCN also demanded respect for black people's cultural differences and acknowledgment of their territorial rights under the approval of Law 70, which recognized collective land rights (Castillo 2007). As a consequence of the forced relocation of the Afro-Colombian population, due to the armed conflict and resistance of certain sectors of displaced persons, the Asociación de Afrocolombianos Desplazados (AFRODES, Displaced Afro-Colombian Association) was created in 1999. Other organizations, such as the Conferencia Nacional de Organizaciones Afrocolombianas (CNOA, National Conference of Afro-Colombian Organizations), sprang up around the defense of ethnic-territorial claims and also took up the defense of gender and racial issues. Finally, black organizations comprising middle-class professionals, students, women, and various other sectors of the Afro-Colombian community sprang up, leading to claims of fragmentation and discontinuity in the black movement (Quintero Ramírez 2011; Urrea Giraldo 2011). Many of these locally based organizations operate like networks of patronage, and only those with the greatest capacity have access to public resources and international aid.

Law 70 and Colombia's declaration as a multiethnic society thus provided a legal-institutional foundation for raising ethnic-based claims to which Afro-Colombians sought to press their grievances, but only after they could present themselves as culturally distinct, as the indigenous had done. However, some scholars, including Zapata Olivella, were critical of these legal expressions because they considered that Colombian elites had upheld a version of mestizaje that favored whitening and that reduced black and indigenous people to mere "ethnic minorities," as if the entire Colombian society was not influenced by African and indigenous elements. In an interview given by Zapata Olivella (2004: 189) before his death, he is very explicit on this issue:

> [The Colombian Constitution] is transcendent: for the first time Colombia is recognized as multiethnic and multicultural. But it is not said which are the ethnics nor the cultures. The Colombian aborigine are not mentioned, neither are the African or Spanish descendants. This definition, taken from UNESCO, avoided the allusion to race, a term that became taboo since Nazism; it was determined that Colombia, as the rest of the world, was multiethnic and multicultural. This definition was supported by writers of the Constitution, stating that in Colombia black minorities exist, and with this statement they ignore the Africanness of the black Colombian. [It would have been correct to refer] to Amerindian-Colombians, to indigenous, to Afro-Colombians, and finally to Hispanic-Colombians. I was the first to talk about Colombian tri-ethnicity. [The Constitution] is thus deficient and creates a racist stigma.

## Historical Estimates of the Black and Indigenous Populations in Colombia

The population censuses of Colombia in 1912 and 1918, the first censuses since the eighteenth century to recognize ethnoracial differences, reported that the black population totaled 6.4 percent and 6.0 percent of the total population respectively and the indigenous population amounted to 6.8 percent and 2.7 percent (see Figure 3.1).[22] In both censuses, census takers established the ethnoracial membership of the respondents on the basis of their appearance. However, by the subsequent census in 1938, the census had stopped collecting information on black Colombians and did not resume the practice until the 1993 census (see Figure 3.1).

At only 1.15 percent of the national population, the 1938 census showed a decline in the indigenous population compared to twenty years earlier. Indig-

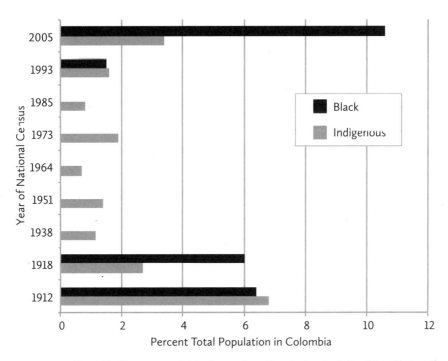

FIGURE 3.1 Size of Indigenous and Afrodescendant Population in Colombian National Censuses

enous status was then established on the basis of language and residency (e.g., living in distant and isolated rural areas). The next two censuses, conducted in 1951 and 1964, reported that the indigenous population was 1.4 percent and 0.7 percent of the total population, using the same criteria. As in the 1910s, these sudden changes in the size of the indigenous population probably reflected the low priority given in counting persons in indigenous communities. By 1973, when efforts were first taken to count indigenous peoples without the earlier indigenous stereotypes, the census reported that the indigenous population had increased to 1.9 percent. However, that year the Colombian census again changed the indigenous criteria to include those who belonged to a "pre-Hispanic" ethnic group within a territory defined by government authorities and where there was a subsistence peasant economy.

Table 3.1 shows estimates of the ethnoracial composition in 1970 by Colombia's most important public geographic institute, the Instituto Geográfico Agustín Codazzi de Colombia (IGAC), which were used by Zapata Olivella (1978).[23] These estimates, which are not well supported statistically, claim that the black population (pure blacks and mulattos) was around 30.0 percent of the national population and the indigenous was 2.5 percent in 1970. In 1985,

TABLE 3.1 Ethnoracial Composition of the Colombian Population in 1970 (%)

| | |
|---|---|
| Pure Blacks | 6.0 |
| Mulattos | 24.0 |
| Mestizos | 47.5 |
| Whites | 20.0 |
| Indigenous | 2.5 |
| Total | 100.0 |

Source: IGAC 1978, quoted by Zapata Olivella 1978

when the census began using ethnic self-identification to count indigenous people, the indigenous population again fell to 0.8 percent of the Colombian population, probably reflecting technical problems in data collection (Urrea Giraldo 2010).

Self-identification criteria were adopted in 1993 to enumerate Afrodescendants, who had not been officially enumerated since 1918. The 1993 census found that 1.6 percent of Colombians identified as indigenous and 1.5 percent as Afrodescendant. The 1993 criteria for Afrodescendant, however, was based on whether respondents identified as belonging to a black community such as the Raizales of San Andres or Palenque of San Basilio, effectively ignoring the majority of urban and rural blacks. In the 1993 census the indigenous and black populations were at 1.6 percent and 1.5 percent respectively (see Figure 3.1). Like the indigenous, black people were counted only on the basis of "cultural" self-identity, while excluding references to racial or phenotypic characteristics, which had the effect of making a great part of the urban and rural black population in Colombia invisible. However, by the 2005 census, the question on blacks combined culture and phenotype into the self-identity question,[24] although it did not distinguish between blacks and mulattos. In this census, 3.4 percent of the population was indigenous and 10.6 percent of the population was considered Afrodescendant, i.e., black, mulatto, Afro-Colombian, Raizal from San Andrés, or Palenquero. (see Figure 3.1).

In 1995 a survey of unknown methodology undertaken by black movement organizations estimated that 26.0 percent of the population was black or mulatto. Interestingly, this number became widely accepted by the Colombian government, the United Nations, and various multilateral organizations (Urrea Giraldo 2011). Meanwhile, the research program Centro de Investigaciones Socioeconomicas de la Universidade del Valle (CIDSE) and Institut de Research pour le Développement (IRD)[25] estimated that 20–22 percent of the national

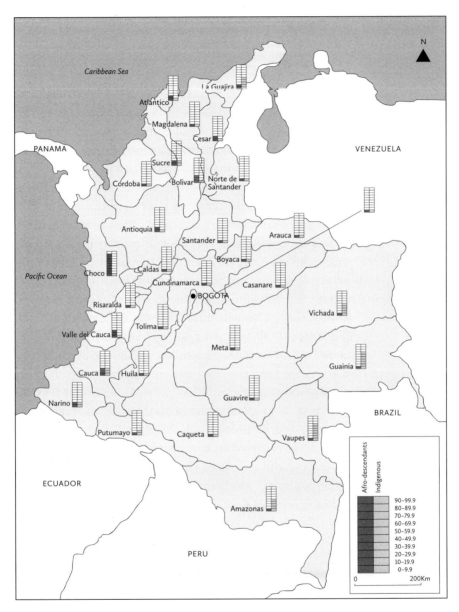

MAP 3.1 Percent Afrodescendant and Indigenous in Colombia, by Department.
Source: Census of Colombia, 2005

population in 2001 was composed of blacks and mulattos on the basis of surveys of thirteen metropolitan areas using self-recognition with photographs of others (Barbary and Urrea Giraldo 2004). The 2010 AmericasBarometer of the Latin American Public Opinion Project (LAPOP) finds blacks and mulattos totaling 12.3 percent of the national total population, and the 2010 Project on Ethnicity and Race in Latin America (PERLA) reports 19.4 percent. Both the LAPOP and PERLA surveys use self-identification. The different estimations of Afrodescendant and indigenous people are a result of the various measures of the demographic weight of ethnic and racial groups, which use different methods of classifying blacks and mulattos, including self-identification and categorization of others and various sampling methodologies.

As Map 3.1 shows, the departments with the largest share of Afrodescendant populations are concentrated on the Pacific Coast (four of the five largest), followed by those on the Caribbean Coast. By percentage, the largest are Chocó (82.1 percent), Bolívar (27.6 percent), Valle del Cauca (27.2 percent), Cauca (22.2 percent), Nariño (18.8 percent), Sucre (16.1 percent), La Guajira (14.8 percent), Córdoba (13.2 percent), Antioquia (11.0 percent), Atlántico (10.8 percent) and Magdalena (9.8 percent). The remaining departments are less than 6.0 percent. However, in absolute terms (not shown on the map), the department of Valle del Cauca with Cali as its capital, has the largest Afrodescendant population with a quarter (25.6 percent) of the national population, followed by Antioquia (13.9 percent), and Bolívar (11.7 percent), with Cartagena as its capital.

Regarding the indigenous population, Map 3.1 shows a distinct territorial distribution from that of Afrodescendants, with the major concentration being in the Southeast. The departments with the highest percent of indigenous population are in the regions of Amazonia and Orinoquia: Vaupés (66.6 percent), Guainía (64.9 percent), Vichada (44.4 percent), and Amazonas (43.0 percent). An exception in terms of location is the departamento of La Guajira on the Caribbean coast which is 45.0 percent indigenous (DANE 2007).

## The PERLA Survey

We present select findings based on the PERLA survey in Colombia in four realms: the dynamics of racial identities, especially regarding the Afrodescendant population; ethnoracial and social class inequalities in the attainment of socioeconomic status; the perception of racial and economic discrimination according to self-identity and skin color; and attitudes toward multicultural policies that benefit the black and indigenous populations in Colombia as well as the participation of black people in problem solving at the community level.

## Identity Dynamics of Afrodescendants

The PERLA survey contains multiple items that assess the ethnoracial membership of contemporary Colombians: a self-identification question similar to the one used by the LAPOP survey in Colombia ("Do you consider yourself indigenous, black, mulatto, white, mestizo, or other?"); the 2005 census question (see note 24); and an open-ended question on racial identity (without providing categories to respondents), origin of ancestors (European, indigenous, African or black, and Asian/Chinese/Japanese), and the ethnoracial identity of parents and romantic partners. As mentioned in the other chapters, the survey also contains several items based on external classifications, as perceived by the survey respondent, including skin color, hair texture, and ethnoracial status (using the same categories of the self-identification question).

Figure 3.2 shows that the estimates of the Afrodescendant population in Colombia vary considerably, depending on the criteria used for counting. Estimates based on PERLA data varied from 19.4 percent obtained by asking the 2005 census question on self-identification, 18.6 percent using the open-ended question on racial identity, and 15.1 percent based on the number of respondents who claimed to have black or African ancestors.[26] Given the size of the data set, there is about a 3 percent range of error, but the relative sizes using these three criteria remain. The percentages obtained using the classification of respondents' hair as kinky and by the external classification of respondents as black or mulatto by the PERLA survey takers and of respondents who claimed at least one black or mulatto father vary for all responders and for both sexes (between 12.2 and 12.4 percent).

Also, only 8.9 percent considered themselves black (*negro*) with another 3.4 percent considering themselves mulatto; 7.6 percent said their parents were both considered black or mulatto. The percentage of people with dark skin (categories 6 to 11) was 9.2 percent, while the percentage of those with dark skin and kinky hair was only 3.4 percent. Figure 3.2 also shows that 15.1 percent of Colombians claim African or black ancestors, but at the same time fewer claim a black/mulatto father (12.3 percent), and also fewer identify as either black (8.9 percent) or mulatto (3.4 percent). The 1991 multicultural constitution allowed people to recognize and express their black and African cultural heritage as more than elements of folklore. The political promotion of these two categories as expressions of ethnic self-identity could explain the stronger tendency for respondents to identify with these categories (between 12.3 and 19.4 percent for both sexes from the PERLA Colombian national sample) and their lower rate of identification with the term mulatto (only 3.4 percent).

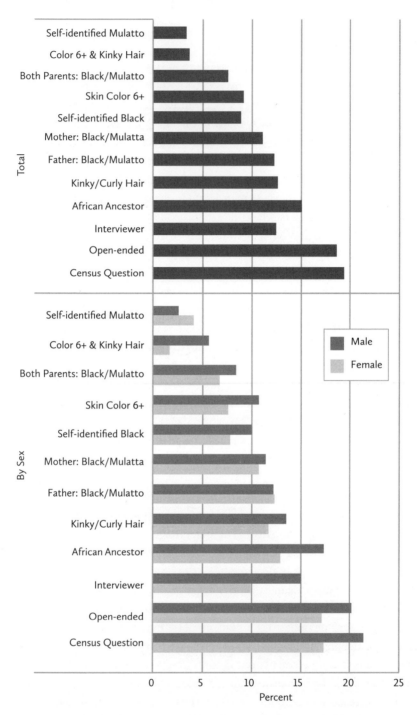

FIGURE 3.2 Percent Afrodescendant according to Various Criteria, Total and by Gender, Colombia

Black feminists such as Angela Davis, Patricia Hill Collins, and bell hooks have underlined the ways in which the category "woman" and norms of femininity, have been constructed based on the experience of white middle-class women and in a white racial imaginary. For this reason, hegemonic norms of femininity can have a whitening effect on black women (Viveros 2012). This effect has been observed in the experience of Indian American women, relating it to colonial history and Western beauty models (Malik 2007). A probable explanation is based on the sexual division of domestic and extradomestic work where feminine attributes tend to be associated with "indoor" occupations and masculine attributes with "outdoor" occupations (most frequently in "open" spaces). Indoor occupations socially require a finer personal presentation, in bodily terms, clothing, and behavior, which is closely linked to whiteness. For characteristics attributed to masculinity, imaginaries of virility and strength come into play, with stronger links associated with darker skin color. Why is this social phenomenon more visible in the Colombian case, compared to other Latin-American societies? In her study on "whitening the region," Applebaum (1999) takes Antioquia and similar regions of the country as a model, pointing to the strong white imaginary (fair skin) in the construction of the nation, which is an idealization of bodies and forms of self-presentation and which clearly differentiates women in Colombia.

The bottom of Figure 3.2 shows that men are more likely to identify themselves as black by parentage or by ancestry, whether they self-identified or were classified by an interviewer. Only one of the twelve bars is larger for women, indicating that women are more likely to self-identify as mulatto (4.1 percent versus 2.7 percent), and for father black/mulatto, the percentages are similar. Interestingly, even when people were classified by others, women were placed in lighter categories than men were. Fewer women were classified in the darkest tones of the color palette (colors 6 to 11) or as black by interviewers, compared to their male counterparts. This gender effect could be related to a social image that associates femininity more strongly with whiteness and masculinity with blackness (Viveros 2002). This phenomenon may also help explain why slightly more respondents (both sexes) identified their fathers as either black or mulatto, compared to their mothers, but also why women have lower percentage of both parents "black or mulatto" than men do (6.8 percent versus 8.4 percent).

Although Figure 3.2 is not broken down by class, the trend in regard to how women perceive themselves and are more likely to be perceived by others, as lighter relative to men, which has been found in other contexts, could suggest that gender and race interact with class. Perhaps whiteness is associated with a femininity of higher social status and blackness and the categories most related to it are associated with a type of femininity that is of lower status. This interaction among gender, skin color, and class is similar to what Bourdieu (1991, 220) describes when discussing the relationship between female or male sexual properties and certain strategies for socioeconomic mobility (as a *reclassement* project), and which operates as if it were a "natural" phenomenon.[27] In order for this effect to function as a necessary condition, there must be correspondence between self-perception and external perception of the other.[28]

Taussig (2009, 40), in his study about the color of the sacred, invites us to think of color as a *medium* and a "polymorph magical substance" which transmits a sense or meaning in the form of sensations, for instance, the repulsion or "chromophobia" that people of refinement have toward bright and savage colors. Taussig indicates that, beginning with the colonial experience and enterprise (245), the Western world imposed the perception that lighter (whiter) colors are associated with a more civilized society (Northern Europe), personifying a prototype for feminine beauty, while darker or "lively" colors are associated with exoticism, a "savage" society (the south), and "rude" individuals ("men in their natural condition").[29] We could then interpret in our results the fact that black women or mulatto women present themselves and are perceived as lighter than black men or mulatto men, as an unconscious mechanism to avoid the stigma of dark skin color. However, in the analysis herein proposed, considering the repulsion felt by the people of refinement towards "vivid" color, it is also possible to consider the racial component as strictly interacting with social class, as a hypothesis for future empirical research.

Next we explore the relationship between skin color and identity. Figure 3.3 shows the average skin color of respondents, categorized by ethnoracial identity.[30] Overall, the data fall into the expected patterns. Those who self-identify as black are darker on average, with a skin color of 7.5 out of 11, compared to those who self-identify as white, with a skin color of about 3. The other categories lie in the middle of the color distribution, with mulattos being the darkest of the intermediate categories at 5. On the other hand, respondents who chose the indigenous and mestizo labels are very similar in skin color, both averaging just above color 4 on the palette. In summary, our findings show a close relationship between ethnoracial self-identification and skin color for blacks and whites in Colombia. For the mestizo and indigenous, the differences in skin color are not significant and the skin color of self-identified mulattos is closer to that of indigenous and mestizo people than to blacks in the PERLA national sample.

This black-mulatto difference would indicate that racial heterogeneity is

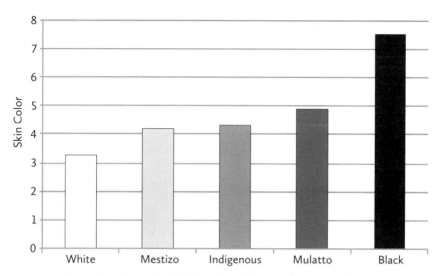

FIGURE 3.3 Mean Skin Color for Self-Identified Ethnoracial Groups, Colombia

important for Afro-Colombians, apparently leading to greater social mobility for mulattos. This phenomenon can be observed best if instead of taking the mean of skin color for each racial category we observe its percentage distribution between the three groups of color as we can see in Figure 3.4.

However, even though the means for skin color are the expected (Figure 3.3), the distributions that are observed in the Figure 3.4 show important variations for the five categories. First, for the entire national sample (1,050 cases), 35.1 percent classified in light colors, 41.0 percent in medium colors, and 23.8 percent in dark colors. Statistically, the variations for the different categories are considerable.

Among those that self-classified as mulatto, 16.3 percent were classified by the interviewer in light colors, 51.2 percent in intermediate colors, and 32.6 percent in dark colors. For those who self-recognized as blacks, 89.3 percent were in dark colors and 10.6 percent in intermediate colors. For those who self-recognized as mestizo, 13.7 percent were classified in dark colors, 31.0 percent in light colors, and 55.4 percent in intermediate colors. Among those that self-identified as white, 4.1 percent were classified in dark colors, 27.8 percent in intermediate colors, and 68.0 percent in light. For the indigenous, 22.2 percent were dark, 46.3 percent were intermediate, and 31.5 percent light.

Thus, there is an important percentage of self-identified mulattos whose skin color is rated light, and at the same time there is a small percentage of self-identified whites with dark skin and a substantial percentage in interme-

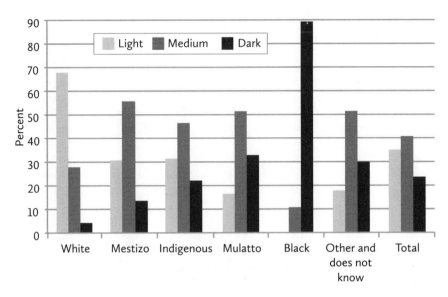

FIGURE 3.4 Ethnoracial Self-Identification by Skin Color Categories, Colombia

diate colors. Among mestizos and indigenous, there are substantial numbers classified in dark colors. This considerable variation between self-recognition and external classification by skin color, especially in the mulatto, mestizo, and indigenous categories (even though in terms of the mean there is a strong correspondence), shows that the pattern of social inequalities is not the same for ethnoracial self-identification as it is for skin color. Thus, as we discuss further on, those who self-identify as mulatto present better indicators in education, occupation, and income than those who self-identify as white and mestizo; but when controlled by skin color, this effect disappears, and the differences in skin color best explain inequalities.

Table 3.2 shows the relationship between the interviewer's external classification and the respondents' own identification, using the same categories. There is greater consistency between self-identification and classification by interviewers in black, mestizo, and white categories than for indigenous and mulatto categories.

The greatest consistency is observed for black at 81.1 percent. Only 44.6 percent of self-identified mulatto and 37.5 percent of self-identified indigenous respondents were classified in these same categories by PERLA survey takers. Indeed, most self-identified indigenous respondents were categorized as mestizo by survey takers (44.6 percent). The findings in Table 3.2 are consistent with the results in Figure 3.3. Nevertheless we could say that, per Table 3.2, indigenous and mulatto categories are more ambiguous when we contrast self-

TABLE 3.2 Consistency in Racial Classification, by Interviewer and
Self-identification (%)

| | White | Mestizo | Indigenous | Black | Mulatto | Total |
|---|---|---|---|---|---|---|
| | | | Interviewer Classification | | | |
| Self-Identification | | | | | | |
| White | 63.0 | 34.1 | 1.5 | 0.4 | 1.1 | 100.0 |
| Mestizo | 21.7 | 66.8 | 1.7 | 4.0 | 5.9 | 100.0 |
| Indigenous | 10.7 | 44.6 | 37.5 | 0.0 | 7.1 | 100.0 |
| Black | 0.0 | 4.9 | 0.4 | 81.1 | 13.7 | 100.0 |
| Mulatto | 19.6 | 23.2 | 1.8 | 10.7 | 44.6 | 100.0 |

Source: PERLA 2010

TABLE 3.3 Origin of Ancestors by Self-Identity (%)

| | European | Indigenous | African/Black | Asian |
|---|---|---|---|---|
| | | Origin of Ancestors | | |
| Self-Identification | | | | |
| Indigenous | 20.6 | 82.9 | 5.7 | 0.0 |
| Black | 7.9 | 19.7 | 80.8 | 1.6 |
| Mulatto | 19.5 | 28.0 | 50.0 | 2.6 |
| White | 21.2 | 19.6 | 7.2 | 0.7 |
| Mestizo | 16.5 | 30.8 | 7.9 | 2.2 |
| Total | 16.5 | 27.8 | 20.0 | 1.7 |

Source: PERLA 2010

identity and interviewer identity, because of the way in which these groups
perceive themselves and are perceived in Colombian society.

If we analyze the origin of family ancestors by self-identity (Table 3.3), it
is interesting to note for the total population of the PERLA national sample
that the most frequent categorization of the origins of family ancestors is indigenous (27.8 percent), followed by the African/black (20.0 percent) and European (16.5 percent). This response pattern reflects the symbolic weight of
the indigenous in the collective memory of the Colombian population and the
acknowledgment of African/black ancestry, with curiously lower recognition
of ancestors of European origins.

Table 3.3 reveals a strong correspondence between self-reported ancestry and ethnoracial self-identity for indigenous (82.9 percent) and black (80.8 percent) persons. Only half (50.0 percent) of self-identified mulattos in the sample recognize African/black ancestry. This is consistent with findings for skin color, where mulattos tend to be more similar in skin color than mestizos and indigenous persons than blacks (see Figure 3.4). Interestingly, a considerable number of whites and mestizos acknowledge African/black ancestry (7.2 and 7.9 percent), although they more often report European and indigenous ancestry, as might be expected. Also, fully a fifth (19.6 percent) of self-identified whites report indigenous ancestry and, surprisingly, a little more than that amount report European ancestry (21.2 percent).

It is striking that 30.8 percent of self-identified mestizos acknowledge indigenous ancestry, while only 16.5 percent recognize European forefathers and just 7.9 percent recognize African/black ancestry. This is consistent with similar skin color averages between mestizos and indigenous persons observed in Figure 3.3, revealing fluidity, in terms of skin color as in origins, between mestizos and the indigenous.

Finally, in the case of self-identified whites, similar proportions as the indigenous claim European ancestry (21.2 percent and 20.6 percent, respectively). Almost 20 percent (19.6) of self-identified whites recognize indigenous ancestors. Thus, self-identified mestizos, whites, and indigenous persons claim a similar Colombian collective imaginary that mixes Spanish and Amerindian origins.

The PERLA survey also contains information on the ethnicity of romantic partners or spouses.[31] Table 3.4 explores the relationship between the respondents' identity and that of their spouse. We find that white and mestizo respondents have the highest degrees of homogamy (61.7 percent and 60.4 percent, respectively), followed by self-identified blacks (57.9 percent). Self-identified mulattos show the highest percentage of homogeneous behavior: 55.6 percent marry "white" partners. It is important to note that these homogamy percentages for white, mestizo, and black people and the higher hypergamy percentage for mulattos must be seen within a Colombian social context of miscegenation, as we discuss in the historical analysis. Self-identified indigenous in the PERLA national sample also shows a high level of hypergamy behavior, because only 22.2 percent marry indigenous partners (Table 3.4); but it is difficult to generalize this finding to all Colombian indigenous people.[32]

Figure 3.4 reveals a relation between ethnoracial identity and color in such a way that self-identified blacks have the darkest color, while whites have the lightest. However, there is much fluidity in skin color for mestizo, mulatto and indigenous respondents, which implies that in everyday life they might be vir-

TABLE 3.4 Race or Ethnicity of Spouse, according to Respondent Self-Identity (%)

| | Racial Identity Assigned to Couple by Interviewee | | | | |
|---|---|---|---|---|---|
| | Indigenous | Black | Mulatto | White | Mestizo |
| Self-Identification | | | | | |
| Indigenous | 22.2 | 8.9 | 4.4 | 35.6 | 28.9 |
| Black | 0.9 | 57.9 | 10.5 | 16.7 | 14.0 |
| Mulatto | 0.0 | 11.1 | 22.2 | 55.6 | 11.1 |
| White | 2.2 | 3.3 | 7.2 | 61.7 | 25.6 |
| Mestizo | 1.1 | 3.7 | 6.0 | 28.8 | 60.4 |

Source: PERLA 2010

tually indistinguishable from each other, particularly in the case of the urban indigenous. In the Latin American context, Colombian society presents a major consistency between classification by others and the self-identity of blacks, while the greatest ambiguity is found between mestizo and indigenous identities. In contrast, for all self-identified groups of the PERLA national sample, including white, we find a lower degree of recognition of European ancestors, compared with a higher recognition of Amerindian or indigenous and African-black ancestors. As a hypothesis, this has to do with the symbolic effects of the new multicultural constitution, where black and indigenous people are increasingly valued.

## Ethnoracial and Social Class Inequalities in the Attainment of Socioeconomic Status

The existence of socioeconomic inequality is widely known in Colombian society. According to DANE, based on data from the 2005 census, and updated through June 2011, 27.8 percent of the Colombian population had at least one unsatisfied basic need (UBN). But for the Colombian black and indigenous populations this reached more than 40 percent and 60 percent, respectively (Urrea Giraldo 2010). On the other hand, according to estimations from the Misión para el Empalme de las Series de Empleo, Pobreza y Desigualdad (MESEP, Mission for the Assembly of the Statistics Series of Employment, Poverty and Inequality),[33] 34.1 percent of the Colombian population was living below the poverty line (PL),[34] with 12.6 percent in extreme poverty. For the black population, more than 55 percent reported living below the poverty line, as did more than 70 percent of indigenous respondents to the census. In the case of extreme poverty, the data show more than 25 percent of black Colombians and more than 40 percent of the indigenous population living in extreme poverty.[35] The Gini indicator of inequality indicates levels of between 0.548 and 0.569 in 2011, depending on the methodology, which makes it among the highest in Latin America (MESEP 2012).

These context data reveal that many sectors of the Colombian population, particularly the black and indigenous populations, do not have the capacity to reach a minimum standard of living to achieve full citizenship, and the data also reveal a great concentration of wealth in Colombia.

## RESPONDENTS' FAMILY BACKGROUND
## BY EDUCATION AND OCCUPATION

In Latin America, economic and sociological studies of social mobility have analyzed changes in educational attainment and the occupational status of children compared to their parents (see, e.g., Filgueira 2001, Filgueira and Peri 2004, Torche and Wormald 2004, Carrasco 2008; and on Colombia, studies by Gaviria 2002, Vivas 2007 and Vivas Pacheco et al. 2012, and Viáfara, Estacio and González 2010, the latter in relation to the racial effect on social mobility in Cali and Bogotá). The focus of these studies is the extent to which processes of upward social mobility, observed through education and occupational status, are reproduced by intergenerational transmission within the family. This perspective has classical precedents in sociology (e.g., Erikson and Goldthorpe 2002 and Bourdieu 1977, 1986 on cultural and educational capital and social reproduction; and Bourdieu and Passeron 1979 on education). In this section we seek to analyze changes in educational attainment and occupational status from parents to children in the PERLA national sample, controlling for the self-identity and skin color of respondents.

Figure 3.5 shows the relationship between parents' education and the identity and skin color of respondents.[36] The results show that the parents of self-identified mulattos have the highest rates of educational attainment (about 8.5 years of formal schooling), followed by the parents of mestizos and whites (about 6 years for each). At the bottom of the scale, we find the parents of black and indigenous respondents (between 4 and 5 years of education for each). However, when we analyze the data by skin color, we see a staircase pattern: the parents of light-skinned respondents, those with the three lightest skin tones, have the highest levels of education (almost seven years on average), followed by the parents of medium- and dark-skinned respondents in descending order.[37]

While the results for parental educational attainment for both mulattos and

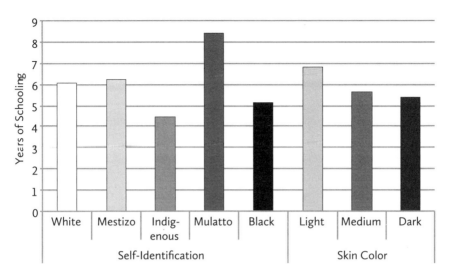

FIGURE 3.5 Mean Years of Parent's Schooling, by Ethnoracial Self-Identification and Skin Color, Colombia

mestizos are unexpected (especially since they are higher than whites), when we examine the data by skin color, we are better able to observe the effect of parent's educational and social inequality according to racial hierarchies: the lighter the respondent, the greater the educational attainment of their parents.

Do these differences in parental educational attainment, according to identity and color, also hold when examining occupational status? Figure 3.6 shows the occupational status of the head of household when the respondent was fourteen years old, categorized by self-identity and skin color.[38] As with education, self-identified mulattos grew up in homes with parents employed in higher-status occupations than other identity groups (21.4 percent). Similarly, the parents of mestizos and whites occupy an intermediate position in terms of occupational prestige (9.5 percent and 7.1 percent, respectively), and black and indigenous respondents occupy the bottom category (4.2 percent and 1.9 percent, respectively), with their parents mostly employed in low-skilled manual occupations such as domestic servitude or construction (Figure 3.6).

Nevertheless, in the case of parental occupation, if we control by skin color there is not a staircase effect because, for darker- and medium-range colors, the percentages are similar or very close and without significant statistical differences in the last two ranges. This means that for skin color the main differences in parental occupation are observed between the light ranges and the medium and dark ranges, because many medium-skinned respondents had parents em-

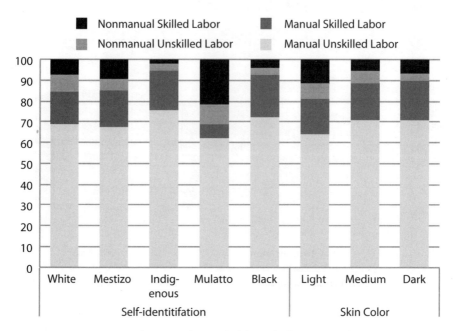

**Legend:** ■ Nonmanual Skilled Labor ■ Manual Skilled Labor ■ Nonmanual Unskilled Labor ▨ Manual Unskilled Labor

FIGURE 3.6 Occupational Group of Household Head when Respondent was 14, by Ethnoracial Self-identification and Skin Color, Colombia

ployed in similar lower-prestige occupations as did dark-skinned respondents. For example, many parents of indigenous respondents whose skin tone is usually classified as medium are employed in manual unskilled occupations.

### DIFFERENCES IN EDUCATION AND OCCUPATIONAL STATUS OF RESPONDENTS BY IDENTITY AND SKIN COLOR

Perhaps the most conclusive evidence of ethnoracial inequality comes from examining the socioeconomic status of respondents themselves. When we analyze the educational attainment of respondents by identity and skin color (Figure 3.7), the mulatto group from the national sample has the highest average (almost twelve years), followed by mestizo and white (both above ten years). Self-identified indigenous and black respondents had the lowest levels of educational attainment (less than ten years). Thus, respondents in the Colombian PERLA national sample who self-identify as mulatto are more educated than those who self-identify with other categories. Nevertheless, analyzing education by skin color reveals a new pattern: light-skinned respondents have the highest level of formal education (almost twelve years), followed by medium-skinned respondents and, lastly, dark-skinned respondents. So, educational

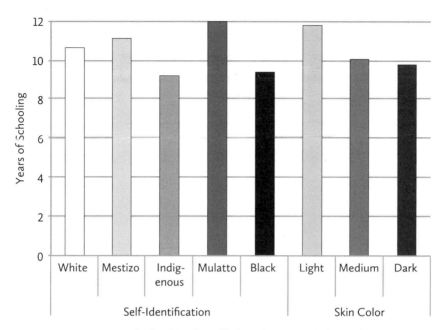

FIGURE 3.7 Mean Years of Schooling, by Self-Identification and Skin Color

inequality corresponds with skin color more than self-identity, in terms of the expected pigmentocracy hypothesis.

When we analyze the other key inequality variable—occupational status— we find that those who self-identify as mestizo or mulatto in the national sample have the highest percentages of participation in nonmanual skilled jobs (Figure 3.8). Similarly, the mulatto group has the highest percentage of nonmanual unskilled labor. On the opposite side, the black group has the highest percentage of manual unskilled labor, but curiously in this case the indigenous group has the lowest percentage of manual unskilled labor. This last group concentrates in manual skilled labor (Figure 3.9), mainly as low-status urban artisans. It is noteworthy that self-identified whites have the lowest probability of being employed in nonmanual skilled labor. Nevertheless, occupational status again shows a staircase pattern, as was the case with education (see Figure 3.7): Light-skinned respondents are more likely to be employed in nonmanual skilled and unskilled labor, and they constitute the lowest percentage of manual unskilled labor: 15.0 percent of those with light skin have nonmanual skilled jobs and 27.7 percent hold nonmanual unskilled occupations versus those of medium color with 10.8 percent in nonmanual skilled and 21.1 percent in nonmanual

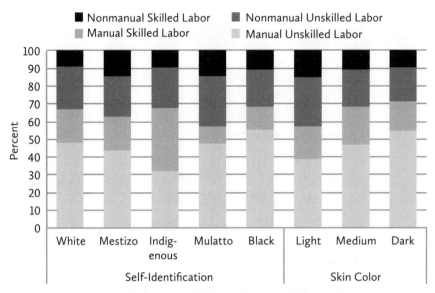

FIGURE 3.8 Occupational Group by Self-Identification and Skin Color

unskilled and those of dark color with 9.8 percent in nonmanual skilled and 19.1 percent in nonmanual unskilled occupations. The "dark" group has the highest percentage of manual unskilled jobs (54.9 percent), and the medium group has an intermediate percentage in this same occupational status (47.0 percent). However, there are differences between medium and dark groups in terms of nonmanual occupations (skilled and unskilled), most clearly observed in the response rates for manual skilled and unskilled occupations: 47.1 percent skilled and 21.1 percent unskilled for medium skin and 54.9 percent and 16.2 percent for dark skin.

If we take only high-status nonmanual occupations[39] of respondents by self-identification and skin color (Figure 3.9), self-identified mulattos are more likely to be employed in high-prestige occupations, followed by mestizo, black, white, and indigenous respondents. As we showed in Figure 3.8, self-identified whites also have a low probability of holding a high-status positions. Skin color shows the expected linear relationship: as skin tone darkens, respondents are less likely to hold high-status nonmanual occupations. If anything, such an association is strongest when analyzing only the top echelon of the occupational structure.

The average monthly income by self-identity and skin color (Figure 3.10), for the Colombian PERLA national sample, shows a trend that follows only one of the previous outcomes: the mulatto group has a higher average income

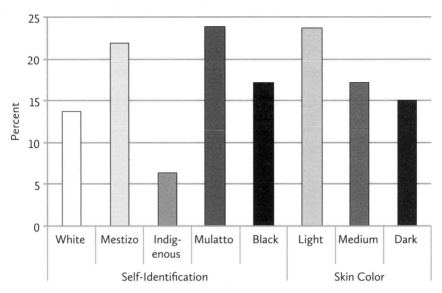

FIGURE 3.9 Percent in High Status Non-manual Occupations, by Ethnoracial Self-Identification and Skin Color, Colombia

(aligning with higher educational attainment and occupational status, as the previous figures show).[40] However, with the other groups the trend is very different: there is little difference in average income among mestizos, indigenous, and whites, all of whose incomes are well below mulattos. The lowest average monthly income is for blacks (553 Colombian pesos). For skin color, Figure 3.10 does not show a clear trend: light and dark persons have the same income average, while the medium group has the lowest, probably because of a lower monthly income for the indigenous, whose skin color is in the medium category. When we examine the data without including indigenous, the skin color trend changes in the expected direction: a descending staircase, with significant differences between light and medium ($1,023,473 versus $648,318 Colombian pesos [2010]), with smaller differences between medium and dark (see Figure 3.11).

Figures 3.4–3.10 explored race-based socioeconomic inequalities in Colombia using both self-identification and skin color. When analyzing the educational attainment and occupational status of our respondents and their parents, the same pattern emerges: race-based inequalities are significantly larger when using skin color than when we use self-identification data. As we showed in this section, we found a staircase pattern where light-skinned Colombians have higher levels of educational attainment and higher occupational status followed by medium-skinned respondents in intermediate positions, and at

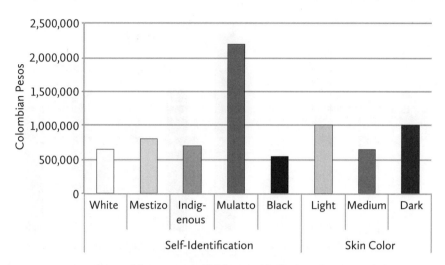

FIGURE 3.10 Mean Monthly Income, by Ethnoracial Self-Identification and Skin Color, in 2010 Colombian Pesos, Colombia

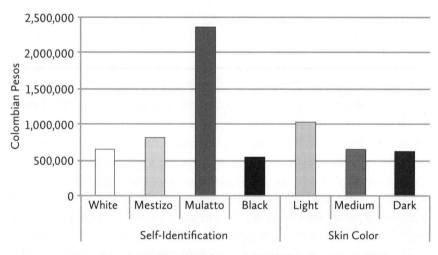

FIGURE 3.11 Mean Monthly Income by Ethnoracial Self-Identification and Skin Color, in 2010 Colombian Pesos, without Self-Identified Indigenous Group, Colombia

the very bottom, those with dark skin tones. In this way we can say there is a pigmentocratic inequality effect in Colombian society.

Despite the main pigmentocratic effect by skin color, respondents who self-identify as mulatto enjoy relatively better conditions for educational attainment and occupational and income opportunity, compared with white and mestizo groups and, of course, compared with black and indigenous groups,

either as households or as individuals. It is necessary to note that this finding reveals a social differentiation process among Afro-Colombians, supported
since the second half of the nineteenth century by the gradual mobility of mulatto elites (Viveros and Gil Hernandez 2010).

## Perceptions of Racial and Economic Discrimination

One of the PERLA survey's greatest contributions is the questionnaire modules
that capture different forms of racial and economic discrimination, but also
others (by sex/gender and sexual orientation, which would be a subsequent
subject in other studies). First, we focus on perception of the interviewed on
events of economic discrimination and skin color that respondents witnessed
versus the discriminatory events that he or she experienced. We then examine
if in the past five years the respondent has ever felt discriminated or treated unfairly because of his or her skin color or by economic status. Then, we investigate the question related to the relative treatment experienced by black people
compared to that experienced by white people. Last, we analyze whether the
idea of "improving the race" is understood by respondents. For this, we control
the perception of discrimination by racial self-identity and by skin color, with
the exception of discriminatory events witnessed versus the ones lived or experienced, which is analyzed only by skin color.

Table 3.5 shows that witnessing versus experiencing discrimination by skin
color[41] is greater for dark respondents on the basis of both economic situation
and skin color. There is a slight decrease in the percentages when comparing
light to medium, and then a great increase from medium to dark. On the other
hand, light and medium groups were less likely to report witnessing skin color
discrimination by economic situation. However, levels are similar for the darkest group.

Also, the reporting of discrimination experiences follows the same trend as
the witnessing of discrimination, with the highest percentage for dark-skinned
respondents but in markedly lower percentages compared to the witnessing
of discrimination. Here, self-reported skin color discrimination for light- and
medium-colored persons is six times and three times as low as self-reported
economic discrimination, but for the darkest group, it is the same and three
times lower. This implies that the skin color and economic discrimination
for the dark group go together, in terms of either witnessed or experienced
discrimination.

Figure 3.12 uses the national and Afrodescendant samples (fifteen hundred
cases total) to answer the question: In the past five years, have you ever felt

TABLE 3.5 Respondents Who Witnessed and Experienced Discrimination, by Economic Level and Skin Color (%)

|  | Economic Situation | Skin Color |
| --- | --- | --- |
| Witnessed |  |  |
| Light | 64.0 | 59.4 |
| Medium | 62.2 | 56.2 |
| Dark | 72.8 | 71.5 |
| Experienced |  |  |
| Light | 26.0 | 4.3 |
| Medium | 29.0 | 9.3 |
| Dark | 31.2 | 23.6 |

Source: PERLA 2010

discriminated or treated unfairly because of your skin color? In Figure 3.12, we show the results by self-identification and skin color. Self-identified blacks clearly stand out as the group that recognized the most color-based discrimination (35 percent), followed by indigenous people (20 percent). In contrast, fewer mulattos, mestizos, and whites claim to have been discriminated against because of their skin color. It is quite interesting that mulattos claim less color discrimination than indigenous, even if indigenous are on average lighter than mulattos (according to Figure 3.12), a finding consistent with other variables such as higher average educational attainment, an important percentage of nonmanual skilled jobs, and higher monthly income.

The skin color results follow a linear trend: darker-skinned respondents claim more color-based discrimination than their lighter-skinned counterparts.

In Figure 3.13, we analyze episodes of discrimination by economic status. Respondents were asked whether they had felt discriminated against in the past five years because of their economic situation. As expected, more respondents overall claimed to have experienced maltreatment because of social class. While the most discriminated groups by class are again blacks, indigenous people, and dark-skinned respondents, many other groups also claim class-based discrimination, including mulattos and mestizos, and even whites and light-skinned respondents.

We now approach the question of external perception of how respondents perceive the relative treatment experienced by black people versus that expe-

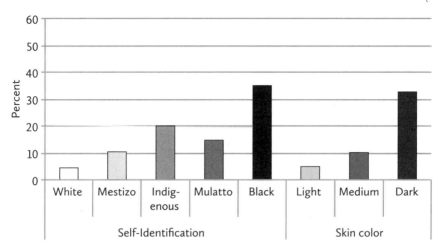

FIGURE 3.12 Self-Reported Skin Color Discrimination by Ethnoracial Self-Identification and Skin Color, Colombia

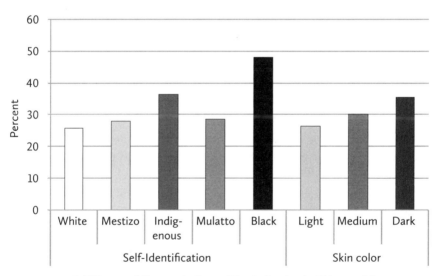

FIGURE 3.13 Self-Reported Economic Status Discrimination by Ethnoracial Self-Identification and Skin Color, Colombia

rienced by white people, rated as better, same, or worse. This question allows us to confront the different perceptions of the subjects, by contrasting two extremes of self-identity: black and white. This question can be seen to constitute an indicator of interracial relations in a particular society.

Figure 3.14 shows the relative treatment that respondents perceive of blacks versus whites (better, same, or worse), by self-identity and skin color for both

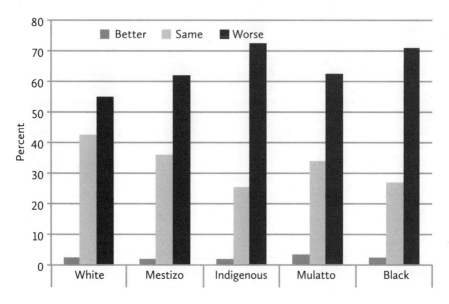

FIGURE 3.14 "Do you think black people are treated better, the same, or worse than white people?" By Ethnoracial Self-Identification and Skin Color, Colombia

samples (fifteen hundred cases). Here we show a systematic staircasing of self-identity and skin color; however, for self-identity, the black and then indigenous groups reveal a greater sensitivity about discrimination against black people. And then, in descending order of sensitivity, we find mulatto, mestizo, and finally white. Examining skin color, the trend follows the same pattern: dark persons perceived worse treatment for blacks (almost 70 percent); meanwhile, light persons reported between 55 and 60 percent. It is interesting to observe that the "better treatment" option has substantially lower percentages across all categories, and fewer responded "same" than "worse."

The endemic expression "improve the race" is a popular saying in various regions of Colombia, not just in areas with a concentrated black or indigenous population but also in other areas and in cities with major interracial miscegenation. In a certain way, this constitutes a legacy of the colonial past that thoroughly expresses an individual whitening strategy in which one of the spouses is of a lighter color than the other. In this way, for the darker spouse, a lighter partner guarantees the "improvement of the race" through their offspring.

Figure 3.15 shows that the responses to whether one has heard that it is important to "improve the race" varies by self-identity and skin color, pointing to a very interesting indirect form of race/skin color discrimination (also with

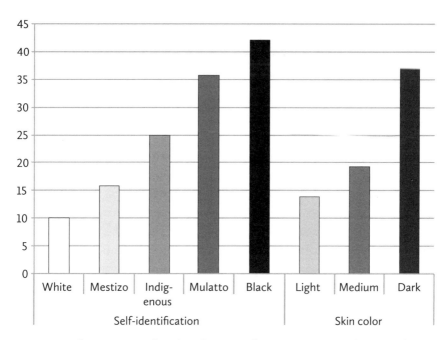

FIGURE 3.15 "Have you ever heard a relative say that it is necessary to 'improve the race'?" Percent Answering Yes by Ethnoracial Self-Identification and Skin Color, Colombia

both samples). The rates of those answering in the affirmative are highest for self-identified blacks (more than 40 percent of agreement), followed by the mulatto group with 35 percent. For the indigenous group, agreement with ever hearing "a relative say that it is necessary to improve the race" is 25 percent; for the mestizo group, the response to this question was 15 percent, and only 10 percent for the white group.

This trend is also strong when analyzing these results by skin color. While more than 35 percent of dark respondents have heard this phrase from a relative, less than 20 percent of medium-skinned respondents, and less than 15 percent of light-skinned Colombians have heard it. It is clear that this indirect form of skin color discrimination is related to racial identification and skin color, which works as a historical strategy for whiteness, as analyzed in the first part of this chapter.

The perception of witnessed or experienced racial and economic discrimination, experiences of these two discriminations during the past five years, the treatment experienced by black versus white, and perceptions of indirect forms of discrimination by skin color, as experienced through the popular phrase "improve the race," which operates alongside a strategy of whiteness (see Table 3.5, Figures 3.12–3.15), give the following outcomes. First, the association between discrimination by skin color and economic situation effects for "dark" respondents tends to be strong, but for "medium" and "light" the skin color effect is weaker than the economic effect. Second, experiences of skin color and economic discrimination during the past five years reveal the same trends, affecting more black and indigenous people and "dark" respondents. Third, self-identified black and indigenous respondents are more likely to perceive worse treatment of black people compared with treatment of white people, followed by treatment of mulattos and mestizos. Fourth, there is a general agreement on having heard from a relative of the necessity to "improve the race," especially among blacks and mulattos and for dark-skinned respondents.

## Attitudes toward Multicultural Policies

Figure 3.16 shows that, in general, Colombians are highly supportive of multicultural policies that benefit both black and indigenous people. More than 90 percent expressed general support for black organizations and for antidiscrimination laws for these ethnic-racial groups. More than 80 percent expressed support for affirmative action, and more than 90 percent of Colombians expressed support for teaching black and indigenous history in schools. Finally, 97.5 percent of Colombians agreed that the government should protect indigenous lands. Although there is support on these issues for both black and indigenous ethnoracial groups, there is a slightly higher support for policies relating to indigenous rights.

The amount of support, with percentages higher than 85 percent regarding all these policies, is striking and paradoxical. What do these high percentages mean? They may be the result of the multiculturalist ideological effect from the 1991 Constitution, through the same public discourse during almost twenty years, at national, regional, and local levels and the creation of ethnic units in all government departments. Nevertheless, ethnoracial minorities have achieved few concrete gains since 1991,[42] especially in the case of blacks but to some extent indigenous people. Consequently, up until now, few whites and mestizos have been negatively affected.[43] A large proportion of the white and mestizo population in Colombia considers the impact of claims made by black and indigenous people as insignificant to private-sector interests or to those of the urban middle-classes (or even of the popular classes). The perceived insig-

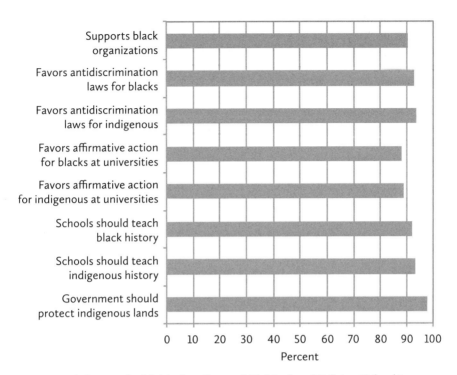

FIGURE 3.16 Support for Multiculturalism and Multicultural Policies, Colombia

nificance of these claims could help explain the broad support that these eight multicultural policies enjoy in Colombia.

In this final section, we turn to the willingness of respondents to participate in local community problem solving. We examine which ethnoracial group is more likely to engage in the resolution of these problems. This topic is important because it provides us with information on levels of solidarity found in local networks (particularly in poor neighborhoods), but it also reveals ways in which differential processes of social mobility work outside local areas for black, indigenous, and white-mestizo populations.

The distribution of percentages in Table 3.6 reveals some interesting results. Self-identified blacks have the highest percentages of collaboration in their communities during the past twelve months as well as outside of this time frame, followed by self-identified indigenous respondents. In contrast, whites, mestizos, and especially mulattos, have lower rates of this form of collaboration.

The data seem to show different strategies of social mobility used by the

TABLE 3.6 "Have you collaborated with a person or group to solve a problem in your community?" By Self-Identification, including Both Samples (%)

| | Collaborated | | | |
| --- | --- | --- | --- | --- |
| | Yes, in past 12 months | Yes, but over a year ago | Never | Total |
| Self-Identification | | | | |
| Black | 27.5 | 24.2 | 48.3 | 100.0 |
| Indigenous | 22.2 | 18.5 | 59.3 | 100.0 |
| White | 21.5 | 14.3 | 64.2 | 100.0 |
| Mestizo | 19.5 | 15.9 | 64.6 | 100.0 |
| Mulatto | 9.3 | 16.3 | 74.4 | 100.0 |

Source: PERLA 2010

respondents' networks, according to socioeconomic living standards. We could say that if self-identified blacks have more cooperation at the community level, this is because of their poor economic situation. In the Colombian situation, this happens in the poorest urban popular neighborhoods, as in the case of the city of Cali, where we also find a white-mestizo population, but it is black people who provide the highest participation through actions that demand state attention at a local level,[44] even though these actions are driven by the fact that they recognize themselves as poor, rather than having a direct ethno-racial connotation. Meanwhile, mulattos experience better living conditions and therefore do not reveal similar patterns of participation at the community level. The mulatto group in both samples, unlike the black self-identity group, favors upward social mobility with little involvement in local community problems.

Findings for black solidarity appearing in Table 3.6 are probably related to blacks' poor socioeconomic conditions, not their ethnicity or race. The PERLA sample shows that, after black people, indigenous people have the highest percentages of community participation at a local level (Table 3.6) compared with the white and mestizo groups. However, as other research has suggested, Colombian indigenous people probably build their solidarity around their "ethnicity," which is an important distinction between indigenous and black ethnics in Colombia. Despite such differences, Afro-Colombians have sought recognition as having an indigenous-like ethnicity.

## Conclusions

Beginning in the colonial period, through the Republican period and the twentieth and twenty-first centuries, Colombia can be characterized as a deeply hierarchical society where both class and race play crucial roles. Instead of destroying the colonial racial and class social order, characterized by castes and other aspects, the new model makes the old class and racial divisions invisible. In the new model, which does not have formal categories of distinction (such as castes), all individuals are apparently free; in practice, however, racial and socioeconomic differences remain more or less intact. Furthermore, over a long period, until well into the twentieth century, women were commonly excluded. Most importantly, physical appearance, particularly skin color, hair texture, body phenotypes,[45] and personal style and dress, operates across all the social dimensions, working directly alongside social class differences. The embodiment of the *habitus* and the body *hexis* (in Bourdieu's 1984 terms) of different social sectors of urban and rural populations since the mid nineteenth century has incorporated pigmentocratic and phenotypic lenses, as part of an unconscious mark of social differences and rules of domination. In this social order, black and indigenous people are at the bottom, white people are on top, and mestizo people in the middle. Sometimes mestizo people are located nearer to whites on the scale, depending on variation in combinations of social class and skin color and other physical aspects. However, in Colombian society this social logic works more in the way of skin color than in terms of self-identity, particularly with white, mestizo, and mulatto categories, for which our findings from the PERLA data differ from the trends established by skin color.

Mestizaje, as an ideology, penetrated liberal republican discourse after the independence wars, throughout the nineteenth century, Regeneración discourse at the end of the nineteenth century and beginning of the twentieth century, and the discourses of the governments of the Liberal Republic in the twentieth century, survived well into the 1980s. The historical arrangement of a racial and social class order was a product of the mestizaje ideology, led by white-mestizo elites, an ideology that was closer to the Argentinean model of miscegenation by whitening.

Despite the national unifying and equalizing idea of miscegenation, the history of indigenous and black social subordination since the colonial period has been very different. The long sociohistorical processes that constructed the ethno-racial imaginary in Colombian society created a representation of otherness linked to the "savage" world of the idealized indigenous. Meanwhile, black people remained "unnamed," at the same time they were also considered "savage" or "primitive"; nevertheless, they do not represent the visible otherness in symbolic terms, as do the indigenous, but rather an invisible otherness. The 1991 Constitution did not significantly modify this representation of otherness in Colombia's ethno-racial imaginary, because indigenous otherness remained through the designation of "multiethnic and multicultural nation." This forced the black population to represent itself as having an ethnicity like the indigenous. In this way, the 1991 Constitution, under the prism of multiculturalism as a new ideology, replaced the idealization of the mestizaje within a secular discourse opposed to the religious speech of the 1886 Constitution, which broke with the last ideological vestiges of the Regeneración of the nineteenth century.

The effects of slavery and the ways in which the Colombian nation has tried to include black people involve several mechanisms of social exclusion that historically have taken different forms. Some of these mechanisms may be represented as expressions of structural racism with institutional effects. However, since the 1991 Constitution, the black movement, like the indigenous movement, has experienced the challenge of becoming statistically visible before the state, civil society, and other social actors, oscillating between emphasizing ethnicity or culture and highlighting race or phenotype. While indigenous people and other minorities, such as the Roma or gypsies, demand an exclusive identity in cultural terms, in the case of the Afro-Colombians the issue is more complex, as race affects many of them in a more direct way.

This chapter has shown that racialization not only affects black people in Colombia but also impacts indigenous people and people with dark skin. More than the Anglo-Saxon definition of race, with fixed frontiers and ancestral marks supported by a heavily institutionalized system, Colombian society's subtle racialization crosses frontiers of class, incorporating socioeconomic differences in a pigmentocratic game. Thus, as a general rule, in Colombia, social classes are colored: individuals and families with the highest levels of capital (e.g., social, cultural, educational, and economic) are "lighter," and those possessed of lower levels of capital are "darker." There are no fixed frontiers, but subtle ranges of colors that directly shape lifestyle, cultural consumption, differentiated access to goods and services, and, most of all, educational and occupational opportunities, and even labor market earning power.[46]

According to the results of the PERLA survey, and considering various alternatives of statistical visibility, the Afrodescendant population in Colombia may be estimated at around 20 percent of the Colombian population. This figure, as reviewed in previous studies, matches the figures of Barbary and Urrea Giraldo (2004). Thanks to black people's claims and their contributions to the construction of the Colombian nation in the past two decades, more Colombians are more likely to accept and recognize their African origin and valorize black and mulatto identities.

The sex/gender dimension is key to understanding how the racialization of social class operates in Colombia. We have been able to capture this with the PERLA survey through the interaction of whiteness and femininity. Racialization is an inequality that is inscribed within a pyramidal and pigmentocratic hierarchical social structure. The results of bibliographic, historiographic, socioanthropological, sociodemographic, and socioeconomic review and the findings from the survey, strengthen this analytical perspective. Results indicate that black women, or darker women in general, face the greatest handicaps in the Colombian social order,[47] followed by black men, and then lighter-skinned men and women. The latter would have the greatest capacity to negotiate social status within society, which allows us to see that social inequality is also significant among the white and mestizo group and that the gaps have become wider.

Institutions of inequality of long duration have perpetuated racial discrimination with results that reproduce the trap of social inequality. Notwithstanding, the PERLA survey reveals that it is easier to detect social inequalities in education and occupational status by examining the effect of skin color rather than by examining racial self-identity. As expected, this statistical pattern is valid for individuals and households.[48] This phenomenon also reproduces itself in perceptions of racial and economic discrimination, although self-identified black persons perceive more discrimination compared to other categories, including the mulatto. In this regard, class differences among Afro-Colombians are expressed subtly through the integration of historical circumstances in skin color. Thus, as indicated in previous studies, there are significant socioeconomic heterogeneities inside the Afro-Colombian population. These heterogeneities are expressed through the mulatto population—even if it is a minority—which has achieved greater and more noticeable advances in social mobility than people with darker skin color. Since the second half of the nineteenth century, because of restricted social mobility for mulatto individuals, white elites have steadily consolidated their hegemony in the social-racial hierarchy. As Zapata Olivella says, "Some blacks have been able to climb to outstanding positions worth the superhuman effort of the parents or the miscegenation with white, but always within the rigid frame of discrimination and prejudice" (Zapata Olivella [1978] 2010: 353).

The presence of small social groups of mulattos that have experienced upward mobility in Colombia intensifies mulattos' ambiguous perceptions toward racial and class discrimination. Although this group is also discriminated against, as the PERLA data indicate, they seem to be much less sensitive to it than groups with darker skin color.

Another interesting finding of the PERLA survey for Colombia is the ambiguity of white and mestizo identities. The results show that self-identified mestizos have higher educational attainment, higher occupational status, and higher income than expected. Apparently, there could be a contradiction here with the pyramidal figure in which white people hold preferential social positions at the top. Notwithstanding, it should be considered that in the identity game, some individuals who are less "white," in terms of skin color, tend to prefer to recognize themselves as "white." Nevertheless, the results for the national sample show that people who self-identified as white were also lighter skinned (on average), allowing us to introduce the hypothesis that within this sample there exists a less-advantaged white population.

The findings on inequality, just like those on perceptions of racial and economic discrimination, reveal a juxtaposition of skin color and social class. As stated by Bourdieu, skin color, like all colors, is value laden and "strongly over-determined" (Bourdieu 1991, 553). In the case of Colombia, these values are expressed in differences in educational attainment and occupational and wage accomplishments of individuals belonging to different ethnic-racial groups. The latter is particularly true throughout the PERLA survey for Colombia, which shows the "dark" population experiences a stronger connection than the medium and light respondents when it comes to skin color and witnessed and experienced economic-status discrimination.

The popular saying "improve the race," in relation to skin color, in particular for black and mulatto identities and, for the "dark" group, is consistent with the Colombian mestizaje ideology. This ideology favors a miscegenation with lighter persons in order to negotiate status improvement in both intimate and public spaces and as a whitening strategy for the following generation. This adage reflects, in an indirect way, the discrimination of darker skin persons in Colombian society.

The apparent support given by most Colombians to multicultural claims of black and indigenous groups relates to the low impact that these social claims have had until now. But this may change in the future, as affirmative action programs targeting the indigenous and black populations start to gain importance in the educational sector and as land claims made by indigenous and black people start to affect the interests of powerful economic groups. It is also noteworthy that the more vulnerable economic situation of black and indigenous respondents makes them more cooperative at a local level, in contrast with mulattos. Unlike indigenous respondents, subjects who self-identified as black take an active part in local community activities, more as a poor population than as an ethnoracial collective. In relation to the mulatto group, upward social mobility is more important.

Lastly, PERLA Colombia data confirm the findings of the revised historiography and the referenced sociological and economic studies, regarding the effect of intersectionality between social class and race. These data reveal that, in the case of Colombian society, social classes have skin colors.

CHAPTER FOUR

# ¿El país de todas las sangres?

## Race and Ethnicity in Contemporary Peru

DAVID SULMONT

JUAN CARLOS CALLIRGOS

Written in 1965, *Todas las sangres* is one of the most important novels of Peruvian author and anthropologist, José María Arguedas (1985 [1965]). In recent
years, politicians and intellectuals have used the phrase "el Perú de todas las
sangres"[1] to refer to the country's ethnic and cultural diversity, evoking the
ideal of a multicultural society where different social groups can live in harmony, maintaining their cultural heritage and enjoying equally the benefits
of economic development. Ironically, in his novel, Arguedas did not describe
a harmonious environment. On the contrary, his story portrays the historical clash between peasants, traditional landowners, and modern businessmen
promoting a mining project in a region of the Peruvian Andes in the mid-
twentieth century. Such a clash occurs in the context of deep-seated tensions
due to differing views of the world and models of economic development.
These different views of the world, with their attendant economic development models, come from indigenous culture; the traditionalist, conservative,
and catholic ideals of *hacendados* (i.e., the owners, of haciendas, or rural estates); the "modernizing" impetus of capitalists; and different forms of social
organization, including the rural community and peasant economy, the semi-
feudal regime of the hacienda, and capitalist exploitation of a mining project.
Arguedas's story has a tragic outcome. The peasants' riot against the mining
project is violently brought down by the government, and their leaders are
executed. This is quite a different outcome from the ideal of social harmony
that the title of the novel evokes nowadays.

Arguedas's work inspired debates in the late 1960s that continue today.[2] It represents a milestone in the discussions on multiculturalism and on the multiethnic nature of Peru. Peruvian society has historically been character- ized by persistent inequality and hierarchical relationships between different ethnic and racial groups. However, during the republican period, economic development and both cultural and political modernizing projects challenged such social relationships and the construction of Peruvian national identity. One of the most important issues surrounding these processes centers on the characteristics of the indigenous population in Peru, especially their precari- ous living conditions and their limited incorporation into Peruvian society as full citizens.

According to the Economic Commission for Latin America (the Spanish ac- ronym is CEPAL), Peru has one the largest populations of indigenous people in the region (CEPAL 2006, 163). Using figures from the 2007 National Census and the 2006 National Continuous Survey (ENCO), by 2007 the indigenous population was estimated at 7.6 million people, approximately 27 percent of the national population, which makes it the second largest indigenous popula- tion in the region, in absolute numbers, only after Mexico. In relative numbers, it is surpassed by only Bolivia and Guatemala.

Map 4.1 shows the percentage of people whose maternal language is an in- digenous one by region (Peru is divided in twenty-five regions), according to the last national census of 2007. The Andean regions in the South (from south to northwest: Puno, Cusco, Apurímac, Ayacucho, and Huancavelica) are the ones with the highest percentages of indigenous people. Historically, those where the Andean regions (around Cusco), where the Inca Empire first expanded in the mid-fourteenth century. It should be noted that the most widespread in- digenous language in contemporary Peru is Quechua, which was the language of the Incas. During the Spanish conquest, the Catholic Church employed the former ruler's language in the evangelization process, contributing to the dif- fusion of Quechua all along the country.

Indigenous people tend to live in poverty. According to the Peruvian Na- tional Institute of Statistics and Informatics (INEI, Instituto Nacional de Esta- dística e Informática 2010b), 55.6 percent of the population that had an indig- enous maternal language lived under the poverty line in 2009. In contrast, only 29 percent of the native Spanish speakers shared this condition. However, the most outstanding differences were in the category of "extreme poverty" (i.e., households that could not satisfy the minimum of nutritional necessities): 26 percent of the population with an indigenous maternal language lived under

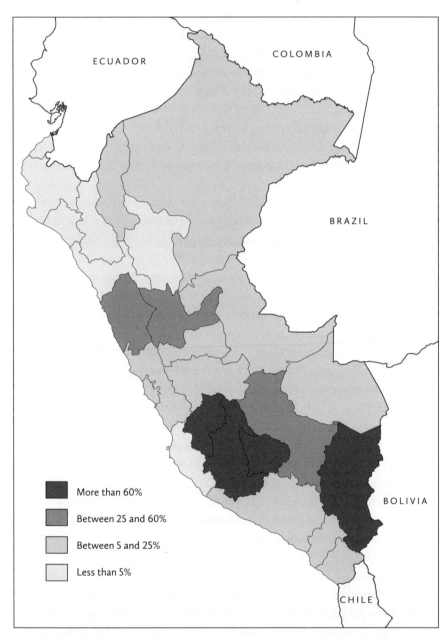

MAP 4.1 Percent Indigenous Language Speakers in Peru, by Province. Source: Census of Peru, 2007

the "extreme poverty line," while only 7.7 percent of native Spanish speakers were in this category.

In addition to socioeconomic inequalities, recent events in Peruvian history have brought the political effects of racial and ethnic inequalities to the forefront. According to the Truth and Reconciliation Commission (Comisión de la Verdad y Reconciliación 2003), the internal armed conflict that took place between 1980 and 2000 produced an estimated seventy thousand fatalities, of which 75 percent were people of indigenous ancestry. This represents the largest number of deaths among the Peruvian indigenous population caused by political violence since Túpac Amaru's anticolonial rebellion in 1780.

On the other hand, since 2002 the country has experienced a new period of economic growth related to the increase in the price and volume of commodities exports, especially minerals.[3] During this period, new social and political conflicts have emerged concerning the impacts (particularly environmental impacts)[4] and redistribution of the benefits of private economic development projects in mining and energy sectors located in rural areas and indigenous lands in the Andes and Amazon regions. These conflicts reflect the tensions between the state, the economic development model, and the country's indigenous population, the majority of which has been excluded socially. Some of these conflicts have had highly dramatic consequences, as in the case of the regional struggle organized by Amazon indigenous organizations in 2009 against government decrees aimed at facilitating private investment in indigenous territories in the Amazon. The government's repression led to a violent clash in June 2009 between the police and the protesters near the Amazon city of Bagua, resulting in the death of twenty-four policemen and ten civilians. This violent event caused the resignation of the prime minister and his entire cabinet and the withdrawal of the government's decrees.[5]

Another less violent symptom of the tensions linked to ethnic and racial inequality in Peru has been the recent widespread notoriety of racially discriminatory practices against indigenous and dark-skinned people who attempted to access certain recreational venues in the capital city (malls, restaurants, discotheques, and movie theaters) that the elite classes usually frequented. These practices have been condemned by the media, public opinion, and certain political authorities that have promoted legal instruments to punish racial discrimination in private and commercial venues.

Presidential elections in the past decade (2000, 2001, 2006, and 2011) have created debates and analysis about the indigenous populations' political representation, particularly the capacity of mainstream political leaders, parties, and institutions to represent the interests and demands of indigenous people (Sulmont 2009; Tanaka and Vera 2009; Tanaka 2011).

In different ways, these examples, among others, express the immediate relevance of inequality and issues of ethnic and racial discrimination in Peruvian society. Politicians, civil society organizations, and scholars have shown a renewed interest in discussing and analyzing problems related to cultural, ethnic, and racial relations in Peru. In some way, the local discussion is related to a global tendency (promoted by social organizations and international institutions like the UN, ILO, and CEPAL, among others) to recognize and expose racism, discrimination, and the living conditions of indigenous, Afrodescendant, and ethnic minority groups in contemporary societies.

The aim of this chapter is to present the results of the Peruvian PERLA survey, analyzing the ideologies and political projects that have framed the social construction of racial and ethnic difference in Peruvian society and their relationships throughout history. The PERLA survey offers a contemporary landscape on the categorization and self-identification practices of social actors from different cultural, ethnic, and racial groups, as well as their socioeconomic inequalities, social mobility processes, and discrimination experiences.

The main argument presented in this chapter is that the "imagined construction" of ethnic and racial differences in Peru has its roots in the different debates and projects of nation building during the nineteenth and the twentieth centuries. These nation-building debates and projects produced a social structure of ethnic and racial boundaries and an "ethnoracial grammar" used by social actors to describe and interpret their differences and inequalities. This grammar is still used in contemporary Peruvian society, contributing to the reproduction of hierarchies and social status, merging socioeconomic inequalities with cultural and racial differences. Although ethnoracial boundaries have become increasingly porous because of the structural transformations associated with economic and political modernization (i.e., the development of the capitalist system and the nation-state building processes), they have not disappeared. As a consequence, for some groups, social mobility in Peruvian society is a process not only of accumulating more economic, educational, or social capital but also of breaking through ethnic and racial boundaries and shifting ethnic or racial identities.

In the first section of the chapter, we discuss the social and historical construction of an ethnoracial narrative in Peruvian society. We present the political and intellectual debates surrounding the definition of "Peruvianhood" and the place of indigenous populations in the Peruvian imagined community, from the years of independence (1821) to the contemporary period. Then, we provide a brief review of how official statistics have reflected ethnic and racial diversity in Peru from the nineteenth century until today, discussing the changes in the official representation of ethnoracial boundaries and their relationship to social and political modernizations processes during the twentieth century. In the third part, we present the results of the PERLA survey, emphasizing the different practices of categorization and ethnoracial self-identification that take place in contemporary Peru and analyzing how these are related to social inequality and discrimination. Finally, we discuss the connections between ethnoracial differences and contemporary political dynamics, especially the capacity of social groups (defined ethnically or racially) to represent their interests in the political arena and have an impact on policies against exclusion and ethnic and racial discrimination.

## Social and Historical Construction

### The Postcolonial Reinvention of the "Indian"

In August 1821, only a month after the declaration of Peru's independence, and years before its consolidation, Libertador General José de San Martín decreed, "In the future the aborigines shall not be called Indians or natives; they are children and citizens of Peru and they shall be known as Peruvians" (Gaceta del Gobierno de Lima Independiente 1950, 67). "Indian" had been a colonial legal and fiscal category that played an important role in the conquest and administration of the American population. It was part of a social structure in which the crown assigned—although not in the rigid manner that has been imagined—different rights and duties to its diverse subjects, based on a notion of "natural inequality." The colonial categories would not survive in the new nation, which was imagined, as Benedict Anderson has aptly stated, as a horizontal community of equals, under the modern principle of individual and universal citizenship (Anderson 1991).

The official and symbolic elimination of the category of "indio," along with other colonial categories, and the promotion of a new identity of Peruanos expressed the assimilatory, liberal, homogenizing, and enlightened impulse of the elites, who must turn "'ex-colonial' subjects into republican citizens with a national future" (Thurner 2003). Following the ideologies of national formation, the creole elites, themselves newly "Peruvian" and influenced by theories of classical liberalism and the premise of a community formed by equals, abolished all colonial categories to form a new community of citizens. The former colonial subjects were not to be "sons" of the king but of Peru and must assume the abstract and individualistic category of "citizens."

The desire of San Martin, born to Spaniards in Argentina in 1778, would have mixed results. On one hand, the term "Indian" was removed from the functioning of the Peruvian state. However, on the other, the term would reappear, reinvented, in the elites' imagination to allude to an inferior being, perhaps inevitably degraded by Spanish colonialism, who was therefore unable to function as a citizen of the new nation. The postcolonial reinvention of "Indian" would differ from the colonial legal and fiscal category: the label would now refer to an allegedly inferior "race" that needed to be redeemed or extinguished, but whose existence imposed a challenge. Peru had an "Indian problem" that it needed to deal with to become a viable, unified, and civilized nation (Kristal 1987).

The subordination of indigenous populations, of course, was not new in the nineteenth century. The colonial administrative system had relied on indigenous elites to extract an indigenous labor force and taxes. An Indian elite was allowed to exist, and the crown recognized its titles of nobility. Not all Indians were poor, obliged to serve in the compulsory labor system (*mita*), or subject to Indian tribute. These privileges and the status of the "noble Indian" were eliminated in the aftermath of Túpac Amaru's uprising (1870–71). Only then would "Indian" become a general label for indigenous peoples, one that would become identified with the peasantry (see, e.g., Spalding 1974).

Racialized views on the Indian as a "miserable race" or as "our unhappy indigenous race" were not simple leftovers from colonial times. Most liberal elites in the nineteenth century considered that the "decrepitude" and "decadence" of *el Indio* had been caused by the unjust, illegitimate, and backward Spanish colonialism, which had destroyed the splendorous Inca civilization, throwing the Indian into his current inferior state (Kristal 1987; Guerrero 1997; Stefanoni 2010). The nation would elevate the Incas to the status of founders of Peru, turning the empire into the nation's glorious past, while placing the indigenous population outside the definition of "Peruanidad" and the exercise of citizenship (Rowe 1954; Walker 1988; Brading 1991; Méndez 1993; Thurner 1997; Larson 2002). Such nationalist ideas departed from a modern notion of "natural equality" and established that the Indian did not inhabit contemporaneity, but was stuck in the colonial past, and constituted a heavy "burden" for the nation. At best, the indigenous population was considered potentially Peruvian: a population to be redeemed, civilized, and integrated into contemporaneity. The pedagogical project of the nation required that elites guide and educate the Indian to civilization and Peruanidad. Enlightened elites had to redeem the Indian because he lacked the necessary characteristics to overcome his desolation. The construction of the Indian as a being to be "Peruvianized" also served to construct elites as civilized and as having the necessary attributes to carry out the civilizing mission.[6]

A similar conception dominated the views on the Afro-Peruvian population. Slavery was progressively limited from 1821 onward,[7] according to the "principles of philanthropy that all governments in the civilized world have adopted."[8] Elites, however, increasingly perceived the Afro-Peruvian population as racially degraded, with instinctive tendencies toward excess, laziness, and dissolute habits. However, this population's considerably smaller size compared to the indigenous relegated them to a less important place in the imagination of nineteenth-century Peruvian elites.

Several authors have regarded racism as an obstacle to the complete fulfillment of the liberal doctrines in Peru (Manrique 1993; 1999). According to this view, racism is part of the heavy burden of the "colonial legacy" and has impeded the modern notion of equality from taking hold. This idea is part of a wider narrative of Latin American exceptionalism that suggests that the region's elites were, and are, not sufficiently modern, liberal, or nationalistic, stubbornly clinging to their colonial positions of hierarchy.[9] Departing from a monolithic idealization of modernity—an idealization that highlights the modern ideals of equality and democracy but obliterates the contradictions of modernity and modern drives for social control, normalization, and discipline—these authors state that modernity developed fully only in Europe. In the profoundly hierarchical Latin American societies, headed by elites unwilling to give up their status, liberalism and modernity were thus "stillborn" (Mallon 1988). Perhaps inadvertently, this scholarship assumes an unambiguous and idealized view of European modernity (and liberalism) as socially, politically, and economically inclusive; in contrast, Latin America can be perceived only as an aberration or deviation. Europe's consolidation of the modern concept of "race" was, in fact, contemporaneous with the rise of the liberal idea of equality and played an important role in rationalizing European colonial expansion in the eighteenth and nineteenth centuries. In the Peruvian case, nineteenth-century racist doctrines about *el indio* or *el negro* were not necessarily derived from colonial ideas of inequality. Rather, just like modern European racism, they departed from modern/liberal conceptions of equality, and served to rationalize social, economic, and political inequalities, as well as to solidify the position of elites.

## "Race" after the War of the Pacific

By the end of the nineteenth century, Peruvian elites had developed racist discourses in relation to indigenous and Afro-Peruvian populations, as well as to immigrants who had arrived from Asia since 1849.[10] However, Peru's defeat by Chile in the War of the Pacific (1879–83), as well as the influence of positivism and the doctrines of scientific racism, produced a radicalization of racist thought in late nineteenth-century Peru. The war left a feeling of defeat, decay, and impotence. Members of Peruvian elites, who expressed doubts over their ability to lead a unified and progressive nation, and about their own racial makeup, adopted the discourses of triumphalism originating in Chile, which highlighted an alleged Chilean racial superiority.[11] Promoting European immigration became a creed among the most notable intellectuals and politicians of the time: Peru's problems, made evident by the quick and devastating defeat in war, had been caused by the absence of a population racially capable of forging an integrated and economically strong nation. Only the immigration of white Europeans could save the country: "Only then will our endemic sickness that is degenerating us into dissolution and which will produce our death if we do not inoculate new elements, start to be modified" (Arona 1971 [1891]).

European immigration had been promoted before the War of the Pacific. Elites believed that Peru must open its boundaries to such immigrants to exert a positive influence in a society marked by the backwardness inherited from Spanish colonialism. In addition, despite their postcolonial notions of *el indio* and *el negro* as degraded races, elites' racial conceptions were flexible, and intellectuals and politicians shared a faith in the civilizing power of progress and education. The "Indian" and the "Negro" could be elevated from their miserable condition by removing the "barriers to progress" introduced by Spanish colonialism.

Peruvian elites had also been selective in appropriating European racial doctrines. They embraced, for instance, the environmentalist conceptions of race derived from French naturalist Jean-Baptiste Lamarck's transformist theories of evolution, which had been discarded in Europe.[12] At the same time, they also discarded the ideas of Georges-Louis Leclerc, Comte de Buffon about natural history and its implications on humans, as well as the observation of Gustave Le Bon that the miscegenation between Spaniards and inferior populations had produced "bastard nations that lack energy and have no future, and which are incapable of contributing to the progress of civilization" (Le Bon, 1889; cf. Prado 1941 [1894], 196). Postcolonial elites had also created their own postulates, some of which were opposed to most European racial theories. In particular, they had stated that miscegenation did not produce degeneration and that "whitening" could help to improve their society. Important intellectuals of the period before the war had stated that Peruvian society's racial diversity was a positive or aesthetically valuable element.[13]

Racist thought would be dramatically transformed by the end of the nineteenth century. The "environmental" arguments, which proposed that races could modify their features through social, cultural, educational, and environmental changes, were replaced by rigidly biological arguments such as those of Clemente Palma. His 1897 thesis, *The Future of Races in Peru* (*El porvenir de las razas en el Perú*), stated that races were not mutable, except through "adequate crossings." Peru required an "ethnic therapeutics," by which the "German race" could give "solidity to the mental life of our race," meaning the "creole race" (Palma 1897, 37). The creole race, or "Peruvian white," had become part of the problem; it was seen as a "lazy race, with poor blood and without muscular vigor. It is a vice-ridden race given over to pleasure and which has courtier's customs" (Prado 1941 [1894], 125), whose history had made it lethargic and unable to develop the country's potential. Peruvian "whites" had acquired an "aversion to work" during colonial times, as well as the vices of idleness and a life of luxury and ostentation (Villarán 1962, 321). Peruvian elites, who previously had discarded some European discourses on race, such as the existence of an idealistic, mystic, and artistic "Latin" race that was inadequate for the virile demands of modernity and the development of industrial capitalism, now revived them. Another racialist argument used to explain the racial "inferiority" of Limeño whites was their long and intimate coexistence with "inferior" Indian and black "races." According to Javier Prado, such inferior races had exerted a pernicious influence on Peru's "Spanish blood." Whites had been exposed to the vices of their black servants, such as their sensuality, theft, superstition, and idleness. Worse yet, black women's "irresistible lust" was transmitted through their maternal milk, since it was common for African Peruvian women to work as wet nurses in elite households (León García 1909, 12). All of a sudden, the population's racial diversity was also perceived as the reason that Peruvians were unable to form a unified nation; miscegenation was seen as pernicious and degenerative, a sickness that could cause social malaises such as delinquency.

The proposals to deal with Peru's "racial problem" were manifold. Those who shared Clemente Palma's radical, nonenvironmentalist stance favored immigration but were open to the massive killing of indigenous people to rid the country of its most noxious elements.[14] European immigrants, however, failed to arrive to Peru in large numbers, in spite of elites' efforts to promote the country as an attractive destination. In fact, the arrival of European immigrants contracted from 1880 to 1930, a period characterized by massive European immigrations to the New World (Bonfiglio 2001). Because of their failure in pursuing the "ethnic therapeutics," most elites persevered in the environmental stance, proposing educational programs and a drastic transformation of the environment to improve the race. A virile, disciplined, population with a "practical sense" was required to adapt the country to the demands of industrial capitalism and for military ends. The preoccupation with population and race reached levels as yet unseen, and "race" was elevated to a variable that explained everything: sciences such as gynecology, puericulture, and the wide branch of medicine called "hygiene" were called on to research ways to "improve the race."

## Hispanismos and Indigenismos

New discourses on Peru's national identity would emerge in the twentieth century. To begin with, anti-Hispanism had been dominant during the nineteenth century because of the need to forge a national identity in opposition to the colonial past and was revived by Spain's attempt to take control of Peruvian guano islands in 1866. But with the appearance of Chile, a new, closer, and more dangerous enemy, this anti-Hispanism lost symbolic weight. In addition, international events, such as the Mexican Revolution, the Russian Revolution, and World War I, urged some Peruvian intellectuals, such as historian José de la Riva Agüero and poet José Santos Chocano, to reconcile Peru with its colonial past and to vindicate what they regarded as the basic and most characteristic elements of Peruvian society, such as Catholicism. Hispanismo was not a local movement. After Spain's loss of its last colonial possessions in 1898, a Hispanoamerican narrative was developed as a discursive attempt to reestablish Spanish pride, emphasizing the grandeur of the colonial past and traditional Hispanic values, in contrast to Anglo-Saxon expansion (Martínez Riaza 1994).

Riva Agüero would vindicate Hispanic values and declare that Peru's character and destiny had been forged in colonial times, which had witnessed the consolidation of the spiritual unity of the nation. He made this declaration facing the threat of an "exaggerated industrialism," which he considered "abject" and an aspect of "economic utilitarianism," forces that could erode social bonds and generate a "total absence of scruples" and a "fierce and hideous egotism . . . that eliminates all enthusiasm and degrades all nobility" (Riva Agüero 1907). Peru was, therefore, racially, culturally, and spiritually Hispanic. Its peculiarity, vis-à-vis the other "daughters" of the Madre Patria was the Inca past and the fact that Peru had been the most important possession of the world's most important metropolis, at least until the mid-eighteenth century. The Spanish conquest was now reinscribed as a favorable event that had brought the benefits of Catholicism to Peru's shores: Peruvians could now be proud of their Inca past but also of their colonial past, which together had bequeathed Peru all of its features.

Hispanismo would find an enthusiastic promoter in the government of President Augusto B. Leguía, known as the Oncenio (between 1919 and 1930). Ironically, Leguía had forced Riva Agüero to abandon the country, and his regime organized the celebration of the centennials of Peru's independence (in 1921, after the Declaration of Independence, and in 1924, after the Battle of Ayacucho, which sealed Spain's defeat in South America); these commemorations of Spanish colonialism's end had an emphatic Hispanista tone and celebrated Spanish colonialism. Thus, in his speech to welcome the representative of the king of Spain, Leguía stated that "we Peruvians are Spaniards by blood, tradition, faith, and language, by all that distinguishes a race" (Ministerio de Relaciones Exteriores 1921). It is evident that this definition of Peruanidad excluded most of Peru's population. It also represents, however, a break from the previous discourse on national identity and the racial characteristics of the country. Only years before, Peruvian elites had a negative conception of Spain's racial legacy corrupted by its proximity to Africa, and by Moor occupation between 711 and 1492, as well as the racial, social, cultural, and economic defects bequeathed to Peru by Spanish colonialism.

Hispanismo cannot be understood, therefore, without taking into account the international context, as well as the indigenista ideas against which it debated. Indigenismos (in plural) were related to the continuation of "Incaist" and the paternalistic and civilizing discourses to "protect" the "Indian," both already present in the nineteenth century. They were also related to the rise of Peruvian archaeology, the formation of provincial intellectual elites—formed sometimes by people with indigenous backgrounds—and to the new vindication of indigenous institutions, such as the community, as viable and useful forms in the modern world. In these cases, the community was seen as evidence of the "associative spirit" of indigenous man, or even of a "communism" that could be used as the base for constructing a future socialist Peru. Indigenista discourses, such as Hildebrando Castro Pozo's, which had a decisive influence on José Carlos Mariátegui's (1928) view on indigenous peoples, ran against liberal recipes that asked for the dissolution of the communities to turn indigenes into individual private proprietors or at least into rural proletarians (Castro Pozo 1924). Such discourses as that of physician and archaeologist

Julio C. Tello vindicated the "indigenous Madre Patria" as "our grand and only mother," in direct challenge to contemporary Hispanista discourses (Presidencia de la República 1925). Many indigenista thinkers and artists reworked the "Indian problem" from socialist or communist perspectives, opposing racist conceptions that were common among Peruvian intellectuals and highlighting the "land problem," that is, the concentration of land in few hands, which was disadvantageous to the indigenous population. Yet, in many cases, indigenismo continued reproducing paternalistic and racialized views on the "Indian," which was still seen as a homogeneous entity and a race to be redeemed.

## The Rise of the Discourse of Mestizaje

The confrontation between Hispanismos and indigenismos would generate, however, a reconciliatory discourse that would exalt miscegenation—mestizaje—as the most important characteristic of Peruvian society. The works of Peruvian intellectual Víctor Andrés Belaúnde (1883–1966) presented the most comprehensive and disseminated view of "integral Peruvianness," formed by a "living synthesis" of elements that had initially been opposed to each other. The racial and cultural-spiritual encounter between the aboriginal and Hispanic races and cultures had produced a Peru that was a spiritual and historic harmonic entity (Belaúnde 1987 [1942]).

The mestizaje discourse was widely disseminated by Peru's school system and is still circulated in Peru today. On the surface, it seemed to transcend the limitations of both Hispanista and indigenista discourses, generating a notion of a shared and reconciled Peruanidad produced by a history marked by the encounter between the races and cultures that generated Peru, and the mutual racial and cultural influence, and the dialectic of their contradictions that ensued. Belaúnde's historical narrative highlights the harmonious encounter of the best indigenous and Hispanic characteristics, which gave Peru a spirit and an encouraging destiny. The Spanish conquest appeared as a positive foundational event, which "adds the Inca Empire to Spain's Empire" in a "historically unbeatable" achievement, in which Spanish conquistadors had "human sympathy" and a "sense of closeness" toward the "primitive tribes." The Dark Legend of Spanish colonialism, dominant during the nineteenth century, was replaced by a view of Spanish colonialism as kindhearted, integrative, and devoted to transcendental ideals (Belaúnde 1987 [1942]).

Belaúnde's "living synthesis" did not transcend the racialist language dominant among Peruvian intellectuals since the nineteenth century. Moreover, mestizaje did not produce a racial and cultural homogeneity among Peruvians:

Belaúnde believed that there are "indigenous masses" living in backwardness who demand a great civilizing effort, similar to what both Incas and Spaniards carried out. He reiterated the idea that "superior" elements must exert a positive influence over "inferior" ones; therefore, although his discourse seems to transcend the exclusions that both Hispanismos and indigenismos generated, it regards elements of Hispanic origin as superior to those of indigenous origin. The effect of the historical narrative is to deny the existence of conflict, gaps, marginalization, and injustice throughout a history that underlines the nation as an integrated and harmonious entity. It also denies the existence of discrimination and racism: the "living synthesis," as a gendered narrative of Peru's history, is the Peruvian version of the "racial democracy" narrative developed by Gilberto Freyre in Brazil.[15]

The mestizaje discourse developed in the 1930s and 1940s influenced such Peruvian historians as José Antonio del Busto and Gustavo Pons Muzzo who reproduced it in school texts, making it an "official discourse" disseminated by the Peruvian state until the early 1980s (Portocarrero and Oliart 1989). It seemed to solve the contradictions of Peruvianness and established an Hispanic-Catholic hegemony more subtly than the Hispanista discourses. It also suggested that Spain integrated Peru into the Western world, exposing it to the benign influence of civilization and modernity. In opposition to Riva Agüero's Hispanismo, aptly regarded by José Carlos Mariátegui as *pasadista* (i.e., an antimodern historical vision that exalted the pre-Bourbon colonial past), the idea of mestizaje as a living synthesis was open to incorporating new and "superior" elements into Peruanidad. By exalting mestizaje as a positive constitutive process, it seemed to include everyone in the definition of Peruvian identity.

While Belaúnde's historical narrative attempted to define Peru as a mestizo nation, mestizaje became a key word to refer to demographic, social, economic, and cultural processes of change in Peru. It was also an objective of the Peruvian state. In 1946, the Peruvian state founded the Instituto Indigenista Peruano, modeled after Mexico's Instituto Nacional Indigenista, to "integrate" the indigenous population, that is, to promote cultural change and economic integration with the market and national society. The institute was underfunded owing to the Peruvian state's weakness and incoherence, but it extended its action through programs of applied anthropology in Ancash, Puno, Apurímac, Ayacucho, and Cusco (Marzal 1986). Albeit with modest results, the institute followed the example of its Mexican counterpart, speaking of the process of "integration" as a mestizaje of the indigenous populations.[16]

At least since the 1940s, mestizaje has also been used in academic circles to refer to "indigenous" rural populations' integration into the market, or to their adoption of "Western" or "modern" cultural elements, or to their migration to the cities. Anthropologists William Mangin and Humberto Ghersi, for instance, used it in this way in their studies of the communities of Vicos and Marcará in Ancash, as did the Cornell University–Peru project of applied anthropology in Vicos. The latter's stated goal was to "bring the indigenous population into the 20th century and integrate them into the market economy and Peruvian society," which was also a way to make "Indians" into mestizos.[17] The anthropology of José María Arguedas also considered that cultural and social mestizaje offered the indigenous people the possibility of improving their lives and freeing themselves from exploitation.[18] Thus, migrations to the city have been interpreted as a process of "de-Indianization," or a process of *cholificación*[19] (where *cholificación* refers to the process of becoming more *cholo*, to use another racialist category of colonial origin, or as a process of mestizaje [see Quijano 1980]).

Diverse studies report that racial labels are used vernacularly to refer to social, cultural, linguistic, and economic positions and hierarchies (Fuenzalida 1971). While racial labels disappeared entirely from the official rhetoric and functioning of the state—the last census to gather information about the "race" of Peruvian population was in 1940—they survived in academic circles and in common language. Perhaps because racial labels were used vernacularly, U.S. anthropologist Julian Steward found it necessary to explain the meanings of Indian and mestizo to North American readers of Volume 2 of his *Handbook of South American Indians*, dedicated to "The Andean Civilizations":

It is necessary to explain the terms Indian and Mestizo. North American readers, who are accustomed to thinking of the former as the designation of the Indian race and the latter as signifying mixed-bloods, may have some difficulty in understanding that in the other American republics these have cultural rather than biological significance. In Ibero-America, Indians and Mestizos are indistinguishable racially, both being predominantly Indian, but the former are characterized by having a preponderance of native culture whereas the latter have assimilated a substantial amount of European culture. The precise differences are a perennial difficulty for the census taker, but in a practical sense it may be said that the Mestizo has been integrated into national life whereas the Indian has not. The latter cannot read or write, does not speak Spanish, and fails to understand European legal, economic, and social systems sufficiently well to cope with them. He is, therefore, characteristically somewhat maladjusted economically and socially. When he makes the adjustments he becomes a Mestizo (Steward 1946: xxviii–xxxxix).

## Race in Contemporary Peru

In Peru, "race" has unstable boundaries and does not allude to "fixed" or permanent realities. The disappearance of race from official language and the rise of a discourse that morally condemns racism have contributed to the lack of fixity. Open expressions of racist ideologies, such as those by Peruvian intellectuals until the 1940s, would not appear with all of their rawness or in outspoken ways; however, racialist language mostly survived in limited or intimate circles. Even now, it erupts in the public sphere in special junctures or may be legitimately used to discuss social processes. In explicit discourse, Peruvians reject racism and consider the use of racial labels offensive and condemnable. There are, however, leftovers of racial discourses that once enjoyed acceptance and legitimacy in Peru. While racial ideologies have not survived the battering of global and local criticisms to racism, some of their elements still play an important role in Peruvians' imagination. Most Peruvians believe, for instance, that races exist, that every person "has" a race or "belongs" to one, even though, as we will see, attributing a racial label is not an exact science. Most Peruvians also believe that races have different physical, intellectual, or moral characteristics. In addition, Peruvians have been trained to classify people into races, that is, to label them according to a race (Callirgos 1993).

Although the labeling process is not permanent or fixed, it is relational and contextual: someone may be labeled a certain way by one individual and in a different way by another. The estimation may include physical criteria, such as skin color, hair characteristics, facial features, the shape of the body, class criteria (as it is said, money whitens), cultural and linguistic criteria (e.g., speaking a cultivated Spanish or speaking an indigenous language), or even geographic criteria (e.g., cities are associated with whiteness or with mestizos, while the rural areas are considered more "Indian"). The process also depends on the person who does the labeling, and on the relationship between who labels and who is labeled. A person is continuously labeled throughout his or her life, and none of the assigned labels will necessarily become lasting. In spite of the fluidity and complexity of these labeling processes, Peruvians are trained to use them, and they determine how individuals relate to each other.

The fact that there are no overt racist intellectual discourses or political discourses but that everyday forms of racial labeling, prejudice, and discrimination prevail is the product of the ambiguous coexistence of antiracist egalitarian and democratic discourses along with discursive elements tainted with racism. While Peruvians are taught the "official truths" that we are all equal before law and that racism is to be reviled, individuals acquire, through subtle but efficient methods, the ability to classify and discriminate racially, and to reproduce historically constructed and emotionally loaded racial prejudices. Since Peruvians learn that the racism instilled in them should be rejected, the manifestations of racism are usually covert, disguised, or appear in conflict situations, for example, when composure is lost, and in insults.

## Ethnicity and Race in Official Peruvian Statistics

According to Rogers Brubaker, the state is a powerful identifier that can enforce an ethnic or racial classificatory system through official mechanisms like national censuses, public records, territory management, administrative procedures, or even the public education curriculum. These processes do not necessarily create "ethnic identities" or "ethnic groups," but they make "certain categories readily and legitimately available for the representation of social reality, the framing of political claims, and the organization of political action" (Brubaker 2004, 54). An official ethnic and racial classificatory system might create an illusion of a society divided into clearly identifiable groups, reinforcing an essentialist view of ethnic or racial differences. By contrast, social and cultural processes show how ethnic or racial identities or categorizations can become quite fluid and porous, changing depending on history, the context of social interactions, or on their relevance for the individuals and groups that might be classified in ethnic or racial terms. In Peru's republican history, population censuses have estimated the size of ethnic and racial groups using different criteria and indicators that reflected the different stages of Peruvian society's conceptualization of ethnicity and race.[20]

In the first stage (1876–1940), population censuses classified people using a set of racial categories associated with physical phenotypes and skin color. After that and since 1940, indicators related to some cultural traits came into use as the concept of "race" was losing its academic and "scientific" status to a more anthropological way of conceptualizing "ethnicity." It is interesting to mention that, following this "culturalist" trend, the 1961 census included a wider set of cultural indicators (for instance, clothing and customs considered indigenous), but these were not used in subsequent censuses. Since 2001, following an international trend in official statistics, the National Household Surveys (Encuestas Nacionales de Hogares; ENAHO) applied by the National Insti-

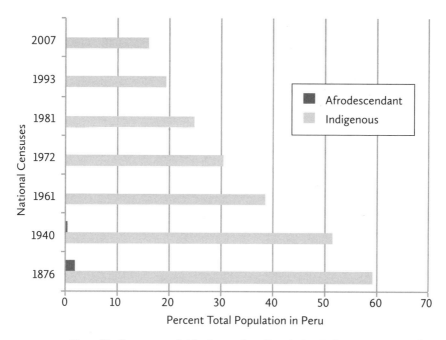

FIGURE 4.1  Size of Indigenous and Afrodescendant Population in Peruvian National Censuses

tute of Statistics and Informatics (INEI) included a self-identification question to identify ethnic groups (see, e.g., Lee 2004; Schkolnik 2009). However, this type of question was not included in the most recent 2007 national census.

During the nineteenth century, four population censuses were implemented (1827, 1850, 1862, and 1876) in Peru, the first three of which had mainly fiscal purposes. The 1876 census was considered the first "modern" census in Peruvian history (Gootemberg 1995, 13). It was conducted during the administration of President Manuel Pardo, who was the head of a liberal political party and the first civilian elected president since independence. The census recorded a total population of 3.7 million inhabitants, and census takers classified respondents according to the following racial categories: white and mestizo (38.6 percent), Indian (57.6 percent), Asian (1.9 percent), and black (1.95 percent) (see Figure 4.1 for indigenous and blacks).

The next national census was held in 1940,[21] recording a national population of 7 million inhabitants. Respondents were classified using the same categories from the 1876 census (Ministerio de Hacienda y Comercio 1944, clxxviii–clxxix). The most important result concerning the racial question in the 1940 census was the inversion of the Peruvian population's racial composition: the percentage of indigenous people decreased from 57.6 percent

TABLE 4.1 Ethnic and Racial Indicators Used in National Censuses and
Estimations of Indigenous Population, 1876–2007

| Census | Indicator | Estimated Indigenous Population (%) | Population Base |
|--------|-----------|-------------------------------------|-----------------|
| 1876 | Racial classification | 57.6 | Total |
| 1940 | Racial classification | 45.9 | Total |
| | Spoken language | 51.6 | Total |
| 1961 | Maternal language | 38.7 | 5 or more years |
| | Customs and clothing | 22.7 | Total |
| 1972 | Maternal language | 30.5 | Total |
| 1981 | Spoken languages | 24.8 | 5 or more years |
| 1993 | Maternal language | 19.5 | 5 or more years |
| 2007 | Maternal language | 15.9 | 3 or more years |

Sources: National Censuses, Instituto Nacional de Estadística e Informática

in 1876 to 45.9 percent in 1940, while the proportion of whites and mestizos rose from 38.6 percent to 52.9 percent (Ministerio de Hacienda y Comercio 1944). However, those patterns not only represent demographic dynamics but also show cultural and ideological processes in Peruvian society. Variations in those figures reflect the changes in ethnoracial boundaries and in the social construction of race and ethnicity associated with socioeconomic transformations, particularly industrialization, urbanization, and the expansion of the education system that Peruvian society experienced during the first half of the twentieth century. The increase of the proportion in mestizo and white categories in the population in comparison with the 1876 census was interpreted in the census report as an indicator of "the rhythm of [racial] fusion . . . revealing a tendency toward the formation of the specific type of national race: the Mestizo, in which racial crossbreeding is synthesized, with a predominance of the ethnic characteristics of whites and Indians" (Ministerio de Hacienda y Comercio 1944, clxxx).

The 1940 census was the last in which a racial question was used to classify the Peruvian population. The census report stated that the observed increases of Spanish speakers and literacy levels among the population were "promising signs of a vigorous social transformation" leading toward a better "demographical and cultural integration or mesticization [sic] of the Peruvian population" (Ministerio de Hacienda y Comercio 1944, clxxxiii). As a consequence of

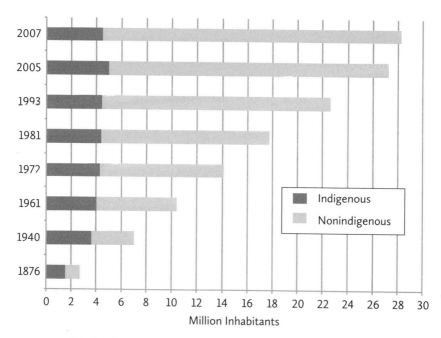

FIGURE 4.2 Total Indigenous and Nonindigenous Population in Peruvian National Censuses

dropping the racial question in subsequent censuses, ethnic groups other than indigenous people (particularly Afro-Peruvians) were made invisible in official statistics for the rest of the twentieth century.

Censuses from 1961 through 2007 also had questions regarding maternal or spoken languages. As we can see in Table 4.1 and Figure 4.1, results indicate a decreasing trend in the proportion of Peruvians speaking indigenous languages (from 51.6 percent in 1940 to 15.9 percent in 2007) and the corresponding increase of Spanish native speakers.

Figure 4.2 shows the evolution of the Peruvian population and the estimates for the indigenous population according to the censuses from 1876 to 2007. Those estimates were calculated using linguistic indicators[22] (with the exception of the 1876 census, where racial categories were used). Interestingly, we can see that since 1961, absolute estimates of indigenous population using this indicator have remained almost constant around 4 million people, despite the fact that numerous demographic studies show that the fertility rate among indigenous populations is much higher than in the general population (Instituto Nacional de Estadística e Informática 2009). This "stagnation" of the indigenous population in absolute numbers cannot be explained by demographic factors alone (like fertility, birth rate, mortality rate, or international immigration). Rather, it reflects social and cultural transformations in twentieth century Peruvian society.

The relative decrease of indigenous-language speakers and the increase of Spanish speakers occurred in parallel with the extension of the education system and the urbanization process that Peruvian society experienced in the second half of the twentieth century. Between 1940 and 1993 the illiteracy rate of the population fifteen years and older decreased from 57.6 percent to 12.8 percent, and in the last census of 2007 it decreased further to 7.1 percent. The urban population increased from 47.4 percent of the total population in 1961 to 59.4 percent in 1972 (Instituto Nacional de Estadística e Informática 2001, 39); by the end of the twentieth century it represented 70.1 percent, and according to the last census of 2007, 79 percent of Peruvians lived in urban areas. Official statistics show that literacy and urbanization are correlated with *disindiginisation* during the twentieth century.

The 1961 census is particularly interesting because, in addition to linguistic indicators (maternal language and spoken languages), data were collected on "regional customs" that sought to also identify indigenous people. Among the data were four items: if the individual "walks barefoot," "uses *ojotas,*" "uses *poncho* or *lliclla,*" or "chews coca leafs."[23] Under the common sense of the epoch, those items were considered ethnic markers because they constituted "customs of the autochthonous indigenous population" (Instituto Nacional de Planificación 1966, VI). According to the census report, 22.7 percent of the respondents showed at least one of those "ethnic markers" in 1961. However, these indicators focused basically on Andean indigenous populations, leaving behind the Amazon region aboriginal groups.

In the past decade, the main methodological innovation for measuring the ethnic and racial dimension in Peruvian society in official statistics was the 2001 inclusion of a self-identification indicator in the National Household Surveys (ENAHO). The question was as follows: "Considering your ancestors and your customs, do you consider yourself: a) indigenous of the Amazon region; b) of Quechua origin; c) of Aymara origin; d) of Black / Mulatto / Zambo origin; e) White; f) of Mestizo origin; g) Other?" In 2006, the INEI's National Continuous Survey (Encuesta Nacional Continua; ENCO)[24] applied this question to respondents aged twelve years and older. Results indicated that 22.5 percent considered themselves of Quechua origin, 2.7 percent Aymara, 1.7 percent from the Amazon, 1.5 percent African descendants (black, zambo, or mulatto), 57.6 percent mestizos, 4.9 percent white, and 9 percent "other." If Quechua, Aymara, and Amazon categories are aggregated, the result is that 27 percent of Peruvians older than twelve years could be identified as "indigenous." If we apply this proportion to the results of the 2007 census, Peru would currently have approximately 7.6 million indigenous people.

An important innovation regarding the issue of ethnicity was introduced in 1993 with the "First Census of Native Communities in the Peruvian Amazon Region." The vast Amazon region in Peru accounts for 62 percent of the national territory but less than 15 percent of the population. It is home to a large variety of native ethnic groups. The census was undertaken by the INEI, in collaboration with representatives of indigenous organizations of the Amazon region. The main tool for this census was an ethnolinguistic map that allowed identifying the different linguistic families in the region and the ethnic groups inside them. According to the 1993 census results, 239,674 people lived in native communities belonging to fifty-three different Amazon ethnic groups (Instituto Nacional de Estadística e Informática 2010a, 17). This represented 1.06 percent of the total population of the country in 1993 (22.6 million), and 5.5 percent of the "indigenous" population, that is, of the population who had a native language as their maternal language at that time (4.4 million). This kind of census was reproduced in 2007, and the Amazon indigenous population was estimated at 332,975 people, representing 1.2 percent of the national population. However, the complexity and ethnic cultural diversity of the Amazon native groups, as well as the geographic difficulties of the region, created methodological doubts about the accuracy of these results.

As we have said, one of the consequences of adopting linguistic indicators in the censuses after 1940 was the statistical invisibilization of other ethnic or racial groups that have Spanish as their maternal language in the twentieth century; examples are mestizos (although many of them might have an indigenous maternal language), whites, and Afro-Peruvians. In the Afro-Peruvian case, the 1876 census classified 1.95 percent of the population as black; this percentage decreased to 0.47 percent in 1940. New estimates of this population had to wait until the twenty-first century, when the self-identification question was included in official social surveys (but not in the 2007 census questionnaire) such as the ENAHO and ENCO. For example, according to the 2006 ENCO, 1.5 percent of the respondents aged twelve years or older identified themselves as Afrodescendants (black, mulatto, or zambo). However, other studies have estimated this proportion at around 5 percent (Benavides et al. 2006). The lack of census information and the relatively low numbers of Afro-Peruvians in the general population make it difficult to perform deeper analysis on the social characteristics of this group using ordinary social surveys (such as ENAHO), particularly because of sample size limitations. To overcome those issues, some surveys, like the 2004 ENAHO (jointly designed by INEI and the Grupo de Análisis para el Desarrollo; GRADE), oversampled in particular geographic areas where Afrodescendants tend to concentrate (Benavides et al. 2006; Valdivia et al. 2007).

Contemporary discussion in Latin America about measuring the population's ethnic characteristics has focused on four dimensions that have oriented the design of national censuses in the region since 2000: self-identification, common origin, culture, and territory (Schkolnik 2009, 67–68). In the Peruvian case, public officials, academics, and several social organizations representing ethnic groups are beginning to engage in a debate on how to include those dimensions in the next census, due in 2017. One of the main challenges is the lack of consensual definitions of the meaning and boundaries of the ethnic or racial categories that official statistics could use to identify ethnic or racial groups.[25] Debates on those issues will confront different positions (academic, cultural, ideological, or political) concerning what constitutes an "ethnic or racial group" or an "indigenous people."

Beyond academic discussions or practices using ethnic and racial variables in surveys and research projects, the production of official statistics, especially in censuses, implies important political decisions about how and why the state or different social and political groups in society may want to present a particular ethnic portrayal of the nation. These include decisions regarding the recognition of citizenship rights (civil, political, and social; individual or collective); the design of public programs (education, health, poverty alleviation, "social inclusion," antidiscrimination, affirmative action programs); or territorial and population management (economic development projects, immigrations policies, reproductive policies). For example, in 2011 the Peruvian government approved a Law of Previous Consultation in order to adapt the national legislation to the provisions of ILO Convention 169 concerning indigenous people's rights. This law establishes a consultation process with indigenous people on economic development projects (mainly private investments in natural resources or energy projects) that might affect indigenous territories. This law's implementation has reactivated a debate about which groups or collectivities should be considered as "indigenous people" in Peru.

## The PERLA survey

### Ethnic and Racial Identity

The Peruvian PERLA survey was distributed between October and November 2010 to a nationally representative sample of fifteen hundred people.[26] One of its principal objectives was to examine and analyze different indicators and quantitative approximations for measuring ethnic and racial categories and self-identification in Peru. The questionnaire included different types of indicators and questions that combined linguistic, cultural, and racial categories. In this section we analyze and discuss the results of these measurements and their implications for the processes of categorization and ethnoracial self-identification in Peruvian society. In Table 4.2 we present all of the different questions and indicators used to identify ethnic and racial groups in the PERLA survey.

In the case of the self-identification type A question, we have grouped the categories "Quechua," "Aymara," and "Amazon" under the single label of "indigenous" for presentation purposes. We used a similar procedure with maternal language (indigenous languages were aggregated into a single category) and the racial self-identification questions. Also, all the categories referring to Afro-Peruvians in the different questions (i.e., blacks, mulattos, and zambos) were aggregated into a single category of Afro-Peruvians. Categorizing the respondents in an aggregated "indigenous" category is a researcher's decision; as Lavaud and Lestage (2009, 66) point out, this decision entails the risk that ethnic measurements using these kinds of survey questions contribute to reproducing social preconceptions of what is "an Indian" or "an indigenous person," transforming a supposedly "scientific" statistical estimation into an ideological and political one. A similar argument can be made concerning Afrodescendants. We are aware of those issues, but they are quite common in any empirical operationalization of ideologically laden concepts. Almost all the statistical measures of indigenous people made by official offices in Latin America suffer from the same problem.

Figure 4.3 shows the distribution of the respondents in the different categories of the first five indicators presented in Table 4.2. We note important variations in the distribution of the racial and ethnic categories among the different indicators. The most outstanding differences relate to the indigenous and mestizos categories. In the first case, the percentage of indigenous varied from 4.7 percent when we used the self-identification type B question to 23.3 percent when the self-identification type A question was used (defined in Table 4.2). Comparing the same questions, mestizos varied from 78.3 percent in the type B question to 60 percent in the type A question.

Figure 4.4 shows the range of estimates of the indigenous population according to the different questions and indicators employed in the PERLA survey. When taking into account the "indigenous" condition of the respondent's parents and ancestors, the percentages of "indigenous people" tended

TABLE 4.2 Ethnic and Racial Indicators Used in Peruvian PERLA Survey

| Indicator | Description |
|---|---|
| External ethnic and racial categorization | Interviewer's perception of the ethnic or racial group of the respondents using the following categories: Indigenous, Mestizo, White, Mulatto, Black, and Others |
| Racial self-identification (open-ended question) | An open-ended question with the following phrasing: "People who live in our country have multiple racial characteristics and origins, could you tell us which is your race?" The interviewer had the instruction to write down the respondent's answers, which were later codified by the fieldwork supervisors. |
| Ethnic and racial self-identification– Type A | This was a similar question than the one used in the ENAHO surveys in Peru: "According to your ancestors and your customs, do you consider yourself from: Quechua origin; Aymara origin; from the Amazon; Black / Mulatto / Zambo; White; Mestizo; Other?" Respondents were asked to choose only one category. Unless indicated otherwise, from now on we will refer to this question as "Ethnic and racial self-identification." |
| Ethnic and racial self-identification– Type B | This question is similar to the previous one, but with some changes in the categories, and it was asked immediately after. The question phrasing was: "Now, considering these options, do you consider yourself a: Mulatto; Black; Indigenous; Mestizo; White; Other?" |
| Maternal language | As we have seen, maternal language is the main indicator used in Peruvian censuses to distinguish indigenous from non-indigenous populations. In the survey the corresponding question was: "Which is the language you learned to speak first during your childhood: Quechua; Aymara; another native language; Spanish; another foreign language?" |
| Parents' ethnic and racial identification | Respondents were asked to identify their parents (mother and father separately) with one of the categories used in the ethnic and racial self-identification question. |
| Ethnic ancestry | Respondents were asked if any of their ancestors were from European, Indigenous, African / Black or Asian origins. In each case they had to answer yes or no. |
| Skin color | To measure skin color, interviewers rated the facial skin color of each respondent according to colors on a skin color palette, which was not shown to the respondents. The palette included eleven skin tones, with "1" being the lightest and "11" being the darkest. The colors of the palette came from internet photographs and the palette was extensively pre-tested in several countries in the region for ease of use by interviewers and to see if it covered the range of colors found in the field. The rating was done just before the beginning of the interview. |

Source: PERLA 2010

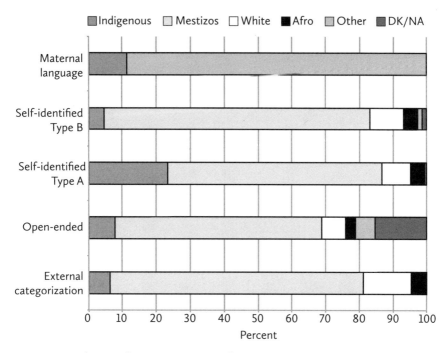

FIGURE 4.3 Ethnoracial Composition according to Various Criteria, Peru

to increase. Almost 40 percent of respondents had some indigenous ancestors other than their parents. If either the father or the mother was identified as an indigenous person, the percentage of respondents that could be categorized as indigenous was 34.7 percent. This compares to 27 percent based on the 2007 Census, as cited earlier, or 32 percent, based on the 2001 CEPAL estimates using maternal language criteria and the 2001 ENAHO survey.

Because of the low incidence of African descendants in the Peruvian population, the sample size of this group in the PERLA survey was quite small and does not allow for more complex statistical analysis. For this reason, most of the comparisons in this chapter are made between indigenous and nonindigenous groups.

As we can see, the methodological alternatives used to estimate the size of ethnic or racial groups in Peru produce very different quantitative results. Some questions, like the self-identification type A, combine categories from dimensions like language or cultural practices (Quechua and Aymara), geography (from the Amazon), and race (white, black, mestizo). In the case of the self-identification type B question (mulatto, black, indigenous, mestizo, and white), the categories refer mostly to the racial dimension. When we compare

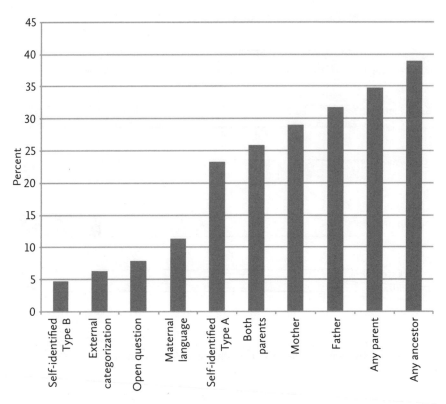

FIGURE 4.4 Percent of Respondents Indigenous or with Indigenous Ancestry Using Various Criteria, Peru

the distribution of respondents among the categories of those two questions (see Figure 4.3), we note important variations in the percentage of people who considered themselves as mestizos. When the choice set was based only on racial categories (like self-identification type B question), the percentage of people who chose the mestizo category was higher (78.3 percent versus 63.3 percent) than in the case when the alternatives included cultural (Quechua or Aymara) and geographic (Amazon) categories related to the indigenous background of the respondents. These results could indicate the social stigma associated with the "indigenous" label, expressly used in the self-identification type B question, which makes this category "unattractive" for many people. As a consequence, facing this kind of "racial" choice set, people may tend either to choose more "neutral" labels like "mestizo" to classify themselves or simply to refuse to answer these kinds of questions (as in the case of the open-ended question on race).

TABLE 4.3 Interviewer versus Self-identification (%)

| | Interviewer Classification | | | | |
|---|---|---|---|---|---|
| | White | Mestizo | Indigenous | Other | Total |
| Self-identification | | | | | |
| White | 66.6 | 30.7 | 1.3 | 1.3 | 100.0 |
| Mestizo | 8.7 | 84.6 | 4.1 | 2.4 | 100.0 |
| Indigenous | 1.4 | 47.8 | 50.7 | 0 | 100.0 |

Source: PERLA 2010

Another interesting result in Figure 4.3 is the low variation in the percentages of people who considered themselves whites or African descendants among the different questions. Self-identification in those categories seems more robust than in the mestizo or indigenous cases, pointing to clearer or more rigid criteria for defining those of white or African descent in Peruvian society.

Table 4.3 illustrates the difficulties inherent in attempting to classify and categorize people into ethnic and racial categories. In this case there was a cross tabulation between self-identification and the interviewers' classification (in both cases using type B categories). Almost a third of the respondents who considered themselves white were classified as mestizos by the interviewers and almost half of the respondents who self-identified as indigenous were classified as mestizos. The high percentage of overlap in the mestizo category comes from the fact that this was the most used category by both respondents and interviewers (see Figure 4.3).

These survey results show the tensions of ethnic and racial self-identification and categorization dynamics in Peruvian society. While people are aware of ethnoracial boundaries, some of those boundaries are still charged with strong social stigma, particularly in the case of the indigenous and nonindigenous distinction. Depending on the nature of the markers used to identify its boundaries, the malleability of the "mestizo frontier" might be interpreted as the product of social, cultural, and political transformations that Peruvian society experienced in the second half of the twentieth century. Most of those changes were marked by a massive upsurge from those of indigenous descent participating at the center of social and political life, largely enabled by processes of immigration, urbanization, the expansion of education, and universal suffrage.

## Color, Ethnicity, and Race

Many people in Peru continue to fuse physical characteristics with social behavior, fixing racial stereotypes in order to categorize individuals. In a 2002 study conducted among high school and university students in Lima, Joanna Drzewieniecki (2004, 20) found that race "is a category that makes a great deal of sense to Peruvian youth. While culture and socioeconomic status matter, young people are aware of skin color and facial features and many perceive an imagined 'racial hierarchy' in Peru running approximately from black to white." As we have seen in Table 4.2, the PERLA survey's design included the phenotypic dimension of ethnic and racial categorization by using a color palette to classify each respondent's skin color. To simplify the presentation of the results, we clustered the different tones in three groups: light (tones 1 to 3); medium (tones 4 to 5); and dark (tones 6 and up). In Figure 4.5 we present the distribution of the respondents in these three groups according to three other ethnic and racial indicators used in the survey: maternal language (indigenous and nonindigenous), ethnic self-identification, and indigenous ancestry (based on the parents' ethnic and racial identification question). In the whole sample, 55.4 percent of respondents were classified with medium color tones, nearly 22 percent were classified with light, and 23 percent with dark tones. If we calculate the "average" of the tones' numeric values, the result would be a color tone of 4.6.

When we compare the distribution of the skin color tones across the categories of the other ethnic and racial indicators, we find important differences. As mentioned previously, maternal language is one of the main indicators that official statisticians use to distinguish indigenous from nonindigenous populations in Peruvian society. Our results show that interviewers classified 22.6 percent of respondents with a nonindigenous maternal language (primarily Spanish) as having light skin color tones. This percentage decreased to nearly 13 percent for those with an indigenous maternal language (Quechua, Aymara, or an Amazonian native language). Similarly, in a comparison between respondents with indigenous ancestry and respondents with nonindigenous ancestry, the former were classified as having darker skin color than the latter. Those results should not be surprising since the question about the indigenous background of one's parents uses categories strongly associated with language ("of Quechua origin," and "of Aymara origin").

However, when we compared groups in the self-identification question, there were not important differences between the skin color distributions of mestizos and indigenous. It appears that self-identification with the indig-

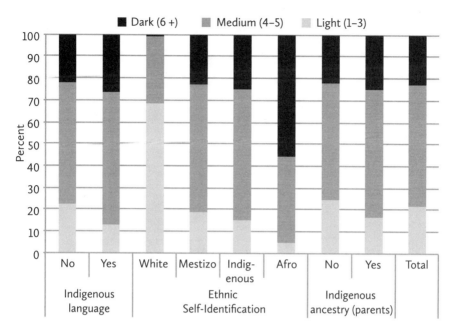

FIGURE 4.5 Respondent's Skin Color by Maternal Language, Ethnic Self-Identification and Indigenous Ancestry, Peru

enous categories (Quechua, Aymara, or from the Amazon) depends more on how people value their cultural characteristics or heritage than their reaction to the phenotypical categorization made by others in the society. On the contrary, white and Afrodescendant self-identification is clearly more associated with skin color differences.

### Ethnicity, Race, and Social Inequalities

As in previous research (see, e.g., Ñopo et al. 2007; Figueroa and Barrón 2005; Trivelli 2005; Valdivia et al. 2007; Thorp and Paredes 2010), PERLA survey data show consistent relationship patterns between socioeconomic inequality and ethnic and racial groups in Peruvian society. We explored some of these inequalities by analyzing three dimensions of social status: educational level, occupational status, and socioeconomic status. We operationalized those variables using the following indicators:

- Average years of formal education
- Percentage of respondents with high-skilled nonmanual occupations (white-collar occupations), excluding housewives and students

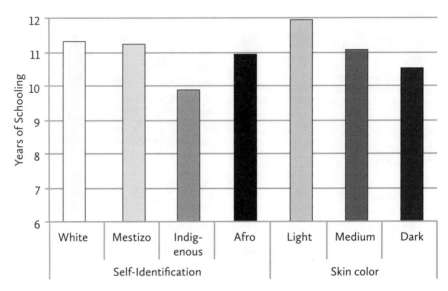

FIGURE 4.6 Mean Years of Schooling by Ethnoracial Self-Identification and Skin Color, Peru

- Percentage of respondents who belonged to the top 25 percent of the socioeconomic status index (calculated according to household equipment and income).[27]

Those indicators will be compared across the categories of two ethnic and racial variables: self-identification (type A) and skin color.

As we see in Figure 4.6, the average years of formal education were higher among whites and mestizos than among indigenous and Afrodescendants. Similarly, when we considered skin color, the average years of formal education were higher among those of lighter skin color and decreased significantly as skin color darkened.

Differences in occupational status had a similar pattern (see Figure 4.7). The percentage of high-skilled white-collar workers was higher for white and mestizos, or people with lighter skin color, than among indigenous, African descendants, or people with darker skin color. When we compared the indicator of socioeconomic status index, we found the same tendency (see Figure 4.8): only 16.3 percent of respondents who self-identified with indigenous categories belonged to the 25 percent of respondents with a higher socioeconomic status, 8.7 percent lower than what could be expected in a homogeneous distribution. The other categories (white, mestizos, and Afrodescendants) had similar proportions to what would be expected. When we analyzed the differences

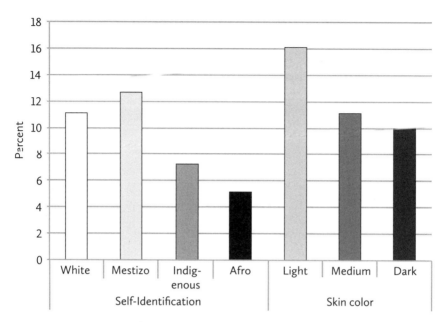

FIGURE 4.7 Percent in High-Status Nonmanual Occupations by Ethnoracial Self-Identification and Skin Color, Peru

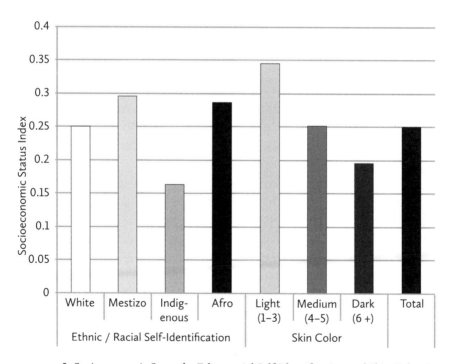

FIGURE 4.8 Socioeconomic Status by Ethnoracial Self-Identification and Skin Color, Peru

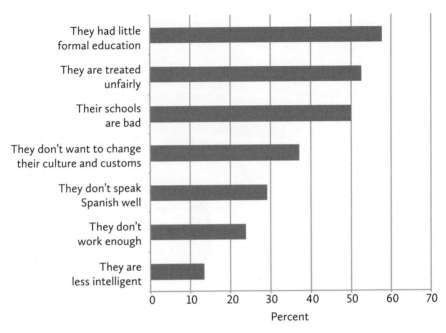

FIGURE 4.9 Reasons Given as to Why the Indigenous Are Poor, Peru

in skin color and their relationship with socioeconomic status, we saw that the probability of being in the top 25 percent decreased as skin color darkened, and vice versa.

These results confirm that socioeconomic inequalities are correlated with ethnic and racial differences in Peruvian society. Another important finding is that differences across groups in indigenous/nonindigenous self-identification categories occur to the same degree as those observed among groups classified by skin color. This may explain why, in the social imaginary, social inequalities related to the acquisition of social assets or cultural capital, or integration to the labor market, merge with cultural characteristics (language or customs) and physical characteristics (skin color), creating stereotypes and ethnic, racial, and "phenotypic" hierarchies. Thus, social inequalities can be understood using both class-based interpretations (the product of the unequal structure of opportunities in a capitalist society) and "racialist" narratives.

In the survey, respondents were asked if they agreed or disagreed with some phrases that represented possible explanations for the social inequalities that affect indigenous people in particular. The specific question was, "According to census data, indigenous people are poorer. How much do you agree with each of the following reasons for that?" Some of the prompted explanations for the indigenous population's level of poverty focused on cultural differences (language, customs) and negative stereotypes about individual characteristics (they are less smart, they don't work enough), while others focused on causes related to the unfair treatment they receive from society or their lack of access to the type of opportunities afforded by a quality education. The phrases that generated higher levels of agreement (see Figure 4.9) were related to unfair treatment and lack of educational opportunities, causes that may be related to discrimination or social exclusion. However, a significant number of respondents agreed with phrases stating that indigenous people's low socioeconomic status is related to their cultural or personal characteristics (intelligence or will to work).

Those last results indicate the overlap between socioeconomic differences and ethnic and racial ones, which reproduce stereotypes that "racialize," "naturalize," or "culturalize" social inequality, stereotypes that are still common among a significant proportion of Peruvians, contributing to the strengthening of ethnic racial hierarchies that still have an important presence in Peru.

## Ethnicity, Race, and Social Mobility

How do race and ethnicity relate to social mobility in Peru? A first hypothesis is that an individual's ethnoracial group might affect the possible range of social mobility: indigenous or "darker" people could experience more limits in their social mobility trajectories, while nonindigenous or "whiter" people might have better chances of reaching higher social status. Another complementary hypothesis is that upward social mobility, when it occurs, might also affect ethnoracial self-identifications or categorizations in the society.

In order to explore these hypotheses empirically, we analyzed intergenerational occupational and educational social mobility across ethnic and color groups in the sample. In the case of occupational mobility, we calculated how many respondents whose fathers had blue-collar occupations reached white-collar occupations (in this case, we are not distinguishing skilled from not skilled white-collar occupations).[28] As we see in Figure 4.10, 24 percent of respondents whose fathers were blue-collar workers had white-collar occupations. However, these percentages were lower for those who self-identified as indigenous (16.3 percent) in comparison to those who self-identified as nonindigenous (26.5 percent); also, percentages decreased as respondents' skin color darkened.

We used the same exercise for comparing intergenerational educational mobility to observe how many respondents whose fathers had a secondary ed-

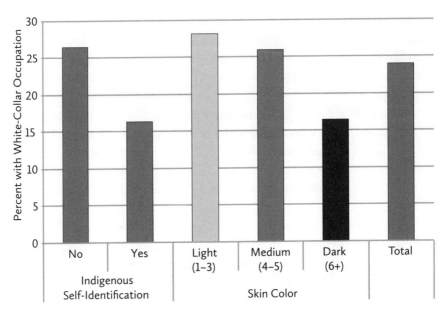

FIGURE 4.10 Percent Attaining White-Collar Jobs among Persons of Blue-Collar Background by Indigenous Self-Identification and Skin Color, Peru

ucation or less reached postsecondary educational levels (Figure 4.11). Across the whole sample, the figure was 35.9 percent, but it was higher among nonindigenous than among indigenous respondents (38.8 versus 27.1 percent), and it decreased as respondents' skin color darkened. In other words, the degree to which children's formal educational level surpassed their fathers was correlated with the respondent's ethnoracial group or category. These results suggest that the nonindigenous or individuals with lighter skin color might get a "plus" in their social mobility trajectories, while the indigenous or people with darker skin color suffer disadvantages in that process.

The second hypothesis states that acquiring increased assets or cultural capital (which, basically, is education) allows people to experience not only upward social mobility but also "upward ethnic racial mobility"; that is, at some level people can "leave" ethnic and racial groups considered by society as "inferior." In previous sections we have argued that the development of the capitalist and market economy, urbanization, and the expansion of the educational system in Peru were correlated with a "de-Indianization" process. This correlation can be explained using either class-based (the expansion of new social classes like the proletariat and the middle class) or racialist (mestizaje or cholificación) narratives of Peruvian modernization in the second half of the twentieth century.

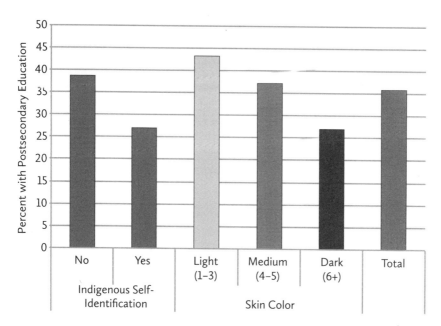

FIGURE 4.11 Percent Attaining Postsecondary Education among Persons of Blue-Collar Background by Indigenous Self-Identification and Skin Color, Peru

In order to see if the survey's data support this argument, we focused only on respondents with some indigenous ancestry (mother or father), which represents 35 percent of the sample. Then we examined how many of those respondents self-identified with an indigenous category across different educational levels ( less-than-secondary, secondary, and postsecondary education). As Figure 4.12 shows, 60.9 percent of respondents with indigenous ancestry self-identified with an indigenous category. However, this percentage was higher among respondents with a secondary education or less (64.1 percent) and decreased for respondents with postsecondary educational attainment (54.9 percent). The results appear to be consistent with the idea that access to higher educational levels comes along with a "de-Indianization" processes.

We performed a similar analysis to compare how the skin color of people with indigenous ancestry varied across educational attainment levels. Figure 4.13 shows that interviewers classified 25 percent of respondents with indigenous ancestry as people with dark skin color, 58.6 percent with medium skin color, and 16.4 percent with light skin color. However, the percentage of respondents with light skin color was significantly higher among people with a postsecondary education (22.9 percent) than among those with a secondary education or less (13.1 percent); inversely, darker skin color was more frequent

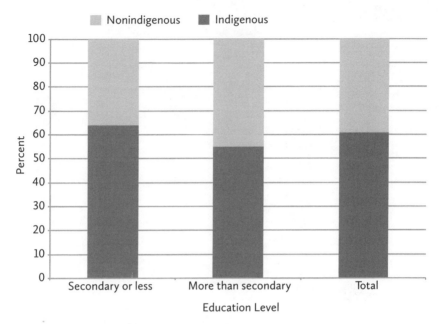

FIGURE 4.12 Self-Identification as Indigenous by Educational Level among Persons with at least One Indigenous Parent, Peru

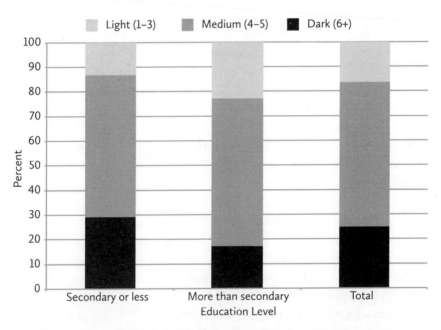

FIGURE 4.13 Skin Color by Educational Level among Persons with at least One Indigenous Parent, Peru

among people with lower educational attainment. These data reinforce the commonly held belief that upward social mobility can "whiten" people with indigenous origins.

It is important to note that interviewers applied the skin color palette before beginning the survey and, therefore, before any knowledge of respondents' educational level. However, this "chromatic" classification was made in a setting of social interaction (in this case, between the respondent and the interviewer),[29] a setting with certain keys or "clues"; interviewers may have "translated" some "visible" indicators other than physical appearance, such as the respondent's neighborhood or residence, the respondent's clothes, or way of speaking, to "skin color." All of these visible indicators provide "cognitive clues," many of which are correlated with socioeconomic variables such as the respondent's educational level.

## Discrimination

One of the PERLA questionnaire's modules was designed to gather information about respondents' experiences with racial or ethnic discrimination, that is, whether they had witnessed discrimination or unfair treatment suffered by other people or had experienced discrimination personally. Strictly speaking, these questions attempted to measure "perceptions" of discrimination, which means that those acts may not have been discriminatory per se, even if they were so interpreted. While surveys are suited to measure perceptions, experimental designs are more suited to measure actual discrimination.[30] However, taking into account the limitations inherent in the PERLA survey method, the results show important associations between discrimination perceptions and the respondents' ethnoracial classification.

Here are the specific questions we analyzed in this section:

- Witnessed discrimination: "Have you seen situations in which another person has been discriminated, treated badly or unfairly because: a) their skin color; b) their economic situation; c) speaking an indigenous language?"
- Experienced discrimination: "In the last five years, have you ever felt discriminated or treated badly or unfairly because: a) your skin color; b) your economic situation; c) the way you talk or your accent?"

Table 4.4 shows the percentage of respondents, by skin color, who witnessed or experienced those situations at least once in the past five years.

TABLE 4.4 Experiences versus Witnessing Discrimination (%)

| | Indigenous Language/Accent | Economic Situation | Skin Color |
|---|---|---|---|
| **Witnessed** | | | |
| Light | 57.6 | 72.4 | 65.3 |
| Medium | 60.5 | 74.4 | 67.3 |
| Dark | 65.4 | 76.8 | 72.4 |
| Indigenous | 72.0 | 79.4 | 70.8 |
| **Experienced** | | | |
| Light | 17.0 | 29.7 | 14.2 |
| Medium | 25.6 | 39.0 | 25.9 |
| Dark | 28.1 | 45.1 | 35.8 |
| Indigenous | 34.8 | 47.1 | 4.3 |

Source: PERLA 2010

Regardless of skin color or indigenous self-identification, witnessing situations of discrimination toward other people was quite common. These perceptions are consistent with the widely held opinion (held by 75 percent of respondents) that Peruvian society is very or somewhat racist.

On the other hand, perceptions of being discriminated against were much less frequent, although underreporting in these cases can be common. Just over 38 percent of all respondents had experienced socioeconomic discrimination, while a quarter of the sample had experienced other types of discrimination (due to skin color or accent). As expected, in all situations, the percentage of people who had felt discriminated against was higher for those who self-identified as indigenous and increased as skin tone darkened. These results show consistency between social status and subjective perceptions: people from ethnic and racial groups most affected by social inequalities were also the ones who felt discrimination more often.

Measures to fight racial or ethnic discrimination had wide support in public opinion. When we asked about affirmative-action-related measures in the PERLA survey (see Figure 4.14), at least 80 percent of respondents agreed with them. Also, a large group of respondents (72.6 percent) supported indigenous organizations. While many of these answers might be considered "politically correct," they still indicate social awareness concerning ethnic and racial discrimination, and the necessity and support for public policies to fight against it.

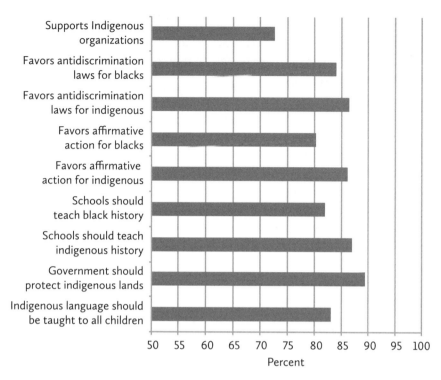

FIGURE 4.14 Support for Multiculturalism and Multicultural Policies, Peru

## Race, Ethnicity, and Politics

Despite the prevalence of important ethnic and racial inequalities, several authors have pointed out the weak politicization of ethnic cleavages in Peruvian society, as well as the absence of important social movements based on ethnic identities (Degregori 1998; de la Cadena 2004; Yashar 2005; Paredes 2008; Thorp and Paredes 2010; Sulmont 2011). This is especially so when we compare Peru with other countries in the region such as Bolivia, Ecuador, Mexico, and Guatemala, where ethnic identities have played an important role in organizing collective action and political demands.

This does not mean that indigenous people in Peru have not played an important role in major processes of collective mobilization, or that they have not claimed fundamental demands in the political arena throughout Peruvian postcolonial history. Between 1958 and 1964, in particular, Peruvian society witnessed large mobilizations of rural communities that were struggling to regain their lands from the haciendas (Degregori 1998). Those struggles were one of the main reasons behind the Agrarian Reform that the military govern-ment undertook in 1969, which confiscated the haciendas and created a new structure of landownership based on agricultural cooperatives formed by peas-ants. However, those cooperatives remained under close control of state offi-cials. In the Andean regions populated mostly by indigenous peasants, peasant movements strongly contested this kind of economic organization; later, in the 1980s, a new wave of peasant mobilizations managed to restructure the owner-ship of the land, turning agricultural cooperatives into self-governed peasant communities (see, e.g., Rénique 2004).

In spite of those processes, as Carlos Iván Degregori (1998) has argued, the political mobilization of Peruvian indigenous communities has, since the sec-ond half of the twentieth century, been organized around demands for bet-ter integration into the national community on the basis of "class categories" (peasants) instead of "ethnic categories." With the exception of the indigenous communities in the Amazon region, which mobilized in 2009 to struggle for their land's rights, indigenous people in Peru have not taken part in politics as "indigenous people" but rather as "peasants" fighting for land or against the hacienda regime, or as "Peruvians" demanding access to social, civil, and politi-cal rights (mainly education, but also social services, public safety, and respect for their right to vote).

Social inequalities that affect indigenous people have been a central topic in Peruvian politics (the "Indian problem" of earlier times was reformulated in the twentieth century as "the problem of landownership") and one of the driving forces of political mobilization and conflict throughout a major part of Peru-vian contemporary history. However, until recent decades, these inequalities and conflicts have not been addressed in terms of ethnic or racial inequalities. Unlike in other Latin American cases, important Peruvian political mobiliza-tions and organizations have usually not been built on ethnic identities.

Summarizing some of the explanations that have been developed for this "Peruvian exception," Maritza Paredes identifies two types of hypothesis in the literature (Paredes 2008). A first explanation focuses on the institutional mechanisms that have limited indigenous people's autonomous organization in national or regional movements on an ethnic basis. The work of Deborah Yashar (2005) exemplifies this approach. Some of the factors that have limited the emergence of ethnic and political organizations are the state's authoritar-ian projects to reform the political and economic structures of the rural sector (such as the cooperatives created during the military government's agrarian reform in 1970); the influence of Marxist political parties in peasant organiza-tions that gave their struggle for land a class perspective rather than an ethnic one; and the effects of the internal armed conflict (1980–2000), which particularly targeted social leaders and political authorities with a peasant origin in rural areas, decapitating local leadership, destroying organizations, and preventing the creation of new ones.

The second type of explanation, found in the works of Marisol de la Cadena (2004) and Carlos Iván Degregori (1998), emphasizes the role of discrimination and "cultural racism" as factors that have prevented political organization and collective action of indigenous people based on ethnic identities. The social stigma of the "indigenous condition" makes this type of identity a burden rather than a useful resource to create collective identities that support some kind of ethnicized social movement. According to Martiza Paredes (2008), the confluence of institutional and political circumstances, as well as cultural structures, created an unfavorable context for indigenous organization on an ethnic basis. Those factors might explain why political mobilization and the recognition of indigenous people's social demands did not result in strong ethnic movements in Peru, unlike in other countries in the region with a significant indigenous population.

Another factor could be the effect of social modernization on ethnic identities. The social experience of immigration in urban centers and access to education, which expanded significantly in the last three decades of the twentieth century, created new channels of social mobility for families and individuals with indigenous backgrounds, and thereby constituted alternative strategies to collective mobilization. These social mobility processes have become means to achieve "ethnic and racial mobility" ("mesticization," "cholification," or the "mixing" of races and cultures) and have been accompanied by acculturation processes that could have "diluted" the centrality of indigenous background and culture as an element of collective identity in new urban contexts.

As mentioned before, although racism and racial discrimination persist in various areas of daily life in contemporary Peru, they operate in a context of fluid identities and porous ethnoracial boundaries, making it difficult to fix rigid ethnic and racial classifications in a modernizing society. In this context, racism and discrimination have become less legitimated social practices, which might open new spaces for younger generations to reinvent the "indigenous condition" and strip it of the stigma of "Indianness." Also, during the past decade, the consolidation of democracy, high rates of economic growth, and the agenda of international institutions have created a different social and political context and new incentives for ethnic mobilization in Peruvian society, where indigenous identities could become useful political and symbolic capital for political organization in the future.

## Conclusions

The empirical results of the PERLA survey in Peru are consistent with findings of several previous studies that show the persistence of socioeconomic inequalities between ethnic or racially categorized groups. Ethnoracial boundaries overlap with socioeconomic status, reproducing ethnic and racial hierarchies as well as social prejudices and stereotypes. An interesting finding of the Peruvian PERLA survey is that the intensity of socioeconomic inequalities across ethnic or racial groups defined by self-identification indicators is similar to the one we find across groups classified by their skin color. Socioeconomic status merges with both cultural and physical differences.

In this context, ethnoracial language is used to refer to socioeconomic positions and broader social processes. Overall, we can say that "Indianness" linked to certain physical, cultural, linguistic, occupational, and geographic characteristics remains synonymous with social stagnation and underdevelopment. Hence, possessing characteristics considered indigenous is a matter of discrimination and mistreatment. In Peru, there has been a sort of equation between racial labels and social positions, identifying, for example, "white" people as upper class. But the equation also works in the opposite direction: a social position can be identified with a racial label, so upward social mobility can become a way to "whiten" people. In this way, racial labels not only refer to phenotypic or cultural characteristics but can also be used to classify a person or a group into a socioeconomic cohort.

However, this fusion of racial labels and social positions is imperfect. Modernization has indeed triggered social mobility processes that translate into spatial mobility (from the countryside to the city), better education, and higher occupational status; they have also weakened ethnoracial boundaries, making them porous and fluid. "The Indians" can become "mestizos" as they acquire higher educational levels, adopt Spanish as their language, migrate to the city, or gain access to higher-skilled jobs, modifying their "ethnic group" in addition to their social status. Something similar seems to happen with skin color: as a person's socioeconomic status rises, other people may see his or her skin color as lighter.

The stigma given to characteristics considered indigenous implies that those who turn away from them suffer less discrimination. For this reason, social advancement in Peru is associated with "de-Indianization," which involves shedding any mark, including changing one's physical appearance, that betrays an "Indian" cultural background. The process of rural to urban migration (which has particular importance since the mid-twentieth century), the expansion of the educational system, and the influence of the media have produced a deep cultural change that has meant leaving behind or redefining lifestyles, customs, traditions, and languages considered indigenous, and adopting those considered acceptable and more prestigious. This process of cultural and geographic change is expressed through a racial language: a person stops being "indigenous" and becomes a "mestizo" or "cholo." Peruvian social sciences have adopted a racialist language, labeling these profound cultural, social, political, and economic changes as processes of "mestizaje" or "cholification."

This complex structure of social, ethnic, and racial differentiation prevents boundaries from being fixed over time. Ethnoracial classification processes (labeling, self-identification) have a "variable geometry" which is reflected in the different possible ways for estimating the size of ethnic and racial groups, depending on the type of indicator that is used. The practical operation of establishing differences is a contextual and relational process which depends on where it is done and who does it; it is therefore difficult to straightforwardly translate ethnic and racial categories into "social identities."

The relationship between socioeconomic inequalities and ethnoracial boundaries has experienced important changes during the twentieth century in Peru, creating a more fluid context for social mobility despite ethnic or racial origins. However, there is an important degree of overlap between race, ethnicity, and socioeconomic status, which contributes to the reproduction of both inequality and classification in hierarchies between groups that are defined ethnically and racially. Certain cultural attributes or physical characteristics are either resources or burdens for social mobility. Whites and mestizos, those with lighter skin color, achieve higher socioeconomic status than indigenous people, Afrodescendants, or people with darker skin. The relationships between inequality, class, ethnicity, and race are multidirectional.

The correlation between class, ethnicity, and race, along with the fluidity and porosity of ethnic racial boundaries, allows modernization processes in Peru to be read using two types of interpretative keys. One is class-based, focusing on the expansion of educational attainment levels, occupational status changes, and socioeconomic mobility in the context of a capitalist society. The second encompasses several "racialist" narratives describing the changes in ethnoracial boundaries in Peruvian society (mestizaje, cholification, race improvement, whitening), using categories and labels inherited from an imagined construction of modern Peru created throughout the nineteenth and early twentieth centuries, when they sought to legitimize the privileged position and the "civilizing" role of the creole elite and the white minority which existed within a majority population of indigenous people.

The racialist language that is still used to identify and interpret social differences has helped reproduce racist attitudes and practices of racial discrimination. However, these practices collide with other processes, namely the products of social modernization: democratization and the expansion of citizenship. People descended from indigenous families (i.e., immigrants coming from the rural settings to the cities, theirs sons, daughters, grandsons, and granddaughters) constitute the majority in the Peruvian population and have reached an important level of economic and political leverage in the society. Their demands for social integration, often formulated in a language of "civil rights," challenge those practices in the public sphere that try to reproduce inequalities as if they were "natural" or that try to set boundaries on the basis of racial or cultural attributes. The recognition of racism and the increasingly public debate on discrimination may be signs that racist practices persist, but they are also signs of racism's illegitimacy in a modernized society.

Another symptom of these processes is the acknowledgment, in both political and academic spheres, that, for groups defined ethnically or racially, socioeconomic inequality does not simply disappear with social and economic development. An example of this is the effort from research and academic institutes and from official state offices[31] to make these differences visible and to design specific policies to address them. Their success, however, remains to be seen.

Given the history of ethnic and racial labeling in Peru, today's situation is paradoxical. As mentioned before, ethnic and racial labels have been disappearing from the public sphere and official processes of the Peruvian state since Peruvian independence. However, in recent years, a global context promoting the use and vindication of ethnicity and race has emerged. This new discursive context, which emphasizes the importance of respecting ethnic and cultural differences and recognizing their value, points to the limits of cultural homogenization policies in achieving national consolidation. Consequently, new discourses of multiculturalism or intercultural dialogue have appeared, as well as new demands for state laws to reflect cultural differences in the allocation of rights and resources.

As mentioned before, Peruvian electoral law is contemplating establishing an "indigenous quota" for the list of applicants to certain public offices. Moreover, a law mandating prior consultation with indigenous people concerning investment projects that could affect their territories was approved in September 2011. The national parliament now has a Commission for Andean, Amazonian and Afro Peruvian People, Environment and Ecology, in charge of discussing legislation related to those matters. The executive branch of the government has a National Institute for the Development of Andean, Amazonian, and Afro Peruvian People, which had been integrated into the recently created (2010) Ministry of Culture; one of the functions of this ministry is to implement the government's policies related to multicultural affairs.

In this context, some social organizations have adopted an ethnic language to frame their social demands. Some of these organizations formally participated in the 2012 discussion about implementing the "previous consultation law," and have also been involved in the debate about including ethnic and racial dimensions within official statistics (Valdivia 2011). Considering the history of ethnic categories in Peru and the lack of clearly defined "ethnic frontiers," using this type of language generates debates even among the groups and movements that already use it. To the extent that incentives exist or are strengthened for politicizing ethnic identities and ethnic and racial boundaries, it is possible that Peruvian society will soon experience greater social demands expressed within an "ethnic" framework, as well as renewed debates about the attributes of "ethnic" or racial groups and the labels to be used to identify or recognize them as social and political actors.

## CHAPTER FIVE

# Mixed and Unequal

## *New Perspectives on Brazilian Ethnoracial Relations*

GRAZIELLA MORAES SILVA

MARCELO PAIXÃO

The idea of racial democracy, which is attributed to Gilberto Freyre (1933), has been traditionally used to portray Brazilian race relations as harmonic and tolerant.[1] Although Freyre did not deny the violence of Brazilian slavery and colonization, he argued that national racial divisions had been overcome by the miscegenation of African slaves, Portuguese colonizers, and the indigenous population.

Early twentieth-century Brazilian arts quickly embraced this image. In literature (e.g., Jorge Amado, Mario de Andrade), music styles (e.g., samba), food (e.g., feijoada), and the arts (e.g., Caribé, Portinari, Di Cavalcanti, Lasar Segall), miscegenation and mixture were celebrated as the national essence. Even in sports, miscegenation and African stock were invoked to explain the success of Brazilian soccer (Rodrigues 1964). In short, during the twentieth century, racial mixture came to be seen as the basis of Brazilian national character and was widely called the tale of the three races. This portrait of Brazil as a racial paradise was further enhanced by Brazil's contrast with pre–civil rights United States. This contrast, which was implicit in Freyre's works, was also supported by studies comparing Brazilian and North American slavery and racial inequalities (e.g., Degler 1971; Tannenbaum 1992 [1946]).

As early as 1950, however, various studies showed that the picture of Brazilian race relations was not so bright. These studies revealed that racial inequalities persisted even in the most developed regions of the country, like São Paulo (Fernandes 1969). They also provided evidence that blacks' and whites' chances of mobility were unequal (e.g., Nogueira and Cavalcanti 1998) and that discrimination against blacks persisted even after upward mobility (e.g., Costa Pinto 1995 [1952]).

In the 1960s and 1970s, the growing availability of statistical data as well as the rising sophistication of statistical methods allowed social scientists to show not only that racial discrimination was persistent in Brazil but also that it affected browns (*pardos*, as those of mixed racial background were described in official statistics) and blacks (*pretos*) almost equally (Hasenbalg 1979; Silva 1978).[2] In other words, there was little evidence that miscegenation was the solution for racial inequality or that mixing was, in Degler's (1971) famous phrase, "an escape hatch." Nevertheless, the idea of Brazil as a country without racial problems was still strong in the national imagination.

Since political democratization in the 1980s, racial inequalities have become much more visible in Brazilian public and policy debates. The black middle class, even if still small, has grown and, largely, adopted a more political racial identification as "negro" (Silva and Reis 2011). A black consumer market has emerged, and black aesthetics have become much more visible in the media (Fry 2005). Noting such changes, Brazilian television networks have also made an effort to portray blacks in a different, more positive light. While previously blacks would appear only as slaves in historical narratives or as maids in modern soap operas (Araujo 2000), today blacks appear as main characters and upper middle-class characters in Brazilian television and cinema. Even if they are still underrepresented in the media, a new and more positive image of blackness has gained currency in the country. Yet studies about the black middle class confirm the persistence of racial discrimination, which cannot be overcome by social mobility (Figueiredo 2002; Silva and Reis 2011).

Joaquim Barbosa, who became the first black member of the Brazilian Supreme Court in 2003, is probably the best-known face of this new black middle class. In 2012 Barbosa was responsible for writing the legal decision in one of the most important corruption cases in Brazilian history, the so-called Mensalão.[3] His decision to convict important government leaders was televised nationwide, making him one of the most popular figures in the Brazilian political scene. For the first time, a black political figure was seriously considered as a potential presidential candidate, although Barbosa denied having political ambitions. In 2013 he became the president of the Supreme Court and *Time* magazine (2013) lauded him as one of the one hundred most influential people in the world. Incidentally, Barbosa has long denounced Brazil's racial discrimination.[4]

But the most conspicuous change in Brazilian race relations is the growing implementation of affirmative action policies. Due largely to strong black mobilization (Paschel 2011), some public universities have implemented race-targeted affirmative action policies, in the form of racial and social quotas, since the early 2000s.[5] Quotas became mandatory in all federal universities, which tend to be the most prestigious and selective in the country, after the Supreme Court declared them legal in 2012 and the legislature passed the law of quotas in 2013.[6]

Today, survey results show that most Brazilians recognize the existence of racial prejudice and discrimination against blacks (Datafolha 1995; 2008). The availability of data on racial attitudes and other aspects of race relations has contributed significantly to this growing awareness. Unlike nearly all the other countries of the region, racial data have been collected in Brazilian censuses since the late nineteenth century,[7] allowing academic research to thoroughly document the persistence of racial inequality for decades, as well as giving support to the demands of social movements. Largely for this reason, and in contrast to other Latin American countries, Brazil's race dynamics have received much academic scrutiny. While this chapter cannot offer a thorough review of this vast literature, which other scholars have already done (Telles 2004), we do make reference to contemporary works and research results that are tackling similar questions.

We note that the PERLA data make at least two broad contributions to this literature, in addition to presenting new data on race identification and perceptions about race relations in Brazil. First, PERLA enables us to compare Brazilian race relations to those of other Latin American countries. The Brazilian race literature has largely been built upon implicit and explicit comparisons to countries of Northern European origin like South Africa and especially the United States (Marx 1998; Moutinho 2004; Nobles 2000; Skidmore 1972; Winant 2001). Such comparisons usually present racial mixture as a unique national characteristic, as either a positive solution or an ideological tool to hide racial inequalities. In this chapter we argue that racial mixture and racial inequalities coexist as equally important facets of Brazilian race relations. Borrowing Lamont and Molnár's concepts (2002), we understand that the key puzzle of Brazilian race relations today is how persistent socioeconomic boundaries can coexist with weak symbolic boundaries among racial groups. PERLA enables us to tackle this puzzle from a different perspective by comparing Brazil to countries with a similar history of racial stratification and mixture (Telles and Sue 2009).

However, Brazil is different from other Latin American countries in that its racial inequalities have been largely acknowledged and evidenced in the past couple of decades; the implementation of affirmative action is proof. Also,

Brazilian racial categories have been largely understood as skin color categories rather than ethnic or cultural categories, which Sansone (2003a) argues makes Brazil distinct from other countries.

PERLA's second important contribution, with the support of the color palette, is an understanding of how racial identification and skin color categories overlap or diverge in the shaping of racial boundaries, racial mobilization, and racial inequalities in Brazil. In addition, as we discuss later, the color palette serves as an important tool for reducing the endogeneity between racial identification and racial outcomes.

In the first section of the chapter, we present an overview of the social history of race relations in Brazil. We discuss the role of race in the nation-building project, right after independence, and the emergence of the idea of "racial democracy" in the early twentieth century, as well as its demise in the second half of the twentieth century. Then, we provide a brief review of how official statistics have reflected ethnic and racial categorization and identification in Brazil since the first census in 1872. In the third section, we present the results of the PERLA survey, with an emphasis on the different practices of categorization and identification in contemporary Brazil, and an analysis of how these are related to social inequality and perceptions of discrimination.

## Brazilian History in Black, Brown, and White

### The Historical Origins of Brazilian Racial Inequality: Independence and Slavery

Two distinctive features of Brazilian history have shaped its race relations. First, Brazil, a Portuguese colony between 1500 and 1822, was the only South American colony that did not have an independence war and the only country that remained united after independence. Second, Brazil was the largest importer of African slaves in the Americas. Behrendt (1999) estimates that between 1519 and 1867, 11,569 million Africans were brought to the Americas, with approximately one-third going to Brazil. Andrews (2004) calculated that 67 percent of the Brazilian population was of African descent by 1800 and maintained that blacks had become part of every sphere of Brazilian social life by the early nineteenth century, though most African-origin peoples (nearly two-thirds) were slaves. From plantations to small business and technical service, nearly all manual and service work was performed by African slaves or their descendants.

Because most Latin American countries abolished slavery by the mid-1800s, shortly after their independence wars, Brazil's absence of wars has been a prevalent explanation for the continuation of slavery until the end of the nineteenth century (e.g., Andrews 2004). Despite growing challenges from abolitionist movements and numerous slave revolts, the slave trade actually intensified through the first half of the nineteenth century until it was finally prohibited in 1850.[8] Slavery, however, lasted for nearly half a century more: Brazil was the last country in the region to abolish it, in 1888.[9]

By the time of abolition, a considerable part of the elite no longer considered slavery economically viable. Many slave owners had spontaneously freed their slaves, and sectors of the rural elite supported abolition (Reis and Reis 1998).[10] In fact, a considerable part of the black and mixed population was already free at the time of abolition (Skidmore 1972).[11]

The early literature comparing slavery in Brazil to other countries has commonly identified the high rates of manumission and close personal relationships between masters and slaves as characteristic of Brazilian slavery (Freyre 1933; Tannenbaum 1992 [1946]). If such characteristics were invoked to praise Brazilians' race relations, the very low survival rates of Brazilian slaves, especially when compared to the United States and even other Latin American countries, contradicts the allegedly beneficent character of Brazilian slavery (Boxer 1963).

## Scientific Racism and Whitening

The establishment of the first Brazilian republican period in 1889 followed the abolition of slavery.[12] While the First Republic (1889–1930) was dominated by liberal economic ideas, hardly any social policy was designed to integrate the newly freed slaves. Even though no blatantly segregationist laws were created, land restriction laws demanding formalized legal papers to prove landownership (Silva 1998), repression of popular cultural and social movements by the 1890 Penal Code (Moura 1988), and massive subsidized European immigration (Skidmore 1990, 25) were strongly influential in excluding blacks from opportunities for social mobility.

In academic and political circles, elites openly debated whitening through immigration as the solution for Brazilians' racial inferiority, just as scientific racism theories endorsed. As a result of these ideas, European immigration was encouraged in the late nineteenth and early twentieth century with the goal of "whitening" the population. At the Brazilian Eugenics Conference in the early 1930s, Roquete Pinto estimated that, by 2012, the racial composition of Brazil would be 80 percent white, 17 percent indigenous, and 3 percent mestizos, with no blacks at all (Schwarcz 1993).

Between 1884 and 1913, approximately 2.7 million white immigrants came to Brazil. Not only did these European immigrants receive subsidized ship passages and other inducements such as land grants, but they also took most of the recently opened industrial jobs in the new economic center of the country, São Paulo: by 1915 the industrial labor force was 85 percent immigrant (Foot-Hardmann and Leonardi 1988). Andrews (2004) and Fernandes (1965) estimated that by 1920 the immigrant population in São Paulo was substantially larger than that of Afrodescendants. In contrast, blacks and browns were (and still are) largely concentrated in the North and Northeast, the poorest regions of the country and, in this period, mostly rural areas.

## Nation Building through Racial Mixture: The Rise of Racial Democracy

During the late 1920s and early 1930s, Brazil experienced political turmoil and important social transformations. Through a bloodless coup d'état, Getulio Vargas, a politician from the South, took power in 1930 and in 1934 was elected and passed a new Constitution, inaugurating what is known as the Brazilian Second Republic. To avoid stepping out of power because of his disagreement with the old regional elites from São Paulo and Minas Gerais, he staged another coup, and inaugurated what is known as the New State (Estado Novo). He remained in power until 1945. Still today, nearly sixty years after his death, Getulio is one of the most popular politicians in Brazil. Getulio's strong popularity (he was known as the father of the poor) was based on his support for inclusive social rights (labor rights, especially), even at the expense of civil rights and political rights. Vargas also had a strong nationalistic ideology, which presented Brazil as the country of the future.

Economically, the 1930 Revolution was related to the decline of the old agrarian elites, who were replaced by new elites, mostly from the industrial and financial sectors. Politically, it meant a state that defined itself as the manager of an industrialization and urbanization process, supporting protectionist policies like import-substitution-industrialization (ISI), which were also adopted in other Latin American countries. Socially, the new government proposed, on a limited basis, new legislation that recognized the need for social policies to integrate the lower classes into the new urban society (*a questão social*). This integration, however, was conducted through top-down models that guaranteed social rights to a minority of workers in the formal and urban sector, mostly industrial and government jobs, while at the same time restricting political and civil rights (Santos 1979). The clearest illustration of these policies is found in the Work Laws of 1943 (Consolidação das Leis do Trabalho, CLT), which instituted centralized models of state-controlled unions.

Understanding the consequences of Vargas's economic and social policies for Brazil's black and brown population is not simple (e.g., Fischer 2008).[13] A farmer from the south of Brazil, Vargas was intellectually influenced by positivist philosophy. At least until the beginning of 1940s, he supported European authoritarian ideologies, such as Mussolini's fascism. In this ideological vein, he maintained immigration restrictions against blacks and Asians and implemented new ones to guarantee and develop "the ethnic composition of the population and the most convenient characteristics of European descent" (Skidmore 1976).

At the same time, as part of his authoritarian project to modernize the country, Vargas strengthened the national labor force's participation in the modern industries. The 1937 authoritarian constitution created quotas for hiring foreign employees (insisting that they should not be more than one-third of any Brazilian firm), which indirectly benefited urban Afro-Brazilians. Even though these changes did not affect the large number of blacks and browns living in rural areas and working in nonregulated occupations, like domestic workers, it benefited many low-income Brazilians, black, brown, and white. Many blacks and browns migrated from rural areas and the Northeast and started working in the industries and other public jobs like gas, electricity, and transportation. Furthermore, the minimum wage, which was adopted in 1940, had an indirect effect as a reference value for the informal labor market where blacks and browns were concentrated because most of the population was in the informal sector, not subjected to the same regulations.

Vargas's nation-building strategy also contributed to the acceptance of Afrodescendant cultural expression, since then considered an essential element of the national identity. For example, the 1940 National Penal Code suspended previous restrictions on popular cultural expressions, such as samba, capoeira, and others related to African traditions. Accepting black cultural expression as fundamentally Brazilian was part of a new understanding of racial mixture as the basis of national identification rather than as a problem to be solved. As discussed in other chapters, this acceptance of ethnoracial minority cultures also mirrored transformations in other countries of the region. In Brazil, this transformation was personified by the alternative narrative presented by Gilberto Freyre, an anthropologist trained at Columbia University, in his 1933 masterpiece *Casa Grande e Senzala* (*Masters and Slaves*).

Freyre presented Brazilian history as the "marriage" of three races—indigenous, Portuguese, and African. The three races were described by their cultural contributions to the unique Brazilian character, a perspective attributed to the influence of Franz Boas's cultural anthropology.[14] Instead of a country cursed by miscegenation, Freyre presented Brazil as a nation blessed by racial mixture, which was a source of tolerance, malleability, and affection. The Portuguese inheritance, in particular, was celebrated. Freyre described the Portuguese, themselves a mixed race, as the most adaptable of the European, capable of assimilating and mixing with native groups.[15] This emphasis on the Portuguese contribution partly explains the ambiguity in Freyre's writings: if on one hand, mixture is praised, on the other it was led and dominated by white Portuguese.

These social and cultural transformations in the 1930s and 1940s were followed by the emergence of a small black middle class, which demanded greater social integration. Yet the discourse of integration usually meant desiring to be part of the nation and sharing opportunities for mobility, while rejecting black traditions and African culture (Andrews 2004). The Black Brazilian Front (Frente Negra Brasileira, FNB), a political party created in the 1930s, expressed these demands. Although it was initially very supportive of the Vargas regime, it was outlawed in Vargas's Estado Novo (1937–45).

The brief return of democracy (1945–64) and the hegemony of development and modernization theories in the years after the Vargas dictatorship strengthened the belief in Brazil as a racial democracy by intensifying structural social mobility and nationalistic discourses about Brazil's economic potential. Brazil's image as a racial democracy was further solidified with comparisons to the segregationist policies and racial conflicts in the U.S. South and to South African apartheid laws during the 1940s and 1950s. Brazil's international reputation reached its highest point in the early 1950s, when UNESCO funded studies in different regions of Brazil to better understand this "racial paradise" (Maio 1999).

## From Racial Democracy to Affirmative Actions

Unfortunately, the results of the UNESCO studies were not so uplifting. Scholars such as Florestan Fernandes, Costa Pinto, and Oracy Nogueira verified the persistence of racial prejudice and inequalities in studies ranging from ethnographies to descriptive statistical analyses.[16] Yet, maybe because of the hegemonic Marxist paradigm in Brazil, the key conclusions of these studies can be summarized in two main points. First, they noted that racial discrimination had largely been replaced by class discrimination, which they believed was the main cause of black exclusion at that time (Fernandes 1965). Second, the authors concluded that discrimination and prejudice in Brazil were not about race, that is, based on ethnic or racial origin as in the United States, but rather about phenotype (Nogueira and Cavalcanti 1998). These findings contested the mainstream racial democracy approach by openly acknowledging Brazil's continuing racial inequalities and racial prejudice. Yet even they underestimated the role and strength of current discrimination, sometimes treating racism as a residual feature that would disappear as Brazilian society modernized or as class relations were transformed through social policies or socialist revolution.[17]

The military coup of 1964 ushered in an era of violent repression, silencing most social and democratic causes, including debates about racial inequalities. The hegemony of the racial democracy narrative proved very efficient in ensuring national unity and stability. On the one hand, it supported a strong national identity based on cultural symbols shared across racial groups. On the other hand, it made racial inequalities almost invisible in national narratives. The mainstream narrative was that Brazil should make "the cake grow before splitting it," a narrative similar to "the rising tides lifts all boats." Such a narrative denied any particularity to racial inequalities and placed the focus on economic growth as the solution to all social problems. Massive urbanization, industrialization, and even stronger economic growth during the Brazilian military dictatorship (1964–88), however, did not prove sufficient to reduce socioeconomic or racial inequalities.

By the end of the military dictatorship, Brazil was considered one of the most unequal countries in the world, with the highest recorded Gini coefficient of 0.633 in 1989 according to the World Bank. But even while the existence of socioeconomic inequalities was accepted, racial inequalities were perceived as residual. The mainstream ideology, shared by the government and popular opinion, was that Brazil did not have a racial problem.

During the 1970s, some black organizations began openly challenging the description of Brazil as a racial democracy, calling it a "myth." Some organizations were based on cultural membership and others were more political. The Movimento Negro Unificado (MNU, or Unified Black Movement) is probably the best-known and was able to mobilize a number of militants (Hanchard 1994).

Also during the 1970s and 1980s, some scholars began to revisit the history of Brazilian slavery, questioning Freyre's widespread arguments about the beneficial character of Portuguese colonization and slavery (e.g., Mattoso 1986). At the same time, statistical studies appeared that relied on the availability of official data on race; these data had been collected through most of the twentieth century, though not every decade, and when it was, it was gathered with distinct methodologies, as we discuss later. Carlos Hasenbalg and Nelson do Silva (1978) produced analyses that evidenced strong and persistent inequalities between whites and nonwhites in Brazil. These studies openly challenged theories that defended the greater possibilities of integration among pardos when compared to pretos, as laid out by Degler's (1971) mulatto escape-hatch theory. The fact that blacks and browns were similarly disadvantaged socioeconomically and that pardos were also of African descent (sometimes assumed but not always correctly) was used by some scholars and black activists as justification to combine these two groups under the label of nonwhites or *negros* (blacks); thus Brazil became known as the country with the largest black population outside Africa.[18]

Democratization during the 1980s encouraged new black organizations to emerge and consolidate. It also strengthened a repertoire of human rights demands and made possible the international funding of local social movements and nongovernmental organizations (NGOs) denouncing racial discrimination in police treatment, health access, media portrayals, and other structural realms. In particular, "celebrations" of one hundred years of abolition (1988) and five hundred years since the discovery of Brazil, or rather its colonization (2000), triggered public demonstrations that scorned such celebrations and gave visibility to black and indigenous causes (Lippi Oliveira 2000; Schwartz 1990).

A turning point in Brazilian race relations was the 2001 United Nations Conference against Racism and Discrimination in Durban, South Africa. Many Brazilian NGOs and social movements attended the Conference against Racism and Discrimination, where they openly denounced the persistence of racial discrimination and inequality in Brazil. Up to that point, the Brazilian government's approach to discrimination had been to deny or understate the issue. Now, for the first time, the Brazilian government acknowledged the country's continuing racial discrimination (Telles 2004).

The Brazilian state began opening itself up to black demands in the past two decades, in part because of domestic pressure (Paschel 2011) but also to preserve its international image (Htun 2004). The government created federal agencies to deal with racial inequalities (Fundação Palmares during the Cardoso administration, and SEPPIR during the Lula administration), passed laws including those granting land rights to communities that were historically lands of fugitive slaves (Quilombolas), and made the history of Africa mandatory in high school curricula (Federal Law Number 10.639).

But the most visible and controversial project of racial redress was the implementation of affirmative action initiatives in the form of racial quotas. Initially implemented in public offices, racial quotas became widespread in access to public universities, including many of the most prestigious in the country. Since they were enacted in the early 2000s, racial quotas have been extensively debated in the Brazilian mass media (e.g., Globo 2006a, 2006b; Kamel 2006; Silva 2007) and academia (Bailey and Peria 2010).[19] Initially, the academic debate focused on the reasons and justifications for implementing racially targeted policies (e.g., Bernardino and Galdino 2004; Hofbauer 2006; Medeiros 2004; Mulholland 2006; Peria 2004). A few authors called such policies the Americanization of Brazilian race relations (e.g., Bourdieu and Wacquant 1999) and charged that they created "dangerous divisions." Such criticisms are largely based on the perspective that race does not exist and that adopting a multicultural approach to address Brazilian racial inequalities is nonsense since people do not perceive themselves as belonging to different cultures. The issue should be about class, not race. Numerous authors responded to these criticisms, insisting on the historical authenticity of ongoing racial inequalities in Brazil and the need for racially targeted policies to address them (e.g., Hanchard 2003; Telles 2003). Other authors have argued that, despite such limits that a multicultural approach may have in Brazil, social policies based on racial identities can play an important role in overcoming racial inequalities (Guimarães 2006; Sansone 2003b).

Now, ten years after the first universities implemented affirmative action policies, the debate has moved to understanding the consequences of such policies. These studies have been divided roughly between those who try to understand how quotas have had an impact on students' self- identification and experiences (Cicalo 2012; Schwartzman and Silva 2012) and those who try to measure the impact of racial quotas on students' performance and graduation rates (e.g., Guimarães 2011; Mello and Amaral 2012; Paiva 2010). Results show that quota students are performing well, and sometimes even better than nonquota students. There is also some evidence of growing racial identification but little evidence of new racial tensions or divisions, even if socioeconomic divisions, which also have a racial element, are much more salient inside the university (Telles and Paixão 2013).

Finally, affirmative action policies have changed substantially in the past decade, from focusing mostly on race to targeting socioeconomic inequalities more broadly. A growing number of universities now have quotas for students from public schools (considered a good proxy for a low socioeconomic background) with the understanding that those quotas should reflect the racial diversity of the state in which the university is located.[20] Therefore, Brazilian affirmative action policies are increasingly understood as policies of socioeconomic inclusion rather than policies of recognition (Paschel 2011; Silva 2006). Although this move from race to class can be interpreted as a backlash against racially targeted policies, a 2012 Supreme Court decision declared racially targeted affirmative action legal, and a federal decree made affirmative action mandatory in all federal universities, using both race and public school quotas (Telles and Paixão 2013). All these changes make it clear that Brazil has officially abandoned its self-image as a racial democracy and adopted policies to redress the historical and current exclusion of blacks.

## Ethnicity and Race in Brazilian Official Statistics

In the debates preceding the implementation of affirmative action, policy makers, social scientists, and journalists relied on official statistics of race.[21] As mentioned earlier, the Brazilian state has classified its population by race during the twentieth century with much more consistency than other Latin American countries.

In the past, states counted their populations by race for political and social control, which was especially the case by colonial powers, in slave economies, in the United States during segregation, or South Africa during Apartheid. In the twentieth century, noncounting by race became progressive either in the name of national integration and color-blindness, as currently in France, Germany, and Spain, or with a discourse of hybridity, as was the case historically in Latin America. The growing use of counting by race and ethnicity in national censuses throughout the world, however, indicates that ethnoracial categorization has returned, but now as state tools for monitoring social inclusion (Morning 2009).[22] In the United States, enumeration by race occurred throughout all of its censuses, as it was clearly critical to its regimes of slavery and segregation, although it would continue after segregation and be defended as a tool for monitoring inclusion by the 1960s (Nobles 2000).

Most Latin American countries were conducting censuses by the end of the nineteenth century. According to Loveman (2013), there were three main reasons why Latin American countries started to take national censuses more seriously in the late nineteenth century (almost a century after the first North American census, in 1790). First, by collecting national statistics on population size and major characteristics, these recently independent countries aimed to present their population as united, as part of the same nation. Second, conducting a census was a way to evidence the existence of a modern bureaucracy, capable of following international rules. For example, according to Loveman, most Latin American censuses made a point of following the prescriptions of the First International Statistical Congress. In other words, conducting a census and having a National Statistical Office were presented as evidence of the "modernism" of newly born Latin American states. Finally, Latin American countries felt they had to challenge nineteenth-century European and U.S. theories of racial degeneration, which presented them as examples of how racial mixture inevitably leads to degeneracy (e.g., Gobineau 1853). Counting their population by race was key to such a goal.

Two opposite strategies demonstrate the centrality of racial classification during these first censuses. On one hand, a few countries chose to underplay the presence of African, Asians, or Indians (the so-called degenerated races) and did not include racial counts. Their census reports simply stated their numerical insignificance, which was used as justification for their exclusion from national statistical descriptions. Argentina, for example, deliberately did not present numbers of blacks and Indians, although more than 50 percent of the population was estimated to be black in 1800 (Andrews 2004). On the other hand, countries like Brazil chose to present their numbers but stressed the growing presence of white or European immigrants as evidence of their racial, and therefore civilizational, improvement.

Since its first census in 1872, Brazil counted by race. The categories used were very similar the ones used today: *preto* (black), *pardo* (brown), and *branco* (white).[23] The population of Brazil numbered nearly 10 million (9,930,478) in 1872, 15.2 percent of whom were slaves: 10.4 percent were classified as blacks and 4.8 percent as browns. The total percentage of whites was 38.1 percent, all of whom were free. The indigenous population, officially classified as *caboclos*, was already a tiny minority at 3.9 percent; all of the indigenous were free.[24] African slaves and their descendants (those classified as pretos and pardos) made up 58 percent of the population. Pardos (browns or, roughly, mixed-race persons) were the largest category at 38.3 percent of the total population, most of whom were free (87.4 percent). Blacks were 19.7 percent of the population, and within that group slightly more than half were slaves (52.9 percent) (Paixão et al. 2011).

Brazil instantiated the centrality of slavery and its overlap with race by the way it depicted its population in tables. According to Loveman (2009), no single table of all Brazilians residents was presented in the 1872 census report. The first table of the report accounted only for the free population, classified according to race (even if the questionnaire asked about color) as branca, parda, preta, and *cabocla de raça indigena* (mixed from indigenous race). Of course such a strategy presented an initial picture of Brazil as much whiter than the total reality, since more than half of the total black population (52.9 percent of

19.7 percent of all blacks) was enslaved. The slave population appeared only a few pages later, divided between brown and black, since whiteness and even indigenous background were perceived as irreconcilable with slavery.

In the 1890 census, Brazil had just become a republic (1889) and abolished slavery (1888). The 1890 census has been criticized for its technical flaws, yet the reduction of the total black population (from 19.7 to 14.6 percent) and the growth of the white population (from 38.1 to 44 percent) were celebrated by all sectors as desirable for progress: whites had become the largest racial group in Brazil.[25]

The 1900 census did not include questions about race or color. There was no census in 1910 and race or color questions were not included in 1920. Although the official justification for excluding race in 1920 was the difficulty, if not impossibility, of an accurate measure of race, a few scholars (e.g., Nobles 2000) attribute the exclusion to a deliberate strategy of hiding the real number of Afro-Brazilians. At this point it was clear that Brazilian immigration policies were not as successful in whitening the population as in neighboring countries like Argentina and Uruguay.

Nobles (2000) also argues that, despite the omission of the race question, race, color, and national origin occupied a central position in all General Department of Statistics (Departamento Geral de Estatística, DGE) publications. Immigration policies were discussed at length in the 1908 report. For the 1920 census, Oliveira Viana, one of the most important supporters of eugenics, wrote the introductory essay in which he presented "optimistic predictions" about the progressive whitening of the Brazilian population. Even though Viana was criticized for his language and "imported" ideas at the time, his overall positive perception about the whitening of the country, which was seen as a sign of progress, seemed to be widely shared by most of the Brazilian elite. In short, the presentation and interpretation of these early censuses were part of an elite project devoted to transforming the Brazilian racial profile.

If whitening was a shared national value among the elite, Brazilian intellectuals had to adapt scientific racism (or eugenics) to the Latin American demographic and economic reality. As Stepan (1991) argued, eugenics in the region had to put almost equal weight on race, political economy, and social policies. If, as in the case of Argentina, guaranteeing racial purity could be presented as a road to progress, that was not the case for most Latin American countries with majority nonwhite populations. In Brazil, racial mixture and social policies were perceived as more viable alternatives. In particular, understanding racial mixture through a positive light—as Gilberto Freyre did in Brazil—had a strong impact in reestablishing the national racial project.

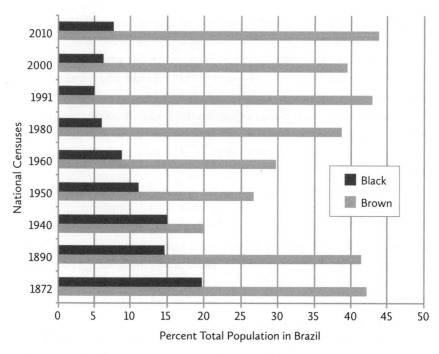

FIGURE 5.1 Size of Black and Brown Population in Brazilian National Censuses

While Brazil had no census in 1930, the introduction to the 1940 census, written by the sociologist and educator Fernando Azevedo, illustrated the strong impact of Freyre's interpretation. Diverging from Oliveira Viana's desire for whitening, Azevedo celebrated Brazil as a country of mixture (Azevedo 1944). Yet, perhaps ironically, census results supported the previous conclusion that the indigenous and blacks were disappearing and seemed to confirm whitening predictions. As Figure 5.1 shows, blacks and browns, who represented 66 percent of the population in 1890, had diminished to 34 percent in 1940 while whites went from 44 percent to 63.5 percent.

Nevertheless, the growing percentage of whites between 1890 and 1940 does not tell us the whole story for several reasons. First, it hides important regional differences. In the early twentieth century, blacks and browns were still a majority in the Central-West, North, and Northeast. Second, differences in censuses and census results have to be analyzed as indicators not only of demographic transformations in the population but also of changing racial identification. Several studies have already shown that in almost every country, demographic transformation (i.e., rates of mortality and birth) cannot account for racial differences (Perz et al. 2008).[26] An analysis focusing on boundary shifting and the expanded definition of whiteness, similar to Loveman and Muniz's (2007) analysis of Puerto Rico at the beginning of the twentieth century or to Carvalho et al. (2004) arguments about the importance of reclassification in the growth of pardos and decline of pretos in Brazil in the following decades (1950–80), would also apply here.

Finally, the 1940 census did not offer the option of identifying as pardo or mestizo, encouraging census takers to choose between white and black. Using Statistical Bureau (IBGE) records, Nobles (2000) argues that the decision to exclude a mixed category derived from the rejection of racist ideas, namely that mixed races would be inferior. When census agents could not classify respondents as white, black, or yellow (a new category created to incorporate the growing population of Asian immigrants), they added a line which was later recoded as pardo. Documents also show a new conception of race, including not only phenotype but also cultural characteristics. Therefore, "well-educated and well-mannered people of mixed race were also considered white, even if clearly brown in appearance" (Nobles 2000, 100).

The 1950 census allowed, for the first time, self-classification of racial identity. People were asked to identify their color and were given four options: *preto* (black), *pardo* (brown), *amarelo* (yellow), and *branco* (white). As Figure 5.1 shows, the percentage of pardos grew in comparison to the 1940 census, but the percentage of blacks shrank. The 1960 census, which relied on the same methodology and categories, showed a similar pattern.

The race question was excluded from the 1970 census. This exclusion has been described as a clear illustration of the 1964 military regime's adoption of the racial democracy. However, the debates around racial inequality that occurred in the IBGE during the 1970s challenge the view of IBGE as a passive institution. The reinclusion of the race question in the 1976 Annual National Household Survey (PNAD) and in the 1980 census (following the 1950 model) further shows that the census bureau was not so submissive to the military ideology (Powell 2011).[27]

The 1976 PNAD, a landmark in studies on Brazil's racial categories, included a special supplement with two questions about color. One was an open-ended question that asked respondents to identify their color, without providing any options to choose from. The other asked respondents to select their color on the basis of the traditional census options (branco, pardo, preto, or amarelo). The results are well known: 136 different color type responses to the open-ended question. This led to the general belief that racial categories were hollow in Brazil, because they were so diverse. Yet nearly 90 percent of respondents chose one of four categories, three of which were the traditional census categories (branco, pardo, or preto).[28] Such a high concentration in official categories supported retaining these categories. The race question has been presented in every Brazilian census since 1980 (i.e., 1991, 2000, and 2010) and every Annual National Household Survey questionnaire since 1976, and has used the same categories: preto, pardo, branco, and amarelo. Having historical data on race has allowed scholars to show the persistence of racial inequalities across time and to analyze the racial dimension of various issues covered in national household surveys such as intergenerational mobility and health.

Nevertheless, debates about racial categories have continued through the late twentieth century and into the early twenty-first century. In 1991 the race question was changed to "What is your race or color?" from "What is your color?," and a new option was included: indigenous.[29] In the 1990s, the black movement exerted a growing pressure to change the census racial categories to a dichotomous classification, excluding pardo and preto and including negro, a more politicized racial category that would encompass all Brazilians with African ancestry. In 1998 the president of the Brazilian Institute of Geography and Statistics, which carries out the census, himself a sociologist, conducted a study similar to the 1976 PNAD (but relying on the Pesquisa Mensal de Empregos, or Monthly Job Study) and came to similar conclusions as those of the 1979 PNAD (Schwartzman 1999). Supported by a special panel, he decided to retain the historical categories of black, brown, and white.

Media, government reports, and sociodemographic studies, however, increasingly grouped blacks and browns together and labeled them negros, influenced by the large number of studies that showed socioeconomic indicators for blacks and browns to be very similar and equally different from those for whites. Combining blacks and browns allowed the media to report that, according to 2010 census data, the percentage of negros in Brazil was higher than that of whites. Besides the race question,[30] the 2010 census also included a question about indigenous language.

The changes in racial demographics, in particular the percentage growth of blacks and browns shown in Figure 5.1, raises questions about the dynamics of racial classification. It also stresses the importance of racial statistics in Brazil, where these changes are much more visible than in other countries of the region. Although counting by race was initially closely related to eugenics ideologies and therefore to racial exclusion, it became a tool for inclusion and identity politics. Documenting racial inequalities through the years has given support to the implementation of racially targeted reform policies. In contrast to other Latin American countries, where not counting by race allowed race to be invisible, Brazil's racial statistics allowed scholars and policy makers to make

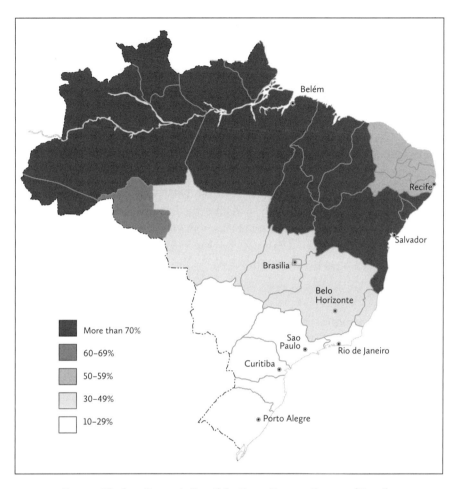

MAP 5.1 Percent Black or Brown in Brazil, by State. Source: Census of Brazil, 2010

race visible and to think about its consequences for social exclusion as well as for the need to target it for social inclusion.

Second, it is clear that transformations in the country's racial distribution are due not only to demographics but also to a transformation in the meaning of racial categories. With this awareness, the IBGE created a national survey in 2008, the Study on Ethnic and Race Characteristics of the Population (Pesquisa sobre as características etnico-raciais da população, PCERP) about Brazilians' perceptions of race.[31] In addition, studies and surveys focusing on race have been conducted in Brazil since the 1990s: Datafolha 1995, 2008; Fundação Perseu Abramo 2003; and Pesquisa Social Brasileira 2003. PERLA Brazil benefits from being able to dialogue with and contribute to these previous results.

Regionally, Map 5.1 uses 2010 Census data to show that the white population is concentrated in the Southeast and South, while nonwhites constitute the numerical majority in the Northeast and North. This racial concentration by region is largely a result of Brazilian development and the association of its labor force with race, In the twentieth century, Brazilian modernization involved large investments in industrialization, which attracted the large majority of mass European immigration (ca. 1880–1930), which Brazilian elites had encouraged to both whiten the country and provide industrial labor. In the centuries before that, enslaved Africans had been brought to work in the most economically dynamic places in the country, particularly in the large plantations of the Northeast. Although such a regional distribution by race remains in place today, the various economic cycles and crises since then have produced intensive internal migration that have attracted many nonwhites to the Southeast and some whites to the Northeast.

## The PERLA Survey

### Ethnic and Racial Identity

The Brazilian PERLA survey was distributed in August 2010 to a countrywide representative sample of one thousand people.[32] One of its main goals was to examine and analyze the impact of different categories and self-identification in Brazil. In this section we analyze and discuss the results of these measurements and their implications for the processes of categorization and ethnoracial self-identification in Brazilian society.

Racial categories have been among the most venerable and contentious topics in the Brazilian literature about race relations. One often hears that it is impossible to know who is black or white (*quem é negro e quem é branco*) in Brazil. The recent implementation of race-targeted public policies has brought this concern to the center of the political stage.

The PERLA survey included multiple ways to approach the ethnic or racial status of respondents, including self-identification in an open-ended format, self-identification when shown a list of ethnic categories, classification of skin color and hair texture by survey takers, and information on parents and ancestors. Figure 5.2 summarizes the results of these multiple indicators for Afro-descendants. It shows that, according to how one operationalizes blackness, the percentage of blacks in Brazil varied from 6 percent of interviewees who self-identified as negros to more than 59.4 percent of respondents who were classified by interviewers as black or brown.

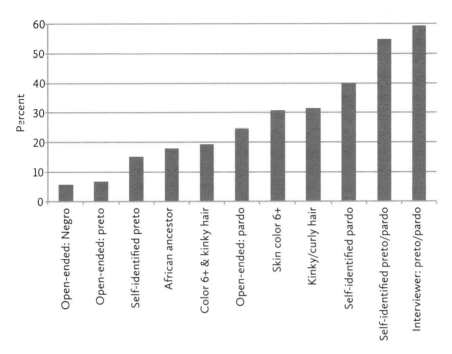

FIGURE 5.2  Percent Afrodescendant according to Various Criteria, Brazil

As noted previously, sociodemographic studies (Henriques 2001; Paixão and Carvano 2008) commonly refer to blacks (in Portuguese, *negro*) as the sum of those who identify as black (*preto*) and brown (*pardo*), because of these two groups' socioeconomic similarities. According to the 2010 census, negros represent 50.7 percent of the Brazilian population, and are thus the majority group. In the PERLA sample, they represented 54.9 percent.

Figure 5.2 also shows that, when respondents were allowed to openly identify by race, only a minority of the population self-identified as either preto or negro, the two possible translations of black. Although the negro category was never used in official census categorization, other surveys have shown that it is increasingly favored by black respondents. As a more politicized category, it is commonly used by black movement activists, although not exclusively. Nevertheless, other national surveys have already shown that, in an open-ended questionnaire format, the percentage of respondents choosing negro was always less than 10 percent; PERLA data similarly showed that 6 percent of respondents so identified. In PERLA's open-ended format, another 8 percent identified as preto, while only one out of the survey's one thousand interviewees chose to identify as Afro-Brazilian.[33] In contrast, 11 percent identified themselves as *moreno* (dark) and 25 percent as pardo.

Another possible way to define who is black in Brazil is to ask about African ancestry or family origin. These two measures, however, yielded very different results. While a bit more than 20 percent of respondents affirmed having African ancestors, more than 60 percent identified one parent as black or brown (data not shown). These results closely resemble those found by Bailey, Loveman, and Muniz. Relying on the 2003 PESB (Pesquisa Social Brasileira), the authors compared a range of classification strategies and found that the percentage of blacks ranged from 31.6 percent when interviewers were forced to choose between black and white to 59.3 percent when respondents were categorized according to the descent rule (i.e., having at least one black or brown parent).[34]

As explained in chapter 1, PERLA also provided data on how interviewers classified interviewees by the color of their skin, using a color palette with eleven shades (ranging from 1 = very light to 11 = very dark) and by their hair type (straight, curly, kinky, and other). As Figure 5.2 shows, 31 percent of the respondents were classified as negro because they were darker than 6 on the scale, 32 percent were so classified because of their hair type (kinky), and 19 percent because of both skin color (darker than 6) and hair (kinky).

In the rest of this section we discuss in detail what we see as PERLA's two main contributions regarding ethnoracial categorization: the overlap between self-classification and classification by others, with a special focus on the original phenotype-based classification; and the different meanings attributed to racial identification.

## Classification by Others versus Identification

One argument commonly presented by those who claim that racial boundaries in Brazil are too blurred to be defined in "black and white" is the difference between self-classification (or identification) and classification by others. While these debates are relevant to the measurement of racial inequalities, as we discuss later, they are also key to implementing racially targeted policies since administrators have used different measures to define who should benefit from the programs (e.g., Mulholland 2006).

PERLA data confirm previous findings that identification and categorization by others largely overlap (Telles and Lim 1998; Telles 2004; Datafolha 1995, 2008; Bailey et al. 2013); these results are in Table 5.1 with the percentage of overlap in bold. Over 80 percent of interviewees who identified as white, black, and brown were categorized the same way by interviewers, with no significant

TABLE 5.1 Interviewees' Racial Identification (Q. 11) versus Interviewers' Categorization (Q. 4) (%)

|  | Interviewers' Classification | | | | |
|  | Branco | Pardo | Preto | Other | Total |
|---|---|---|---|---|---|
| Self-identification | | | | | |
| Branco | **83.0** | 13.2 | 0.8 | 3.0 | 100.0 |
| Pardo | 6.5 | **82.6** | 8.8 | 2.0 | 100.0 |
| Preto | 1.3 | 9.2 | **88.1** | 1.3 | 100.0 |

Source: PERLA 2010

difference among racial groups.[35] For blacks and browns, those above the bold were lightened by interviewers. For whites and browns, those below the bold were darkened.[36]

Such a strong overlap is understandable because interviewers and interviewees used similar criteria to define racial categorization. In previous surveys, most interviewees explained their choice of racial identification/categorization by their skin color (e.g., Fundação Perseu Abramo 2003; PESB 2002; PCERP 2008). Other phenotypic traits, like the shape of the lips and nose, and hair type, were also commonly mentioned. According to the 2008 PCERP, 60.5 percent of interviewees defined their racial identity by phenotypic traits, followed at some distance by family origin (28.4 percent) and culture or tradition (6.5 percent).[37] These findings confirm the centrality of phenotype and skin color in the definition of racial categories in Brazil (Banton 2012).

In view of skin color's centrality, the use of a color palette allowed us to differentiate perceptions about skin color from perceptions about race (See chapter 1 for discussion of its use, including its innovations and limitations).

The boxplot graph in Figure 5.3 confirms the importance of skin color in racial classification by interviewers. In this graph, the box represents the middle 50 percent of cases and the ends of the whiskers represent where 95 percent of the cases fall. Again, there is much overlap between interviewers' use of the official IBGE racial categories and their perception of skin color according to the color palette. Most persons (70.3 percent) who were rated light (between 1 and 3 on the color palette) identified as white. Among those who identified as browns, the dispersion was greater, yet 52.4 percent of brown respondents were classified as having a medium skin tone (either 4 or 5 on the palette). The remaining 47.6 percent were ranked as dark (32.5 percent) twice as frequently

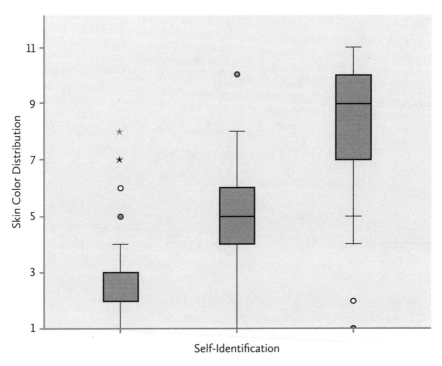

FIGURE 5.3 Boxplot Showing the Skin-Color Distribution of Persons Who Self-Identified as White, Brown, and Black, Brazil

as light (15.1 percent).[38] The consistency was even stronger among those who identified as black, more than 90 percent of whom were ranked as dark skinned (6 or more).[39] In short, Brazil showed great consistency between *census* racial categories, especially those of black and white, and the color classification of respondents based on the color palette. When viewed in comparison to other countries discussed in this book, this overlap is even more striking and should not be minimized.

Interviewers' classification of hair type also strongly overlapped with racial identification using IBGE categories, although not as strongly as with skin color ranking. Those who self- identified as white also tended to be classified as having straight hair (69.7 percent) and those who were identified as black tended to be classified as having kinky hair (77.3 percent). Once again, browns were more spread out: 33 percent were classified as having kinky hair, 38.6 percent as having curly hair, and 25.4 percent as having straight hair. In short, racial categories and phenotype traits (hair or skin color) also overlapped in Brazil, although less so among browns (data not shown for hair and census self-classification).

## Different Dimensions of Racial Identification

The low rates of open-ended self-identification as negro and the strong overlap between racial identification or categorization and skin color have been interpreted very differently in the literature about Brazilian race relations. On one extreme, it has been understood as evidence of lack of black consciousness or even a desire for whitening. More optimistic (or naïve) interpreters have seen it as evidence of blurred racial boundaries, or the celebration of racial mixture. Yet, as Guimarães (2012) argued, it would be misleading to believe that the Brazilian racial classification and identification system is reduced to skin color.

PERLA allows us to think about this issue in a more sophisticated way, taking into account different meanings and dimensions of racial identification (Ashmore et al. 2004). In the survey, we asked questions about the attachment, importance, and centrality of racial identification as well as about the sense of interdependence among the respondent and other people from the same ethnoracial group.

Figure 5.4 shows that nearly all interviewees had pride in their racial identity (83.3 percent). Pride was slightly more frequent among browns (87.2 percent) and blacks (92.7 percent) than among whites (78.7 percent).[40] The majority of interviewees (66 percent) also agreed (or agreed completely) with the statement that belonging to their racial group determined many aspects of their lives, even if less emphatically. Those who identified as black tended to agree more often (75 percent), but the majority of whites and browns also agreed (63.2 percent and 64.4 percent, respectively).[41]

By racial group, interviewees were roughly divided regarding their perceptions of the interdependence of their lives with others in their racial group. Approximately half of whites (48.8 percent), browns (45.2 percent), and blacks (50 percent) agreed with the statement, "What happens to members of my racial group influences my own life."

Yet racial identification lost its strength when compared to national identification. When asked to choose between racial and national identification, only a small minority of white (3.3 percent), brown (6.2 percent) and black (10.5 percent) interviewees choose racial identification, with only a small (although statistically significant) reduction of national identification among those who identified as black.

This can be seen as illustrating the insights of the racial dominance literature regarding the interface between race and national identities. Sidanius and his coauthors (2001, 847–48) seemed to interpret similar results in the Dominican Republic as the false consciousness of their black respondents, who sup-

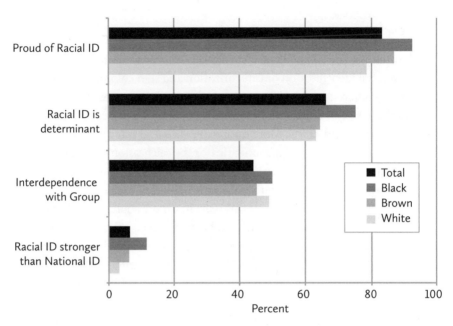

FIGURE 5.4 Multiple Dimensions of Racial Identity by Racial Self-Identification according to IBGE Racial Categories, Brazil

ported a nation that had historically excluded them through what they termed "inclusionary discrimination."[42] An alternative interpretation maintains that, although racial identification is central, it does not preclude acknowledging racial mixture as an important and positive feature of Brazilian society. PERLA results show that most interviewees across racial groups (more than 80 percent) believed Brazil to be a mixed country, in contrast to the less than 10 percent who believed the country to be mostly negro (8 percent) or Portuguese (7 percent). In addition, 78.8 percent agreed that racial mixture is a good thing for Brazil (data not shown). These results are confirmed by other national surveys and more qualitative studies that have pointed to the centrality of racial mixture in Brazil, which has successfully eroded cultural boundaries, even if not reducing racial inequalities (Silva and Reis 2012; Telles and Sue 2009).

Our results also confirm that, even if racial identification is perceived as important and racial inequality and discrimination are acknowledged in Brazil (as surveys such as PESB 2003, Datafolha 1995 and 2008, and data in this chapter show), these perceptions do not translate into racial differences or divisions, because blacks and whites do not see themselves as belonging to different collectivities. PERLA's questions about similarities and differences among racial groups show that, with the exception of the indigenous, Brazilians tended not

TABLE 5.2  Similarities and Differences among Racial Groups (%)

|  | Treatment of kids | Culture and Habits | Sexual Practices |
|---|---|---|---|
| Whites who perceive **negros** as different (or very different) in: | 16.9 | 24.9 | 9.9 |
| Browns who perceive **negros** as different (or very different) in: | 11.1 | 16.5 | 7.0 |
| Blacks who perceive **brancos** as different (or very different) in: | 16.6 | 20.3 | 12.9 |
| Browns who perceive **brancos** as different (or very different) in: | 14.9 | 14.3 | 9.1 |
| Whites, browns, and blacks who perceive **Indigenas** as different (or very different) in: | 60.0 | 80.0 | 50.0 |

Source: PERLA 2010

Note: Groups based on racial self-identification IBGE categories.

to identify strong cultural differences between racial groups. According to Table 5.2, of those who identified as white, only a numerical minority believed that negros were different or very different in the way they treat their children (16.9 percent), in their culture and habits (24.9 percent), and in their sexual practices (9.9 percent). Among those who identified as brown, perceptions of difference toward negros regarding this question were even lower, 11.1 percent, 16.5 percent, and 7 percent, respectively. Among those who identified as black, few believed that whites were different or very different in the treatment of their children (16.6 percent), in their culture and habits (20.3 percent), and in their sexual practices (12.6 percent). Likewise, among those who identified as brown, only a minority identified differences toward whites in the way they treat their children (14.9 percent), in culture (14.3 percent), and in sexual practices (9.1 percent).

In contrast, whites, blacks, and browns similarly believed indigenous people to be different or very different in the treatment of their children (60 percent), in their culture and habits (80 percent), and in their sexual practices (50 percent). These findings confirm Wade's (1997) contention that in Latin America, indigenous, unlike blacks, are the "cultural other," at least for the Brazilian case (Table 5.2).

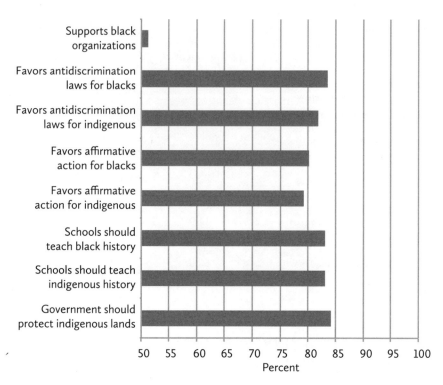

FIGURE 5.5 Support for Multiculturalism and Multicultural Policies, Brazil

Sansone (2003a) argued that this lack of cultural boundaries between blacks and whites reduced racial identification to individual and superficial choices, something similar to symbolic ethnicity, or what he calls "blackness without ethnicity." Because race does not create group solidarity, Sansone's interpretations might lead to the conclusion that, although people recognize the importance of race and are proud of their racial background, they may reject multicultural policies, racially targeted policies, and black mobilization.

However, as we show in Figure 5.5, most Brazilians support affirmative action, antidiscrimination laws, and the teaching of black and indigenous history. A large majority of respondents (more than 80 percent), without significant differences across racial groups, agreed with race-targeted policies to improve the situation of blacks.[43] Nearly all respondents (more than 90 percent) also agreed with the teaching of black and African history, the protection of land rights of traditional black communities (*quilombolas*), and more rigorous laws to punish those who discriminate. Other national surveys conducted since the implementation of affirmative action policies (e.g., Fundação Perseu Abramo 2003; PESB 2003; and Datafolha 2008) have found similar results. In fact, comparing the 1995 Datafolha survey results with the 2008 Datafolha results, Guimarães (2007) argued that support for racially targeted policies had increased in the past decade in Brazil.

Again using innovative questions, PERLA also asked respondents about their perceptions on black political mobilization. A small majority of interviewees (59.8 percent) agreed or agreed completely that black people should organize politically to fight for their rights, without significant difference among those who identified as white, brown, or black (56.5, 52.1, and 59 percent, respectively). Nevertheless, only 35 percent of interviewees had heard about any such organization (data not shown).[44] These results suggest that black mobilization, even if supported by a considerable majority, is still largely invisible in Brazil.

This widespread support for black mobilization and racially targeted policies shows that most Brazilians were not concerned about the possible "dangerous divisions" that Fry and Maggie (2007) have warned about and which he and other critics of racially targeted initiatives have seen as a threat (e.g., the various authors of articles in Fry et al. 2007 and Kamel 2006). This widespread popular support might be a result of the growing visibility of studies and public statistics that consistently demonstrate the persistence of racial inequality, as we argue in the next section.

## Racial Inequalities in Brazil

As discussed previously, evidence for racial inequalities in education, income, access to jobs, and social mobility have been gathered in Brazil since the 1950s' UNESCO studies. They were further verified in the pioneering works of Silva (1978) and Hasenbalg (1979) in the 1970s. Relying on official statistics and regression analysis, Hasenbalg and Silva showed that the effect of race was significant and independent of that of class, and that racial inequalities were stronger between whites and nonwhites than between blacks and browns.

Since then, racial inequalities have been documented in nearly all realms of social life (e.g., Paixão and Carvano 2008; Paixão et al. 2011). Although some of these inequalities may be attributed to changes in identification within and across generations (e.g., Schwartzman 2007), studies have shown that racial inequality in opportunities for social mobility are strong and persistent (e.g., Hasenbalg and Silva 1988). Although there is some evidence that educational inequality between whites and nonwhites has declined in the past twenty-five years (e.g., Marteleto 2012), several studies have shown that racial inequalities are even stronger on the top of the socioeconomic structure, which can contribute to further racial disparities (e.g., Campante et al. 2004; Osorio 2008; Santos 2005).

Nearly all of the recent studies on Brazilian racial inequalities—which are so numerous that reviewing them here is impossible—benefit from having official statistics on race and color. This is an important difference between Brazil and the other countries discussed in this book. In countries where there are no public statistics on race, PERLA makes an important contribution to exposing racial and ethnic inequalities. However, these inequalities are well known in Brazil. Moreover, Brazilian census and household surveys, with their large number of cases, are much more suitable than PERLA for analyzing persistent socioeconomic inequalities.

Yet exactly because they use official statistics, most of these studies relied on a single categorical measure of race, identification according to census categories.[45] In contrast, as we described, PERLA used different types of racial classification and thus adds significantly to the literature by comparing inequality across these different types of racial categorization. Such authors as Bailey et al. (2012) have undertaken recent and similar efforts.

The hypothesis that racial inequality in Brazil might be strongly related to the criteria used for racial classification and identification dates back to the 1950s, when Charles Wagley (1952) proposed the idea of "social race" in his studies of the Recôncavo da Bahia. The hypothesis of social race refers to the impact of socioeconomic status on race identification and categorization and proposes that color or race as measured in demographic surveys would be influenced by the socioeconomic status of each individual and would darken or lighten according to whether the individual's socioeconomic status is lower or higher, respectively. For example, a person would classify herself in lighter categories as she gains upward mobility. As a consequence, the strong correlation between race and class was due to the impact not only of race on socioeconomic outcomes but also of socioeconomic status on racial categorization. This interrelationship created a difficult problem of endogeneity in trying to isolate the causal impact of race in socioeconomic outcomes.

It has also led several authors to claim that, in comparison to the United States where race is based on hypodescent (or "one drop" rules), Brazilian racial boundaries would be more imprecise because they are highly influenced by socioeconomic status. In addition, Brazilians would be able to move across distinct racial categories when socially mobile. For example, in his mulatto escape-hatch hypothesis, Degler (1971) claimed that upwardly mobile mulattos would be able to whiten.

Another consequence of this "racial mobility" is that demographic research would inevitably overestimate color or racial inequalities, since lower-income whites would be seen as darker while higher-income blacks would be whitened (a trend exemplified by the popular expression "money whitens"). Indeed, Schwartzman (2007) found that more educated nonwhites were likely to marry whites, and more educated interracial couples were more likely to label their children white than less educated interracial couples, thus creating intergenerational whitening and confirming the "money whitens" hypothesis.

Nevertheless, comparing 1996 and 2006 PNAD data, Schwartzman also showed that the effects of whitening have declined, perhaps related to the recent shifts in Brazilian racial politics. Relying on the 1995 Datafolha census, Bailey and Telles (2006) showed that identifying as negro was significantly correlated with higher levels of education. In contrast, identifying as moreno was correlated with lower levels of education and with living in areas with a lower percentage of whites. Similarly, Marteleto (2012) attributed part of the reduction of educational inequality between browns and blacks between 1982 and 2007 to the darkening of more educated browns. These results may indicate an important change in contemporary Brazil: education, and therefore income, can now darken browns rather than whiten them.

In order to compare the impact of different types of racial categories in measuring racial inequalities, we recall that PERLA used four types of racial categorization: racial self-identification according to census categories; racial categorization by interviewer according to census categories; racial categorization by interviewer according to color palette scale; and a joint measure of categorization by interviewer according to the color palette and hair type. Because the first measure is the only one derived directly from interviewees, we contrast it to the other three types of interviewer classification. This first measure is also comparable to official statistics.[46] The comparisons relying on the color palette and on phenotype are the most important contributions, because of their originality as a measure of racial categorization and their possibility of reducing the Brazilian endogeneity of racial categorization and socioeconomic status. In these comparisons, the interviewee's average schooling was used as a proxy for socioeconomic status. We chose this indicator because of its lower potential for dispersion in relation to the average; other socioeconomic indicators such as earnings or occupation would be subject to either high variance or dispersion, which would be especially problematic given the sample size.[47]

Before comparing these different categorization types, we stress that educational inequalities between those classified as lighter and darker were significant in PERLA analyses regardless of the racial categories used (with one exception, described later, concerning occupational status and the color palette). Therefore what we propose here is not to discuss the fact of ethnoracial categorization and discrimination but to analyze its underestimation (or overestimation) when relying on official statistics.

## Racial Self-Identification and Classification by Others

In the literature, the contrast between racial self-identification and classification by interviewers has traditionally been fundamental to discussing the impact of whitening (Telles and Lim 1998; Valle e Silva 1994). Scholars have argued that if more educated blacks tended to whiten themselves, racial inequalities measured by heteroclassification would be smaller than the ones found in official statistics. Therefore, comparing categorization by interviewers and self-categorization would be a way to measure the tendency (or lack of) of higher-status blacks to whiten. The first studies had divergent results. Silva's (1994) findings for the city of São Paulo in 1986 found that interviewer's classification tended to reduce racial inequality, supporting the hypothesis that money whitens. However, Telles and Lim's (1998) nationally based study from 1995 data showed that racial inequalities in income were greater when interviewer classification was used.[48] More recent studies have tended to confirm Telles and Lim's findings (e.g., Bailey et al. 2012), indicating that official data, which is presumably based on self-identification, underestimate racial inequalities. Our comparison of respondents' average education level by self-identification and interviewer classification are shown in Figure 5.6 (Telles 2004).

The strong overlap between interviewee and interviewers classification explains why the apparent differences are small. Nevertheless, racial inequalities in average years of schooling were slightly stronger when PERLA used interviewer categorization according to census categories. Using interviewees' racial self-identification, the average years of education for whites were 7.9, for browns 6.8, and for blacks 6.9. Using interviewers' racial classification, whites had 7.8 average years of education, browns 6.8, and blacks 6.5. Therefore, whites' and browns' average years of study were fundamentally the same with the self-identification and interviewer categorization, and the difference between them remained statistically significant.[49] The difference between whites and blacks grew and remained statically significant.[50] With the interviewer classification, the difference between blacks and browns increased, although the difference was not statistically significant.

Recalling an earlier analysis, we found a strong correlation between the census categories and the ranking of skin color according to the color palette (see Figure 5.3 and its related discussion), although not as strong as interviewer

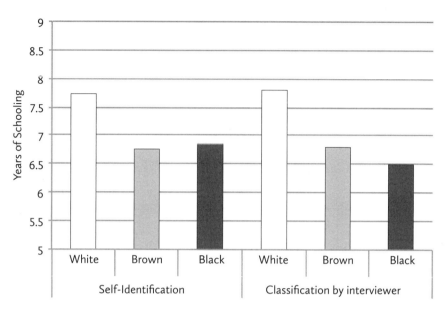

FIGURE 5.6 Mean Years of Schooling by Racial Self-Identification and Classification by Interviewer, Brazil

classification according to census categories (Table 5.1). Nevertheless, small differences might have a significant impact in the measurement of inequalities. Figure 5.7 shows a comparison of average years of education by racial self-identification and interviewer categorization according to the color palette. Once again, the color tones were combined into three groups: light (tones 1–3; 355 records), medium (tones 4–5; 337 records), and dark (tones 6–11; 308 records).

As we saw with interviewer categorization, those who self-identified as white and those who were categorized as lighter had similar levels of schooling. As in the previous set of findings there were clear differences between the lighter and darker groups. While the education status of browns and blacks, according to the census, was similarly lower (with a difference of nearly one year of education when compared to whites), respondents classified by the interviewer as medium and dark according to the palette had more striking differences between themselves in years of education. Those whose skin color was ranked medium had an average of 7.0 years of education, only 0.7 less than those who were ranked as light and higher than those who self-identified as browns. In contrast, those whose skin color was rated as dark had, on average, 6.3 years of education, or nearly 1.6 years less than those rated as light and

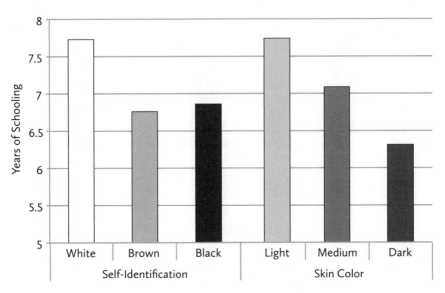

FIGURE 5.7 Mean Years of Schooling by Racial Self-Identification and Skin Color, Brazil

0.6 less than those who self-identified as black; only the differences between the light and dark groups were statistically significant.

We used the color palette to analyze another important measure of inequality, access to white-collar jobs. Figure 5.8 shows contrasting percentages of those in high-status nonmanual occupations by racial self-identification and interviewer categorization according to the three groupings of the palette colors.

Light-colored respondents had the highest percentage of high-status, nonmanual occupations (33.5 percent), similar to those who identified as white (33 percent). Those who self-identified as pardos were similar to those rated as medium color (22.5 and 2.3 percent, respectively). Likewise, those who identified as preto and those who were rated as dark were the least likely to be in high-status, nonmanual occupations (20 percent for both).

These results support Nogueira's (1998 [1954]) classic findings that discrimination in Brazil was more about phenotype than about racial background or ancestry. Nogueira, however, defined phenotype not only on skin color but also on facial features and hair texture. Usually, straight hair is more socially valued in Brazilian society, whereas curly and kinky hair tends to be stigmatized or disdained.

Because PERLA asked survey takers to classify respondents' hair type, we are able to analyze other phenotypic traits beyond skin color. PERLA interviewers

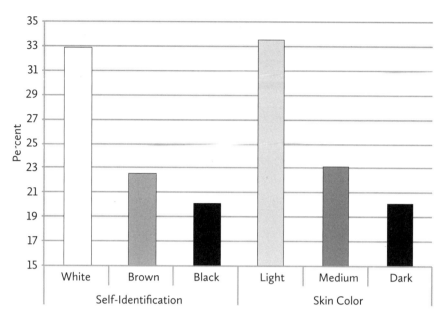

FIGURE 5.8 Percent in High-Status Nonmanual Occupations by Racial Self-Identification and Skin Color, Brazil

classified hair type using the following categories: straight (353 cases), curly (271 cases), and kinky (294 cases).[51] Looking at hair type alone (table not shown), we find a positive correlation between straighter hair and higher average years of education. Straight hair respondents had the highest level of educational attainment (7.6 years), those with curly hair occupied an intermediate position (7.2 years), and those with kinky hair presented the lowest levels of formal schooling (6.4 years).

More interestingly, we explored the correlation between a combined measure of phenotype, which joined palette-based skin color classification and hair type, and educational achievement. Combining the three skin color groups with the three hair types, we created six groups: light—straight hair (204 records); light—curly and kinky hair (123 records); medium—straight hair (118 records); medium—curly and kinky hair (183 records); dark—straight and curly hair (104) records); and dark—kinky hair (186 records). Figure 5.9 summarizes the results.

Respondents who were classified as lighter with straight hair had more years of education, on average, than those who were lighter without straight hair, who were better off than those ranked darker with straight hair, and so on, to those who were classified as dark with kinky hair. The difference in average

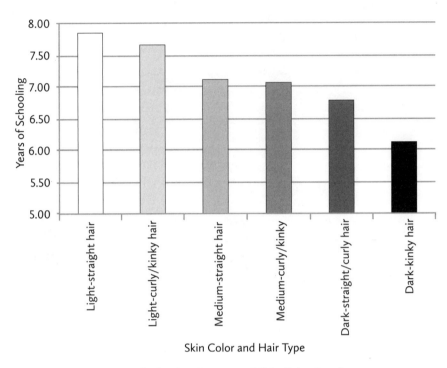

FIGURE 5.9 Mean Years of Schooling by Hair and Skin Color, Brazil

schooling years between those who were classified as light— straight hair and those classified as dark—kinky hair was nearly two years. Perhaps because of the small number of cases, only the difference between the two extremes was statistically significant.

Although these results have statistical limitations, they still offer important insights on previous theories about racial classification and inequality in Brazil. They suggest the hypothesis of a Brazilian pigmentocracy, in which darker individuals with kinky hair are on the bottom and lighter individuals with straight hair are on the top. Results in Figures 5.7, 5.8, and 5.9 also indicate that interviewers' categorization relying on the color palette was more strongly correlated to socioeconomic outcomes, especially average educational attainment, than interviewee's identification or interviewer's categorization using census racial categories. Therefore, racial or color inequality is probably underestimated in official statistics.

Two mechanisms, likely occurring simultaneously, might explain these findings. Low-socioeconomic-status browns might reject black categories and lighten themselves in search of status or simply because they are lighter than average in their social network. Ethnographic studies have shown low-income respondents' preference for mixed categories (e.g., Sheriff 2001). Also, high-socioeconomic-status browns might be darkening themselves as a result of the important transformation in Brazilian racial politics or, again, as a consequence of context, (i.e., they are darker than average in their social network). Black and brown professionals' stronger perception of discrimination gives further support to the latter hypothesis (Silva and Reis 2011). The increase in the relative size of the black and brown populations in the last census alongside the decline in racial inequality according to government statistics (Paixão and Carvano 2008) also suggests this latter mechanism.

Yet all these findings tell us little about the mechanisms that produce racial inequalities. Some scholars still question the role of race (and racial discrimination) as an independent variable in explaining racial inequalities, attributing current racial inequalities instead to history, educational inequalities, and broader socioeconomic exclusion (e.g., Fry 2005; Harris et al. 1993; Schwartzman 1999). In the next section, we discuss PERLA's contributions to the debate about perceptions of discrimination in Brazil.

## Racial Inequality without Racial Discrimination?

Most studies examining perceptions about race relations emphasize a key contradiction: in surveys, Brazil appears to be a racist country without racists (Datafolha 1995, 2008; Fundação-Perseu-Abramo 2003). Similarly, PERLA found that nearly all respondents believed there to be substantial racism in Brazil but did not see themselves as racist and did not express blatant racist attitudes. PERLA also confirmed that most respondents consistently affirmed their commitment to racial integration: 97.9 percent stated that they would not mind if their children went to a school in which the majority of students was black, 96.2 percent said that they would not mind if their children married a black person, 83.2 percent affirmed feeling comfortable with people from all races, and 81.4 percent said that they would like to have a black president (data not shown).[52]

Respondents, however, were more divided in acknowledging unequal treatment toward blacks. When asked if blacks in Brazil are treated better, similar to, or worse than whites, PERLA respondents were slightly more likely (considering a 4 point margin of error) to believe that blacks are treated worse than whites (54.0 percent) than to believe that they are treated equally (44.3 percent).[53] There were some statistically significant differences across racial identification groups: blacks (54.3 percent) tended to identify unequal treatment more often than whites (46.4 percent) and browns (46.4 percent).[54] Yet, these differences were not as large as in other contexts (such as the United States or South Africa) where stigmatized groups mostly acknowledge racial discrimination.

When the question was asked as an affirmation of equality of treatment, respondents were equally divided, although slightly more believed in racial equality: 44.7 percent agreed that all people in Brazil are treated equally regardless of their skin color or race (versus 32 percent who disagreed) and 44 percent of respondents agreed that blacks receive the treatment they deserve in Brazil (versus 31.9 percent who disagreed).[55] As with the other questions, there were no notable differences across groups by racial self-identification.[56]

In short, although respondents accepted the existence of racial inequality and even racial prejudice, they were more ambiguous about the existence of discrimination, here understood as inequality or unfairness in treatment—a new paradox suggesting a racially unequal country without racial discrimination. PERLA data allow us to further explore these Brazilian paradoxes by exploring dimensions previously neglected, such as different explanations for Brazilian racial inequality, perceptions of racial advantages and disadvantages, and the relationship between perception and experiences with discrimination, racial self-identification, and interviewers' skin color classification.

## The Sources of Racial Inequality

If respondents were ambiguous toward unequal treatment but acknowledged racial inequality, how would they explain the persistence of black poverty in Brazil? PERLA asked this question, giving respondents a few options that were not mutually exclusive: because blacks do not work hard enough, are not as intelligent, are treated unfairly, do not want to change their culture, have less schooling, and attend bad or inefficient schools. Figure 5.10 summarizes the results.

Once again, respondents were divided about unfair treatment, although they tended to recognize it more often than other causes of inequality. Nearly half of the respondents (40.3 percent) agreed (or agreed completely) that discrimination (defined as unfair treatment) is one of the causes of racial inequality in Brazil. A similar percentage (41.8 percent), however, disagreed (or disagreed completely) with such a statement. As Figure 5.10 shows, however, unfair treatment was by far the most cited and least rejected explanation for racial inequality. It was followed by attending bad schools (accepted by 23.3 percent, rejected by 60.4 percent), low levels of education (accepted by 19 percent, rejected by 65.7 percent), lack of desire to change their culture (accepted by 13.6

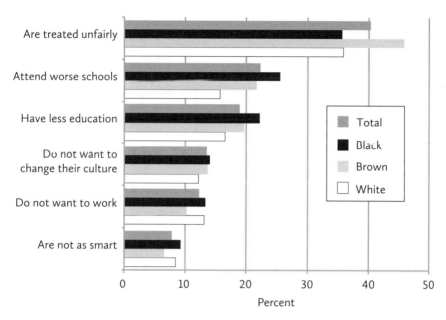

FIGURE 5.10 Reasons Given as to Why Blacks Are Poor, Brazil

percent, rejected by 67.7 percent), lack of work ethic (accepted by 12.3 percent, rejected by 80.2 percent), and lower intelligence (accepted by 7.9 percent, rejected by 85.3 percent). Figure 5.10 also shows that these perceptions did not vary much across those who identified as white, black, and brown, although browns identified unfair treatment slightly more often.[57] Overall, Brazilians across racial groups still seem divided in their acknowledgment of racial discrimination, even while rejecting other explanations for racial inequalities.

## Unveiling the Brazilian Racial Hierarchy

These results confirm Bailey's (2002; 2009a) findings regarding the equal propensity of blacks and whites in Brazil to endorse structural accounts of racial inequality—a finding especially striking in contrast to the United States, as discussed by the author. To further investigate this issue, the Brazilian survey included a series of questions, not included in the other sites, about the advantages and disadvantages of being white or black in Brazil. These questions allowed us to capture perceptions about the Brazilian racial hierarchy without using such loaded terms as "privilege," "injustice," and "discrimination." Table 5.3 summarizes our findings.

TABLE 5.3 Advantages and Disadvantages about Being White, Black, and Indigenous (Multiple Choice) (%)

| | Advantages in Being | | | Disadvantages in Being | | |
|---|---|---|---|---|---|---|
| | White | Black | Indigenous | White | Black | Indigenous |
| Jobs | **50.1** | 6.4 | 3.4 | 1.9 | **41.5** | **33.8** |
| Opportunities | **45.2** | 6.3 | 4.4 | 3.0 | **39.4** | **29.7** |
| Looks | 18.2 | 11.6 | 4.7 | 3.0 | 8.4 | 10.5 |
| Happiness/ well-being | 10.5 | 11.9 | 14.1 | 3.0 | 4.6 | 5.8 |
| Aptitude for music and sports | 7.8 | 20.6 | 4.9 | 3.2 | 4.8 | 6.2 |
| Favored in public policies | 14.0 | 5.8 | 10.2 | 2.6 | 11.0 | 13.9 |
| Other | 2.0 | 1.3 | 1.5 | 3.2 | 1.7 | 0.9 |
| None | 1.2 | 2.6 | 2.2 | 3.1 | 1.2 | 1.3 |
| Do not know/ want to answer | 29.1 | 48.7 | 62.7 | 77.8 | 38.3 | 47.8 |

Source: PERLA 2010

We note first in Table 5.3 that the benefits about being white related to structural advantages (jobs and opportunities), while for the black and indigenous they were largely based on stereotypes (better musicians, better in sports, happier). Disadvantages tended to show opposite responses: they were more structural (fewer jobs and opportunities) for blacks and indigenous, while more stereotypical for whites (worse musicians and worse in sports). Finally, we found no evidence of a backlash against affirmative action policies: only 5.8 percent of interviewees identified blacks as having any advantage in public policies, while 14 percent mentioned whites as being favored by public policies, and there were no significant differences among those who identified as white, brown, or black (Table 5.3).

In addition, and maybe more importantly, the questions had strikingly different rates of giving no response (which in general were very low throughout the PERLA questionnaire). More than 80 percent of respondents declined to identify any disadvantages related to being white in Brazil. In contrast, about 40 percent did not mention disadvantages to being black, and 50 percent identified no disadvantages to being indigenous. In identifying advantages, the findings were reversed: nearly 50 percent of respondents did not know or did not want to mention advantages to being black in Brazil, and 65 percent did not know or did not mention advantages to being indigenous. In contrast, less than 30 percent could not mention advantages to being white. In short, while some interviewees did not perceive unequal treatment, the advantages of whiteness and structural disadvantages of blackness seemed to be largely accepted.

## Experiences with Discrimination

Despite acknowledging the advantages and disadvantages about being black, white, or indigenous, 72.2 percent of interviewees believed that skin color did not affect their lives positively or negatively.[58] Although blacks identified color as a negative influence slightly more often than the other racial groups, there were no significant differences across them.

Nevertheless, 71.3 percent of respondents also said that their socioeconomic background had no influence in their lives. Therefore, rather than an affirmation of racial equality and fairness, these denials of the influence of class and race in one of the most unequal countries of the world might result from the strength of an ideology of individualism and self-reliance, already proven to be surprisingly powerful in some Latin American societies (Scalon 2004).

When asked directly about their experiences of discrimination, those who identified as black, brown, and white showed significant differences, as illustrated in the first rows of Table 5.3. Nearly half of those who identified as black (46 percent) reported having experienced or witnessed situations in which people were treated unfairly because of the color of their skin (even though 31.7 percent of them reported only a few instances).[59] In contrast, 28.7 percent of whites and 26.3 percent of browns said they had experienced or witnessed such a situation. For classification according to the color palette, those classified as light, who witnessed skin color discrimination less often (24.1 percent), contrast with those classified as medium and dark, who saw it more often (31.1 and 37.4 percent, respectively). These are statistically significant differences.

Interestingly, differences were also significant (although not as strong) among those who claimed to have experienced or witnessed situations in which people were treated unfairly because of their socioeconomic status, as shown in Table 5.4. While 42.8 percent of those identifying as black affirmed having witnessed discrimination due to socioeconomic status, 30.9 percent of browns and 29.2 percent of whites stated the same. Looking at classification according to the color palette, 26.0 percent of those judged to be light, 31.4

TABLE 5.4 Percent experienced or witnessed situations in which someone was discriminated due to the color of their skin or their socioeconomic status

| | Economic Situation | Skin Color |
|---|---|---|
| Witnessed by Racial Self-dentification | | |
| White | 29.2 | 28.7 |
| Brown | 30.9 | 26.3 |
| Black | 42.8 | 46.0 |
| Experienced by Racial Self-identification | | |
| White | 18.8 | 7.7 |
| Brown | 22.8 | 10.0 |
| Black | 30.7 | 36.9 |
| Witnessed by Color Palette | | |
| Light | 26.0 | 24.1 |
| Medium | 31.4 | 31.1 |
| Dark | 40.2 | 37.4 |
| Experienced by Color Palette | | |
| Light | 18.3 | 6.6 |
| Medium | 21.4 | 8.2 |
| Dark | 29.7 | 26.8 |

Source: PERLA 2010.

Note: Percentage of yes, at least a few times, by racial identification according to IBGE categories.

percent of those considered medium, and 40.2 percent of those considered dark had witnessed situations of socioeconomic discrimination. In spite of these differences across ethnoracial groups, it is impressive that only a third of respondents reported having ever experienced or witnessed situations of socioeconomic discrimination in such an unequal country as Brazil.

When asked directly about personal experiences of discrimination (bottom rows of Table 5.4), the differences between those who identified as black and those who were classified as dark was stronger in comparison to those who identified as brown and white. While 7.7 percent of whites and 10 percent of browns said they had experienced discrimination due to their skin color, 36.9

percent of blacks said the same.[60] In addition, respondents who identified as black mentioned skin color discrimination most frequently, while whites and browns acknowledged discrimination due to socioeconomic status more commonly.

We found the same pattern when we analyzed perception of discrimination by classification according to the color palette. About one-quarter (26.8 percent) of respondents rated as dark reported having experienced discrimination at least a few times; this percentage fell to 8.2 percent among those classified as medium and to 6.6 percent for the groups ranked lighter. Even if interviewers' classification of interviewee skin color does not explain everything, it certainly points to the importance of this variable.[61]

These results also indicate that respondents who self-identified as black saw discrimination more often than respondents whom interviewers rated as dark-skinned. The debate about the endogeneity between racial identification and measurement of perception of discrimination makes this particularly interesting (Pager and Shepherd 2008) and tends to confirm the importance of racial identification beyond skin color. In other words, the perception of racial discrimination might increase the likelihood that people identify as black rather than as brown. Because identification as brown (or mixed) can be perceived as downplaying the role of racial discrimination, as claimed by black movement activists, people who see themselves as experiencing discrimination might be more likely to identify as negro, as discussed more qualitatively in Silva and Leão (2012). Nevertheless, the differences between those who identified or were seen as lighter and the others were significant in both cases. Even if more racially conscious blacks acknowledge discrimination more often, the advantages of whiteness are still visible.

It is important to consider, however, that because the impact of skin color can be contextual and relative, it might have different effects in different social groups. Therefore, the high perception of discrimination among those identifying as black should not be interpreted as an overestimation. For example, people considered to have a medium shade of skin color may be considered dark in particular situations where others are overwhelmingly light-skinned or white; this may, in turn, affect their racial identification. In addition, as discussed, the profile of discrimination in Brazil has become highly elitist; those who are able to cross certain socioeconomic boundaries might experience discrimination more strongly. Studies about the Brazilian black middle class, for example, have shown that this group tends to report higher rates of discrimination and identify more often as negro and that those two processes are interconnected (Silva and Reis 2011). In short, although discrimination seems to vary by skin color, how your skin color is perceived (as light, medium, or dark) also may vary according to the context. In an upper-middle-class or elite environment, a medium-skinned person might be considered dark, while that same person in a working-class environment might be considered medium or even light.

Finally, qualitative data show that discrimination is much more common than acknowledged (Figueiredo 2002; Sheriff 2001). Therefore, the reports of discrimination presented here, based on self-identification and skin color classification, probably underestimate the frequency and impact of everyday discrimination, which is a key mechanism for the reproduction and persistence of Brazilian racial inequalities discussed earlier.

## Conclusions

With the PERLA survey results, we hope to have contributed to developing a few key issues in the Brazilian academic debate concerning the different dimensions and forms for defining blackness in Brazil, the persistence of racial inequalities across these definitions, and the perceived role of discrimination in explaining these inequalities. In analyzing PERLA data, we benefited from and were also challenged by the rapidly growing (quantitatively and qualitatively) academic literature about race in Brazil. It gave us strong parameters for supporting our findings but also challenged us to specify the originality of our findings, perhaps more so than in the other chapters of this book.

Broadly, we believe that the Brazilian PERLA data analyses provide original insights about the large consistencies, small inconsistencies, and multiple dimensions of racial categories and measurement in Brazil; the centrality of skin color in shaping racial identification and stratification; and the multiple relationships among racial categories, racial inequalities, and perceptions of racial unfairness and discrimination. In this conclusion, we review these findings.

Regarding racial categories, PERLA confirms the impact of different types of measures in defining who is black in Brazil. The data provided unique evidence that perception of skin color (and, to a lesser extent, phenotype traits) and racial categorization or identification largely overlap in Brazil—a finding especially striking in contrast to the other cases discussed in this book.

Yet, such a finding should not lead us to believe that racial categories in Brazil are simply about skin color: PERLA's novel results about the strength of the evaluation, attachment, and importance of racial identification confirm the relevance of Guimarães's (2012) warning against a simplified understanding of race in Brazil. If it is true that cultural boundaries among racial groups are not salient and that national identification appears as more important than racial identification, PERLA showed that most Brazilians legitimize black political organizations to fight for black rights as well as most policy initiatives targeting blacks. The support for black mobilization and racially targeted policies might result from the growing visibility of studies and public statistics that evidence the persistence of racial inequality, debunking the suggestion that Brazilians see the strengthening of black identification as a threat to national unity.

Following other recent studies (e.g., Bailey et al. 2012), PERLA also confirms that regardless of the type of racial category, racial inequality between white/lights and nonwhites/blacks/darks remains significant in Brazil. But one of the most original contributions of PERLA is the contrast between inequality measured by census categories and by phenotype. By using interviewer-based racial classification according to the color palette and hair type, the PERLA data suggest Brazilian racial or color inequalities more strongly than other studies, which have used census categories for capturing race.

Maybe more importantly, the color palette also allowed us to discuss the endogeneity between race and class categories in Brazil (the so-called social race hypothesis) from a new standpoint. Because interviewer categorization relying on census categories might also be biased by socioeconomic status, asking about skin color and phenotype is a strategy for reducing this endogenous effect and better perceiving the impact of race or color on socioeconomic status. The stronger racial inequalities found when relying on the color palette strengthen the arguments that race or color matter, regardless of socioeconomic status, and that the official categories probably underestimate the racial gap.

Despite the widespread evidence of racial inequalities and the general acknowledgment of the existence of racism and racial prejudice in Brazil, PERLA showed that Brazilian interviewees were ambiguous in their perception of racial discrimination and unfairness. Respondents were largely divided in their acknowledgment that race or skin color causes differential treatment in Brazil. Even though unfair treatment was the most cited cause of black poverty, few respondents were ready to accept that race was important in shaping people's (and their own) life chances.

Nevertheless, PERLA responses to a question about advantages and disadvantages of being black and white showed a broader acknowledgment of the burden of blackness. Most respondents were quick to point to structural advantages of whiteness and had a harder time discussing any disadvantage of whiteness. In contrast, the disadvantages of blackness were concentrated in structural features (work, networks) while the advantages were fewer and more stereotypical (better musicians, better in sports).

These findings gain new and more precise contours once we look more closely at perceptions about racial unfairness and discrimination and how they vary according to racial identification. Those who identified as preto, the darkest group in the official categories used systematically and by IBGE, revealed more pride in their racial identity and believed that race affected their lives in different ways, both positively and negatively. In comparison to those who identified as white and brown, blacks also affirmed their attachment to black identification, compared to national identification, even though the great majority still chose national over racial identification.

These differences are probably related to the stronger perception of racial discrimination within the group that identified as black/preto. These respondents more frequently recognized racial discrimination. They also perceived racial discrimination more frequently than class discrimination, which whites and browns perceived more often. If the use of racial self-identification makes it harder to assess a causal direction (is it from black identification to perception of discrimination, or vice versa?), categorizing persons as dark, according to interviewer assessments on the basis of the color palette, partly confirmed the centrality of race or color in shaping perceptions of discrimination and also the correlation of racial identification and acknowledgment of discrimination, beyond skin color. Therefore, those who identified as black, regardless of their skin color, are also the ones who identified racial discrimination more often. Nevertheless, racial discrimination was just as frequent among those who were rated as medium and dark according to the palette, evidencing once more the advantages of whiteness or light skin.

As Pager and Shepherd (2008) discussed, perceptions of discrimination are not a completely reliable measure of discrimination since they can underestimate or overestimate discrimination. Evidence from more qualitative studies matched with the consistent and persistence statistical evidence of racial inequalities points to the former: discrimination is probably much higher in Brazil than what respondents reported.

Statistical visibility is also probably the reason why policies targeting racial inequalities are much more developed in Brazil than in other countries of the region. More visibility of racial discrimination and a better understanding of how racial inequalities recur will help to develop mechanisms to fight them.

Our analysis of the Brazilian PERLA data helps us to understand better the puzzle of Brazil's strong socioeconomic and weak symbolic racial boundaries by opening the black box of racial identification and categorization and contrasting different measure of inequality, discrimination, and cultural distance.

In contrast to the other Latin American countries where racial mixture ideologies became synonymous with the widespread denial of racial identification, Brazilians' strong perception that "race matters" joined with their elastic perception of racial differences to create a particular racial mixture ideology, one in which "races" still exist.

## CHAPTER SIX

# A Comparative Analysis of Ethnicity, Race, and Color in Latin America Based on PERLA Findings

EDWARD TELLES

RENÉ D. FLORES

As the preceding chapters have shown, ethnicity and race have taken many paths throughout Latin America, exemplified here by the four important cases of Brazil, Colombia, Mexico, and Peru. For nearly two hundred years, these nation-states have defined themselves largely with respect to ethnicity and race and their dilemmas about how to include or exclude black, indigenous, and mixed race persons. Today, these countries tend to seek their inclusion as they have become democratic and multiculturalist, to different degrees. However, there has been little empirical data to understand the basic questions of Latin American multiculturalism such as, Who is black or indigenous and how much ethnoracial inequality is there? The near universalization of a census item on ethnoracial self-identification in Latin America is an important accomplishment of black and indigenous social movements and the new multiculturalism, as it has helped to raise the visibility of ethnoracial minorities and enables researchers to assess inequalities. However, these census questions may miss dimensions of race and ethnicity such as skin color or ethnoracial categorization by others, which may also structure inequalities.

Moreover, there are many other topics that censuses and other official sources do not cover, particularly those which gauge public opinion. What do national populations think of black and indigenous peoples or their movements? What about social policies to redress ethnoracial inequalities? How common are experiences of discrimination? We have sought to advance our understanding of these critical questions, as governments and civil society increasingly engage ethnoracial issues throughout Latin America.

After five years of work by the Project on Ethnicity and Race in Latin America (PERLA), which involved the design and implementation of representative surveys and the analysis of the results, we have provided an in-depth examination of ethnicity and race in four of the largest countries in Latin America. In the preceding chapters, we have provided analyses of patterns of ethnoracial identity, inequality, discrimination, and public opinion on ethnoracial issues in these countries, all set within their particular historical and social context. Although our research has been implicitly comparative in that we set out a common research design and have engaged a common set of research questions with similar surveys, analyses, and tables, these country chapters have been written as stand-alone investigations for each country.

In each chapter we have shown key historical commonalities and differences among the four countries in the types of systems of social hierarchy (e.g., slavery) that they established; in the nation-building discourses their elites crafted, including whitening, mestizaje, and multicultural narratives and policies; and in the types of black and indigenous social movements they have experienced. The comparative nature of this project sets it apart from similar studies, which often examine only one country or at most a subregion of Latin America. In the remainder of this final chapter, we directly compare and summarize some of the most important findings based on the PERLA survey data, which we show in tables using bivariate analysis. We list five general conclusions for this book, summarizing important differences and similarities across the four countries.

## Five Key Findings from the PERLA Surveys

*1. Race/ethnicity is multidimensional and can be measured in multiple ways including how ethnoracial questions are worded, which categories are used, and who answers the question. These have implications for population counts of ethnoracial groups and estimates of ethoracial inequality (Measurement).*

We found widely ranging estimates of the size of ethnoracial groups in Latin America, depending on how the ethnoracial data were captured. Such methods have major implications for census data collection, which is arguably the primary ethnoracial social policy in the four countries. Whereas national censuses commonly include only one or two questions to estimate the country's ethnoracial composition, the PERLA survey included multiple ethnoracial items. These items employ various questions and response categories. Moreover, they rely on self-identification or on interviewer classification. One could argue for the validity of all these approaches. Certainly, we would argue that the one or two questions included in official data could never fully capture the complex ways in which ethnicity and race operate in the region. Thus an important aim of our project is to show that race and ethnicity can be measured in several ways and that these different ways to capture ethnicity and race are consequential. Our findings thus provide important information for census bureaus and both official and private surveys for gathering such data.

Ethnoracial identities are highly ambiguous and sensitive to the nature of the survey question and can lead to a wide range in estimates of the size of the indigenous and Afrodescendant populations. PERLA data show that one of the reasons behind these changes in the estimated population sizes is that individuals often identify in an ethnic category distinct from the one others use to categorize them. Further, individuals might identify in different categories according to the wording of the question asked. Ironically, relying on individual self-identification, a common census practice, returns the smallest population estimates for indigenous people in Mexico and Peru. In contrast, questions about parents or ancestors result in the largest numbers of indigenous people identified as such in both countries. In the case of Afrodescendants, however, self-identification and external classification produced the largest population estimates in Colombia and Brazil. This appears to validate these countries' census questions and highlights the closer connection between physical features and identity for Afrodescendants, compared to indigenous people, who are more easily classified as mestizo with cultural assimilation.

While only a minority of Mexicans and Peruvians identifies as indigenous, close to half of the population in both countries acknowledges having indigenous ancestors. Nevertheless, despite their self-reported indigenous ancestry, most respondents in this region identify as mestizo, even when they possess indigenous cultural traits such as speaking an indigenous language. This highlights the capacity of the mestizo category to encompass individuals with multiple cultural and physical characteristics, a peculiarity that may be rooted in its historical origin as a unifying category in nineteenth-century nation-building efforts. We argue that the Mexican state, and to a lesser extent the Peruvian, was successful in promoting and implementing a single national ethnic identity of mestizo, resulting in relatively small black, white, and indigenous minorities. Not only does a large proportion of Mexicans identify as mestizo (65 percent), but many Mexicans (74 percent) were also classified externally as such by our survey takers. This also suggests that mestizo has become Mexico's de facto ethnicity, its unmarked national category. In all three Spanish-speaking countries, most persons identifying in any ethnoracial category call themselves mestizo. As we would expect, we observed a greater tendency for people of medium skin color to identify as mestizo, but many in both the lightest and darkest skin color categories also identify as mestizo. In addition, mestizo identification is strongly related to education: the most educated are more likely to identify with the elite-created nationalist category of mestizo, while self-identified whites tend to be poorer.

While a substantial part of what we know in the social sciences about race and ethnicity in Latin America comes from the Brazilian case, the comparative evidence presented in this book suggests that this country is far from the norm. The alleged ambiguity of racial categories in Brazil, sometimes measured as the level of agreement between identity and external categorization (Telles and Lim 1998), has generated substantial scholarly attention, as in the classic work by Marvin Harris (Harris 1964; 1970). However, this kind of ambiguity is actually substantially lower in Brazil relative to the rest of the examined countries. As the Brazilian chapter shows, in every racial category, more than 80 percent of people self-identified in the category where interviewers placed them. In contrast, consistency was lower in the other three countries. For example, only 37 percent of self-identified indigenous people were classified as such by interviewers in Mexico and Peru, and in Colombia the comparable figure was 51 percent.

This greater ambiguity in Mexico and Peru may be attributable to the fact that the dominant ethnic boundary in these countries is the especially porous boundary dividing indigenous from nonindigenous. On the other hand, in both Brazil and Colombia, Afrodescendants seem to be more easily identified by others, except perhaps for Colombian mulattos. This seems to confirm the common idea that while cultural differences are a crucial component of indigeneity, physical traits, which are more easily distinguishable in an interview context, are most important for defining who is "black" (Hooker 2005).

While we find relatively high levels of agreement in Brazil between self-identity and external categorization, we also document a high degree of ambiguity about who is Afrodescendant when we use other ethnoracial indicators such as information about ancestors, hair type, skin color, and an open-ended question on racial classification. Estimates of the Afrodescendant population in Brazil can range by a factor of ten times, ranging from only 5.6 percent of the population identifying as black (*preto*) in an open-ended question to 59.4 percent of the population, when interviewers classify respondents as black or brown (*pardo*). On the other hand, the variation for Colombia is smaller. While external categorization produces the largest number of Afrodescendants in

Brazil, self-identity actually trumps physical appearance in Colombia. For the Colombian case, we find that the government definition of blackness, used in the census questionnaire, produces the largest estimates of Afro-Colombians, 25 percent of the sample population.

The capacity of Afrodescendants to move between racial categories seems to be more limited than for the indigenous, perhaps because of physical constraints.[1] This is not to say that skin color does not affect the life chances of indigenous people or persons of indigenous ancestry. Quite the opposite: one of the most consistent findings across the four countries is that individuals with darker skin tones are of lower socioeconomic status than their lighter-skinned counterparts. In other words, there might be substantial ambiguity about who is indigenous (and, to a lesser extent, Afrodescendant), but there is little disagreement about who is dark-skinned. In this sense, indigenous people might be able to pass as mestizos, but their dark skin color could still be a liability in the labor market or in other areas (Flores and Telles 2012; Villarreal 2010), as our findings for inequality suggest.

Despite the importance of mestizaje, and the mixed-race category of mestizo, a small but significant number of citizens continue to identify primarily as white, including about 10 percent of Mexicans and 25 percent of Colombians (see Telles and Flores 2013 for an analysis of self-identification as white in seventeen countries). Interestingly, among the four countries in this study, only Brazil uses the category white in its census. Aside from Brazil, the census and official surveys in the other three countries distinguish only ethnoracial minorities and not whites or mestizos. In other words, though local governments no longer officially endorse the ethnoracial category of "white," it still survives among the population. In our view, this highlights the power of social processes to maintain ethnoracial identities even when they seemingly contradict the mestizaje ideologies of these countries. At the same time, whiteness in Latin America is conceived in different ways than in the United States. Unlike their U.S. counterparts, self-identified whites in our samples do not subscribe to notions of racial purity but often recognize nonwhite parents and ancestors.

While Brazil and Mexico may be paired up as the most fully developed mestizaje systems or "racial democracies," they in fact represent two very different racial systems. Unlike Brazilians, contemporary Mexicans seemed unfamiliar with the notion of race, according to our survey takers in Mexico. Indeed, fully 45 percent of them could not state their race in an open-ended format. In contrast, the social discourse of race and racial differences seems to be much more prevalent in Brazil, where the census has more consistently collected ethnoracial data and where social movements have been successful in using social science data on racial inequality to argue for racially based policies such as affirmative action (Telles 2004; Bailey 2008).

The identity dynamics outlined in the book shed light on the complexities surrounding the measurement of ethnic and racial inequality in Latin America. The Mexican state, through its Ministry of Public Education and other cultural channels, has emphasized the mestizo category as the national identity category, which has apparently resulted in people of higher socioeconomic status being more likely to identify as mestizo, as our data show, because they acquire this identity with increased education, even if they have lighter skin tones. Hence, a white identity is correlated with a lower socioeconomic profile in Mexico and Colombia. In Peru, the socioeconomic profiles of self-identified whites and mestizos are remarkably similar. Only in Brazil are people who self-identify as white more socially advantaged than self-identified nonwhites. This again highlights the uniqueness of Brazil, where its mestizaje discourse (racial democracy) did not directly promote a national hybrid category for its dominant population perhaps because it received a large number of European immigrants relatively recently. This is reflected in the census tradition of distinguishing whites from other groups. As a result, the light-skinned descendants of European settlers, some with nonwhite admixture, who have accumulated considerable resources, continue to identify as white. In contrast, as the Mexican chapter argues, the mestizaje ideology in Mexico not only sought to "Mexicanize" the indigenous population but also attempted to convert European descendants into mestizos.

*2. Estimates of inequality based on ethnoracial classification do not consistently support expectations of pigmentocracy (Categorical Pigmentocracy).*

Inequality in Latin America may be characterized as a pigmentocracy, but our data do not consistently support this finding based on ethnoracial categories. As we discussed in the introduction, we expected to find whites at the top of the social hierarchy with indigenous peoples and the descendants of African slaves at the bottom, with mixed-race persons in the middle. PERLA findings, which permit us to examine inequality using alternative ways of racially classifying the population, generally support this assertion but especially with skin color and only partially with ethnoracial self-identification, as Figure 6.1 and Table 6.1 reveal.

In Table 6.1 we compare ethnoracial inequality using the PERLA data. The rows provide information for leading indicators of education and occupation, divided by country. The columns present information for persons who identify themselves as white, as mestizo or pardo in the case of Brazil, or as the target

TABLE 6.1 Inequality by Country and Ethnoracial Group (%)

| | White | Mestizo/Pardo | Preto (BR)/Negro (CO)/ Indigenous (MX, PE) |
|---|---|---|---|
| **With secondary education** | | | |
| Brazil | 20 | 12 | 6 |
| Colombia | 12 | 21 | 11 |
| Mexico | 8 | 6 | 5 |
| Peru | 23 | 21 | 17 |
| **With primary education (excluding current students)** | | | |
| Brazil | 28 | 36 | 36 |
| Colombia | 27 | 26 | 29 |
| Mexico | 56 | 63 | 71 |
| Peru | 19 | 13 | 23 |
| **In white-collar occupations** | | | |
| Brazil | 31 | 25 | 22 |
| Colombia | 23 | 27 | 25 |
| Mexico | 20 | 30 | 27 |
| Peru | 45 | 34 | 33 |
| **Domestic worker, farmer, or peasant** | | | |
| Brazil | 14 | 18 | 21 |
| Colombia | 33 | 36 | 37 |
| Mexico | 40 | 28 | 45 |
| Peru | 8 | 8 | 12 |

Source: PERLA 2010

minority, which is preto in Brazil, negro in Colombia, and indigenous in Peru and Mexico.

The table reveals several interesting results. First of all, those in the target minority, shown in the third column, are almost always of lower status than whites and mestizos. In Colombia, Mexico, and Peru, however, mestizos were sometimes of higher status than whites. This is consistent with the findings by Telles and Flores (2013): more highly educated persons are most likely to

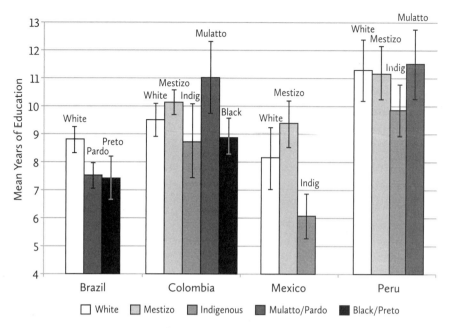

FIGURE 6.1 Mean Years of Education by Ethnoracial Self-Identification in Brazil, Colombia, Mexico, and Peru

choose mestizo identities in Mexico and Peru but white identities in Peru. The Mexican state's promotion of the national ideology of mestizaje through official textbooks implies that more educated people are more exposed to such narratives. This in turn induces a negative correlation between socioeconomic status and a white identity in Mexico, where mestizos are the best off of all groups in self-identified ethnoracial categories.

In agreement with previous studies, we found that pardos and pretos in Brazil are equally disadvantaged (Telles 2004). However, we also found that Afrodescendants in Colombia do not necessarily share the same fate. Colombian mulattos have on average two more years of formal education than self-identified whites. These findings are illustrated in Figure 6.1. The vertical bars at the top of the histograms show that even when there seems to be ethnoracial inequality in the direction of a pigmentocracy, the differences are not always statistically significant based on our samples. However, our data on skin color show a clear pigmentocracy suggesting that ethnoracial data based on self-identification is less reliable than external evaluation and especially color, when assessing ethnoracial inequality.

As Table 6.1 shows, self-identified indigenous people consistently had the lowest socioeconomic profile in Mexico, Peru, and Colombia, as measured by educational attainment and occupational status. The especially low socio-economic status of the indigenous reflects the structural mechanisms that continue to reproduce indigenous poverty, including discrimination, land dispossession, and state disinvestment. It also calls attention to the double-edged sword of cultural distinction. In other words, while contemporary Latin American states are especially willing to recognize special rights for indigenous people on the basis of their perceived cultural differences (Paschel 2010), such cultural differences in language, customs, and practices are often penalized in settings where most official institutions continue to operate in the Spanish language and view indigenous culture, while folkloric, as anachronistic and even backward. Indeed, in our analysis of public opinion, we found that many Latin Americans, including 40 percent of Mexicans, attribute indigenous poverty to the indigenous peoples' unwillingness to "change their culture or customs" (see Telles and Bailey 2013 for analysis of what conditions the populations of Latin American countries attribute to indigenous and black poverty).

*3. Skin color is a more consistent but overlooked dimension of inequality in Latin America (Continuous Pigmentocracy).*

Contrary to Table 6.1, which showed mestizos as being of higher status than whites in Mexico and Colombia, Table 6.2 clearly shows a pigmentocracy in all four countries when the population is sorted by actual skin color and Figure 6.2 vividly illustrates pigmentocracies in each of the four countries, when using skin color as the measure of race. Table 6.2 and Figure 6.2 show that the lightest-skinned persons tended to be the most advantaged. In all the PERLA countries, skin color was a more reliable predictor of racial inequality with the exception of Brazil, where identity and appearance tend to be more correlated. In all four countries, light-skinned people, regardless of their identity, had higher levels of education and higher occupational status than their darker counterparts. This confirms the growing evidence on the importance of physical appearance or external categorization rather than self-identification in measuring inequality (Flores and Telles 2012; Telles and Lim 1998; Villarreal 2010). Although it is fundamental to perceptions and understandings of race, color is often ignored and is assumed to be encapsulated in the traditional ethnoracial categories. However, the data from Table 6.2 and Figure 6.1 suggest that color differences may reveal more inequality than the categorical ethnoracial identities. This suggests that the ethnoracial categories used by the national censuses hide important color distinctions, which are popularly made and cognitively assessed but are often not named in ethnoracial categories.

In short, we find that inequality based on skin color is consistent in all coun-

TABLE 6.2  Inequality by Country and Color Group (%)

| | Light (1–3) | Medium (4–5) | Dark (6+) |
|---|---|---|---|
| **With university education (excluding students)** | | | |
| Brazil | 22 | 14 | 6 |
| Colombia | 20 | 15 | 13 |
| Mexico | 11 | 4 | 4 |
| Peru | 26 | 18 | 15 |
| **With primary education (excluding students)** | | | |
| Brazil | 29 | 31 | 39 |
| Colombia | 20 | 31 | 31 |
| Mexico | 55 | 66 | 73 |
| Peru | 14 | 17 | 22 |
| **In white-collar occupations** | | | |
| Brazil | 30 | 26 | 23 |
| Colombia | 28 | 23 | 26 |
| Mexico | 36 | 28 | 18 |
| Peru | 39 | 34 | 31 |
| **Domestic worker, farmer, or peasant** | | | |
| Brazil | 13 | 16 | 24 |
| Colombia | 29 | 42 | 35 |
| Mexico | 24 | 36 | 49 |
| Peru | 7 | 10 | 12 |

Source: PERLA 2010

tries. Dark-skinned people are consistently located in lower socioeconomic statuses than their light-skinned counterparts. Telles and Steele (2012) and Telles, Flores, and Urrea (forthcoming) show, using a larger group of countries, that the color-education correlation persists even after accounting for other factors including class origins. In contrast, when ethnoracial membership is assessed using self-identity, inequality estimates are less consistent and sometimes produce unexpected results. For example, self-identified mestizos are better off than self-identified whites in Mexico and Colombia (Telles and Flores 2013), and we also found that mulattos are better off than whites in Colombia. This confirms that externally assessed ethnoracial classification results

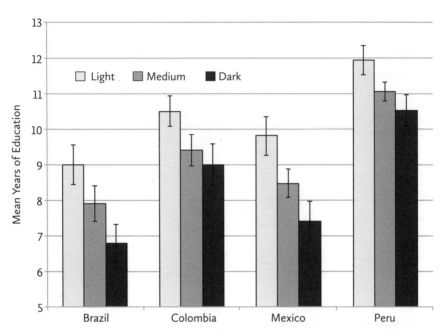

FIGURE 6.2 Mean Years of Education by Skin Color in Brazil, Colombia, Mexico, and Peru

in greater inequality than relying on self-identity, as Telles and Lim (1998) and Bailey, Loveman, and Muniz (2012) found for the case of Brazil. The fact that ethnic and racial inequality is more connected to external appearance than to self-identity implies that societal discrimination may be an important mechanism producing these socioeconomic gaps. At least for assessing inequality, we find that external classification produces greater estimates of inequality than self-identification (Telles, Flores, and Urrea forthcoming).

We found that Afrodescendants have higher socioeconomic status than the indigenous, but given that the indigenous are numerical minorities even among persons in the color categories in which they are concentrated, the general correlation between color and socioeconomic status is hardly affected. Persons of medium brown color who are likely to have a large amount of indigenous ancestry are not as poor as those with the darkest brown color, who are likely to have a large amount of African blood, with the exception that persons that self-identify as indigenous—those who tend to speak an indigenous language and reside in rural areas—are at the bottom of the social pyramid.

Until recently, economists and other social scientists tended to understand social inequalities as colorless or raceless in Latin America, often overlooking the apparent ethnoracial dimensions of these differences. Recent work, however, has revealed the extent to which race is imbued in societal inequality. Only in the past decade have most Latin American countries begun to collect national census data that permit an examination of inequalities by ethnicity and race. The incipient analysis of inequalities based on this new data has begun to challenge the dominant inequality paradigm based on class, even outside of Brazil. Our findings on inequality have underscored these new findings of ethnoracial inequality throughout Latin America.

*4. Ethnoracial discrimination is commonly experienced and witnessed in Latin America (Perceived Discrimination).*

Mestizaje and racial democracy ideologies commonly state that racial discrimination is not prevalent in Latin America. Because of extensive race mixing, these ideologies claim, racism and racial divisions have been extirpated from the region. However, our data show that many contemporary Latin Americans report both experiencing racial discrimination and seeing it happen to others. Although these reports are based on perceptions of discrimination rather than actual discrimination, which is hard to measure, they tell us a great deal about the popular recognition of discrimination, experienced personally or seen by others. Perceptions of racial discrimination have been reported for Brazil (Turra and Venturi 1995; Telles 2004; Bailey 2009b), but little is known for the other countries (see Ñopo et al. 2007 and Barbary and Urrea 2004 for exceptions). At the opposite end of the spectrum from Brazil is Mexico, where our finding of widely acknowledged discrimination seems surprising given that elites and the media continue to defend mestizaje and ignore issues of racial discrimination. While it seemed that color discrimination was often denied in Mexican academic circles, we found that many ordinary Mexicans report feeling discrimination based on their color (like language in the case of the indigenous), and many more report that they have seen color (or language) discrimination against others.

Large numbers of respondents in the four countries reported actual discrimination against themselves or having experiences of witnessing discrimination against others. Although reports of class discrimination tended to be the highest, reports of discrimination by color or by language or accent were not far behind. This suggests that, despite claims by some that class is the central stratifying variable in Latin America, many Latin Americans also experience racial discrimination. Even in Mexico, where the notion that racism is a foreign concept not practiced by Mexicans is especially powerful, color-based discrimination was widely reported. Thus, popular reports seem to contradict notions that are based on official ideologies as the chapter on Mexico suggests and as Sue (2013) showed in her ethnography of Veracruz, Mexico, where personal experiences of color-based discrimination often coexist with internalized ideas of nonracism (Sue 2013).

These findings suggest that even though mestizaje ideologies have been relatively successful in cementing the perception that "pure" races no longer exist since most people are "mixed," contemporary Latin Americans still perceive differential treatment based on their phenotype. This raises a caution for theorists in the United States who believe that interracial marriages or biological mestizaje by themselves will solve the race problem. The Latin American case shows that a general belief in widespread racial intermixing does not preclude ethnoracial discrimination (Telles and Sue 2009). Racial discrimination could shift to maltreatment on the basis of appearance and color, even in societies that emphasize common "mixed" descent. Hence, members of the same mixed family might have quite different experiences based on their own appearance even if they share the same racial ancestry (Telles 2004). We showed that large numbers of Latin Americans seem to recognize that.

Table 6.3 shows the percentages of respondents who reported discrimination and who witnessed discrimination, by both country and ethnoracial group. This table shows more consistent patterns of reported discrimination by race than the status inequalities shown in Table 6.1. Based on reports of discrimination against themselves, the data in the top three panels of Table 6.3 show that the target minority clearly reports greater discrimination than mestizos (or pardos in Brazil) and that mestizos report more discrimination than persons who identify as white. In the case of Brazil, for example (first row of data), pretos were more than three times as likely as pardos to report experiencing discrimination (34.2 vs. 9.8 percent).

The pattern by color is not surprising, but it is also true for language and class. The finding for language for Colombia shows that the target minority (negros) reports language or accent discrimination like that affecting the indigenous in Mexico and Peru. The difference between pretos and the other groups is slighter in Brazil, where linguistic differences by ethnoracial group are probably nonexistent except to the extent to which they are associated with regional and class distinctions. In terms of reporting discrimination against others, the bottom three panels show a similar pattern with a few exceptions, which are not that surprising since the actual discrimination was experienced by others.

Table 6.4 replicates Table 6.3 but with color distinctions. Again, the differences go in the expected direction, and the gap between the darkest and the medium group is sometimes considerably large. These results mirror the find-

TABLE 6.3  Reported Discrimination by Country and Ethnoracial Group (%)

| | White | Mestizo/ Pardo | Preto (BR)/Negro (CO)/ Indigenous (MX, PE) |
|---|---|---|---|
| **Reporting discrimination by color** | | | |
| Brazil | 6 | 10 | 34 |
| Colombia | 4 | 9 | 28 |
| Mexico | 9 | 14 | 20 |
| Peru | 16 | 21 | 31 |
| **Reporting discrimination by language or accent** | | | |
| Brazil | 11 | 13 | 16 |
| Colombia | 17 | 18 | 29 |
| Mexico | 13 | 19 | 25 |
| Peru | 18 | 20 | 30 |
| **Reporting discrimination by class** | | | |
| Brazil | 18 | 22 | 28 |
| Colombia | 25 | 27 | 31 |
| Mexico | 23 | 35 | 35 |
| Peru | 25 | 35 | 44 |
| **Witnessing discrimination by color** | | | |
| Brazil | 28 | 25 | 42 |
| Colombia | 58 | 59 | 74 |
| Mexico | 49 | 62 | 58 |
| Peru | 68 | 67 | 70 |
| **Witnessing discrimination by language or accent** | | | |
| Brazil | — | — | — |
| Colombia | — | — | — |
| Mexico | 41 | 57 | 55 |
| Peru | 48 | 57 | 68 |
| **Witnessing discrimination by class** | | | |
| Brazil | 28 | 30 | 39 |
| Colombia | 62 | 65 | 73 |
| Mexico | 56 | 74 | 67 |
| Peru | 74 | 73 | 76 |

Source: PERLA 2010

Note: Columns aggregate Agrees and Strongly Agrees.

ings for Table 6.3. The darkest group in Brazil reports experiencing nearly three times as much color discrimination as the medium group (top line of data in Table 6.4), though the color differences tend to be even greater than for those based on ethnoracial discrimination. Cross-nationally, these findings, as well as those in Table 6.3, reveal that discrimination in Peru tends to be especially great, although it may also be that Peruvians are especially sensitive to discrimination, though it is not clear why. Interestingly, color and language discrimination are reported by large proportions of the Mexican population, as in the other countries, despite the tendency by many elites to deny that it occurs.

*5. Most Latin Americans support ethnic and race-based social movements and public policies to promote black and indigenous people (Minority Support).*

With the region's turn to official multiculturalism, we know little about whether the general public actually supports the state-sponsored multicultural policies that have proliferated in the region. For example, how willing is the public to accept policies that seek to promote blacks and indigenous people and cultures such as bilingual education and affirmative action? Given the socialization of many Latin American adults, particularly in Brazil and Mexico, in the ideology of mestizaje, do these new ideas of multiculturalism resonate among the general population? What is the level of awareness and support of indigenous and black social movements? These questions are particularly important today as the region democratizes and when public opinion polling should thus be a key democratic input, as it captures the sentiments of the national population.

Table 6.5 shows that most Latin Americans support ethnoracial movements and multicultural policies that seek to advance the culture and socioeconomic status of ethnoracial minorities. In all countries, as Table 6.5 shows, more than 80 percent of respondents supported affirmative action policies for indigenous people and Afrodescendants in education. We found similar high percentages of people supporting the protection of indigenous lands and the teaching of indigenous and Afro history at schools. Interestingly, we found slightly higher support for policies targeting indigenous people rather than blacks in all countries except Brazil (where the level of support for both groups was similar). Perhaps, indigenous people are perceived as more deserving than their black counterparts, as Hooker (2005) suggests. This could also be related to the fact that Latin American governments have more often recognized the contribution of indigenous cultures to their nations while often ignoring those of Afrodescendants.

TABLE 6.4 Reported Discrimination by Country and Color Group (%)

| | Light (1-3) | Medium (4-5) | Dark (6+) |
|---|---|---|---|
| Reporting discrimination by color | | | |
| Brazil | 7 | 9 | 26 |
| Colombia | 4 | 9 | 24 |
| Mexico | 13 | 13 | 26 |
| Peru | 14 | 26 | 36 |
| Reporting discrimination by language or accent | | | |
| Brazil | 13 | 13 | 14 |
| Colombia | 15 | 19 | 27 |
| Mexico | 17 | 19 | 25 |
| Peru | 17 | 26 | 28 |
| Reporting discrimination by class | | | |
| Brazil | 18 | 21 | 29 |
| Colombia | 26 | 29 | 31 |
| Mexico | 33 | 31 | 40 |
| Peru | 30 | 40 | 46 |
| Witnessing discrimination by color | | | |
| Brazil | 22 | 31 | 35 |
| Colombia | 59 | 56 | 71 |
| Mexico | 66 | 56 | 55 |
| Peru | 65 | 68 | 73 |
| Witnessing discrimination by language or accent | | | |
| Brazil | | | |
| Colombia | | | |
| Mexico | 63 | 52 | 48 |
| Peru | 58 | 62 | 67 |
| Witnessing discrimination by class | | | |
| Brazil | 25 | 31 | 37 |
| Colombia | 64 | 62 | 73 |
| Mexico | 74 | 68 | 65 |
| Peru | 72 | 75 | 77 |

Source: PERLA 2010

Note: Columns aggregate Agrees and Strongly Agrees.

TABLE 6.5 Support for Ethnoracial Social Movements and Policies (%)

| | Brazil | Colombia | Mexico | Peru |
|---|---|---|---|---|
| Indigenous political organizations[a] | — | — | 61 | 73 |
| Black political organizations[a] | 51 | 91 | — | — |
| Affirmative action for indigenous | 79 | 89 | 92 | 86 |
| Affirmative action for blacks | 80 | 88 | 87 | 80 |
| Affirmative action for poor people | 82 | 90 | 94 | 87 |
| Antidiscrimination laws for indigenous | 82 | 94 | 89 | 87 |
| Antidiscrimination laws for blacks[a] | 84 | 94 | — | 84 |
| Laws to protect indigenous lands | 84 | 98 | 90 | 89 |
| Laws to protect black lands[a] | 81 | 97 | — | — |
| Teaching indigenous history in schools | 83 | 93 | 92 | 87 |
| Teaching black history in schools[a] | 83 | 94 | — | 82 |

Source: PERLA 2010.

Note: Columns aggregate Agrees and Strongly Agrees.

[a]This question was not included in the questionnaires of one or more countries.

Our findings may be surprising to some because of the assumption that, by insisting first and foremost on identification with the nation, discourses of racial democracy and mestizaje have fostered widespread opposition to such group-specific policies. Nevertheless, even in Mexico there is substantial support for indigenous movements and for policies that promote the indigenous.

Such high levels of support are rather striking, especially when compared to the opposition that similar programs provoke in other settings such as the United States. How can we explain this puzzle? Perhaps indigenous and black movements have been successful in mobilizing public opinion in their favor in recent years, especially given the near absence of Afrodescendant and indigenous peoples in the middle class, while in the United States such mobilization has lost its effect in the face of mounting anti-affirmative action forces. We believe that part of the answer may lie in the fact that race-based redistributive policies have been mostly symbolic in the region with the exception of Brazil. The bolder and more comprehensive affirmative action policies enacted by the Brazilian government have actually had substantial redistributive effects, resulting in increased white middle-class opposition to them (Cicalo 2012; Telles 2004). Still, though, we need to question the idea that mestizaje discourses are inherently opposed to the claims of distinct ethnoracial groups. Though such discourses have often essentialized and marginalized these groups and treated them as relics of the past, they have often recognized their contributions to national cultures. In doing so, they may have fostered some degree of acceptance and support for them.

At the same time, though most respondents support ethnoracial political movements, such support is lower relative to other multicultural policies indicating that some Latin Americans have mixed feelings about these movements. Ethnic-based political organizations receive substantially less support in Mexico and Brazil, the two countries with the longest history of indigenous and black political movements. In the case of Brazil, only 51.2 percent of Brazilians support black political organizations. Perhaps the political organization of such a large segment of the population might seem threatening to many non-black Brazilians, especially since redistribution policies could potentially have a wide social impact. Mexicans expressed the lowest levels of support for indigenous organizations (61 percent), lower than in Peru (72.6 percent),[2] perhaps, as the Mexican chapter argues, because the media promotion of an armed Zapatista uprising in the 1990s reduced mainstream support for indigenous political mobilizations. Quite tellingly, the Mexico chapter shows such support is lower in areas with a history of indigenous mobilization.

These attitudes reflect public opinion on the ground but not necessarily the opinions of policy makers who may pay little attention to public opinion. As we noted before, the Mexico-Brazil comparison is particularly illustrative. Although these two countries have had the strongest versions of mestizaje, their ethnoracial policies have moved in almost opposite directions in the past few decades. Brazil has broken with its racial democracy ideology for the most part and has gone as far as instituting affirmative action in most public universities, and there is wide public recognition of the existence of racial discrimination. In contrast, Mexican elites have continued to defend mestizaje, and there seems no chance that Mexican institutions will develop ethnoracial affirmative action programs anytime soon, even as some mestizaje tenets are beginning to be challenged within civil society and the constitution asserts that it is pluriethnic. Peru and Colombia arguably lie somewhere in between.

## Final Words

In sum, we have shown that the ethnoracial composition of each of these four countries is affected by how data on ethnoracial statistics are collected, including the ethnoracial categories used, how questions are phrased, and who does the classification (respondents or interviewers). Moreover, we have demonstrated the presence of ethnoracial inequality, particularly by skin color. We have also shown that the populations of these four large Latin American countries often perceive ethnoracial discrimination, and we have demonstrated that inequality and discrimination continue to operate regardless of how such data are collected. Finally, we have shown that the public is generally aware of and supportive of policies to address the disadvantages of indigenous and Afrodescendant peoples.

Although elements of racial mixture ideologies were considered progressive because they sought national unity across often divisive ethnoracial boundaries, they also denied or downplayed the persistent social disadvantages faced by dark-skinned people. In the past two decades or so, their veracity and power as social principles have begun to diminish. Our findings, based on nationally representative surveys from the Project on Ethnicity and Race in Latin America, reveal the ethnoracial inequalities and discrimination in the region regarding black, indigenous, and dark-skinned persons in general. Despite decades of denial through ideologies like mestizaje, pigmentocracy is a fact throughout Latin America, as we found in these four important but diverse countries.

But we see possibility too. Multiculturalism has brought greater recognition of ethnoracial distinctions, and ordinary citizens understand the presence of widespread ethnoracial inequalities—and support social policies for redressing inequalities and exclusion. We can only hope that, with multiculturalism, Latin American countries go beyond mere recognition of Latin America's ethnic diversity to create thorough and effective social policies that address the deep-seated ethnoracial inequalities in the region. Only through concerted government policies are the tide of injustice and the privileging of light skin likely to change. We hope that our findings from the Project on Ethnicity and Race in Latin America have provided information for further diagnosing these pigmentocracies and for policy makers and academics to engage in a richer discussion of race and ethnicity in Latin America today.

# NOTES

## CHAPTER 1

1. The Colombia survey was designed to slightly overrepresent Afrodescendants in that PERLA sample.

2. One could raise concerns that the skin of persons with low educational levels (e.g., agricultural workers) might become darker with exposure to sun and thus create a different explanation associating color with education. However, in separate analyses, PERLA found that color was a strong predictor of education among persons in indoor occupations, where sun exposure is limited (see www.perla.princeton.edu/palettetest).

3. The actual colors of the palette can be viewed at http://perla.princeton.edu/surveys /perla-color-palette.

4. Bourdieu (1984, 553) notes that one of the dimensions of symbolic capital in differentiated societies consists of ethnicity, with names and skin color as markers, which function as positive or negative symbolic capital.

5. Certainly, some Latin American countries had relatively weak mestizaje ideologies, if any, and other ideologies or systems were more influential. Argentina largely shunned mestizaje, pursued whitening, and eventually attracted the largest number of European immigrants in the region (Helg 1990; Andrews 1980). Still other ethnic situations included the clearly separate development of Latino and indigenous societies in Guatemala (Grandin 2000) and the explicit racial segregation and exclusion found in Cuba and Panama (Sawyer 2006; Conniff 1985). Colombia had a relatively weak mestizaje ideology that had strong elements of whitening, and Brazil and Mexico were particularly strong.

6. Perhaps ideas of assimilation in the United States come closest to Latin American ideas of mestizaje, but this concept has historically been applied to European Americans, while African Americans have been segregated in urban areas (Denton and Massey 1993) and Native Americans have been segregated in rural reservations (Snipp 1989). Ideas of mixed-racedness and the related notion of the mestizaje were common in the United States at least prior to 1920, when the census stopped collecting such data (Sollors 2000; Nobles 2000), though these ideas are again becoming important (Telles and Sue 2009).

7. Multiculturalism in Latin America generally, and sometimes in Canada and the United States, involves the claims of black and indigenous minorities, which is quite distinct from that involving immigrants who have mostly chosen to move from their ancestral homelands. In this sense Afro–Latin Americans and indigenous peoples can make relatively strong normative claims for special rights and protections (Kymlicka 1995).

8. However, Cuba has not made its microdata for any of its censuses publicly available, precluding most systematic sociological analysis.

## CHAPTER 2

1. In capitals in the original.

2. Polysemy means that the concept has a "hard core" of meaning, but that other meanings can become activated according to the context in which the word is used.

3. However, there are also new versions that have begun to question the dramatic decrement of the indigenous population in the New Spain (Gruzinski 2000).

4. Since indigenous people feared such a loss of autonomy, many of them did not support the independence war (Reina 2000).

5. Unlike other Latin American countries, such as Brazil, Cuba, Argentina, or Uruguay, the state policies to attract European immigration to Mexico were not as successful.

6. Indigenismo was a broad social, economic, and political movement that became influential after the Mexican Revolution. It critiqued the harsh government policies of the Porfirio Diaz's regime toward the indigenous, including forced assimilation and open warfare, and lauded the contribution of indigenous cultures to the Mexican nation. In practice, however, indigenista government policies were also aimed at the cultural assimilation of indigenous populations (see Villoro 1996 [1950]; de la Peña 2005; Saldívar 2008).

7. During this period, Franz Boas led a group of anthropologists from the American Anthropological Association who attempted to mitigate racism across the world, particularly in the United States. As a Columbia University professor, he influenced several generations of anthropologists, who eventually held academic posts throughout the American continent (Lowie 1947).

8. During the 1930s, thousands of migrant workers from Mexico were deported from the United States. In turn, the Mexican government created a commission in charge of resettling these migrants. Gamio worked as a consultant for this commission. He believed that international migration had been a process of "natural selection" and, thus, the returned migrants would help to modernize Mexico (see Walsh 2004).

9. Gonzalo Aguirre Beltrán (1989, 19) posits that when Gamio was studying at Columbia University, Boas came to realize that he could apply many of his ideas to eliminate racism in Mexico.

10. Manuel Gamio was responsible for the first efforts to classify the indigenous people after the colonial period, but in terms of culture, not "caste" or "race." Shortly after the end of the Mexican Revolution, Gamio attested to the presence of forty distinct indigenous cultures in the country based on linguistic criteria (Gamio 2010 [1916]; see also de la Peña 2002).

11. In addition to literacy primers and indigenous language grammar books, the

members of the Summer Institute of Linguistics were active missionaries who wanted to learn more non-Western languages to translate religious texts and convert the indigenous people, most of whom were Catholics, to the Protestant or evangelical religions.

12. In 1989 Mexico signed the OIT 169 Convention that was translated in the amendment of Article 4 of the constitution.

13. For a deeper understanding of the multicultural policies in Mexico, see Olivé 1999.

14. A good example is what is happening in the state of Veracruz, where the Veracruz Cultural Institute sponsors an annual Afro-Caribbean festival (Martínez Montiel 1993a).

15. In the case of demands made by Afro-Mexican organizations to include a question in the 2010 census, the answer was negative: it was felt that the majority of Mexicans would not understand the category Negro. On the other hand, our findings in the Costa Chica show that the self-identification term Negro is the emic category for the Afrodescendants.

16. We are considering an indigenous "pan-ethnic" category that does not specify the ethnolinguistic group the individual belongs to. For the purposes of our analysis it is important to differentiate between those who self-identify as indigenous and those who consider themselves as Nahuas, Mixtecs, Mayans, etc. In the results of the 2010 census on population and housing, one-third of those who identified themselves as speakers of a Mexican indigenous language did not self-identify as indigenous. Furthermore, only one-third of the participants who self-identified as indigenous admitted to speaking a vernacular language.

17. We have decided to use the term "customs" instead of "culture" given that it was easier for most of the people who participated in the survey to understand.

18. The predicted probabilities were calculated based on a logit regression predicting identification as mestizo, while holding all other individual and contextual variables constant at their means, including, e.g., age, gender, skin tone, and area of residence.

19. In the first section of this chapter we made reference to the importance of schooling and national textbooks in the construction of a national mestizo identity. This could explain the reason why people who have spent more time at school tend to consider themselves mestizos versus those with less formal schooling.

20. This ideology has become popular through the saying, "The North (white) works, the Center (mestizo) thinks, and the South (indigenous) rests." This phrase was used repeatedly by President Felipe Calderón, during his reelection campaign in 2006, to promise more investment and modernization in the South of Mexico. Calderón used this phrase as an example of false and biased ideas.

21. In the perception of interviewers, respondents in the Northwest had a skin tone of 3.95 on average and those in the Northeast 4.5, while those living in the South ranked 5.15.

22. This calculation is based on a logistic regression model predicting identification as "Indigenous."

23. In the section on the history of interethnic relations in Mexico, we briefly discuss the War of Castes in Mexico and the consequences it had in reinforcing stereotypes regarding the danger posed by indigenous groups in some regions of the country.

24. For a description of Oportunidades (the Program for Human Development), see CONEVAL 2010.

25. The difference of 4.7 percentage points was statistically significant ($p = 0.001$).

26. In Mexico the existing programs are minor in scale and discretionary; there is no law that enforces quotas or compensatory measures. Thus, despite their acceptance, affirmative measures for indigenous and Afrodescendants have remained largely out of the public debate (unlike the U.S. or Brazilian cases).

27. To calculate this, we used logistic regression analysis to predict supporting this policy. We included several sociodemographic controls, including age, gender, ethnoracial identity, community size, and state of residence. The negative association between education and supporting indigenous language instruction for all children remained significant even after including these controls in the regression model.

28. It appears that language for them is the reproduction of their identity and a place of resistance.

29. In our own survey, 35 percent of respondents believed that indigenous people are poor in Mexico because they have poor Spanish skills and 39 percent believed that their poverty is due to their unwillingness to change their culture and traditions.

30. While 63 percent of Mexicans in other regions supported indigenous political organizations, only 53 percent of respondents living in southern states did so.

31. Based on logistic regression analysis predicting the support of indigenous organizations for political goals.

32. There is strong evidence for these kind of family bonds, especially between internal migrants (see Martínez Casas 2007; Lavaud and Lestage 2009).

33. We should bear in mind the massive support received by the Zapatista movement in 2001 en route from Chiapas to Mexico City. A series of articles on this march and its repercussions on legislation can be found in Gutiérrez 2001.

34. The Asociación Popular de los Pueblos de Oaxaca came about in the summer of 2006 in the state of Oaxaca in the south of Mexico. For several months the state capital faced serious clashes between this ethnic and social movement and local authorities. For a more complete version of this indigenous movement and its consequences in the South, see Salceda 2011.

35. This category includes (1) Profesional, intelectual y científico (abogado, profesor universitario, médico, contador, arquitecto, ingeniero, etc.); (2) Director (gerente, jefe de departamento, supervisor); (3) Técnico o profesional de nivel medio (técnico en computación, maestro de primaria y secundaria, artista, deportista, etc.).

36. These differences were statistically significant ($p < 5$).

37. There were other ideological mechanisms sponsored by the Mexican government in order to reinforce the mestizaje ideology. The importance of the nationalist mural painting done by distinguished artists like Diego Rivera is well known (see O´Gorman 2002).

CHAPTER 3

1. *Cabildo* is an institution of Spanish colonial origins that dates back to the Middle Ages. It designates the government of a rural or urban community, which is elected by the community's own people. The Spanish crown also adapted this institution to indigenous people in *resguardos* and extended it to the black population under the modality

of black cabildos with religious purposes. About its use on the black population, and also the repression against these cabildos, see de Friedemann 1984a, 1984b.

2. On the laws concerning black people included in the compilation, see Navarrete 2005.

3. There were differences in marriage regulations of indigenous and black people. While whites were allowed to marry indigenous women, marriage to blacks or mulattos was widely opposed, as evidenced in several documents of the national historical files.

4. As reported in transitory Article 55 of the Constitution and developed according to Law 70, issued in 1993.

5. Colombia's current territory was not considered during the sixteenth century as a colony by the Spanish administration but was recognized instead as part of the kingdom, governed directly by the monarch, as the crown was the sole owner of the lands and seas that were to be discovered and conquered. So, between 1550 and 1717, a vast territory that includes various countries today (Colombia, Venezuela, Ecuador, Panama, and even Costa Rica) was called The New Kingdom of Granada. From the year 1717 the crown created in this wide territory the Viceroyalty of Nueva Granada, which came to an end in 1810 following the struggles for independence.

6. Sugarcane cultivation associated with the sugar mills in Department of Valle del Cauca does not date to the colonial period (Colmenares 1983 and Urrea Giraldo 2010).

7. Sometimes slaves were employed in haciendas that combined both livestock raising and sugarcane cultivation, as in Mompox and Cartagena. The Jesuit *haciendas* such as Llano Grande, Vijes, and Japio thus represent mixed models of this combined form. (Tovar 1988, 49). Also, see Colmenares (1983), *Las haciendas de los jesuítas en el Nuevo reino de Granada*.

8. It is necessary to point out that whites were not defined as castes but as a source of castes.

9. Even though the Manumission Law was approved on July 21, 1851, it was only in effect on January 1, 1852, after the Slavery Abolition law.

10. *Resguardos* date back to the colonial period, when the Spanish king granted lands to indigenous communities. Therefore, it is a figure that arises during the Spanish colonial legislation, is ratified by Law 89 of 1890, and finally is guaranteed by 1991 Constitution.

11. The period from 1863 to 1878 was dominated by radical liberals who sought a republican, secular, tolerant, and modern nation, and it was followed by the period known as Regeneración (1878–1900), in which a centralist regime was established through the division of powers (executive, legislative, and judicial). During that period, the 1886 Constitution decreed that every public authority has a divine origin, and Regeneración established Catholicism as the official religion in the Colombian nation and Catholic marriage as the only one recognized by the civil law. Through the 1887 Concordat with the Vatican (which was also approved by Law 35 of 1888), the church was given multiple privileges in the economic sphere (tax exemptions) and a wide interference in education at a national level and particularly in territories with a high concentration of indigenous and black populations, where it practically exercised state representation. On the other hand, Colombia's centralized government was given the power to print money and in-

tervene in the economy in various ways. The 1886 Constitution continued as the law of the land until the 1991 Constitution.

12. An indigenous group's reservation that has its own government, recognized by the state, was called *cabildo*, and its lands were the indigenous people's collective property.

13. The last three categories, pardos, zambos, and blacks, contained both free individuals and slaves. Likewise, during the colonial period there was a distinction between the *bozal* black and the *criollo* black: the first was the newly arrived from Africa, the second was the enslaved black born in the New World (Navarrete 2005).

14. "All races . . . have [in our country] a place, and they can be seen in their physical and moral development, and nothing is more curious than the multiple phenomena of the combinations of types, moral trends and attitudes derived from the coexistence of so many races, some of them pure but somehow modified by the influence of the place where they live, others related between them for more or less intense crossings" (Samper 1969 [1861], 83, quoted by Leal 2010, 403).

15. "The various or varied races and castes (are) all located in the place that best benefits the blood, the traditions, the industry, and the energy of each one." Samper 1969 [1861], 99, quoted by Leal 2010, 407.

16. The project was promoted during the period of the Liberal Republic (1930–46) and thereafter during the first years of the presidential period of Ospina Perez, who presided over the Conservative Republic (1946–53) until his murder in 1948.

17. Almost all the black and mulatto intellectuals of the time were sympathetic with the Gaitanist cause, whether they were professionals (generally lawyers and doctors), black artisans, or politicians belonging to the liberal party in Colombia's main regions with greater concentration of black population.

18. Uribe 1994, 30–34, 36–40. On this issue, see also Green 2000, 117.

19. Zapata Olivella 1978; Múnera 1998. Also, Múnera, 2010.

20. See Viveros 2012b for a detailed and reflexive biography about this black intellectual.

21. E.g., Asociación Integral Campesina del Atrato (Integral Peasant Association of Atrato River); Consejo Comunitario Mayor de la Asociación Campesina Integral del Atrato (Major Community Council of Integral Peasant Association of Atrato River); Consejos Comunitarios de Comunidades Negras en la Cuenca del Pacífico (Community Councils of Black Communities in the Pacific Basin).

22. DANE 2007. Colombia: una nación multicultural, su diversidad étnica. www.dane .gov.co/censo/. 2007.

23. Collected in Zapata Olivella 2004 and Zapata Olivella 2010.

24. The question in the Colombian 2005 census on self-ethnic identification is the following: "According to your culture, people, or physical features, are you or do you recognize yourself as being . . . indigenous, Roma or gypsy, Raizal, Palenquero, black, mulatto, Afro-Colombian, None of the above, NS [Doesn't know] and Not in refs. [Doesn't answer]?" The categories "raizal," "Palenquero," and "black/mulatto/Afro-Colombian" correspond to Afrodescendant category. On the other hand, as the PERLA findings for Colombia show, the census's alternative answer, "None of the above," was preferred by the self-ethnic-racial identities "white" and "mestizo."

25. It was a research program about the Colombian Southwest black population by

CIDSE's Facultad de Ciencias Sociales y Económicas and IRD of the French government (1996–2004).

26. The 2005 census showed 10.6 percent. However, the percentages for both sexes of the PERLA survey are 23.5 percent for the census question; 20.0 percent for African/black origin ancestry; 23.8 percent for color palette from 6 to 11; 19.5 percent for the open question on race (excluding NS and NR); 20.1 percent for black/mulatto categories given by interviewer; and 18.5 percent for black/mulatto self-identity.

27. "Sex properties are as inseparable from class properties as the yellow from lemon is inseparable from its acidity: a class is defined in its most essential for the place and value that it gives to both sexes and to its socially constituted dispositions. This is what makes possible the existence of so many ways to live femininity as there are classes and fractions of class, and that the division of labor between sexes takes completely different forms, both in the practice and the representations, within the different social classes" (Bourdieu 1991, 106).

28. In this case there must be correspondence between the survey takers and the interviewees; for this reason the whitening "makeup" is part of femininity *habitus*, where different perceptions (ego and alter) meet.

29. Color must then be conceived as inseparable from the object that it colors (Taussig 2009, 250); this means that it is more than a simple property that is socially built. Therefore, the people of "color," belonging to "primitive" people, of nonwhite skin, would come to be perceived, like their ornaments, their clothes, their paintings, etc., as different from the "white," and the people with darker skin by this "property" will be represented as of lower status.

30. The color palette includes a range of eleven shades. On the palette, the averages for the self-identity categories fall into this sequence: "white," "mestizo," "indigenous," "mulatto," and "black."

31. It refers to the racial identity given to the couple by the interviewee, but with self-identity of the ego (as interviewee), with the same ego self-identity racial categories.

32. The PERLA Colombian national sample for the indigenous people, as other surveys done in the country, are biased, because they are small and don't take into account the indigenous people living in rural areas, especially in indigenous territories such as *resguardos*, that are usually situated far from urban areas. So, the PERLA data about indigenous people are more representative of urban indigenous.

33. Coordinated by the National Department of Statistics (DANE) 2012.

34. The index, built on one level, is "consumption-based," measured by the expenditure required to access a minimum standard of nutrition and other very basic needs. This necessary expense is called purchasing power parity (PPP). World Bank 1999.

35. All the estimations for this chapter are made by Urrea and Viáfara, supported in Urrea and Viáfara 2007.

36. Figure 3.5 shows the average of school years reached by both parents of the ego (the interviewed), controlling to the left the racial self-identity and to the right the skin color of the latter.

37. This different pattern of schooling average reached by the ego's parents, between self-identity and skin color, has to do with the small size of mulatto self-identity in the PERLA national sample.

38. Figure 3.6 shows the occupational status of the head of household when the ego (the interviewed) was fourteen, controlling to the left the racial self-identity and to the right the skin color of the latter.

39. (1) Professional, intellectual, and scientific (e.g., lawyer, university professor, doctor, accountant, architect, engineer); (2) Director (manager, head of department, supervisor); (3) Technician or medium-level professional (computer technician, primary and secondary teacher, artist, sports men/women).

40. Again, here there is a sample effect, due to the mulatto self-identity group selected, which in this case shows a relative upward social mobility process.

41. Table 3.5 allows knowing, on the one hand, the discriminatory events by skin color and economic condition observed by the ego, on the other, if the ego has experienced some discriminatory event. In Table 3.5, skin color is the only control variable.

42. In the case of indigenous people, it is possible that they have lost public support because of recent large-scale indigenous social movements that have managed to get the national government to negotiate with them. Through these negotiations, they have made successful gains, including the recovery of lands and funding of resguardos.

43. These negative aspects, for instance, have to do with the ceding of land owned by whites and mestizos to indigenous people and Afrodescendants because of collective property rights granted by the 1991 Constitution. However, when lands meant to be ceded have rich mineral resources or the potential for excellent agricultural and livestock use, their ownership has been contested by white-mestizo landowner groups and multinational and large national companies, which have often taken such lands by force with the help of paramilitary armies. This land conflict, however, is not generalized to the whole country, but only to certain rural areas of black and indigenous population, and for this reason it doesn't affect, yet, the wide public opinion of the whole Colombian population. In the field of superior education there already starts to appear complaints of white-mestizo students that do not agree with the politics of differential quotas for admission to public universities in favor of indigenous and black people, even though this last politic is still very weak and restrictive in percentages over the total admitted university student population. If this last university policy was ever extended is possible that it would generate some resistance from the white-mestizo student population.

44. See the findings of the EHSIISAS 2010 (Encuesta de Hogares del Sistema de Inclusión Social de la Alcaldía de Cali: household survey of Social Inclusion System of the Municipality of Cali) about higher participation of black people in different community activities and organizations at the neighborhood level, compared with white and *mestizo* people living in the same neighborhoods.

45. Such phenotypes include type of nose, lips, and cheekbones, and sometimes body type.

46. As we can see in Figure 3.10, when the indigenous group of the sample is left out, due to the fact that this self-identity group with low incomes is located in the medium rank of skin color, the trend of labor incomes by skin color is the expected outcome according to the pigmentocratic hypothesis.

47. And most likely also Indian women and dark-skinned *mestizo* women are also handicapped, but this study has focused on Afrodescendant population.

48. The average income was the only variable that did not show an expected behavior in terms of skin color, due to the characteristics of the mulatto group within the national sample. Also, in the case of indigenous people captured in urban areas, many fell under the category of manual skilled labor, which indicates the high predominance of lower status artisan jobs.

CHAPTER 4

1. "El Peru de todos las sangres" literally translates as "Peru, the country of all bloods," although *sangres* might be translated as races or breeds, as well as bloods. The title *El Pais de Todas las Sangres?* might thus be translated as *The Country of All the Races?* in reference to Arguedas's book *All the Races* (*Todas las sangres*).

2. Arguedas's novel has been subject to intense debates in the Peruvian social sciences related to the issues of social modernization in the context of a hierarchical and multicultural society (see, e.g., Rochabrún 2011). Arguedas's centennial was commemorated in 2011 with several symposiums and seminars discussing his contribution to the understanding of multicultural relations in contemporary Peru.

3. Peruvian GNP in 2009 was 59 percent higher than in 2001.

4. As an example, we can mention that in the November 2011 Ombudsman Office report on social conflicts in the country, out of 220 identified conflicts, 57 percent were related to socioenvironmental issues (Defensoría del Pueblo 2011).

5. Peru has a presidential system. The president designates a prime minister and a cabinet of ministers in charge of the government. This cabinet can be dismissed at any moment by the president.

6. For an example, see the paradigmatic definition of "Indian" in Juan Espinosa's 1857 "Republican Dictionary" (Espinosa 1857).

7. After the independence proclamation on July 28, 1821, San Martin disenfranchised the slaves' newborns. Slavery was finally abolished by President Ramon Castilla on December 3, 1854.

8. Decree issued by José de San Martin, on November 24, 1821 (Gobierno del Perú 1831).

9. For *dependentista* views of Peruvian elites, see Bonilla and Spalding 1972; Yepes 1972; Bonilla 1974; Cotler 1978; Bonilla 1980; Tantalean 1983; Pásara 1988. Similar essentialist views of Peruvian elites were expressed in Salazar Bondy 1964. For similar views of Latin American elites, see Stein and Stein 1970; Halperin Donhi 1986; Peloso and Tenenbaum 1996.

10. The first immigrants from China arrived in Peru in 1849, imported as workers for the sugar and cotton estates and for the extraction of guano in the islands of Peru. Their working conditions were close to semislavery. Anti-Asian racism reached levels of paranoia when Chinese workers relocated to Lima, after the end of their initial contracts. The importation of Asian workers had been accepted as a "necessary evil" due to lack of "arms," but their settlement in the heart of the city of Lima, in the vicinity of its main central market, had not been not foreseen. See Rodriguez Pastor 1989.

11. For a discussion of Chilean racialist discourse, see Maureira 2004. For an analysis sensitive to racialized and gendered images in Chilean discourse during the war, see McEvoy 2000; 2011.

12. For an explanation on environmental conceptions of race, see Stepan 1996.

13. Painter Benito Laso compared Peruvian society to a painter's palette, richly adorned by colors. Intellectual Manuel Atanasio Fuentes, for his part, compared Lima's population to a colorful "field of flowers," aesthetically superior to the "uniform and monotonous" fields (Fuentes 1867, 77–78; Laso 1859).

14. Clemente Palma was explicit in his proposal to build the nation *a cañonazos* (by military means) to get rid of a "useless" and "decrepit" race.

15. Some paradigmatic examples of Brazil as a racial democracy are Pierson 1942; Freyre 1945, 1946; Tannenbaum 1947; Wagley 1952.

16. See the "Plan nacional de integración de la población aborigen" published by the Instituto Indigenista Peruano (Instituto Indigenista Peruano 1965. For an analysis, see Degregori et al. 1978.

17. See Mangin 1955; Ghersi 1959; Holmberg 1966. For information about the Cornell-Peru Project, visit the website at https://courses.cit.cornell.edu/vicosperu/vicos-site/cornellperu_page_1.htm.

18. This vision can be seen in his articles: "El complejo cultural del Perú," "Puquio, una cultura en proceso de cambio," and "Evolución de las comunidades indígenas" (Arguedas 1975). The articles were originally published in 1952, 1956, and 1957.

19. *Cholo* is generally a term used to denote an indigenous person with urban experience and some degree of education (Paredes 2008, 8). Anibal Quijano (1980) considered the *cholos* a transitional social group, constituted by indigenous immigrants from rural areas who settle in urban centers during the twentieth century. In fact *cholo* is a polysemic category; depending on the context, it may have a positive or negative connotation, and it is used both in private and public discourses. For example, the former president Alejandro Toledo presented himself as "El Cholo" (his wife called him once "mi cholo sano y sagrado").

20. A recent publication from David Sulmont and Nestor Valdivia published a comprehensive review of the indicators, categories, and questions used in censuses and other official statistics to measure the ethnic and racial dimension of Peruvian society (Sulmont and Valdivia 2012). See also Valdivia 2011.

21. Some partial censuses were held during the first decades of the twentieth century, but they were circumscribed to specific regions.

22. The indigenous are people who speak an indigenous language or whose maternal language is an indigenous one.

23. *Ojotas* are a sort of rudimentary sandals commonly used by peasants in rural areas in Peruvian Andes. *Poncho* (for men) and *lliclla* (for women) are considered "typical" clothing of indigenous people in the Andes.

24. ENCO was an official survey designed following the model of the ENAHO but applied to a much larger sample and during a longer period of time (one year). This design allowed better statistical representation of small geographic circumscriptions in the country. This kind of survey and sample format was applied only in 2006.

25. For a deeper discussion on those matters, see Valdivia 2011.

26. Sample error was estimated at +/-2.53 percent, with 95 percent confidence. Sampling was probabilistic in its first stages (localities, household clusters, and households). The last stage of selecting individuals inside a household was done using quotas for sex

and age groups. Sampling and fieldwork were performed by IPSOS APOYO, a specialized firm in market and survey research.

27. Variables used in the status index are: (a) estimated household per capita average monthly income; (b) household equipment; and (c) number of light bulbs in the household. Variables (a) and (b) were converted into quartile-range variables. The new variables were summed with variable (c) into an index_1 variable. Index_1 variable was converted into a new quartile-range variable. Each range was coded as: (1) bottom 25 percent; (2) mid-bottom 25 percent; (3) mid-upper 25 percent; and (4) top 25 percent.

28. Analyzing only high-skilled white collar occupations would have resulted in too few cases to reach statistical significance.

29. All the interviews were done in the respondent's home.

30. For recent experiments on race and discrimination in Peru, see Ñopo et al. 2010; Galarza et al. 2011.

31. Particularly the official statistics institutes and some ministries associated with social and cultural policies: Social Inclusion and Development; Health, Education, and Culture.

## CHAPTER 5

1. The term "racial democracy" was coined much later, in the 1970s. The general idea of racial democracy, however, can be seen in Freyre's early writings, like *Masters and Slaves* from 1933. For a more detailed discussion of the concept of racial democracy, see Guimarães 2001.

2. Throughout this chapter, readers should understand brown as a translation of the Brazilian census category pardo. As for the category black, when it appears in comparison or alongside the term brown, it refers to census category prete, but when on its own it refers to the general designation for people of African descent in Brazil.

3. *Mensalão* refers to an alleged monthly payment by the federal government of the Workers Party (PT) to deputies and senators so they support federal government initiatives.

4. For more on Joaquim Barbosa's trajectory, see Telles 2012.

5. As discussed later, most universities now have socioeconomic quotas that also take race representation into account.

6. On average, public universities in Brazil are much more selective and prestigious than private universities and an important path to social mobility. In addition, they are tuition free, making them the most attractive option for higher education. Public universities are roughly equally divided between state and federal universities. With the exception of the state of São Paulo, federal universities are more prestigious than state universities.

7. As discussed in detail later, race data were collected in the 1872 and 1890 censuses during the nineteenth century. In the twentieth century, race data were collected in 1940, 1950, 1960, 1980, 1991, and 2000. In 2010 the question was also included for the first time in the census basic questionnaire (as opposed to the sample questionnaire).

8. The prohibition of the slave trade was officially declared in 1850 through the law of Eusébio de Queiroz (himself a notorious slave trader). But it is widely known that it continued at least until 1852.

9. As Andrews (2004) points out, Caribbean countries like Cuba and Puerto Rico also did not have independence wars and followed the same pattern.

10. Reis and Reis (1999) show the disagreement among rural elites and their influence on slave abolition. For example, in São Paulo, the area where coffee plantations were growing faster at the end of the nineteenth century, slave owners were more interested in hiring immigrants than keeping their slaves.

11. Citing Robert Brent Toplin, "The Movement for the Abolition of Slavery in Brazil, 1880–1888" (Ph.D. diss., Rutgers University, 1968), Skidmore states, "As the abolitionist campaign continued, the slave population dwindled from a million and a half in 1872 to half a million in 1888" (1972, 2).

12. After Independence, in 1824, Brazil was ruled by emperors, descendants of the Portuguese king.

13. Fisher (2008) discusses in detail the impact of the Vargas regime for Brazilian urban poor in Rio de Janeiro, analyzing a few differential impacts for blacks and browns.

14. Although Freyre studied at the anthropology department of Columbia in which Boas was a professor, he was never his student. Recent studies show that, until the 1920s, Freyre was affiliated with hegemonic eugenic ideas and that his ideological transformation was sudden after he had returned to Brazil (Pallares-Burke 2005).

15. Freyre defended such a perspective even more strongly during the 1970s, when he supported the Salazar dictatorship and the continuation of Portuguese colonization in Africa due to its "exceptional" character. This resignification of the Portuguese contribution to Brazil is even more striking if we consider that, in the 1908 census report, Bulhões de Carvalho had presented the Portuguese as the least-desired immigration group in the Brazilian whitening effort.

16. As Telles (2003) discussed, other authors such as Marvin Harris and Thales de Azevedo were closer to the racial democracy paradigm. Here, however, we are focusing on the studies conducted by Brazilian scholars, which are widely read nowadays.

17. One exception is Costa Pinto (1952), who argued that modernization could actually strengthen Brazilian racial tensions.

18. The rejection of the category nonwhite in favor of negro is based on the preference of a category that emphasizes something shared among members of the aggregated category instead of something that focuses on their shared deprivation of whiteness.

19. Bailey and Peria (2010) discuss in detail the divide in Brazilian academia regarding affirmative action with a special focus on their different images of the Brazilian nation, their distinct diagnoses of the mechanisms behind nonwhite underrepresentation in Brazilian universities, their opposing prognoses for a remedy via racial quotas, and their diverse motivations for entering the debate. They conclude by stating that despite disagreements there is widespread agreement on the rejection of the biology of race and on the recognition of racism.

20. In the 2010 census, the proportion of blacks and browns in Brazilian states varied from 76.16 in Bahia to 15.35 in Santa Catarina.

21. For example, Peria (2004) discusses in detail how the law that first implemented racial quotas in the Rio de Janeiro State largely relied on official statistics publicized through the media during the Durban Conference.

22. Rallu and his coauthors (2004, cited in Morning 2008, 243) propose a similar ty-

pology for the reasons why racial categories are included or excluded in national statistics: enumeration for political control, nonenumeration in the name of national integration, discourse of national hybridity, and enumeration for antidiscrimination.

23. In this first census, there was also *caboclo* (indigenous-white mix) but current analyses join pardos and caboclos. For a detailed discussion about the pros and cons of joining pardos and caboclos, see Oliveira 1999.

24. The indigenous population might be underestimated and included in the pardo category. Nevertheless, it was largely reduced by mortality (due to European infections, resistance to colonization, and slavery) but also by the massive entrance of European settlers and African slaves during the previous three centuries. For more on indigenous census counting, see Oliveira 1999.

25. Loveman (2009) argues that this change, however, could be a result of a methodological flaw. In the 1890 census the categories of mixed race were changed: instead of pardos and caboclos, the census asked about *mestiços* and caboclos, which, she maintains, was a term less associated with blackness.

26. In the census of 1940, interviewers classified people between white and black or yellow (a new category, created to account for the Japanese immigrants in the South and Southeast region). It is only in 1950 that interviewers were asked to self-declare their own classification according to given categories of white (*branco*), black (*preto, pardo*), and yellow (*amarelo*).

27. The decision to follow the 1950 model was partly based on a 1976 study that compared how people responded to the color question when asked openly.

28. The other category was *moreno*. This also triggered an important debate about the use of the *moreno* category as a census category. See Harris 1995; Harris et al. 1993; Telles 1995.

29. Despite an increase in the percentage of indigenous people between 1991 and 2000, which doubled from 0.2 to 0.4 percent, indigenous and yellow have remained less than 2 percent of the Brazilian population.

30. Before that, a question about indigenous language was included only in a sample of the census population that answered a longer questionnaire.

31. The PCERP (Pesquisa das Características Étnico-Raciais da População) was a survey conducted in 2008 in six metropolitan areas in the five regions of the country (plus Brasília, the political capital) to "broaden the understanding of official statistics in relation to ethnoracial issues" (p. 17). It interviewed a total of 15,110 Brazilians or households. The report can be found at http://www.ibge.gov.br/home/estatistica/populacao/ caracteristicas_raciais/default_raciais.shtm

32. Sample error was roughly estimated at +/- 4%, with 95 percent confidence. Sampling was probabilistic in its first stages (localities, household clusters, and households). Sampling and fieldwork were performed by Instituto Análise (http://institutoanalise .com/), a specialized firm in market and survey research.

33. There was no significant association between identifying as negro with gender, age, region of birth, or years of education. Yet this might be due to the low number of nonwhite interviewees with higher education.

34. According to Bailey et al. (2012), the PESB "follows the model of the American General Social Survey (GSS). The data are based on a nationally representative sample

covering the five regions of Brazil and all persons aged 18 and over. The complete sample consists of 2,364 persons sampled across 102 municipalities."

35. The categories of yellow and indigenous have less overlap but also very few cases for any significant inference.

36. Among those who were recategorized, half were whitened and half were darkened. Analyzing the overlap of self-identification and identification by others, Telles and Lim (1998) concluded that interviewers are more likely to darken lower-income interviewees and to lighten those with higher incomes; therefore a higher level of racial inequality in income is perceived when identification by others is used (compared to self-identification), something we explore later.

37. According to the PCERP report IBGE (2011), a total of 73.8 percent of interviewees chose skin color as one of the dimensions of their racial identity, and 47.6 percent mentioned it as the most important; 53.5 percent mentioned other physical traits (lips or nose shape, hair type), and 12.9 percent chose it as the first option.

38. We follow the definition of *light*, *medium*, and *dark* used throughout this book to allow for comparisons. Yet, if we included those classified as 3 and 6 (according to the color palette) as medium, we would have nearly 90 percent of all respondents who identified as brown, showing those who identified as brown were indeed closer to the medium of the palette classification.

39. Because there is so much overlap between self-identification and identification according to the interviewer, the distribution based on self-identification is very similar and will not be considered here.

40. Frequencies for those who identify as yellow (73.3 percent) and indigenous (100 percent) are similarly high, but the numbers are too small (N = 30 and 19, respectively) for any significant conclusion.

41. A similar question at PCERP 2008 ("Does race or color influence people's lives?") found similar results: 63.7 percent of the respondents said yes.

42. Sidanius, Pena, and Sawyer (2001) analyzed the black Caribbean context, where, in the Dominican Republic, for example, blacks and whites feel strongly committed as part of the nation, and blacks were found to be even more committed than whites. This contrasts with the United States, where blacks are less committed to the American identification than whites.

43. In PERLA, the support for affirmative action programs is even higher than in previous studies (Bailey 2002, 2004; Guimarães 2007). This may be due to PERLA's formulation of the question: "Do you agree that universities should guarantee spots for *qualified* black students?" In the other surveys, the word *qualified* was not included, and the acceptance rate was around 60 percent. The same question regarding indigenous qualified students and poor qualified students also had very high rates of agreement.

44. Due to a mistake in the application of the questionnaire, the questions about willingness to participate in a black organization and about the perception of a threat to national unity or conflict were posed to only the 33.4 percent of respondents who had heard about a black organization, or 334 interviewees. Among those 35 percent, only a small minority (20 percent or 7 percent of the total) would be willing to participate in black organization. As expected, blacks would be more willing to participate (33.3 percent), but a small number of whites (17.2 percent) and browns (16.2 percent) also said

"yes." The threat to national unity, a common issue raised by intellectuals concerned with the rise of identity politics in Brazil (e.g., Fry et al. 2007), did not seem to concern interviewees. Almost no interviewees view black political organizations as a hazard to national unity. The low perception of racial conflict appears as a better explanation for the low interest in participating in black organizations: 71 percent of those who were asked (25 percent of the total) believe that there is very little or no conflict among blacks and whites in Brazil.

45. With the exception of the 1976 PNAD, the 1998 PME, and the 2008 PCERP, IBGE studies all rely on self-identification according to census categories.

46. Nevertheless, it should be noted that IBGE classification is a mix of self-identification (of the main questionnaire respondent) and classification by others (the main respondent's categorization of the other household residents).

47. In addition, the average years of schooling for the 2010 PERLA sample was 7.1, very similar to the official 2009 PNAD-IBGE data (Pesquisa Nacional por Amostra de Domicílios [National Research by Household Sample], of the Brazilian Institute of Geography and Statistics), 7.2. For more about the PNAD 2009 indicators, see http://www.ibge.gov.br/home/presidencia/noticias/noticia_visualiza.php?id_noticia=1717&id_pagina=1.

48. This has been attributed either to the possibility that the relation changed over time or that the effect in São Paulo is not reproduced nationally. Osorio (2008) also cites the research, Pesquisa Nacional de Demografia e Saúde, as a study in which the classification of color or race of the individuals occurred by means of the self- and heteroclassificatory system. However, in this study, the author does not mention the discrepancy between one form and another of classification controlled by the socioeconomic condition of the interviewees.

49. Approximately 0.9, $p = 0.004$.

50. Difference in average years of education between blacks and whites in survey takers classification is 1.26, $p = 0.003$.

51. There were also twenty-six cases of bald interviewees who were excluded in light of the small number and the lack of analytical interest.

52. A few statements, however, showed surprisingly high agreement rates: 13.9 percent said they already heard the expression "improve the race," and 37.8 percent agree that blacks should marry whites to improve the race. Differences among those who identify as black, white, or brown are not significant. Survey experiments conducted by PESB also show that blatant racism might be hidden behind politically correct statements. See chapters 10 and 11 in Almeida 2007.

53. Only sixteen interviewees (1.7 percent) thought blacks were treated better.

54. Pearson Chi square = 23,237 (df 12, $p = 0.026$).

55. Note that more than 20 percent of respondents answer they did not agree or disagree to both questions, which could be interpreted as being unsure, so likely not to recognize discrimination.

56. Interestingly, however, in the latter question, those respondents who identified as brown acknowledged unequal treatment more often than all other groups (34.2 percent disagree vs. 39.5 percent who agree), a pattern confirmed in other questions, which challenges the common description of browns as racially alienated (Munanga 2008; Silva and Leão 2012).

57. When the same questions are made about indigenous people, the perception of injustice increases: 62 percent believe that indigenous are treated worse than whites. Unfair treatment also appears as the most common explanation for indigenous poverty: 40.8 percent agree (or agree completely) that indigenous are treated worse than whites (versus 41.3 percent who disagree or disagree completely). But for indigenous people, culture comes second: 33.6 percent point to the fact that because indigenous do not want to change their culture they remain poor (versus 45.4 percent who disagree). The other explanations follow the same pattern as blacks, even if relying on blatant racism more often. Although the frequency of blatantly racist statements (e.g., indigenous are not as smart or are lazy) is higher, 29.3 percent blame bad or inefficient schools (versus 50.9 percent who disagree), 29.9 percent point to lower educational attainment (versus 53.4 percent who disagree), 19 percent believe they do not work hard enough (versus 69.9 percent who disagree), and 16.5 percent believe that the indigenous are, on average, less intelligent than whites (versus 72.5 percent who disagree). In addition, 23.2 percent point to the fact that indigenous people do not speak Portuguese as well as whites (versus 56.5 percent who reject that explanation). There were no significant differences among respondents who identify as white, brown, and black.

58. This finding seems contradictory in light of the nearly 70 percent who thought that their color or race was a determinant in many aspects of their lives, as shown in Figure 5.4. This apparent paradox can be attributed to different understanding of racial identification and skin color and demands further research.

59. The options of response were *never, at least a few times, sometimes, often*. In the analysis we differentiate between *never* and *a few times*.

60. Interviewees were asked if they had experienced discrimination due to the color of their skin and according to other characteristics like gender and economic situation. The reply options were *never, a few times, sometimes, often*. Among blacks, most say they experienced discrimination a few times (25.5 percent versus 9.2 percent *sometimes*, and 2.1 percent *often*).

61. We did not find significant differences in perception of discrimination by gender, age, or socioeconomic status. But this might be related to the small number of cases.

CHAPTER 6

1. The one exception to this trend seems is Colombian mulattos, who seem much more able to move across racial and ethnic boundaries than either blacks in Colombia or pardos and pretos in Brazil; 53.4 percent of those who self-identified as mulatto were classified as either mestizo or white by survey takers.

2. These differences are statistically significant at the 95 percent level.

# REFERENCES

Aboites, Luis. 1998. *El agua de la nación: Una historia política de México 1888–1946.* Mexico City: CIESAS.

Acuña León, María de los Angeles, and Doria Chavarría López. 1991. "Endogamia y exogamia en la sociedad colonial cartaginesa, 1738–1821." *Revista de Historia* 23:107–44.

Agudelo, Carlos. 2005. *Retos del multiculturalismo en Colombia: Política y poblaciones negras.* Medellín: La Carreta Social.

Aguilar, Rosario. Forthcoming. "Los tonos de los desafíos democráticos: El color de piel y la raza en México." *Política y Gobierno.* Mexico City: CIDE.

Aguirre Beltrán, Gonzalo. 1944. "The Slave Trade in Mexico." *Hispanic American Historical Review* 24:412–31.

———. 1967. *Regiones de refugio.* Vol. 46. Mexico City: Instituto Indigenista Interamericano.

———. 1982. *El proceso de aculturación.* Ediciones de la Casa Chata. Mexico City: CIESAS.

———. 1989. *Cuijla: Esbozo Etnográfico de un Pueblo Negro.* Mexico City: Fondo de Cultura Económica.

———. 1992 [1957]. *Obra Antropológica VI. El Proceso de aculturación y Cambio Socio-cultural en México.* Mexico City: Gobierno del Estado de Veracruz / Universidad Veracruzana / INI / FCE.

Albán, A. 2010. "Racialización, violencia epistémica, colonialidad lingüística y re-existencia en el proyecto moderno-colonial." In *Debates sobre ciudadanía y políticas raciales en las Américas Negras*, edited by Claudia Mosquera Rosero-Labbé, Agustín Laó-Montes, and César Rodríguez Garavito. Bogotá: Universidad Nacional de Colombia.

Almario, Óscar. 2010. "Los negros en la independencia de la Nueva Granada" In *Indios, negros y mestizos en la independencia*, edited by Heraclio Bonilla. Bogotá: Editorial Planeta.

———. 2010b. "Anotaciones sobre una posible periodización de las representaciones raciales en Colombia." In *Debates sobre ciudadanía y políticas raciales en las Américas*

*Negras,* edited by Claudia Mosquera Rosero-Labbé, Agustín Laó-Montes, and César Rodríguez Garavito. Bogotá: Programa Editorial.

Almeida, Alberto Carlos. 2007. *A Cabeça do Brasileiro.* Rio de Janeiro: Record.

Anderson, Benedict. 1991. *Imagined Communities: Reflections on the Origin and Spread of Nationalism.* London: Verso.

Andrés Gallego, José. 2005. *La esclavitud en la América española.* Madrid: Encuentro.

Andrews, George Reid. 1980. *The Afro-Argentines of Buenos Aires, 1800–1900.* Madison: University of Wisconsin Press.

———. 2004. *Afro-Latin America, 1800–2000.* Oxford: Oxford University Press.

———. 2010. *Blackness in the White Nation: A History of Afro-Uruguay.* Chapel Hill: University of North Carolina Press.

Angosto-Ferrández, Luis Fernando, and Sabine Kradolfer. 2012. *Everlasting Countdowns: Race, Ethnicity and National Censuses in Latin American States.* Newcastle upon Tyne: Cambridge Scholars Publishing.

Appelbaum, Nancy. 1999. "Whitening the Region: Caucano Mediation and 'Antioqueño Colonization' in Nineteenth-Century Colombia." *Hispanic American Historical Review* 79, 4:631–67.

Appelbaum, Nancy, Anne Macpherson, and Karin Alejandra Rosemblatt, eds. 2003. *Race and Nation in Modern Latin America.* Chapel Hill: University of North Carolina Press.

Araújo, Joel Zito. 2000. *A negação do Brasil: o negro na telenovela brasileira.* São Paulo: SENAC.

Arboleda, Sergio. *La república en la América española.* 1972 [1869]. Bogotá: Imprenta Banco Popular.

Arguedas, José María. 1975. *Formación de la cultura nacional indoamericana.* Mexico City: Siglo XXI.

———. 1985 [1965]. *Todas las sangres.* Lima: Horizonte.

Arias Vanegas, Julio. 2007. "Seres, cuerpos y espíritus del clima: ¿Pensamiento racial en la obra de Francisco José de Caldas?" *Revista de Estudios Sociales* 27:16–30.

Arona, Juan de. 1891. "Pedro Paz Soldán y Unánue." *Páginas diplomáticas del Perú,* 204. Lima, Impr. de la Escuela de ingenieros.

———. *La inmigración en el Perú: Monografía histórico-crítica.* 1891. Lima: Impr. del Universo de C. Prince.

Ashmore, Richard, Kay Deaux, and Tracy McLaughlin-Volpe. 2004. "An Organizing Framework for Collective Identity: Articulation and Significance of Multidimensionality." *Psychological Bulletin* 130:80–114.

Atria, Raúl. 2004. *Estructura ocupacional, estructura social y clases sociales.* Vol. 96. United Nations Publications.

Azevedo, Fernando de. 1944. *A cultura brasileira.* 2nd ed. São Paulo: Campanhia editora nacional.

Bailey, Stanley. 2002. "The Race Construct and Public Opinion: Understanding Brazilian Beliefs about Racial Inequality and Their Determinants." *American Journal of Sociology* 108:406–39.

———. 2004. "Group Dominance and the Myth of Racial Democracy: Antiracism Attitudes in Brazil." *American Sociological Review* 69:728–44.

———. 2008. "Unmixing for Race Making in Brazil." *American Journal of Sociology* 114:577–614.

———. 2009a. "Public Opinion on Nonwhite Underrepresentation and Racial Identity Politics in Brazil." *Latin American Politics and Society* 51.4:69–99.

———. 2009b. *Legacies of Race: Identities, Attitudes, and Politics in Brazil*. Stanford University Press.

———. 2013. "Measures of 'Race' and the Analysis of Racial Inequality in Brazil." *Social Science Research* 42, no. 1: 106–19.

Bailey, Stanley, and Michelle Peria. 2010. "Racial Quotas and the Culture War in Brazilian Academia." *Sociology Compass* 4.8:592–604.

Bailey, Stanley, and Edward Telles. 2006. "Multiracial versus Collective Black Categories: Examining Census Classification Debates in Brazil." *Ethnicities* 6:74–101.

Baker, Lee D. 2010. *Anthropology and the Racial Politics of Culture*. Durham: Duke University Press.

Banton, Michael. 2012. "The Colour Line and the Colour Scale in the Twentieth Century." *Ethnic and Racial Studies* 35:1109–31.

Barbary, Olivier, and Fernando Urrea Giraldo. 2004. *Gente negra en Colombia: Dinámicas sociopolíticas en Cali y el Pacífico*. Colciencias, Lealon, Medellín: CIDSE, IRD.

Barth, Fredrik. 1969. *Ethnic Groups and Boundaries: The Social Organization of Culture Difference*. (Results of a symposium held at the University of Bergen, 23rd to 26th February 1967.) Bergen: Universitetsforlaget; London: Allen & Unwin.

Barragán, Esteban. 1997. *Con un pie en el estribo: Formación y deslizamientos de las sociedades rancheras en la construcción de México Moderno*. Zamora: El Colegio de Michoacán.

Bartolomé, Miguel, and Alicia Barabas. 1990. *La presa Cerro de Oro y el Ingeniero el Gran Dios*. Mexico City: INI.

Bartra, Armando, and Gerardo Otero. 2007. "Rebeldía Contra el Globalismo Neoliberal y el Tlcan en el Mexico Rural: ¿Del Estado Coporativista a la formacion Politico-cultural del Campesinado?" *Revista Textual* 50.

Basave, Agustín. 2007. *El nacionalismo*. Mexico City: Nostra Ediciones.

Behrendt, Stephen. 1999. "Transatlantic Slave Trade." In *Africana: The Encyclopedia of the African and African American Experience*, edited by K. Appiah and H. L. Gates Jr. New York: Basic Civitas.

Behrman, Jere, Alejandro Gavira, and Miguel Székely. 2001. "Intergenerational Mobility in Latin America." *Journal of the Latin American and Caribbean Economic Association* 2, no.1: 1–44.

Behrman, Jere R., Alejandro Gaviria, and Miguel Székely. 2001. "Intergenerational Mobility in Latin America." *Economia* 2, no. 1: 1–31.

Belaúnde, Víctor Andrés. 1987 [1942]. *Peruanidad*. Lima: Comisión del Centenario de V. A.

Benavides, Martín, Máximo Torero, and Néstor Valdivia. 2006. *Más allá de los promedios: Afrodescendientes en América Latina. Pobreza, discriminación social e identidad: El caso de la población afrodescendiente en el Perú*. Washington, D.C.: Grade, Banco Mundial.

Bernardino, Joaze, and Daniela Galdino. 2004. "Levando raca a serio: acao afirmativa e Universidade," in *Colecao Politicas da Cor*. Rio de Janeiro: DP&A.

Bonfiglio, Giovanni. 2001. *Presencia europea en el Perú*. Lima: Fondo Editorial del Congreso del Perú.

Bonfil Batalla, Guillermo. 1981. *Utopía y revolución*, Mexico City: Nueva Imagen.

———. 1990. *México profundo: Una civilización negada*. Mexico City: Grijalbo; Consejo Nacional para la Cultura y las Artes.

Bonilla, Heraclio. 1974. *Guano y burguesía en el Perú*. Lima: Instituto de Estudios Peruanos.

———. 1980. "El problema nacional y colonial del Perú en el contexto de la Guerra del Pacífico." *Desarrollo Economico*: 49–70.

Bonilla, Heraclio, and Karen Spalding. 1972. "La independencia en el Perú: las palabras y los hechos." In *La independencia en el Perú*, edited by Heraclio Bonilla. Lima: Instituto de Estudios Peruanos.

Bost, Suzanne. 2003. *Mulattas and Mestizas: Representing Mixed Identities in the Americas, 1850–2000*. Athens: University of Georgia Press.

Bourdieu, Pierre. 1977. "Cultural Reproduction and Social Reproduction." In. *Power and Ideology in Education*, edited by J. Karabel and A. H. Halsey. New York: Oxford University Press.

———. 1984. *Distinction: A Social Critique of the Judgement of Taste*. Translated by Richard Nice. Cambridge: Harvard University Press.

———. 1986. "The Forms of Capital." In *Handbook of Theory and Research for the Sociology of Education*, edited by J. G. Richardson. New York: Greenwood.

———. 1988. *La Distinción*. Madrid: Editorial Taurus.

Bourdieu, Pierre, and Jean Claude Passeron. 1979. *The Inheritors: French Students and Their Relation to Culture*. Chicago: University of Chicago Press.

Bourdieu, Pierre, and Loïc Wacquant. 1999. "On the Cunning of Imperialist Reason." *Theory, Culture, and Society* 16:41–58.

Boxer, C. R. 1963. *Race Relations in the Portuguese Colonial Empire, 1415–1825*. Oxford: Clarendon Press.

Boyer, Richard. 2000. *Colonial Lives: Documents on Latin American History, 1550–1850*. New York: Oxford University Press.

Brading, David. 1991. *The First America: Spanish Monarchy, Creole Patriots and the Liberal State, 1492–1867*. Cambridge: Cambridge University Press.

———. 1993 [1973]. *Los orígenes del nacionalismo mexicano*. Mexico City: Era.

Brown, Michael K., Martin Carnoy, Elliot Currie, Troy Duster, David B. Oppenheimer, Marjorie M. Schultz, and David Wellman. 2003. *Whitewashing Race: The Myth of a Color-Blind Society*. Berkeley: University of California Press.

Brubaker, Rogers. 2004. *Ethnicity without Groups*. Cambridge, Mass.: Harvard University Press.

———. 2009. "Ethnicity, Race, and Nationalism." *Annual Review of Sociology* 35:21–42.

Buchenau, Jurgen, et al. 2009. *State Governors in the Mexican Revolution, 1910–1952*. Rowman & Littlefield.

Callirgos, Juan Carlos. 1993. *El racismo: La cuestión del otro (y de uno)*. Lima: DESCO, Centro de Estudios y Promoción del Desarrollo.

Campante, Filipe, Anna Crespo, and Phillippe Leite. 2004. "Desigualdade Salarial entre Racas no Mercado de Trabalho Urbano Brasileiro: Aspectos Regionais." *Revista Brasileira de Economia* 58:185–210.

Canache, Damarys, Matthew Hayes, Jeffery J. Mondak, and Mitchell A. Seligson. 2014. "Determinants of Perceived Skin-Color Discrimination in Latin America." *Journal of Politics* 76, no.2: 506–20.

Candelario, Ginetta. 2007. *Black behind the Ears: Dominican Racial Identity from Museums to Beauty Shops*. Durham: Duke University Press.

Carrasco, G. 2008. "Influencia del capital cultural, capital económico y capital social basado en la familia sobre el rendimiento de los estudiantes: un análisis comparativo." Convenio de Investigación 2006–PBA 13.

Carvalho, José Alberto Magno de, Charles H. Wood, and Flávia Cristina Drumond Andrade. 2004. "Estimating the Stability of Census-based Racial/Ethnic Classifications: The Case of Brazil." *Population Studies* 58, no. 3: 331–43.

Castellanos Guerrero, Alicia. 2000. "Antropología y racismo en México." *Desacatos. Racismo* 4:53–79. Mexico City: CIESAS.

Castellanos Guerrero, Alicia, Jorge Gómez Izquierdo, and Francisco Pineda Castillo. 2007. "El discurso racista en México." In *Racismo y discurso en América Latina*, edited by Teun A.Van Dijk. Barcelona: Gedisa.

Castellanos Guerrero, Alicia, and Juan Manuel Sandoval, eds. 1998. *Nación, racismo e identidad*. Mexico City: Nuestro Tiempo.

Castillo, Luis Carlos. 2007. *Etnicidad y nación: El desafío de la diversidad en Colombia*. Cali: Programa Editorial de la Universidad del Valle Convenio de Investigación 2006–PBA 13. Consorcio de Investigación Económica y Social. Lima: DESCO.

Castro Pozo, Hildebrando. 1924. *Nuestra comunidad indígena*. Lima: El Lucero.

Caumartin, Corinne, G. Gray Molina and Rosemary Thorp. 2010. "Inequality, Ethnicity, and Political Violence in Latin America: The Cases of Bolivia, Guatemala, and Peru." In *Horizontal Inequalities and Conflict: Understanding Group Violence in Multiethnic Societies*, edited by F. Stewart. London: Palgrave Macmillan.

CEPAL. 2006. *Panorama social de América Latina 2006*. Santiago de Chile: CEPAL.

Cicalo, André. 2012. *Urban Encounters: Affirmative Action and Black Identities in Brazil*. New York: Palgrave Macmillan.

Colmenares, Germán. 1983. *Sociedad y Economía en el Valle del Cauca*. Vol. 1. Cali: terratenientes, mineros y comerciantes. Siglo XVIII. Biblioteca Banco Popular. Bogotá: Textos Universitarios.

———. 1997. *Historia económica y social de Colombia, 1537–1719*. In *Obra completa*. Tercer Mundo Editores. Bogotá: Universidad del Valle. Banco de la República. COLCIENCIAS.

Comisión de Esclarecimiento Histórico. 1999. *Memoria del silencio: Informe de la Comisión para el Esclarecimiento Histórico*. Ciudad de Guatemala: CEH; Comisión de la Verdad y Reconciliación.

Comisión de la Verdad y Reconciliación. 2003. *Informe final*. Lima: CVR.

CONEVAL. 2010. "Cuadro 13. Incidencia, número de personas y carencias promedio en los indicadores de pobreza en la población que habla lengua indígena, 2008–2010." In *Medición de la pobreza, Estados Unidos Mexicanos*. Available at http://www

.coneval.gob.mx/cmsconeval/rw/pages/medicion/Pobreza_2010/Anexo_estadistico
.es.do.

Conniff, Michael L. 1985. *Black Labor on a White Canal: Panama, 1904-1981*. Pittsburgh: University of Pittsburgh Press.

Cope, R. Douglas. 1994 [1980]. *The Limits of Racial Domination: Plebeian Society in Colonial Mexico City, 1660–1720*. Madison: University of Wisconsin Press.

———. 2007. *Ethnicity and Race: Making Identities in a Changing World*. Pine Forge Press.

Costa Pinto. 1995 [1952]. *O Negro no Rio de Janeiro: Relações de raça numa sociedade em mudança*. Rio de Janeiro: UFRJ.

Cotler, Julio. 1978. *Clases, estado y nación en el Perú*. Lima: Instituto de Estudios Peruanos.

Cottrol, Robert J. 2013. *The Long Lingering Shadow: Slavery, Race and Law in the American Hemisphere*. Athens: University of Georgia.

Crabtree, John, and Laurence Whitehead, eds. 2008. *Unresolved Tensions: Bolivia Past and Present*. Pittsburgh, Pa.: University of Pittsburgh Press.

DANE. 2007. *Colombia: una nación multicultural. Su diversidad étnica*. www.dane.gov .co/censo/. Accessed July 15, 2011.

Daniel, Reginald. 2006. *Race and Multiraciality in Brazil and the United States: Converging Paths?* University Park: Pennsylvania State University Press.

Datafolha. 1995. *Dataset: Racismo cordial: A mais completa análise sobre o preconceito de cor no Brasil*. São Paulo: Editora Atica.

———. 2008. "Dataset: Racismo Confrontado." In *Folha de São Paulo, November 23*. São Paulo.

de Azevedo, Fernando. 1996 [1943]. *A cultura brasileira*. 3rd ed. Rio de Janeiro: IBGE.

Defensoría del Pueblo. 2011. "Reporte de conflictos sociales No. 93. Noviembre. Adjuntía para la Prevención de Conflictos Sociales y la Gobernabilidad." Lima: Defensoría del Pueblo. http://www.defensoria.gob.pe/conflictos-sociales/home.php. Accessed December 21, 2011.

Degler, Carl N. 1971. *Neither Black nor White: Slavery and Race Relations in Brazil and the United States*. New York: Macmillan.

Degregori, Carlos Iván. 1998. "Movimientos étnicos, democracia y nación en Perú y Bolivia." In *La construcción de la nación y la representación ciudadana en México, Guatemala, Perú, Ecuador y Bolivia*, edited by C. Dary. Ciudad de Guatemala: FLACSO.

Degregori, Carlos Iván, Mariano Valderrama, and Marfil Francke. 1978. *Indigenismo, clases sociales y problema nacional: La discusión sobre el "Problema indígena" en el Perú*. Lima: CELATS.

de la Cadena, Marisol. 2000. *Indigenous Mestizos: The Politics of Race and Culture in Cuzco, Peru, 1919–1991*. Durham: Duke University Press.

———. 2004. *Indígenas mestizos: Raza y cultura en el Cusco*. Lima: Instituto de Estudios Peruanos.

de la Fuente, Alejandro. 2001. *A Nation for All: Race, Inequality, and Politics in Twentieth-Century Cuba*. Chapel Hill: University of North Carolina Press.

de la Peña, Guillermo. 1997 [1996]. "¿Un concepto operativo de lo indio?" In *Estado del desarrollo económico y social de los pueblos indígenas de México*, 24–25. Mexico City: Instituto Nacional Indigenista: PNUD.

———. 2002. *Antropología sociocultural en el México del milenio: Búsquedas, encuentros y transiciones*. Mexico City: Fondo de Cultura Económica.

———. 2005. "Social and Cultural Policies toward Indigenous Peoples: Perspectives from Latin America." *Annual Review of Anthropology* 34:717–39.

del Popolo, Fabiana. 2001. *Características sociodemográficas y socioeconómicas de las personas de edad en América Latina*. Santiago: Naciones Unidas, CEPAL, Proyecto Regional de Población CELADE-FNUAP (Fondo de Población de las Naciones Unidas), Centro Latinoamericano y Caribeño de Demografía (CELADE), Division de Población.

———. 2008. *Los pueblos indígenas y afrodescendientes en las fuentes de datos: Experiencias en América Latina*. Santiago del Chile: Comisión Económica para América Latina y el Caribe, CEPAL.

del Popolo, Fabiana, and Susana Schkolnik. 2012. "Indigenous People and Afro-Descendants: The Difficult Art of Counting." In *Everlasting Countdowns: Race, Ethnicity and National Censuses in Latin American States*, edited by Fernando Angosto Ferrandez and Sabine Kradolfer. Cambridge: Cambridge Scholars Publishing.

Denton, Nancy A. and Douglas Massey. 1993. *American Apartheid: Segregation and the Making of the Underclass*. Cambridge: Harvard University Press.

de Roux, Gustavo. 1991. "Orígenes y expresiones de una ideología liberal." In *Boletín Socioeconómico*, no. 22. Centro de Investigaciones y Documentación Socioeconómica CIDSE, Facultad de Ciencias Sociales y Económicas. Cali: Universidad del Valle.

———. 2010. "Políticas públicas para el avance de la población afrocolombiana: Revisión y análisis." Programa de las Naciones Unidas para el Desarrollo (PNUD).

Desmond, Matthew, and Mustafa Emirbayer. 2009. "What is Racial Domination?" *Du Bois Review* 6.

Dirección General del Estadística. 1930 [1993]. *Censo de Población*. Mexico City: INEGI.

Drzewieniecki, Joanna. 2004. "Peruvian Youth and Racism: The Category of Race Remains Strong." Presentation at the meeting of the Latin American Studies Association in Las Vegas.

Duchet, Michele. 1975. *Antropología e historia en el Siglo de la as Luces*. Mexico City: Siglo XXI.

ENADIS. 2010. www.conapred.gob.mx/EDNADIS2010.

Eriksen, Thomas. 1995. *Small Places, Large Issues: An Introduction to Social and Cultural Anthropology*. London: Pluto Press.

Erikson, Robert, and John H. Goldthorpe. 2002. "Intergenerational Inequality: A Sociological Perspective." *Journal of Economic Perspectives* 16, no. 3: 31–44.

Escobar Latapí, Augusto, and Mercedes González de la Rocha. 2005. *Evaluación cualitativa de mediano plazo del Programa Oportunidades en zonas rurales. Evaluación externa de impacto del Programa Oportunidades 2004*. Cuernavaca: INSP. Available at http://www.sedesol.gob.mx/work/models/SEDESOL/Resource/1681/1/images/evaluacion_cualitativa.pdf.

Espinosa, Juan. 1857. *Diccionario republicano*. Lima: Imprenta Libre.

Fernandes, Florestan. 1965. *A integracao do negro na sociedade de classes*. São Paulo: Dominus Editora.

———. 1969. *The Negro in Brazilian society*. New York: Columbia University Press, 1969.

Ferrández, Luis Fernando Angosto, and Sabine Kradolfer. 2012. "Race, Ethnicity and National Censuses in Latin American States: Comparative Perspectives." In *Everlasting Countdowns: Race, Ethnicity and National Censuses in Latin American States*, edited by Luis Fernando Angosto Ferrández and Sabine Kradolfer. Cambridge: Cambridge Scholars Publishing.

Figueiredo, Angela. 2002. *Novas elites de cor: estudo sobre os profissionais liberais negros de Salvador*. São Paulo: Annablume.

Figueroa, Adolfo, and Manuel Barrón. 2005. "Inequality, Ethnicity and Social Disorder in Peru." Crise Working Paper 8. Oxford: University of Oxford.

Filgueira, Carlos. 2001. *La actualidad de viejas temáticas: Sobre los estudios de clase, estratificación y movilidad social en América Latina*. Santiago: CEPAL.

Filgueira, Carlos H., and Andrés Peri. 2004. "América Latina: los rostros de la pobreza y sus causas determinantes." *Serie Población y Desarrollo,* 54. Santiago: CEPAL.

Fischer, Brodwyn M. 2008. *A Poverty of Rights: Citizenship and Inequality in Twentieth-Century Rio de Janeiro*. Palo Alto: Stanford University Press.

Flores, René D., and Edward Telles. 2012. "Social Stratification in Mexico: Disentangling Color, Ethnicity, and Class." *American Sociological Review* 77:486–94.

Florescano, Enrique. 1996. *Etnia, estado y nación: Ensayo sobre las identidades colectivas en México*. Mexico City: Aguilar.

Flórez, Carmen Elisa, Carlos Medina, and Fernando Urrea Giraldo. 2001. "Understanding the Cost of Social Exclusion due to Race or Ethnic Background in Latin American and Caribbean Countries." Paper presented at the meeting Todos Contamos: Los Grupos Étnicos en los Censos, Cartagena de Indias, Colombia.

Flórez, F. 2010. "¿Hijos de la barbarie o de la ciudadanía? Negros y mulatos en el marco del primer centenario de la Independencia de Cartagena, 1911–1941." In *Debates sobre ciudadanía y políticas raciales en las Américas Negras*, edited by Claudia Mosquera Rosero-Labbé, Agustín Laó-Montes, and César Rodríguez Garavito. Bogotá: Universidad Nacional de Colombia.

Fontana, Lorenza. 2013. "Why Are Bolivian Indigenous People Statistically Disappearing?" The Sheffield Institute for International Development: Sheffield UniversityOctober 8, 2013.

Foot-Hardmann, Francisco, and Victor Leonardi. 1988. *História da indústria e do trabalho no Brasil*. São Paulo: Ática.

Francis, Andrew M., and Maria Tannuri-Pianto. 2013. "Endogenous Race in Brazil: Affirmative Action and the Construction of Racial Identity among Young Adults." *Economic Development and Cultural Change* 61, no.4: 731–53.

French, Jan Hoffman. 2009. *Legalizing Identities: Becoming Black or Indian in Brazil's Northeast*. Chapel Hill: University of North Carolina Press.

Freyre, Gilberto. 1933. *The Masters and the Slaves: A Study in the Development of Brazilian Civilization*. Berkeley: University of California Press.

———. 1945. *Brazil: An Interpretation*. New York: Alfred Knopf.

Friedemann, Nina S. de. 1984a. "Estudios de negros en la antropología colombiana: presencia e invisibilidad." In *Un siglo de investigación social*, edited by Nina S. de Friedemann and Jaime Arocha. Bogotá: Etno.

———. 1984b. "Negros en Colombia: identidad e invisibilidad." *América Negra* 3:25–35.

Friedlander, Judith. 1975. *Being Indian in Heuyapan*. New York: St. Martin's Press.

Fry, Peter. 2005. *A persistencia da raca: Ensaios antropologicos sobre o Brasil e a Africa Austral*. Rio de Janeiro: Civilização Brasileira.

Fry, Peter, and Yvonne Maggie. 2007. *Divisões perigosas: Políticas raciais no Brasil contemporâneo*. Rio de Janeiro: Civilização Brasileira.

Fuentes, Manuel. 1867. *Lima: Apuntes históricos, descriptivos, estadísticos y de costumbres*. Paris: Librería Firmín Didot.

Fuenzalida, Fernando. 1971. "Poder, etnía y estratificación social en el Perú actual." In *Perú Hoy*, edited by José Matos Mar et al. Mexico City: Siglo XXI.

Fundação Perseu Abramo. 2004. "Dataset: Racismo no Brasil: percepções da discriminação e do preconceito racial no século XXI." Rosa Luxemburg Stiftung: 174. São Paulo: Editora Fundação Perseu Abramo.

Gaceta del Gobierno de Lima Independiente. 1950. "Decreto del 27 de agosto de 1821." In *Gaceta del Gobierno de Lima Independiente*. La Plata: Universidad Nacional de la Plata.

Galarza, Francisco, Liuba Koga, and Gustavo Yamada. 2011. *Discriminación en el mercado laboral de Lima: Un análisis experimental*. Presentation at the Seminario sobre la Discriminación en el Perú: Entre el estado y el mercado. Universidad del Pacífico, 6 Oct. 2011. Lima: Universidad del Pacífico. Available at http://www.up.edu.pe/ciup/Paginas/JER/Detalle.aspx?IdElemento=227.

Galván, Luz Elena. 2010. *Las disciplinas escolares y sus libros*. Mexico City: CIESAS.

Gamio, Manuel. 2010 [1916]. *Forjando patria*. Boulder: University Press of Colorado.

Gaviria, Alejandro. 2002. *Los que suben y los que bajan: Educación y movilidad social en Colombia*. Bogotá: Fedesarrollo-Alfaomega.

General Directorate of Statistics. 1930. *Quinto censo de población. 15 de mayo de 1930. Resumen General*. Mexico City.

Ghersi, Humberto. 1959. "El indígena y el mestizo en la Comunidad de Marcará." *Revista del Museo Nacional* 28, no.1:118–88.

Gleizer, Daniela. 2012. *El exilio incómodo: México y los refugiados judíos 1933–1945*. Mexico City Universidad Autónoma Metropolitana.

Globo. 2006a. "Documento Contrario a Lei de Cotas e ao Estatuto de Igualdade Racial." In *O Globo*. Rio de Janeiro.

———. 2006b. "Manifesto em Favor da lei de cotas e do Estatuto de Igualdade Racial." In *O Globo*, 13. Rio de Janeiro.

Gobierno del Perú. 1931. *Colección de leyes, decretos y órdenes publicadas en el Perú desde su independencia en el año de 1821 hasta 31 de diciembre de 1834*. Vol. 1. Lima: Imprenta José Masías.

Gobineau, J. A. 1853. *Essai sur l'inégalité des races humaines*. Paris: Belfon.

Goldberg, David Theo. 2002. *The Racial State*. Oxford: Blackwell.

Gómez, Laureano. 1970 [1928]. *Interrogantes sobre el progreso de Colombia*. Bogotá: Editorial Revista Colombiana.

González Casanova, P. 1965. *La democracia en México*. Tlalpan: Ediciones ERA.

González Navarro, Moisés. 1968. "El mestizaje mexicano en el periodo nacional." *Revista Mexicana de Sociología*, 30, no.1 (January–March): 35–52.

———. 1970. *Raza y tierra: La guerra de castas y el henequén*. Mexico City: El Colegio de México.

González Sousa, Luis. 2001. *La agenda nacional después de la marcha zapatista*. Mexico City: Ed. Rizoma.

Gootemberg, Paul. 1995. *Población y etnicidad en el Perú republicano (siglo XIX): Algunas revisiones*. Documento de trabajo 71. Lima: Instituto de Estudios Peruanos.

Goyer, Doreen S., and Eliane Domschke. 1983. *The Handbook of National Population Censuses: Latin America and the Caribbean, North America, Oceania*. Westport, Conn.: Greenwood Press.

Graham, Richard, ed. 1990. *The Idea of Race in Latin America, 1870–1940*. Austin: University of Texas Press.

Grandin, Greg. 2000. *The Blood of Guatemala: A History of Race and Nation*. Durham: Duke University Press.

Gravlee, Clarence C. 2005. "Ethnic Classification in Southeastern Puerto Rico: The Cultural Model of Color." *Social Forces* 83, no. 3: 949–70.

Green, W. John. 2000. "Left Liberalism and Race in the Evolution of Colombian Popular National Identity." *The Americas* 57, no. 1: 95–124.

Gruzinski, Serge. 2000. *El pensamiento Mestizo*. Barcelona: Ediciones Paidós.

Guerrero, Andrés. 1997. "The Construction of a Ventriloquist's Image: Liberal Discourse and the 'Miserable Indian Race' in late 19th Century Ecuador." *Journal of Latin American Studies* 29, no. 3: 550–90.

Guimarães, Antonio Sérgio. 2001. "Democracia racial: O Ideal, o Pacto, e o Mito." *Novos Estudos do CEBRAP* 61:147–62.

———. 2006. "Globalization, Cultural Imperialism or Analytical Categories: Translating Race Categories Worldwide." 16th World Congress of Sociology.

———.2007. "New Ideological Inflections in the Study of Racism in Brazil." In UCLA-Harvard Interdisciplinary Roundtable Conference on Racial, Ethnic and Caste Discrimination and Remedial Measures in Global Perspective. Los Angeles: UCLA.

———. 2011. "Inclusão social nas universidades brasileiras: o caso da UFBA." In *As cores da desigualdade*, vol. 1, edited by D. Fernandes and D. Hedal, 19–41. Belo Horizonte: Fino Traço.

———. 2012. "The Brazilian System of Racial Classification." *Ethnic and Racial Studies* 35:1157–62.

Gullickson, Aaron. 2005. "The Significance of Color Declines: A Re-Analysis of Skin Tone Differentials in Post–Civil Rights America." *Social Forces* 84, no. 1: 157–80.

Gutiérrez Gonzalez, Abril, and Jesús Ramírez Cuevas, eds. 2001. *Una mirada a la marcha de la dignidad indígena*. Mexico City:Gobierno del Estado de Morelos.

Gutiérrez, Ramón A. 1991. *When Jesus Came, the Corn Mothers Went Away: Marriage, Sexuality, and Power in New Mexico, 1500–1846*. Palo Alto: Stanford University Press.

Hale, Charles A. 1968. *Mexican Liberalism in the Age of Mora, 1821–1853*. New Haven: Yale University Press.

Hale, Charles R. 2002. "Does Multiculturalism Menace? Governance, Cultural Rights and the Politics of Identity in Guatemala." *Journal of Latin American Studies* 34, no. 3: 485–524.

Halperin Donhi, Tulio. 1986. *Historia contemporánea de América Latina*. Madrid: Alianza Editorial.

Hanchard, Michael George. 1994. *Orpheus and Power: The Movimento Negro of Rio de Janeiro and São Paulo, Brazil, 1945–1988*. Princeton, N.J.: Princeton University Press.

———. 2003. "Acts of Misrecognition: Transnational Black Politics, Anti-imperialism and the Ethnocentrisms of Pierre Bourdieu and Loïc Wacquant." *Theory, Culture, and Society* 20:5–29.

Hannaford, Ivan. 1996. *Race: The History of an Idea in the West*. Washington, D.C.: Woodrow Wilson Center Press.

Harris, David R., and Jeremiah Joseph Sim. 2002. "Who is Multiracial? Assessing the Complexity of Lived Race." *American Sociological Review*: 614–27.

Harris, Marvin. 1956. *Town and Country in Brazil*. New York: Columbia University Press.

———. 1964. *Patterns of Race in the Americas*. New York: Walker.

———. 1970. "Referential Ambiguity in the Calculus of Brazilian Racial Identity." *Southwestern Journal of Anthropology* 26, no. 1: 1–14.

———. 1995. "A Reply to Telles." *Social Forces* 73:1613–14.

Harris, Marvin, Josildeth Consorte, Joseph Lang, and Bryan Byrne. 1993. "Who Are the Whites? Imposed Census Categories and the Racial Demography of Brazil." *Social Forces* 72:451–62.

Hasenbalg, Carlos Alfredo. 1979. *Discriminação e desigualdades raciais no Brasil*. Rio de Janeiro: Graal.

Hasenbalg, Carlos, and Nelson do Valle e Silva. 1988. *Estrutura social, mobilidade e raça*. São Paulo: Vértice.

Heath, Shirley Brice. 1986. *La política del lenguaje en México: De la colonia a la nación*. Mexico City: CONACULTA / INI.

Helg, Aline. 1990. "Race in Argentina and Cuba, 1880–1930. Theory, Policies and Popular Reaction." In *The Idea of Race in Latin America, 1870–1940*, edited by Richard Graham. Austin: University of Texas Press.

Henriques, Ricardo. 2001. "Desigualdade racial no Brasil: evolução das condições de vida na década de 90." *IPEA*. Available at http://repositorio.ipea.gov.br/bitstream/11058/1968/1/TD_807.pdf.

Hering Torres, Max Sebastián. 2007. "Raza: Variables Históricas." *Revista de Estudios Sociales* (26): 16–27.

———. 2010. "Colores de Piel: Una revisión histórica de larga duración." In *Debates sobre ciudadanía y políticas raciales en las Américas Negras*, edited by Claudia Mosquera Rosero-Labbé, Agustín Laó-Montes, César Rodríguez Garavito. [Cali, Colombia]: Universidad del Valle, Programa Editorial.

Hernández, Aída, Teresa Sierra, and Sarela Paz. 2003. *Los indígenas en tiempos del PAN: Neoindigenismo, resistencia y identidades*. Mexico City: CIESAS.

Hernández, Aída, ed. 2004. *El estado y los indígenas en tiempos del PAN: Neoindigenismo, legalidad e identidad*. Mexico City: CIESAS.

Hill, Michael D. 2010. "Myth, Globalization, and Mestizaje in New Age Andean Religion: The Intic Churincuna (Children of the Sun) of Urubamba, Peru." *Ethnohistory* 57, no. 2: 263–89.

Hofbauer, Andreas. 2006. "Ações afirmativas eo debate sobre racismo no Brasil." *Lua Nova* 68:9–56.

Hoffmann, Odile. 2008. "Entre etnización y racionalización: Los avatares de la identificación entre los afrodescendientes en México." In *Racismo e identidades: Sudáfrica y afrodescendientes en las Américas*, edited by Alicia Castellanos Guerrero, 163–75. Mexico City: UAM-Iztapalapa.

Holmberg, Allan. 1966. *Vicos, método y práctica de antropología aplicada*. Lima: Editorial Estudios Andinos.

Holt, Thomas C. 2000. *The Problem of Race in the Twenty-First Century*. Cambridge, Mass.: Harvard University Press.

Homede, Nuria, and Antonio Ugalde. 2009. "Twenty-Five Years of Convoluted Health Reforms in Mexico." *Plos Medicine* 6, no. 8 (August). Available at http://www .plosmedicine.org/article/info:doi/10.1371/journal.pmed.1000124.

Hooker, Juliet. 2005. "Indigenous Inclusion/Black Exclusion: Race, Ethnicity and Multi-cultural Citizenship in Latin America." *Journal of Latin American Studies* 37:285–310.

Howard, David John. 2001. *Coloring the Nation: Race and Ethnicity in the Dominican Republic*. Oxford, U.K.: Signal Books.

Htun, Mala. 2004. "From 'Racial Democracy' to Affirmative Action: Changing on State Policy on Race in Brazil." *Latin American Research Review* 39:60–89.

Hu-DeHart, Evelyn. 1984. *Yaqui Resistance and Survival: The Struggle for Land and Autonomy, 1821–1910*, Madison: University of Wisconsin Press.

IBGE. 2011. *Características étnico-raciais da população*. Rio de Janeiro: IBGE.

Instituto Indigenista Peruano. 1965. *Plan nacional de integración de la población aborigen (Perú)*. Lima: Instituto Indigenista Peruano.

Instituto Nacional de Estadística e informática. 2001. *Perú: Estimaciones y proyecciones de población, 1950–2050*. Lima: INEI.

———. 2009. *Perú: Fecundidad y sus diferenciales por departamento, provincia y distrito, 2007*. Lima: INEI.

———. 2010a. *Perú: Análisis etnosociodemográfico de las comunidades nativas de la Amazonía, 1993 y 2007*. Lima: INEI.

———. 2010b. *Perú: Perfil de la pobreza por departamentos: 2005–2009*. Lima: INEI.

Instituto Nacional de Planificación. *IV Censo Nacional de Población 1961*. Lima: INP.

Ishida, Kanako. 2003. "Racial Intermarriage between Indígenas and Ladinos in Guatemala." Master's thesis, UCLA.

Jablonski, Nina G. 2012. *Living Color: The Biological and Social Meaning of Skin Color*. University of California Press.

Jaramillo Uribe, Jaime. 1994. "La personalidad histórica de Colombia." *La personalidad histórica de Colombia y otros ensayos*. Bogotá: El Áncora Editores.

Kamel, Ali. 2006. *Não Somos Racistas.* Rio de Janeiro: Nova Fronteira.

Katzew, Ilona. 2004. *La pintura de castas: Representaciones raciales en el México del Siglo XVIII.* Madrid: Consejo Nacional para la Cultura y las Artes.

Kellogg, Susan. 1995. *Law and the Transformation of Aztec Cultura, 1550–1700.* Tulsa: University of Oklahoma Press.

Keith, Verna M., and Cedric Herring. 1991. "Skin Tone and Stratification in the Black Community." *American Journal of Sociology,* no. 3:760–78.

Kertzer, David I., and Dominique Ariel, eds. 2002. *Census and Identity: The Politics of Race, Ethnicity and Language in National Censuses.* Cambridge University Press.

Klein, Herbert S. 1987. *Escravidão africana América Latina e Caribe.* São Paulo: Editora Brasiliense.

Knight, Alan. 1990. "Racism, Revolution and Indigenismo: Mexico, 1910–1940." In *The Idea of Race in Latin America,* edited by Richard Graham. Austin: University of Texas Press.

———. 2004. *Racismo, Revolución e Indigenismo. México 1910–1940.* Puebla: Universidad Benemérita Autónoma de Puebla BUAP.

Kristal, Efrain. 1987. *The Andes Viewed from the City: History and Political Discourse on the Indian in Peru, 1848–1930.* New York: Peter Lang.

Kymlicka, William. 1994. *La política vernácula: Nacionalismo, multiculturalismo y ciudadanía.* Barcelona: Paidos.

———. 1995. *Multicultural Citizenship: A Liberal Theory of Minority Rights.* Oxford: Clarendon Press.

Lamont, Michèle, and Virág Molnár. 2002. "The Study of Boundaries in the Social Sciences." *Annual Review of Sociology* 28:167–95.

Larson, Brooke. 2002. *Indígenas, élites y estado en la formación de las Repúblicas Andinas.* Lima: IEP, PUCP.

———. 2004. *Trials of Nation Making: Liberalism, Race, and Ethnicity in the Andes, 1810–1910.* Cambridge: Cambridge University Press.

Laso, Francisco. 1859. "La paleta y los colores." *La Revista de Lima* 1:231.

Lasso, Marixa. 2007. "Un mito republicano de armonía racial: Raza y patriotismo en Colombia, 1810–1812." *Revista de Estudios Sociales* 27:32–45.

———. 2006. "Race War and Nation in Caribbean Gran Colombia, Cartagena, 1810–1832." *American Historical Review* 11, no. 2: 336–61.

Lavaud, Jean-Pierre, and Françoise Lestage. 2009. "Contar a los indígenas (Bolivia, México y Estados Unidos)." In *El regreso de lo indígena: retos, problemas y perspectivas,* edited by Valerie Robin Azevedo and Carmen Salazar Soler. Lima: IFEA / CBC.

Leal, C. 2010. "Usos del concepto de 'raza' en Colombia." In *Debates sobre ciudadanía y políticas raciales en las Américas negras,* edited by Claudia Mosquera Rosero-Labbé, Agustín Laó-Montes and César Rodríguez Garavito. Bogotá: Programa Editorial.

Le Bon, Gustave. 1889. *Les premières civilisations.* Paris: C. Marpon et E. Flammarion.

Lee, Taeku. 2004. "Social Construction, Self-Identification and the Survey Measure of Race." Presentation. Annual meeting of the American Political Science Association. Chicago.

León García, Enrique. 1909. *Las razas en Lima: Estudio demográfico.* Lima: Universidad Mayor de San Marcos, Facultad de Medicina.

Lippi Oliveira, Lucia Maria. 2000. "Imaginário histórico e poder cultural: as comemorações do Descobrimento." *Revista Estudos Históricos* 14:183–202.

Lipschütz, Alexander. 1994. *El Indoamericanismo y el problema racial en las Américas*. Santiago: Editorial Nascimento.

Lomnitz, Claudio. 2005. *Las salidas del laberinto: Cultura e ideología en el espacio nacional mexicano*. Mexico City: Joaquín Mortiz.

López de Mesa, Luis. 1920. *Los problemas de la raza en Colombia*. Bogotá: Linotipos El Espectador.

Loveman, Brian. 1993. *The Constitution of Tyranny: Regimes of Exception in Spanish America*. Pittsburgh, Pa.: University of Pittsburgh Press.

Loveman, Mara. 2009. "The Race to Progress: Census-Taking and Nation-Making in Brazil." *Hispanic American Historical Review* 89, no. 3: 435–70.

———. 2013. "Census Taking and Nation Making in Nineteenth-Century Latin America." In *State and Nation Making in Latin America and Spain: Republics of the Possible*, edited by M. Centeno and A. E. Ferraro, 307–29. Cambridge: Cambridge University Press.

———. 2014. *National Colors: Racial Classification and the State in Latin America*. Oxford: Oxford University Press.

Loveman, Mara, and Jeronimo Muniz. 2007. "How Puerto Ricans Became White: Boundary Dynamics and Intercensus Racial Reclassification." *American Sociological Review* 72:915–39.

Loveman, Mara, Jeronimo Muniz, and Stanley Bailey. 2012. "Brazil in Black and White? Race Categories, the Census, and the Study of Inequality." *Ethnic and Racial Studies* 35:1466–83.

Lowie, Robert H. 1947. *Primitive Society*. Colección Martin Diskin. New York: Liveright Publishing Corporation.

Mainwaring, Scott, and Aníbal Pérez-Liñán. 2014. *The Rise and Fall of Democracies and Dictatorships: Latin America since 1900*. Cambridge: Cambridge University Press.

Maio, Marcos Chor. 1999. "O projeto Unesco e a agenda das relações raciais no Brasilnos anos 40 e 50." *Revista Brasileira de Ciências Sociais* 14:141–58.

Malik, Savita. 2007. "The Domination of Fair Skin: Skin Whitening, Indian Women and Public Health." San Francisco State University, Department of Health Education. Culminating Experience. http://savitamalik.myefolio.com/uploads/the%20domination%20of%20fair%20skin%20paper%20final%20copy.pdf. Accessed July 10, 2013.

Mallon, Florencia. 1988. "Economic Liberalism: Where We Are and Where We Need to Go." In *Guiding the Invisible Hand: Economic Liberalism and the State in Latin America*, edited by Joseph Love and Nils Jacobsen. New York: Praeger.

———. 1992. "Indian Communities, Political Cultures, and the State in Latin America, 1780–1990." *Journal of Latin American Studies* 24:35–53.

Mangin, William. 1955. "Estructura social en el Callejón de Huaylas." *Revista del Museo Nacional* 24, no. 1:174–89.

Manrique, Nelson. 1993. *Vinieron los Sarracenos: El universo mental de la conquista de América*. Lima: DESCO.

———. 1999. *La piel y la pluma: Escritos sobre literatura, etnicidad y racismo*. Lima: SUR-CIDIAG.

Mareletto, Leticia. 2012. "Educational Inequality by Race in Brazil, 1982–2007: Structural Changes and Shifts in Racial Classification." *Demography* 49:337–58.

Mariátegui, José Carlos. 1928. *Siete ensayos de interpretación de la realidad peruana*. Lima: Minerva.

Martí, José. 1965. *Páginas Escogidas*. Vol. 1. La Havana: Editora Universitaria.

Martínez-Alier, Verena. 1974. *Marriage, Class and Colour in Nineteenth-Century Cuba: A Study of Racial Attitudes and Sexual Values in a Slave Society*. Cambridge: Cambridge University Press.

Martínez Casas, Regina. 1998. "Los avatares de las políticas lingüísticas en México." *Revista Latina de Pensamiento y Lenguaje* 6, no.2: 1–19.

———. 2002. "La invención de la adolescencia: los otomíes urbanos en Guadalajara." *Diario de Campo* 23 (December): 23–35.

———. 2006. "Diversidad y educación intercultural." In *Multiculturalismo: Desafíos y perspectivas*, edited by Daniel Gutiérrez Martínez. Mexico City: Siglo XXI.

———. 2007. *Vivir invisibles: La resignificación de los otomíes urbanos en Guadalajara*. Mexico City: CIESAS.

———. 2010. *Profesionalización de jóvenes indígenas: El caso del IFP en México*. Informe técnico. Mexico City: CIESAS.

Martínez Casas, Regina, and Olivier Barbary. Forthcoming. L'émergence et l'explosion de l'appartenance indigène autodéclarée dans les recensements mexicains de 2000 et 2010.

Martínez Casas, Regina, and Eugenia Bayona Escat. 2010. "Juntos pero no revueltos: Los arreglos familiares de los indígenas urbanos en Guadalajara." In *Familia y tradición: Herencias tangibles e intangibles en escenarios cambiantes*, edited by Nora Edith Jiménez Hernández. Zamora, Michoacán: El Colegio de Michoacán.

Martínez Casas, Regina, and Angélica Rojas. 2010. "Etnicidad y escuela en niños y jóvenes otomíes, mixtecos y purépechas en México." In *Epistemología de las identidades: Reflexiones en torno a la pluralidad*, edited by Daniel Gutiérrez Martínez. Mexico City: UNAM.

Martínez Montiel, Luz María. 1993a. "La cultura africana: Tercera raíz." In *Simbiosis de culturas: Los inmigrantes y su cultura en México*, edited by Guillermo Bonfil Batalla. Mexico City: FCE.

———. 1993b. *Presencia africana en Centroamérica*. Mexico City: SEP.

Martínez, María Elena. 2009. *Genealogical Fictions: Limpieza de Sangre, Religion, and Gender in Colonial Mexico*. Palo Alto: Stanford University Press.

Martínez Novo, Carmen. 2006. *Who Defines Indigenous?: Identities, Development Intellectuals and the State in Northern Mexico*. New Brunswick, N.J.: Rutgers University Press.

Martínez Riaza, Ascensión. 1994. "El Perú y España durante el Oncenio. El Hispanismo en el discurso oficial y en las manifestaciones simbólicas, 1919–1930." *Histórica* 18, no. 2: 335–63.

Martínez-Echazábal, Lourdes. 1998. "Mestizaje and the Discourse of National/Cultural Identity in Latin America, 1845–1959." *Latin American Perspectives*: 21–42.

Marx, Anthony. 1998. *Making Race and Nation: A Comparison of South Africa, the United States and Brazil.* Cambridge: Cambridge University Press.

Marzal, Manuel. 1986. *Historia de la antropología indigenista: México y Perú.* Lima: Pontificia Universidad Católica del Perú.

Massey, Douglas. 2008. *La racionalización de los migrantes mexicanos en Estados Unidos: Estrateficación racial en la teoría y en la práctica.* Zacatecas: Red Internacional de Migración y Desarrollo.

Massey, Douglas, and Magaly Sánchez. 2010. *Brokered Boundaries: Creating Immigrant Identity in Anti-immigrant Times.* New York: Russell Sage Foundation.

Matta, Roberto da. 1984. *O que faz o brasil, Brasil?* Rio de Janeiro: Salamandra.

Mattoso, Katia de Queirós. 1986. *To Be a Slave in Brazil.* New Brunswick, N.J.: Rutgers University Press.

Maureira, Hugo. 2004. "Valiant Race, Tenacious Race, Heroic, Indomitable and Implacable: The War of the Pacific (1879–1884) and the Role of Racial Ideas in the Construction of Chilean National Identity." Presentation. Ponencia presentada en la Conferencia de Estudiantes de ILASSA sobre América Latina, February 2004.

McCaa, Robert, Stuart B. Schwartz, and Arturo Grubesich. 1979. "Race and cClass in Colonial Latin America: A Critique." *Comparative Studies in Society and History* 21, no. 3: 421–33.

McEvoy, Carmen. 2000. "'Bella Lima ya tiemblas llorosa del triunfador chileno en poder': Una aproximación a los elementos de género en el discurso nacioanalista chileno." in *El hechizo de las imágenes: Estatus social y etnicidad en la historia peruana,* edited by Narda Enríquez. Lima: Pontificia Universidad Católica del Perú.

———. 2011. *Guerreros civilizadores: Política, sociedad y cultura en Chile durante la guerra del Pacífico.* Lima: CEB.

Medeiros, Carlos Alberto. 2004. *Na lei e na raca: Legislacao e relacoes raciais, Brasil– Estados Unidos.* Rio de Janeiro: DP&A.

Meisel, Adolfo, and Maria. Aguilera D. 2003. "Cartagena de Indias en 1777: Un análisis demográfico." In *150 años de la abolición de la esclavización en Colombia: Desde la marginalidad a la construcción de la nación.* VI Cátedra Anual de Historia Ernesto Restrepo Tirado. Ministerio de Cultura, PNUD, CERLALC, Convenio Andrés Bello, Fundación Beatriz Osorio Sierra, Museo Nacional de Colombia. Bogotá: Distribuidora y Editora Aguilar, Altea, Taurus, Alfaguara, S.A.

Mello, Marcelo Pereira, and Shirlena Campos de Souza Amaral. 2012. "Cotas para negros e carentes na educação pública superior: Análise do caso UENF, de 2004 a 2010." *InterScience Place* 1:25–49.

Méndez, Cecilia. 1993. *Incas sí, Indios no: Apuntes para el estudio del nacionalismo criollo en el Perú.* Lima: Instituto de Estudios Peruanos.

MESEP: Misión para el Empalme de las Series de Empleo, Pobreza y Desigualdad (Mission for the Assembly of the Statistics Series of Employment, Poverty and Inequality). 2012. "Pobreza monetaria en Colombia: Nueva metodología y cifras 2002–2010. Resultados segunda fase de la Mesep." DNP (Departamento Nacional de Planeación) y DANE (Departamento Nacional de Estadística). Bogotá. https://www.dnp.gov.co/LinkClick.aspx?fileticket=sWVVQZ7fQH4%3D&tabid=337. Accessed July 15, 2013.

Miller, Marilyn Grace. 2004. *Rise and Fall of the Cosmic Race: The Cult of Mestizaje in Latin America*. Austin: University of Texas Press.

Mina, Mateo. 1975. *Esclavitud y libertad en el valle del Río Cauca*. Bogotá: Fundación Rosca de Investigación y Acción Social.

Mina, W., comp. 2011. *Manuel Zapata Olivella: Africanidad, Indianidad, Multiculturalidad*. Santiago de Cali: Universidad del Valle, Universidad de Cartagena.

Ministerio de Hacienda y Comercio, Direccion Nacional de Estadística. 1944. *Censo nacional de población y ocupación 1940*. Vol. 1. Lima.

Ministerio de Relaciones Exteriores. 1921. "Respuesta de Leguía al mensaje de Alfonso XIII, Rey de España." In *Discursos y documentos oficiales en el primer centenario de la Independencia Nacional MCMXXI*. Lima: Imprenta Torres Aguirre.

Montoya, Juan, and Orían Jiménez. 2010. "¿Racismo sin raza? Esclavitud, discriminación y exclusión en el Nuevo Reino de Granada, 1573–1808." In *Debates sobre ciudadanía y políticas raciales en las Américas Negras*, edited by Claudia Mosquera Rosero-Labbé, Agustín Laó Montes, and Cesar Rodriguez Garavito. Bogotá: Universidad Nacional de Colombia. Facultad de Ciencias Humanas. Centro de Estudios Sociales–CES/Universidad del Valle.

Mora, José María. 1950. *México y sus revoluciones*. Mexico City: Porrúa.

Moreno Figueroa, Mónica. 2008. "Negociando la Pertenencia: Familia y Mestizaje en México." in *Raza, etnicidad y sexualidades: Ciudadanía y multiculturalismo en América Latina*, edited by Peter Wade, Fernando Urrea Giraldo, and María Viveros. Bogota: Centro de Estudios Sociales / Universidad Nacional de Colombia.

———. 2010. "Distributed Intensities: Whiteness, Mestizaje and the Logias of Mexican Racism." *Ethnicities* 10, no. 3: 387–401. Available at http://dx.doi.org/10.1177/1468796810372305.

Moreno Morales, Daniel Eduardo. 2008. "Ethnic Identity and National Politics." Ph.D. diss., Vanderbilt University.

Morning, Ann. 2008. "Ethnic Classification in Global Perspective: A Cross-national Survey of the 2000 Census Round." *Population Research and Policy Review* 27, no. 2: 239–72.

———. 2009. "Toward a Sociology of Racial Conceptualization for the 21st Century." *Social Forces* 87:1167–92.

Moura, Roberto. 1988. *Tia Ciata e a Pequena África no Rio de Janeiro*. Rio de Janeiro: Funarte.

Moutinho, Laura. 2004. *Razão, cor e desejo: Uma análise comparativa sobre relacionamentos afetivo-sexuais inter-raciais no Brasil e na Africa do Sul*. São Paulo: UNESP.

Mulholland, Timothy M. 2006. "O sistema de cotas para negros na Universidade de Brasília." Pp. 183–85 in *Ação afirmativa e universidade*, vol. 1, edited by J. Feres Junior and Z. Jonas. Brasília: UnB.

Múnera, Alfonso. 1998. *El fracaso de la nación: Región, clase y raza en el Caribe colombiano (1717–1821)*. Bogotá: Banco de la República: Ancora Editores.

———. 2005. *Fronteras imaginadas: la construcción de las razas y de la geografía en el siglo XIX colombiano*. Bogotá: Editorial Planeta.

———. 2010. "Negros y mulatos en la independencia de Cartagena de Indias: Un balance." In *Indios, negros y mestizos en la independencia*, edited by Heraclio Bonilla. Bogotá: Editorial Planeta.

Muniz, Jeronimo. 2012. "Preto no branco? Mensuração, relevância e concordância classificatória no país da incerteza racial." *Dados* 55:251–82.

Nascimento, Abdias do. 1979. *Mixture or Massacre? Essays in the Genocide of a Black People*. Buffalo, N.Y.: Afrodiaspora.

Navarrete, María Cristina. *Génesis y desarrollo de la esclavitud en Colombia*. Cali: Programa Editorial. Universidad del Valle, 2005

Nobles, Melissa. 2000. *Shades of Citizenship: Race and the Census in Modern Politics*. Stanford, Calif.: Stanford University Press.

Nogueira, Oracy, and Maria Laura Viveiros de Castro Cavalcanti. 1998. *Preconceito de marca: As relacoes raciais em Itapetininga*. São Paulo: EDUSP.

Ñopo, Hugo, Jaime Saavedra, and Máximo Torero. 2007. "Ethnicity and Earnings in a Mixed Race Labor Market." *Economic Development and Cultural Change* 55, no. 4: 709–34.

Ñopo, Hugo, Alberto Chong, and Andrea Moro, eds. 2010. *Discrimination in Latin America: An Economic Perspective*. Washington D.C.: Inter-American Development Bank–World Bank Publications.

O'Gorman, Edmundo. *El arte o de la monstruosidad y otros escritos*. Mexico City: Planeta, 2002.

Olivé, León. 1999. *Multiculturalismo y pluralismo*. Mexico City: Paidos Universidad Nacional Autónoma de México.

Oliveira, João Pacheco de. 1999. "Entrando e Saindo da 'mistura': os indígenas nos censos nacionais." In *Ensaios em antropologia histórica*, edited by J. P. d. Oliveira. Rio de Janeiro: UFRJ.

Omi, Michael, and Howard Winant. 1994. *Racial Formation in the United States: From the 1960s to the 1990s*. New York: Routledge.

Osorio, Rafael Guerreiro. 2008. "Is All Socioeconomic Inequality among Racial Groups in Brazil Caused by Racial Discrimination?" Working Paper no. 43. Brasilia: UNDP–International Poverty Centre.

Pager, Devah, and Hana Shepherd. 2008. "The Sociology of Discrimination: Racial Discrimination in Employment, Housing, Credit, and Consumer Markets." *Annual Review of Sociology* 34:181–209.

Paiva, Angela. 2010. *Entre dados e fatos: Ação afirmativa nas universidades públicas brasileiras*. Rio de Janeiro: Editora PUC.

Paixão, Marcelo JP, and Luiz M. Carvano. 2008. *Relatório anual das desigualdades raciais no Brasil, 2007–2008*. Rio de Janeiro: Editora Garamond.

Paixão, Marcelo, Irene Rossetto, Fabiana Montobanele, and Luiz M. Carvano, eds. *Relatório anual das desigualdades raciais no Brasil, 2009–2010*. Rio de Janeiro: Garamond.

Palacios, Jorge. 1978. "La esclavitud y la sociedad esclavista." In *Manual de historia de Colombia*. Vol. 1, chap. 9. Bogotá: Colcultura.

Palma, Clemente. 1897. *El porvenir de las razas en el Perú*. Lima: Imprenta Torres Aguirre.

Palmer, Ingrid. 1976. *La alimentación y la nueva tecnología agrícola*. Mexico City: Sepsetentas.

Palomar, Cristina. 2004. "En cada charro un hermano." Ph.D. diss., CIESAS-Occidente.

Paredes, Maritza. 2008. "Weak Indigenous Politics in Peru." Crise Working Paper no. 33. Oxford: University of Oxford.

Pásara, Luis. 1988. *Derecho y sociedad en el Perú*. Lima: El Virrey.

Paschel, Tianna S. 2010. "The Right to Difference: Explaining Colombia's Shift from Color-Blindness to the Law of Black Communities." *American Journal of Sociology* 116, no. 3: 729–69.

———. 2011. "States, Movements and the New Politics of Blackness in Colombia and Brazil." Ph.D. diss., University of California, Berkeley.

Patiño, Beatriz. 2011. *Riqueza, pobreza y diferenciación social en la Provincia de Antioquia durante el siglo XVIII*. Grupo de Investigación en Historia Social. Clio. Editorial Universidad de Antioquia, Medellín.

Patrinos, Harry, and G. Psachoroupoulos. 1994. *Indigenous People and Poverty in Latin America: An Empirical Analysis*. Washington, D.C.: World Bank.

Patterson, Orlando. 2005. "Four Modes of Ethno-Somatic Stratification: The Experience of Blacks in Europe and the Americas." In *Ethnicity, Social Mobility, and Public Policy: Comparing the USA and UK*, edited by G. C. Loury, T. Modood, and S. M. Teles. Cambridge: Cambridge University Press.

PCERP. 2008. Características étnico-raciais da população. Rio de Janeiro: IBGE. Available at http://www.ibge.gov.br/home/estatistica/populacao/caracteristicas_raciais/PCERP2_008.pdf

———. 2011. Pesquisa das caracteristicas étnico-raciais da população brasileira. Report in references: IBGE.

Peloso, Vincent, and Barbara Tenenbaum, eds. 1996. *Liberals, Politics, and Power: State Formation in Nineteenth-Century Latin America*. Athens: University of Georgia Press.

Peria, Michelle. 2004. "Acao afirmativa: Um estudo sobre a reserva de vagas para negros nas universidades publicas brasileiras. O caso do Estado do Rio de Janeiro." *Social Anthropology*, Museu Nacional/Federal University of Rio de Janeiro: UFRJ.

Peru Ministerio de Relaciones Exteriores. 1922. *Discursos y documentos oficiales en el primer centenario de la independencia nacional*. Lima: Imprenta Torres Aguirre.

Perz, Stephen G., Jonathan Warren, and David P. Kennery. 2008. "Contribution of Racial Ethnic Reclassification and Demographic Processes to Indigenous Population Resurgence: The Case of Brazil." *Latin American Research Review* 43:7–33.

PESB. 2002. Pesquisa Social Brasileira. Consorcio de Informações Sociais. Available at: http://www.nadd.prp.usp.br/cis/DetalheBancoDados.aspx?cod=B11.

Petrucelli, Jose. 2012. "Ethnic/Racial Statistics: Brazil and and Overview of the Americas." In *Everlasting Countdowns: Race, Ethnicity and National Censuses in Latin American States*, edited by Luis Fernando Angosto Ferrández and Sabine Kradolfer. Cambridge: Cambridge Scholars Publishing.

Pierson, Donald. 1942. *Negroes in Brazil: A Study of Race Contact at Bahia*. Chicago: University of Chicago Press.

Pisano, Pietro. 2012. *Liderazgo político "negro" en Colombia, 1943–1964*. Bogotá: Ediciones Universidad Nacional de Colombia, Facultad de Ciencias Humanas, Departamento de Historia.

Piza, Edith, and Fúlvia Rosemberg. 1999. "Cor nos censos brasileiros." *Revista USP* 40.

Posada Carbó, Eduardo. 2006. *La nación soñada: Violencia, liberalismo y democracia en Colombia*. Barcelona: Editorial Norma.

Portes, Alejandro, and Kelly Hoffman. 2003. "Latin American Class Structures: Their Composition and Change during the Neoliberal Era." *Latin American Research Review* 38, no. 1: 41–82.

Portocarrero, Gonzalo, and Patricia Oliart. 1989. *El Perú desde la escuela*. Lima: Instituto de Apoyo Agrario.

Powell, Brenna Marea. 2009. "Grey Area: Defining Race and the Struggle for Equality in Brazil." Cambridge, Mass.: Harvard University, Government and Social Policy Program.

———. 2011. "Contours of the Group: Using Internal Group Dynamics to Explain Ethnic Outcomes in Brazil, Northern Ireland, and the United States." Ph.D. diss., Harvard University.

Prado, Javier. 1941 [1894]. *Estado social del Perú durante la dominación española (estudio histórico—sociológico)*. Lima: Librería e Imprenta Gil.

Presidencia de la República. 1925. "Discurso del Doctor Julio C. Tello, Director del Museo." *El Perú en el Centenario de Ayacucho. Recopilación efectuada por la Secretaría del señor Presidente de la República de los discursos pronunciados en las ceremonias conmemorativas*. Lima: Editorial Garcilaso.

Quijano, Aníbal. 1980. *Dominación y cultura: Lo cholo y el conflicto cultural en el Perú*. Lima: Mosca Azul.

Quintero Ramírez, Óscar. 2011. "Los afro aquí: Dinámicas organizativas e identidades de la población afrocolombiana en Bogotá." *Boletín de Antropología* 24, no. 41: 65–83.

Reina, Leticia. 2000. *Los retos de la etnicidad en los estados-nación del siglo XXI*. Mexico City: CIESAS.

Reis, Elisa P., and Eustáquio Reis. 1998. "As Elites Agrárias e a Abolição da Escravidão no Brasil." In *Processos e Escolhas*, edited by E. P. Reis, 137–82. Rio de Janeiro: Contracapa.

Rénique, José Luis. 2004. *La batalla por Puno: Conflicto agrario y nación en los Andes Peruanos 1866–1995*. Lima: Instituto de Estudios Peruanos-Sur, Casa de Estudios del Socialismo.

Republica Dominicana. 2012. *La variable étnico-racial en los censos de población en la República Dominicana*. Santo Domingo: Oficina Nacional de Estadística.

Riva Agüero, José de la. 1907. "Prólogo a problemas ético sociológicos del Perú." *El Comercio*, November 3.

Riva Palacio, Vicente. 1884. *México a través de los siglos*. 5 vols. Mexico City: Editorial Cumbre.

Roca, Carlos Toranzo. 2008. "Let the Mestizos Stand Up and Be Counted." In *Unresolved Tensions: Bolivia, Past and Present*, edited by John Crabtree and Laurence Whitehead. Pittsburgh: University of Pittsburgh Press.

Rochabrún, Guillermo, ed. 2011. *¿He vivido en vano? La mesa redonda sobre Todas las Sangres, 23 de junio de 1965*. Lima: Instituto de Estudios Peruanos; PUCP.

Rodrigues, Mário. 1964. *O negro no futebol brasileiro*. Rio de Janeiro: Editôra Civilização Brasileira.

Rodriguez, Clara E. 2000. *Changing Race: Latinos, the Census, and the History of Ethnicity in the United States*. New York: New York University Press.

Rodríguez Garavito, César, Juan Camilo Cárdenas Juan David Oviedo M. Sebastián Villamizar S. 2013. *La discriminación racial en el trabajo: Un estudio experimental en Bogotá Documentos 7*. Centro de Estudios de Derecho, Justicia y Sociedad, Dejusticia Carrera 24 N° 34–61. Bogotá: D.C.

Rodriguez Pastor, Humberto. 1989. *Hijos del Celeste Imperio (1850-1900): Migración, agricultura, mentalidad y explotación*. Lima: Instituto de Apoyo Agrario.

Rojas, Cristina. 2000. *Civilización y violencia. La búsqueda de la identidad en la Colombia del siglo XIX*. Bogotá, Editorial Norma.

Roth, Wendy. 2012. *Race Migrations: Latinos and the Cultural Transformation of Race*. Stanford, Calif.: Stanford University Press.

Rowe, John. 1954. "El movimiento nacional Inca del siglo XVIII." *Revista Universitaria* 107:17–47.

Sáenz, Moisés. 1939. *México integro*, Lima: Torres Aguirre.

Safford, Frank. 1991. "Race, Integration, and Progress: Elite Attitudes and the Indian in Colombia, 1750-1870." *Hispanic American Historical Review* 71, no. 1: 1–33.

Salazar Bondy, Sebastián. 1964. *Lima la horrible*. Lima: Populibros Peruanos.

Salceda, Juan Manuel. 2011. "La(s) APPO(s): Prácticas políticas y juegos del lenguaje en movimiento, 2006-2009." Ph.D. diss., Social CIESAS.

Saldívar, Emiko. 2006. "Estrategias de atención a la diferencia: El programa de educación intercultural de la Ciudad de México." In *El triple desafío: Derechos, instituciones y políticas para la ciudad pluricultural*, edited by Pablo, Molina Yanes and OscarVirginia y González, 99–124. Mexico City: Gobierno del Distrito Federal / UACM.

———. 2008. *Prácticas cotidianas del estado: Una etnografía del indigenismo*. Mexico City: UIA / Plaza y Valdés.

Samper, José María. 1969 [1861]. *Ensayo sobre las revoluciones políticas y la condición social de las repúblicas colombianas (hispano-americanas)*. Bogotá: Universidad Nacional.

Sánchez Albornoz, Nicolás. 1973. *La población de América Latina: Desde los tiempos precolombinos al año 2000*. Madrid: Series Alianza Universidad.

Sanders, James E. 2007. "Pertenecer a la gran familia granadina: Lucha partidista y construcción de la identidad indígena y política en el Cauca, Colombia, 1849-1890." *Revista de Estudios Sociales* 26:28–45.

Sansone, Livio. 2003a. *Blackness without Ethnicity: Constructing Race in Brazil*. New York: Palgrave MacMillan.

———. 2003b. "Multiculturalismo, Estado e modernidade—as nuanças em alguns países europeus e o debate no Brasil." *Dados* 46:535–56.

Santos, José Alcides Figueiredo. 2005. "Efeitos de classe na desigualdade racial no Brasil." *Dados* 48:21–65.

Santos, Wanderley Guilherme. 1979. *Cidadania e justiça: A política social na ordem brasileira*. Rio de Janeiro: Campus Ltda.

Saperstein, Aliya, and Andrew M. Penner. 2012. "Racial Fluidity and Inequality in the United States." *American Journal of Sociology* 118, no. 3: 676–727.

Sariego, Juan Luis. 1988. *Enclaves y minerales en el Norte de México*. Mexico City: CIESAS.

Sawyer, Mark Q. *Racial Politics in Post-revolutionary Cuba*. Cambridge: Cambridge University Press, 2006.

Scalon, Maria Celi. 2004. *Imagens da desigualdade*. Belo Horizonte, MG: Editora UFMG.

Schkolnik, Susana. 2009. "La inclusión del enfoque étnico en los censos de población de América Latina." *Notas de Población-Cepal* 89:57–100.

Schwarcz, Lilia. 1990. "De festa também se vive: Reflexões sobre o centenário da abolição em São Paulo." *Estudos Afro-Asiáticos* 18:13–26.

———. 1993. *O espetáculo das raças: Cientistas, instituições e questão racial no Brasil (1870–1930)*. São Paulo: Companhia das Letras.

Schwartzman, Luisa. 2007. "Does Money Whiten? Intergenerational Changes in Racial Classification in Brazil." *American Sociological Review* 72:940–64.

Schwartzman, Luisa Farah, and Graziella Morães Dias da Silva. 2012. "Unexpected Narratives from Multicultural Policies: Translations of Affirmative Action in Brazil." *Latin American and Caribbean Ethnic Studies* 7, no. 1: 31–48.

Schwartzman, Simon. 1999. "Fora de foco: Diversidade e identidades etnicas no Brasil." *Novos Estudos CEBRAP* 55:83–96.

Sheriff, Robin E. 2001. *Dreaming Equality: Color, Race, and Racism in Urban Brazil*. New Brunswick, N.J.: Rutgers University Press.

Sidanius, Jim, Yesilernis Peña, and Mark Q. Sawyer. 2001. "Inclusionary Discrimination: Pigmentocracy and Patriotism in the Dominican Republic." *Political Psychology* 22:827–51.

Sieder, Rachel. 2002. *Multiculturalism in Latin America: Indigenous Rights, Diversity, and Democracy*. Houndmills, U.K.: Palgrave Macmillan.

Sierra, Justo. 1947. *Conversaciones, cartas y ensayos*. Mexico City: Secretaría de Educación Publica.

———. 1949. *Educación e historia*. Washington, D.C.: Unión Panamericana.

Silva, Graziella Morães Dias. 2006. "Ações afirmativas no Brasil e na África do Sul." *Tempo Social* 18:131–65.

———. 2007. "Recent Debates on Affirmative Action." *ReVista: Harvard Review of Latin American Studies* 6:56–60.

Silva, Graziella Moraes Dias, and Elisa P. Reis. 2011. "Perceptions of Social Mobility, Inequality and Racial Discrimination among Black Professionals in Rio de Janeiro." *Latin American Research Review* 46:55–78.

———. "Multiple Meanings of Racial Mixture." 2012. *Ethnic and Racial Studies* 35:382–99.

Silva, Graziella Moraes, and Luciana T. Leão. 2012. "The Paradox of Mixing: Identities, Inequalities and Perceptions of Discrimination among Brazilian Browns." *Revista Brasileira de Ciências Sociais* 27, no. 80: 117–33.

Silva, Hédio, Jr. 1998. "Crônica da culpa anunciada." In *A cor do medo*, edited by
D. D. D. Oliveira, E. C. Geraldo, R. Barbosa de Lima, and S. A. d. Sá. Brasília: UnB.

Silva, Nelson do Valle. 1978. "Black-White Income Differentials: Brazil, 1960." Ph.D.
diss., University of Michigan.

———. 1994. "Uma nota sobre 'raça social' no Brasil." *Estudos Afro-Asiáticos* 26:67–80.

Skidmore, Thomas. 1972. "Toward a Comparative Analysis of Race Relations since
Abolition in Brazil and the United States." *Journal of Latin American Studies*
4:1–28.

———. 1974. *Black into White: Race and Nationality in Brazilian Thought*. New York:
Oxford University Press.

———. 1976. *Preto no branco: raça e nacionalidade no pensamento brasileiro*. São Paulo:
Paz e Terra.

———. 1990. "Racial Ideas and Social Policy in Brazil, 1870–1940." In *The Idea of Race
in Latin America, 1870–1940*, edited by R. Graham, 7–36. Austin: University of Texas
Press.

———. 1993. *Black into White: Race and Nationality in Brazilian Thought*. Durham:
Duke University Press.

Snipp, C. Matthew. 1989. *American Indians: The First of This Land*. New York: Russell
Sage Foundation.

Solano, Sergio Paolo. 2011. "Raza, trabajo y honorabilidad en Colombia durante el
siglo XIX." In *Infancia de la nación: Colombia durante el primer siglo de la República*.
Bogotá: Pluma de Mompox.

Sollors, Werner, ed. 2000. *Interracialism: Black-White Intermarriage in American
History, Literature, and Law*. Oxford: Oxford University Press.

Spalding, Karen. 1974. *De indio a campesino: Cambios en la estructura social del Perú
colonial*. Lima: Instituto de Estudios Peruanos.

Stavenhagen, Rodolfo. 2001. *La cuestión étnica*. Mexico City: COLMEX.

Stefanoni, Pablo. 2010. *"Qué hacer con los indios": Y otros traumas irresueltos de la
colonialidad*. La Paz: Plural Editores.

Stein, Stanley, and Barbara Stein. 1970. *The Colonial Heritage of Latin America: Essays
on Economic Dependence in Perspective*. Oxford: Oxford University Press.

Stepan, Nancy Leys. 1991. *The Hour of Eugenics: Race, Gender, and Nation in Latin
America*. Ithaca, N.Y.: Cornell University Press.

Steward, Julian, ed. 1946. *Handbook of South American Indians*. Vol. 2: *The Andean
Civilizations*. Washington, D.C.: United States Government Printing Office.

Stubbs, Josefina, and Hiska N. Reyes. 2006. *Más Allá de los Promedios: Afrodescendientes
en América Latina: Resultados de la Prueba Piloto de Captación en la Argentina*.
Universidad Nacional de Tres de Febrero: World Bank.

Sue, Christina. 2007. "Race and National Ideology in Mexico: An Ethnographic Study
of Color, Mestizaje and Blackness in Veracruz." Ph.D. diss., University of California,
Los Angeles.

———. 2013. *The Land of the Cosmic Race: Race Mixture, Racism and Blackness in Mexico*.
New York: Oxford University Press.

Sulmont, David. 2009. "Líneas de frontera y comportamiento electoral en el Perú:
Diferencias sociales y tendencias del voto en las elecciones presidenciales peruanas

1980–2006." In *Cambios Sociales en el Perú: 1968–2008*, edited by Orlando Plaza. Lima: PUCP-CISEPA.

———. 2011. "Race, Ethnicity and Politics in Three Peruvian Localities: An Analysis of the 2005 CRISE Perceptions Survey in Peru." *Latin American and Caribbean Ethnic Studies* 6, no. 1:47–78.

Sulmont, David, and Néstor Valdivia. 2012. "From Pre-modern 'Indians' to Contemporary 'Indigenous People': Race and Ethnicity in Peruvian Censuses, 1827–2007." In *Everlasting Countdowns: Race, Ethnicity and national censuses in Latin American States*, edited by Luis Fernando Angosto Fernández and Sabine Kradolfer. Newcastle upon Tyne: Cambridge Scholars Publishing.

Takaki, Ronald. 1990 [1979]. *Iron Cages: Race and Culture in 19th-Century America*. New York: Oxford University Press.

Tamez González, Silvia, and Catalina Eibenschutz. 2008. "Popular Health Insurance: Key Piece of Inequity in Health in Mexico." *Revista de Salud Pública* 10:133–45.

Tanaka, Martín. 2011. "Peruvian 2011 Elections: A Vote for Moderate Change?" *Journal of Democracy* 2, no. 4: 75–83.

Tanaka, Martín, and Sofía Vera. 2009. *Clivajes estructurales históricos y coyuntura económica en la elección presidencial del 2006*. Ponencia presentada en el 2do Congreso Latinoamericano de Wapor. Lima.

Tannenbaum, Frank. 1992 [1946]. *Slave and Citizen: The Negro in the Americas*. New York: A. A. Knopf.

Tantalean, Javier. 1983. *Política económico-financiera y la formación del estado: Siglo XIX*. Lima: CEDEP.

Taussig, Michael. 2009. *What Color Is the Sacred?* Chicago: University of Chicago Press.

Telles, Edward E. 1995. "Who Are the Morenas?" *Social Forces* 23:1609–11.

———. 2003. "U.S. Foundations and Racial Reasoning in Brazil." *Theory, Culture, and Society* 20:31–47.

———. 2004. *Race in Another America: The Significance of Skin Color in Brazil*. Princeton, N.J.: Princeton University Press.

———. 2007. "Race and Ethnicity and Latin America's United Nations Millennium Development Goals." *Latin American and Caribbean Ethnic Studies* 2:185–200.

———. 2012. "Barbosa Gomes, Joaquim Benedito (Brazil)." *Dictionary of Caribbean and Afro–Latin American Biography*. New York: Oxford University Press. Available at https://sites.google.com/a/oup.com/reference/Home/dcalab.

Telles, Edward, and Stanley Bailey. 2013. "Understanding Latin American Beliefs about Racial Inequality." *American Journal of Sociology* 118, no. 5: 1559–95.

Telles, Edward E., and René Flores. 2013. "More than Just Color: Whiteness Nation and Status in Latin America." *Hispanic American Historical Review* 93, no. 3: 411–49.

Telles, Edward, René Flores, and Fernando Urrea Giraldo. Unpublished. "Why Skin Color Is a Better Predictor of Schooling Than Ethnoracial Identity in Latin America." Presented at the International Sociological Association meetings, Yokohama, 2014.

Telles, Edward, and Denia Garcia. 2013. "Mestizaje and Public Opinion in Latin America." *Latin American Research Review* 48, no. 3: 130–52.

Telles, Edward, and Nelson Lim. 1998. "Does It Matter Who Answers the Race Question? Racial Classification and Income Inequality in Brazil." *Demography* 35, no. 4: 465–74.

Telles, Edward, and Marcelo Paixão. 2013. "Affirmative Action in Brazil." *LASA Forum* 44, no. 2: 10–11.

Telles, Edward, and Tianna Paschel. Forthcoming. "Beyond Whitening: Color Elasticity, Status and Nation in Latin American Racial Classification." *American Journal of Sociology.*

Telles, Edward, and Liza Steele. 2012. "Pigmentocracy in the Americas: How is Educational Attainment Related to Skin Color? *Insights* 73. Latin American Public Opinion Project, Vanderbilt University.

Telles, Edward, and Christina Sue. 2009. "Race Mixture: Boundary Crossing in Comparative Perspective." *Annual Review of Sociology* 35:129–46.

Thorp, Rosemary, and Maritza Paredes. 2010. *Ethnicity and the Persistence of Inequality: The Case of Peru.* New York: Palgrave Macmillan.

Thurner, Mark. 1997. *From Two Republics to One Divided: Contradictions of Postcolonial Nationmaking in Andean Peru.* Durham: Duke University Press.

———. 2003. "Peruvian Genealogies of History and Nation." In *After Spanish Rule: Postcolonial Predicaments of the Americas*, edited by Mark Thurner and Andrés Guerrero. Durham: Duke University Press.

Torche, Florencia, and Seymour Spilerman. 2009. "Intergenerational Influences of Wealth in Mexico." *Latin American Research Review* 44, no. 3: 75–101.

Torche, Florencia, and Guillermo Wormald. 2004. "Estratificación y movilidad social en Chile: Entre la adscripción y el logro." *Serie Políticas Sociales* 98: División de Desarrollo Social, CEPAL, Santiago de Chile: 78.

Tovar, Hermes. 1988. *Hacienda colonial y formación social.* Barcelona: Sendai.

Trivelli, Carolina. 2005. *Los hogares indígenas y la pobreza en el Perú: Una mirada a partir de la información cuantitativa.* Lima: IEP.

Turra, Cleusa, and Gustavo Venturi. 1995. *Racismo cordial.* São Paulo: Editora Ática.

Urías, Beatriz. 2007. *Historias secretas del racismo en México.* Mexico City: Tusquets.

Urrea Giraldo, Fernando. 2010. "Cap. 2: COLOMBIA. Dinámica de reestructuración productiva, cambios institucionales y políticos y procesos de desregulación de las relaciones asalariadas: El caso colombiano." In *Trabajo y modelos productivos en América Latina: Argentina, Brasil, Colombia, México y Venezuela luego de las crisis del modo de desarrollo neoliberal*, compiled by Enrique De la Garza Toledo and Julio Cesar Neffa, 137–200. 1st ed. Buenos Aires: Consejo Latinoamericano de Ciencias Sociales; CLACSO.

———. 2011. "Notas sobre la dinámica organizativa de las poblaciones afrocolombianas." Unpublished.

Urrea Giraldo, Fernando, and Carlos Viáfara López. 2007. *Pobreza y grupos étnicos en Colombia: Análisis de sus factores determinantes y lineamientos de políticas para su reducción.* Bogotá: Departamento Nacional de Planeación.

Valdivia, Néstor. 2011. *El uso de categorías étnico/raciales en censos y encuestas en el Perú: Balance y aportes para una discusión.* Lima: GRADE.

Valdivia, Néstor, Martín Benavides, and Máximo Torero. 2007. "Exclusión, identidad étnica y políticas de inclusión social en el Perú: el caso de la población indígena y la población afrodescendiente." *Grupo de Análisis para el Desarrollo (Grade), Investigación, políticas y desarrollo*, 603–55.

Van Cott, Donna Lee. 2000. *The Friendly Liquidation of the Past: The Politics of Diversity in Latin America*. Pittsburgh, Pa.: University of Pittsburgh Press.

Van den Berghe, Pierre L. 1967. *Race and Racism: A Comparative Perspective*. New York: Wiley.

Vasconcelos, José. 1982 [1925]. *La raza cósmica*. Mexico City: Siglo XXI.

Vaughn, Bobby. 2001a. "Mexico in the Context of the Transatlantic Slave Trade." *Diálogo* 5:14–19.

———. 2001b. "Race and Nation: A Study of Blackness in Mexico." Ph.D. diss., Stanford University.

———. 2005. "Afro-Mexico: Blacks, Indigenous, Politics and the Greater Diaspora." In *Neither Enemies nor Friends*, edited by Anani Dzidzienyo and Suzanne Oboler. New York: Palgrave Macmillan.

Vázquez, Josefina. 1970. *Nacionalismo y educación en México*. Mexico City: COLMEX.

Viáfara, Carlos, Alexander Estacio, and Luisa González. 2010. "Condición étnico-racial, género y movilidad social en Bogotá, Cali y el agregado de las trece áreas metropolitanas en Colombia: un análisis descriptivo y econométrico." *Revista Sociedad y Economiá* (Cali), no. 18: 113–36.

Villa Rojas, Alfonso. 1955. *Los mazatecos y el problema indígena de la cuenca del Papaloapan*. Mexico City: INI.

Villarán, Manuel Vicente.1962. "Las profesiones liberales en el Perú." *Páginas escogidas*. Lima: Talleres Gráficos P. Villanueva.

Villarreal, Andrés. 2010. "Stratification by Skin Color in Contemporary Mexico." *American Sociological Review* 75, no. 5: 652–78.

Villoro, Luis. 1996 [1950]. *Los grandes momentos del indigenismo en México*. Mexico City: FCE.

———. 1998 [1984]. *El proceso ideológico de la Revolución de Independencia*. Mexico City: FCE.

Vinson, Ben, III. 2004. *Afroméxico: El pulso de la historia de la esclavitud en México, una historia recordada, olvidada y vuelta a recorder*. Mexico City: Fondo de Cultura Económica.

Vivas, Harvy. 2007. "Educación, background familiar y calidad de los entornos locales en Colombia." Ph.D. thesis, Universitat Autònoma de Barcelona UAB.

Vivas Pacheco, Harvy, Juan Byron Correa Fonnegra, and Jorge Andrés Domínguez. 2012. "Potencial de logro educativo, entorno socioeconómico y familiar: Una aplicación empírica con variables latentes para Colombia." *Sociedad y Economía* 21:99–124.

Viveros, Mara. 2002. *De quebradores y cumplidores: Sobre hombres, masculinidades y relaciones de género en Colombia*. Bogotá: Universidad Nacional de Colombia, Bogotá.

———. 2012. "Género y racismo: Reflexiones a partir de investigaciones colombianas." In *Memorias eventos Proyecto Dignificación de los afrocolombianos y su cultura a través de la cátedra de estudios afrocolombianos*, edited by María Isabel Mena. Bogotá: Documentos para el Debate.

Viveros, Mara, and Franklin Gil Hernández. 2010. "Género y generación en las experiencias de ascenso social de personas negras en Bogotá." *Maguaré* 24:99–130.

Viveros, Mara and Franklin Gil Hernández. 2012. "Género y racismo: Reflexiones a partir de investigaciones colombianas." In *Memorias eventos Proyecto Dignificación de los Afrocolombianos y su Cultura a través de la Cátedra de Estudios Afrocolombianos*, edited by María Isabel Mena. Bogotá: Documentos para el Debate.

Von Vacano, Diego A. 2012. *The Color of Citizenship: Race, Modernity and Latin American/Hispanic Political Thought.* Oxford: Oxford University Press.

Wade, Peter. 1993. *Blackness and Race Mixture: The Dynamics of Racial Identity in Columbia.* Baltimore: Johns Hopkins University Press.

———. 1997. *Race and Ethnicity in Latin America.* London: Pluto Press.

———. 2000. *Music, Race and Nation: "Música Tropical" in Colombia.* Chicago: University of Chicago Press.

———. 2005. "Rethinking Mestizaje: Ideology and Lived Experience." *Journal of Latin American Studies* 37, no. 2: 239–57.

———. 2009. *Race and Sex in Latin America.* London: Pluto Press.

Wagley, Charles, ed. 1952. *Race and Class in Rural Brazil.* Paris: UNESCO.

Walker, Charles. 1988. "The Patriotic Society: Discussions and Omissions about Indians in the Peruvian War of Independence." *Americas* 55, no. 2: 275–98.

Walsh, Casey. 2004. "Eugenic Acculturation: Manuel Gamio, Migration Studies and the Anthropology of Development in Mexico, 1910–1940." *Latin American Perspectives* 31, no. 5 (September):118–45.

———. 2011. "Managing Urban Water Demand in Neoliberal Northern Mexico." *Human Organization* 70, no. 1: 54–62.

Whitten, Norman E. 2004. "Symbolic Inversion, the Topology of El Mestizaje, and the Spaces of Las Razas in Ecuador." *Journal of Latin American Anthropology* 8, no. 1: 52–85.

Wimmer, Andreas. 2013. *Ethnic Boundary Making: Institutions, Power, Networks.* New York: Oxford University Press.

Winant, Howard. 2001. *The World Is a Ghetto: Race and Democracy since World War II.* New York: Basic Books.

World Bank. 2012. "GDP per capita, PPP (Current international $)" http://data .worldbank.org/indicator/NY.GDP.PCAP.PP.CD (accessed 15 June)

Yankelevich, Pablo. 2009. "La arquitectura de la política de inmigración en México." In *Nación y extranjería* edited by Pablo Yankelevich, 187–230. Mexico City: Universidad Nacional autónoma de México.

Yashar, Deborah J. 2005. *Contesting Citizenship in Latin America: The Rise of Indigenous Movements and the Postliberal Challenge.* Cambridge Studies in Contentious Politics. Cambridge: Cambridge University Press.

Yepes, Ernesto. 1972. *Perú 1820–1920: Un siglo de desarrollo capitalista.* Lima: Instituto de Estudios Peruanos.

Zapata Olivella, Manuel. 1978. "Identidad del Negro en América Latina." *Revista Rotaria* 18 (June): 45–9. Pereira: Gráficas Olímpicas.

———. 2004. Entrevista periódico EL TIEMPO. Publicada en su edición del 28/05/2004.

———. 2010. *Por los senderos de sus ancestros: Textos escogidos, 1940–2000*. Bogotá: Ministerio de Cultura.

Zavala, Silvio, José Miranda, and Alfonso Caso. 1954. *Métodos y resultados de la política indigenista en México*. Memorias del Instituto Nacional Indigenista, vol. 6, Mexico City: INI.

Zenteno, René, and Patricio Solís. 2006. "Continuidades y discontinuidades de la movilidad ocupacional en Monterrey." *Estudios Demográficos y Urbanos* 21, no. 3: 515–46.

# ABOUT THE AUTHORS

JUAN CARLOS CALLIRGOS is professor of social sciences at the Catholic University of Peru. He is an anthropologist with a Ph.D. in history. He has carried out research on ethnicity and racism, gender and masculinities, and national identity. He has authored *El racismo: La cuestion del otro (y de uno)*.

RENÉ D. FLORES recently received a Ph.D. in sociology and social policy at Princeton University and is now a Robert Wood Johnson Fellow at the University of Michigan. His research interests include international migration, race and ethnicity, social stratification, and ethnic conflict, with a focus on the United States, Latin America, and Spain. His work has appeared in the *American Sociological Review* and the *Hispanic American Historical Review*.

REGINA MARTÍNEZ CASAS is an anthropologist and linguist at the Center for Research and Advanced Study in Social Anthropology (CIESAS), where she coordinates the Graduate Program of Indo-American Linguistics. Her research and teaching interests are in indigenous education, interethnic relations, anthropological linguistics, and the history of social-anthropological theory. In 2007 she authored *Vivir invisibles: La resignificación cultural entre los otomíes urbanos de Guadalajara*.

MARCELO PAIXÃO is a professor at the Institute of Economics at the Federal University of Rio de Janeiro. He is also coordinator of the Laboratory for Economic, Historic, Social and Statistical Analysis of Race Relations (LAE-SER), which has produced the *Annual Report on Racial Inequality in Brazil* for 2007–8 and 2009–10. In 2014 he authored *A lenda da modernidade encantada: Por uma crítica ao pensamento social brasileiro sobre relações raciais e projeto de Estado-Nação*.

EMIKO SALDÍVAR is associate researcher and lecturer at the University of California, Santa Barbara, and previously she was a professor at the Universidad Iberoamericana in Mexico City. Her work focuses on race and ethnicity in Mexico with a special emphasis on state formation and indigenous people. She is the author of *Practicas cotidianas del estado: Una etnografia del indigenismo*.

GRAZIELLA MORAES SILVA is professor of sociology and department chair at the Federal University of Rio de Janeiro (UFRJ) and an associate of the Interdisciplinary Center for Inequality Studies (NIED) and the Graduate School of Anthropology and Sociology (PPGSA). She has recently written articles about the experiences and attitudes of black professionals in Brazil and South Africa, which have been published in *Latin American Research Review* and *Ethnic and Racial Studies*.

CHRISTINA A. SUE is an assistant professor of sociology at the University of Colorado, Boulder. Her research focuses on race, ethnicity, and immigration, with a regional focus on the United States and Latin America. Her work has been published in the *American Journal of Sociology*, the *Annual Review of Sociology*, and *Ethnic and Racial Studies*. In 2013 she authored *Land of the Cosmic Race: Race Mixture, Racism, and Blackness in Mexico*.

DAVID SULMONT is a professor of sociology at the department of social sciences and director of the Institute of Public Opinion at the Catholic University of Peru (PUCP). He has published several articles on race and ethnicity in Peru and is currently a member of the Technical Committee on Ethnic Statistics of the National Statistics ad Computational Institute.

EDWARD TELLES is professor of sociology, director of the Center for Migration and Development at Princeton University, and principal investigator of PERLA. He has written widely on race and ethnicity in Latin America and on immigration and assimilation in the United States. In 2004 he authored *Race in Another America: The Significance of Skin Color in Brazil*.

FERNANDO URREA GIRALDO is a sociologist and emeritus professor at the Universidad del Valle in Cali, Colombia. He has published research on urban indigenous populations; the black middle class; development and labor; and race, ethnicity, and sexuality. In 2004 he coauthored *Gente negra en Colombia: Dinámicas sociopolíticas en Cali y el Pacífico*.

CARLOS AUGUSTO VIÁFARA LÓPEZ is associate professor in the department of economics at the Universidad del Valle. He has published widely on economic and social development; poverty; access to education, labor markets, and social mobility; and policies for racial inclusion. He has participated in various government initiatives regarding policies for the Afro-Colombian population, most recently as high commissioner for the Inclusion of Afro-Colombians for Santiago de Cali.

MARA VIVEROS VIGOYA is professor of anthropology and researcher at the School of Gender Studies at the Colombian National University. She has published widely on sexuality, masculinity and health, mobility and racial inequality, multiculturalism in Latin America, and the black middle classes. Among her many books, she has authored *De quebradores y cumplidores: Sobre hombres, masculinidades y relaciones de género en Colombia.*

# INDEX

NOTE: Figures and tables are indicated by *f* and *t*.

Arguedas, José María, 126–27, 140, 245
  (n. 2)
Asian immigrants: in Brazil, 187, 249
  (n. 26); in Peru, 245 (n. 10)
Asociación de Afrocolombianos
  Desplazados (AFRODES, Displaced
  Afro-Colombian Association), 91
Asociación Popular de los Pueblos de
  Oaxaca, 240 (n. 34)
Assimilation, 237 (n. 6)
Attitudes, racial, in methodology, 14
Aymara, in Bolivian census, 8
Azevedo, Fernando, 186
Azevedo, Thales de, 248 (n. 16)

Barbosa, Joaquim, 173
Barth, Frederik, 30
Belaúnde, Victor Andrés, 138, 139
Black Brazilian Front (Frente Negra
  Brasileira, FNB), 179
Black Club of Colombia, 91
Blacks. See Afrodescendant(s)
Boas, Franz, 18, 37, 43–44, 79, 179, 238
  (n. 7), 248 (n. 14)
Bolivia: Afrodescendant population in,
  26t; census in, 8; indigenous popula-
  tion of, 127; mestizaje in, 20
Bourdieu, Pierre, 12, 237 (n. 4)
Bozal, 242 (n. 13)
Brading, David, 41
Brazil: affirmative action in, 173–74,
  179–83, 181–83, 198–99, 248 (n. 19), 250
  (n. 43); African slaves imported to, 1;
  Afrodescendant population in, 26t, 28,
  186–87; Afrodescendants in, 173–74,
  178–83, 191–92, 199; ambiguity in,
  221; arts in, 172; Asian immigrants in,
  187; census in, 9, 25, 174, 183–90, 186f,
  189f; choice of, for PERLA, 5; cultural
  differences between racial groups in,
  perception of, 196–97, 197t; democratization in, 173, 181; discrimination
  in, 174, 179–80, 211–14, 212t, 231t,
  233t, 251 (n. 56), 252 (n. 57); economic
  development in, 177–78; education

in, 174, 182, 201–2, 203–4, 204f, 225f,
  228f, 247 (n. 6), 248 (n. 19); ethnoracial
  categories in, 175; Eusébio de Queiroz
  law in, 247 (n. 8); First Republic in,
  176; in Freyre, 178–79; Fundação
  Perseu Abramo in, 189, 193, 198, 207;
  identity in, 190–92, 191f; independence
  of, 175–76; indigenous organization
  support in, 71; indigenous people in,
  197, 197t; inequality in, 172–73, 180,
  199–202, 207–9; interdependence
  within racial groups in, 195, 196f; labor
  in, 178; leftist government in, inequality and, 23; Marxism in, 179; Mensalão
  in, 173; mestizaje in, 19, 20, 177–79, 185,
  222–23; mestizo in, 187; multiculturalism in, 198–99, 198f; national identification in, racial identification vs.,
  195, 196f; New State in, 176; otherness
  in, 197, 197t; Paraguayan War and, 17;
  PERLA in, 190–214, 191f, 193t, 194f,
  196f, 197t, 198f, 203f, 204f, 205f, 206f,
  209f, 210t, 212t; Portugal and, 17; pride
  in, 195, 196f; public policy on inequality in, support for, 69, 198–99, 198f,
  234t; race in, 178–79; racial democracy
  in, 177–83; Racial Equality Statute in,
  30; racial hierarchy in, 209–11, 210t;
  racial identification in, dimensions
  of, 195–99, 196f, 197t, 198f; racism in,
  207–8, 252 (n. 57); scientific racism
  in, 176–77; Second Republic in, 177;
  self-identification in, 192–94, 193t,
  194f, 202–7, 203f, 204f, 205f; skin color
  in, 175, 187–88, 193–94, 194f, 202, 203f;
  slavery in, 17, 175–76, 247 (n. 8), 248
  (n. 10); social mobility in, 173, 199,
  200–201, 247 (n. 6); Supreme Court in,
  173; Vargas and, 177, 178; white immigration to, 177; whitening in, 176–77,
  185, 190, 201, 202; white population in,
  in colonial period, 16; whites in,
  184–85, 190
Brazilian Eugenics Conference, 176
Brubaker, Rogers, 142

Buffon, Comte de, 134
Busto, José Antonio del, 139

as New Granada, 84, 241 (n. 5); otherness in, 122; PERLA in, 96–120; poverty
in, 105–6; public policy attitudes in,
multicultural, 118–20, 119f, 120t, 234t;
racism in, 81–82; Regeneración regime
in, 86–87, 241 (n. 11); *resguardos* in,
86, 87, 240 (n. 1), 241 (n. 10); runaway
slaves in, 85; self-identification in, 94,
101f, 102f, 103, 103t, 222, 242 (n. 24);
skin color in, 98f, 99–102, 101f, 122;
slavery in, 81, 82, 85–86, 122, 241 (n. 9);
social mobility in, 86, 101, 119–20;
whiteness in, 82, 124; whitening in,
19, 88–89, 92, 99; white population in,
in colonial period, 16; women in, 123
Colonization: in Colombia, 84–87; in
ethnoracial history, 15–16; labor and,
38–39; of Mexico, 38–39; sex ratios and,
15; whitening and, 15–18
Color. *See* Skin color
Color palette, for skin color, 11–13, 243
(n. 30)
Commission for Andean, Amazonian,
and Afro Peruvian People, Environ-
ment, and Ecology (Peru), 170
Community collaboration, in Colombia,
119–20, 120t
"Compiled Laws of the Indian Kingdoms"
(Colombia), 81
Conferencia Nacional de Organizaciones
Afrocolombianas (CNOA, National
Conference of Afro-Colombian
Organizations), 91
Conservative governments, 23
Coordinación Nacional de Comunidades
Negras (National Coordination of
Black Communities) (Colombia), 91
Córdoba, Diego Luis, 82
Costa Rica: Afrodescendant population
in, 26t; census in, 8; mestizaje in, 19;
white self-identification in, 59
Criollos: in Colombia, 86, 242 (n. 13);
mestizaje and, 15
Cuba, 17, 18, 25, 26t, 238 (n. 8)
*Cultura criolla*, 56

Darwinism, 42, 238 (n. 8)
Data Opinión Publica y Mercados, 5
Davis, Angela, 99
Degregori, Carlos Iván, 166, 167
Democratic Action Movement (Colombia), 91
Democratization, 22, 23, 173, 181
Dewey, John, 44
Díaz, Porfirio, 41, 238 (n. 6)
Discrimination: in Brazil, 174, 179–80,
211–14, 212t, 231t, 233t, 251 (n. 56), 252
(n. 57); in Colombia, 113–18, 114t, 115f,
116f, 117f, 231t, 233t; democratization
and, 23; education and, 66t, 67t;
identity and, 67t; "inclusionary,"
195–96; inequality without, 207–8;
language and, 65, 66, 66t; mestizaje
and, 230; in Mexico, 65–68, 66t, 67t,
231t, 233t; perception of, 65–68, 113–18,
114t, 115f, 116f, 117f, 229–32, 231t; in
Peru, 129, 163–64, 164t, 165f, 231t, 233t;
questions on experience of, in research
methodology, 14; scientific, 18; self-
identification and, 10; skin color and,
66t, 67, 67t, 68f, 113–18, 114t, 115f, 116f,
117f, 163–64, 164t, 165f, 212–14, 212t; in
United States, 65. *See also* Racism
Dominican Republic, 21, 25, 26t, 195–96

Economic development, 22, 177–78
Ecuador, 9, 26t
Education: in Brazil, 174, 182, 201–2,
203–4, 204f, 225f, 228f, 247 (n. 6),
248 (n. 19); in Colombia, 225f, 228f;
discrimination and, 66t, 67t; family
background and, 106–8, 107f, 108f;
indigenous identity and, in Mexico, 64;
of indigenous people in Mexico, 44–45;
mestizo identity and, 223; mestizo
self-identification and, 57f; in Mexico,
225f; occupation and, 106–8, 107f,
108f; in Peru, 155–56, 156f, 162f, 225f,
228f; return on, 73; skin color and, 74,
74f, 75f, 106–8, 107f, 108–9, 108f, 109f,
155–56, 156f, 161f, 162f, 202, 203–4, 203f,

204f, 228f; social mobility and, 160. *See also* Affirmative action

Elites: in Brazil, 176; castas system and, 40; in Colombia, 86, 88, 92; independence and, 1; indigenous alliances with, in Mexico, 41; mestizaje and, 88; in Mexico, 40, 41, 42–43; nation-building and, 17; in Peru, 131, 132, 134–35; as white, 83; whitening and, 1, 18, 88

El Salvador, Afrodescendant population in, 26t

Employment. *See* Occupation

ENAHO. *See* Encuestas Nacionales de Hogares

ENCO. *See* Encuesta Nacional Continua

*Encomienda*, 84–85

"Encomiendas," 38

Encuesta Nacional Continua (ENCO), 146, 147, 246 (n. 24)

Encuestas Nacionales de Hogares (ENAHO), 142–43, 146, 147–48

Ethnicity: in Brazilian official statistics, 183–90, 186f, 189f; defined, 30; as multidimensional, 219–23; in Peruvian official statistics, 142–48, 143f, 144t, 145f; race vs., 30–31; skin color and, 154–55, 155f; as social construct, 32–33; social interactions and, 30–31; social mobility and, 159–63, 160f, 161f, 162f. *See also* Race; Skin color

Ethnic statistics, official, 24–29; in Brazil, 183–90, 186f, 189f; in Peru, 142–48, 143f, 144t, 145f. *See also* Census

Ethnic therapeutics, 135, 136

Ethnoracial categories: in Brazil, 175, 190–92, 191f, 201–2; in census, 8–10, 24; inequality and, 223–26, 224t, 225f; and measurement of race/ethnicity, 219–23; mestizaje and, 21–22; in official statistics, 24–29; in Peru, 142–48, 143f, 144t, 145f, 168; polysemy of, 53–54; poverty and, 105–6; self-identification with, 9–10, 28; skin color in, 10–14, 175; as term, 30. *See also* Ethnicity; Race

Ethnoracial composition: of Colombia, 94t; of Mexico, 53f; of Peru, 151f. *See also* Ethnoracial categories: in Brazil

Ethnoracial grammar, 130

Ethnoracial history, in Latin America, 14–24

Ethnoracial movements, in Colombia, 90–92

Eugenics, 176, 185. *See also* Neo-Lamarckian genetics; Scientific racism

Eusébio de Queiroz law, in Brazil, 247 (n. 8)

Family: differing experiences within, 230; education and, 106–8, 107f, 108f; mestizo identity and, in Mexico, 57; occupation and, 106–8, 107f, 108f; self-identification and, in Colombia, 103–4, 103t; self-identification and, in Mexico, 58f

Femininity, 99–100, 123. *See also* Women

Fernandes, Florestan, 179

"Fifth race," 37

"First Census of Native Communities in the Peruvian Amazon Region," 147

First International Statistical Congress, 184

FNB. *See* Black Brazilian Front

*Forging a Fatherland* (Gamio), 36

Free Womb law (Colombia), 82

French Intervention (Mexico), 42

Freyre, Gilberto, 18, 20, 139, 172, 178–79, 185, 248 (nn. 14–15). *See also* Racial democracy

Friendship, in Mexico, between indigenous and nonindigenous citizens, 72–73, 73f

Fundação Perseu Abramo, 189, 193, 198, 207

Gaitán, Jorge Eliecer, 87, 88–89, 242 (n. 17)

Gallego, Andrés, 85

Gamio, Manuel, 18, 20, 36, 37, 43–44, 77, 78, 79, 238 (n. 8), 238 (n. 10)

Gender, 98*f*, 99–100, 123. *See also* Women

Genetics, neo-Lamarckian, 18, 134

Ghersi, Humberto, 140

Grammar, ethnoracial, 130

Gran Colombia, 17

Guatemala: Afrodescendant population in, 26*t*; census in, 8; indigenous population of, 127; intermarriage in, 22; mestizaje in, 237 (n. 5)

Guelaguetza celebrations, 32

*Haciendas*, 126, 165–66

Hair, 97, 98*f*, 194, 204–6, 206*f*

Hale, Charles, 23–24

*Handbook of South American Indians* (Steward), 140–41

Harris, Marvin, 33, 221, 248 (n. 16)

Hasenbalg, Carlos, 181

Hispanismo, in Peru, 19–20, 136–38

History, ethnoracial, in Latin America, 14–24

Honduras, Afrodescendant population in, 26*t*

hooks, bell, 99

Identity: Afrodescendant, dynamics of, in Colombia, 97–105, 98*f*, 101*f*, 102*f*, 103*t*, 105*t*; as ambiguous, 220; in Brazil, 190–92, 191*f*; dimensions of, in Brazil, 195–99, 196*f*, 197*t*, 198*f*; discrimination and, 67*t*; geography and, in Mexico, 59–60, 61, 62*f*, 239 (n. 21); indigenous, in Mexico, 61–64; mestizo, in Mexico, 56–58, 58*f*; pride and, 195, 196*f*; skin color and, 100–102, 101*f*

IGAC. *See* Instituto Geográfico Agustín Codazzi de Colombia

Immigration: to Argentina, white, 18; to Brazil, white, 177, 185; Chinese, 245 (n. 10); Japanese, to Brazil, 249 (n. 26); mestizaje and, 78; to Peru, Chinese, 245 (n. 10); to Peru, white, 134, 135–36; restrictions, in Mexico, 78; sex ratio and, 15; social mobility and, 167; whitening and, in Mexico, 88

Import-substitution-industrialization (ISI), 177

"Improve the race": in Brazil, 251 (n. 52); in Colombia, 116–17, 117*f*, 124

"Inclusionary discrimination," 195–96

Independence: of Brazil, 175–76; of Colombia, 86; elites and, 1; in ethnoracial history, 17–18; of Mexico, 40–43; of Peru, 131, 137; whitening and, 15–18

Indian, as category in Peru, 131, 132

Indigenismo: institutionalization of, 44–45; in Mexico, 43–45, 238 (n. 6); in Peru, 136–38

Indigenous organizations, support for, 70*f*, 71

Indigenous people: activism of, 23; Afrodescendant vs., 32–34; as ambiguous, 222; Bolivian population of, 127; in Brazil, 197, 197*t*; as census category, 8–9, 28, 48–49; in Colombia, 82–84, 89; Colombian population of, historical estimates of, 92–96, 93*f*, 94*t*, 95*f*; colonial population of, 16; criteria used to identify, 51–52, 51*f*; as culturally distinct, 32; customs as markers of, 146; democratization and, 23; education level and self-identification as, in Mexico, 64; education level and self-identification as, in Peru, 161*f*; education of, in Mexico, 44–45; elite alliances with, in Mexico, 41; *encomienda* and, 84–85; experiences, 31–34; friendships with, by nonindigenous, in Mexico, 72–73, 73*f*; Guatemalan population of, 127; identity as, in Mexico, 61–64; indicators used for, 150*t*; as laborers in Colombia, 84; language and, 31, 44–45, 49, 49*f*, 61, 62–63, 63*f*, 70, 145–46; as mestizo, 32; Mexican independence and, 40–41; in Mexican population, 50*f*, 51*f*, 53*f*; in Mexico, 38–40, 40–41, 47–48, 48–53, 49*f*, 61–64, 68–70, 69*f*, 70*f*; occupations among, in Peru, 160*f*; otherness of, 46, 83; in Peru, 131–33, 149–51, 151*f*, 152*f*, 153*t*,

168–71; in Peruvian politics, 165–67; Peruvian population of, 127, 128*f*, 143*f*, 145–46, 145*f*; population numbers, 28; Porfiriato and, 42–43; poverty among, explanations of, 68–69, 69*f*, 158–59, 158*f*, 240 (n. 29); poverty among, in Peru, 127–29; rebellions in Mexico, 41; romanticization of, 46; segregation of, 39; self-identification of, 51–52, 62*f*, 154–55, 155*f*; skin color and self-identification as, in Mexico, 55*f*; Zapatista rebellion and, 47

*Indio* category, 25, 131–32

Inequality: in Brazil, 172–73, 180, 199–202, 207–9; in Colombia, 105–13, 107*f*, 108*f*, 109*f*, 110*f*, 111*f*, 112*f*; in Mexico, 42, 45, 65, 69, 73–76, 74*f*, 75*f*, 76*f*; in Peru, 129–30, 155–59, 156*f*, 157*f*, 158*f*, 166; pigmentocracy and, 4, 223–26, 224*t*, 225*f*; public policy on in Mexico, support for, 69–70, 70*f*; skin color and, 13, 226–29, 227*t*, 228*f*; socioeconomic status attainment and, 105–13, 107*f*, 108*f*, 109*f*, 110*f*, 111*f*, 112*f*; without discrimination, 207–8

"Inquisition Laws," in Colombia, 81–82

Institutionalization, of indigenismo, 44–45

Instituto Análise, 5

Instituto Geográfico Agustín Codazzi de Colombia (IGAC), 93, 94*t*

Instituto Indigenista Peruano, 139

Instituto Nacional Indigenista (INI), 45, 139

Interdependence, within racial groups in Brazil, 195, 196*f*

Intermarriage, 22; in Colombia, 82, 241 (n. 3); in Mexico, 71–72, 72*f*

International Labor Organization Convention 169, 24–25, 239 (n. 12)

Interviewer identification, self-identification vs., 54*t*, 103*t*

IPSOS Apoyo, 5

ISI. *See* Import-substitution-industrialization

Japanese immigrants, in Brazil, 249 (n. 26)

Jaramillo Uribe, Jaime, 83, 87, 89

Kaqchikel, in Guatemalan census, 8

Katz, Friedrich, 41

Kiche, in Guatemalan census, 8

Labor: in Brazil, 178; in Colombia, 84; colonization and, 38–39, 84; in Mexico, 38–39

Land ownership, in Colombia, 86–87, 244 (n. 43)

Language: discrimination and, 65, 66, 66*t*; indigenous peoples and, 31, 44–45, 49, 49*f*, 61, 62–63, 63*f*, 70, 145–46; mestizaje and, 37, 44–45; in Mexico, 49, 50; self-identification and, 62–63, 63*f*; teaching of indigenous, in Mexico, 70, 70*f*

LAPOP. *See* Latin American Public Opinion Project

Laso, Benito, 246 (n. 13)

Latin American Public Opinion Project (LAPOP), 96, 97

Law 70 (Colombia), 91–92

Le Bon, Gustave, 134

Leclerc, Georges-Louis, 134

Leftist governments, 23

Leguía, Augusto B., 137

Liberal Reforms (Mexico), 42

Lipschutz, Alejandro, 3–4

Mangin, William, 140

Manumission Law (Colombia), 241 (n. 9)

Mariátegui, José Carlos, 139

Marriage. *See* Intermarriage

Marxism: in Brazil, 179; in Peru, 166–67

Masculinity, 99

Mayan-Yucatec language, 63, 63*f*

Mensalão, 173, 247 (n. 3)

Mestizaje: ambiguity and, 21; in Argentina, 19, 237 (n. 5); Argentinian model of, in Colombia, 88; assimilation and, 237 (n. 6); in Bolivia, 20; books on,

in Peru, 154–55, 155–56, 155f, 156f; race vs., 10–11; self-identification and, 55f, 100–102, 101f, 102f, 104–5, 193–94, 194f, 202–7, 203f, 204f, 205f; social mobility and, 101, 200; socioeconomic status and, 156–58, 157f; sun exposure and, 237 (n. 2); whiteness and, 56

Slavery: abolition of, in Colombia, 82, 85, 241 (n. 9); in Brazil, 17, 175–76, 247 (n. 8), 248 (n. 10); in Colombia, 81, 82, 85–86, 122, 241 (n. 9); in Dominican Republic, 21; mestizaje and, 20–21; in Mexico, 39; in Peru, 133, 245 (n. 7)

Slaves, runaway, 85

Social determinism, 12

Social distance, 1, 68–73, 69f, 70f, 72f, 73f. *See also* Otherness

Social interactions, ethnicity and, 30–31

Social mobility, 32; in Brazil, 173, 199, 200–201, 247 (n. 6); in Colombia, 86, 101, 119–20; immigration and, 167; in Mexico, 70; in Peru, 159–63, 160f, 161f, 162f, 169; skin color and, 101, 200

"Social race," 200, 215

Socioeconomic status: affirmative action and, 182–83; inequality and, 105–13, 107f, 108f, 109f, 110f, 111f, 112f; skin color and, 156–58, 157f; social mobility and, 200–201

Spain, *castas* system under, 15–16

Spanish immigrants, in Mexico, 78

Spanish language, 31, 63

Spouses, self-identification and, 104, 105t

Statistics, official ethnic, 24–29; in Brazil, 183–90, 186f, 189f; in Peru, 142–48, 143f, 144t, 145f. *See also* Census

Steward, Julian, 140–41

Study on Ethnic and Race Characteristics of the Population (Pesquisa sobre as características etnico-raciais da população, PCERP), 189, 249 (n. 31)

Sun exposure, skin color and, 237 (n. 2)

Supreme Court of Brazil, 173

Symbolic capital, 237 (n. 4)

Tello, Julio C., 138

*Todas las sangres* (Arguedas), 126–27, 245 (n. 2)

Torres, Demosthenes, 30

Townsend, William C., 45

Truth and Reconciliation Commission, 129

Tzotzil language, 63, 63f

United Nations Conference on Racism, 23, 24–25, 181

United Nations Economic Commission on Latin America and the Caribbean (CELADE), 9

United States: African Americans in, 65, 250 (n. 42); assimilation in, 237 (n. 6); census in, 183, 237 (n. 6); colonization of, 15; discrimination in, 65; fluidity of racial categories in, 21–22; mestizaje and, 21; multiculturalism in, 238 (n. 7); race in, 29; segregation in, 19, 183; social mobility in, 234; war with Mexico, 42; whiteness in, 21

Uruguay: Afrodescendant population in, 26t; census in, 8; mestizaje in, 19; white self-identification in, 59

Valdivia, Nestor, 246 (n. 19)

Valle e Silva, Nelson do, 181

Van den Berghe, Pierre, 33

Vargas, Getulio, 177, 178

Vasconcelos, José, 36–37, 43, 79

Venezuela, 18, 25, 26t

Wagley, Charles, 200

War of the Castes, 63

War of the Pacific, 134–36

Whiteness and whites: in Argentina, 59; in Brazilian census, 184–85, 190; in *casta* system, 16; civilized society and, 100; in Colombia, 82, 124; in Costa Rica, 59; femininity and, 99–100, 123; geography and self-identification as, in Mexico, 60,

60*f*; historical proportion of, 16; immigrants, attraction of, in independence period, 18; independent nation-building and, 17–19; mestizo vs., 9; in Mexican population, 53*f*; in Mexico, 58–59, 58–60, 60*f*, 77–78; as nonindigenous, 60; in Peru, 16, 135; skin color and, 55*f*, 56; women and, 99

Whitening, 15–18; in Brazil, 176–77, 185, 190, 201, 202; in Colombia, 19, 88–89, 92, 99; elites and, 1, 18, 88; in ethnoracial history, 17–18; femininity and, 99; gender and, 99; "improve the race" and, 116–17, 117*f*, 124, 251 (n. 52); in Mexico, 43, 88; in Peru, 163, 168; scientific racism in, 18, 176–77

Women, 123; Afrodescendant, 98*f*, 135; in Colombia, 123; and colonial period sex ratio, 15; whiteness and, 99

Yashar, Deborah, 166

Zambo, 242 (n. 13).
Zapata Olivella, Manuel, 89–90, 92, 93, 123
Zapatista rebellion, 23, 45–46, 47, 71